DATE DUE

MR 31 '98			
AP 27 '98			
Fe 27 '98			
NO 12 '98			
JY 14 '99			
RENEW			
AG 3 '99			
NO 29 '99			
DE 1 0 00			
FE 1 2 '09			
DE 1 6 '09			

DEMCO 38-296

DEBUSSY
MAN AND ARTIST

Other Books by
OSCAR THOMPSON

PRACTICAL MUSICAL CRITICISM, 1934
HOW TO UNDERSTAND MUSIC, 1935
A TABULATED BIOGRAPHICAL HISTORY OF MUSIC, 1936
THE AMERICAN SINGER—100 YEARS OF SUCCESS IN
    OPERA, 1937

CLAUDE DEBUSSY
(From a photograph inscribed to Arthur Hartmann)

DEBUSSY
MAN AND ARTIST

By

OSCAR THOMPSON

Author of
The American Singer, Practical Musical Criticism,
How to Understand Music, A Tabulated
Biographical History of Music

ILLUSTRATED

DODD, MEAD & COMPANY
NEW YORK   1937

COPYRIGHT, 1937
BY DODD, MEAD AND COMPANY, INC.

PRINTED IN THE UNITED STATES OF AMERICA
BY THE VAIL-BALLOU PRESS, INC., BINGHAMTON, N. Y.

To George

IN MEMORY OF OLD
DISCUSSIONS OF NEW
REVELATIONS

O. T.

August 14, 1937

FOREWORD

THIS is the first American biography of Achille-Claude Debussy. When the author began his labors on it in the summer of 1932, there existed no Debussy biography in the English language, a curious circumstance in view of the popularity of Debussy's compositions and the many articles devoted to both the music and the man in newspapers and magazines. In 1908, ten years before the composer's death, two small volumes appeared almost simultaneously in Great Britain, Mrs. L. S. Liebich's *Claude-A. Debussy* and William H. Daly's *Debussy, A Study in Modern Music*. Each was designed primarily as an introduction to the music, and such material as was presented in the biographical sections of these volumes was of the sketchiest. Several important chapters of Debussy's story were still to be lived; and much that had happened in the years immediately preceding the publication of these studies of the living artist was not yet ripe for the telling. Daly, indeed, begins with the statement: "Of the outward life of Debussy, there is, thus far, not much to relate." With so obvious a void in English biographical literature to be filled, it was again curious that so long a period elapsed after the composer's death in 1918 before any one of an accumulation of French biographies was issued in translation. But in 1933 the most authoritative and at that time the latest of the successive Lives, *Claude Debussy et son temps* (English title, *Claude Debussy: His Life and Works*), by Léon Vallas, was imported in an altogether admirable English version by Maire and Grace O'Brien. Three years later the career and the compositions were studied anew from the English vantage point, in the compact and informative *Debussy* of Edward Lockspeiser. For reasons of his own, Vallas chose not to tell all he knew. "I have avoided all biographical details," he states in his preface, "the publication of which might be deemed premature and indiscreet. The secrets of his [Debussy's] private life belong to those who share it and bear his name." Lockspeiser found no such necessity to draw the veil; and the author of this book feels that the time has come for Debussy to be dealt with as openly as Beethoven or Wagner. The second Mme. Debussy has followed the first to the grave, where Debussy's beloved daughter has been resting nearly as long as he. Nothing that may be disclosed at this date can tarnish his memory or cast any shadow on anyone who bears his name, certainly not on the only sister, now living in Paris, or the two younger brothers, one in Paris, the other an agriculturist in the South of France. The time for personal, social, and moralistic aspersions of any kind having long since passed, only a reflected glory can shine on the children of Mme. Bardac-Debussy by her earlier marriage, who must consider it their great good fortune to have been brought into intimate association with "Claude de France."

The author, in working along his own lines these past five years, has accumulated a vast debt, nevertheless, to both Vallas and Lockspeiser, the former particularly, that is freely and gratefully acknowledged; together with obligations to Debussy's Austrian biographer, Ernst Decsey, and to André Suarès, Gabriel Astruc, René Peter, and others in France, whose personal and public writings about Debussy have been drawn on without stint for factual and anecdotal material and for descriptions of Debussy as they knew him.

CONTENTS

x . CONTENTS

ILLUSTRATIONS

PART I

THE MAN AND THE ARTIST

THE MAN AND THE ARTIST

SOMETHING feline in his nature was noted, again and again, by those who knew Achille-Claude Debussy. He was catlike and solitary, as he was artistic and amorous. Wrote André Suarès: "Just as the cat rubs itself against the hand which strokes it, Debussy caresses his soul with the pleasure which he invokes." Claude spoke of music as feminine. In his own musical creation he sought out facets of beauty to which that gender might be attached. Certainly he made no show of masculinity in the muscular sense of the word, as exemplified by some of his contemporaries, particularly those who aspired to the Wagnerian Valhalla. But of many descriptions that have come to the author of this volume from many sources, not one bears an intimation that Debussy was an effeminate creature. Feline, not feminine, is the adjective most used to suggest his walk, his manner, his particular kind of acrid wit, his playfulness, his sulks, and, most of all, the voluptuousness that colored his whole relation to life and art. He was a hedonist, a sybarite, a sensualist. But his career was one of toil and narrow means. The prodigal in him got him into difficulties that he might otherwise have avoided, but his extravagances were small, like the opportunities therefor. Successive affairs of the heart, each of the irregular order that the French condone readily enough, but quite generally regard as no subject for biographical fact-finding, were the chief of these extravagances, so far as any or all of them may have affected his career. Plainly there was no want of virility in Debussy's attitude toward the affections. The man who set the *Chansons de Bilitis* of Pierre Louÿs and who conceived the Prélude to Mallarmé's *L'Après-midi d'un faune* was an epicure, but no epicene. Physically, said Georgette Leblanc, who described him as he appeared

3

at the time of his first meeting with Maurice Maeterlinck, he gave the impression of having been built for strength—a strength he had no occasion, and no incentive, to acquire. Debussy was lazy in all except his art. Until sickness sapped his vitality and weakened his will, he worked steadily and conscientiously at composition. Otherwise, life was nothing for a display of energy. He was no great reader. He was much less an athlete, a sportsman, or a soldier. The notion which found its way into an English publication during his lifetime, that he had served in the army or any auxiliary thereto, has no foundation in fact. Debussy's life was sedentary and altogether civilian.

As for cats, he liked them and they were his house pets during the successive liaisons that preceded and attended his two marriages. His friend René Peter is authority for the statement that the cats were always angoras, and always gray. Moreover, since they were taken in one at a time, the name of any cat encountered in the Debussy domicile was always Line. Peter reports having seen three of them fall from a window on different occasions, and, contrary to tradition, they perished thereby. Each was replaced by another of the species. And the newcomer was always Line. Debussy's fondness for cats extended even to a variety that would have shattered to bits if subjected to the falls which seem to have had so fatal a fascination for the angoras. Several versions are told of a tale having to do with his desperate need of funds for the ordinary necessities of a particular day. Hungry, he left his abode to raise a little money. One account is that he borrowed from a friend, another that he hawked an early piano piece that had turned up unexpectedly among discarded manuscripts. In either case the upshot was that he returned to his quarters, not with a bundle of edibles, but with a porcelain cat, for which he had expended the entire proceeds of his sortie in search of funds.

A natural Bohemian, a man of Montmartre by instinct and

habit, it was inevitable that Debussy should be one of the celebrities who frequented the famous café that in its title paid public tribute to the dignities of catship, the historic Chat Noir. With the Brasserie Pousset, the Chez Weber, and the Reynolds bar, it supplied the kind of background that many best remember when they think of "Claude de France." There was sobriety in his conduct, as in his music. But he relished late hours in places where painters, writers, stage folk, and musicians congregated. He could be solitary as well as catlike there, too. But he knew well many of the notables who frequented such places and he was similarly well known. Not all were symbolists, impressionists and neo-fantasts of the sister arts. The ever-redoubtable Clemenceau dined with Debussy, Gabriel Fauré, Paul Dukas, Pierre Lalo, and a few mere generals and inconsequential public officials at the Chateaubriand restaurant on the evening in 1908 when his "great ministry" fell. The Tiger adored Mozart; *Così fan Tutti* and *The Magic Flute* particularly were manna for his indomitable spirit. Then there was Mata Hari, the seductive Dutch dancer, whom the French were compelled to shoot as a war spy. Debussy knew her ordinarily well, as did Massenet and Saint-Saëns. If cabinet ministers, ambassadors, advocates, and soldiers could be caught by her charms, was it strange that the list should include also a few poets and musicians? But Debussy, it must be remembered, was an invalid when the menace of Mata Hari became an issue of national rather than personal safety.

A gutter cat of forged iron, its back hunched, was the sign of the Chat Noir, as first established at 84 Boulevard Rochechouart. Rodolfe Salis, the proprietor, was a clever caricaturist, and in the words of Gabriel Astruc, "a painter without a future." He had been a student at the École des Beaux-Arts, and he dressed his waiters in costumes of the green of academicians' palms. At the counter was enthroned Mme. Salis, "a blonde and kindly Joconde." All began promisingly, with the King of the Hellenes and the Crown Prince of the Belgians among patrons and the "Hydro-pathes" attending the "literary Fridays" held at the place, with painters not to be outdone in attendance by poets, when, of an evening, waiters fought with some roving apaches, with the result that a man was killed. The legend is that by accident during the scuffle the proprietor brought a heavy chair down on the cranium of one of his most faithful servitors. At any rate, Salis moved his Chat Noir, including the well-hunched sign, to the Rue de Laval, afterward the Rue Victor Masse. There Debussy found it in the time of his nocturnal loiterings in haunts of smoke and argumentation. There were three floors, reached by means of a staircase decorated with framed drawings, and the walls were hidden under canvases of painters who frequented the house. In an old studio on the top floor—not to be reached without libations en route—was a shadow theater, the frame of which rested on an upright piano. Perhaps a hundred persons could be accommodated there. Henri Rivière, the painter, manufactured the figures and designed the decors, crawling through what Astruc describes as a "regular rathole" to get at the strings. With Debussy, there frequently sat in this room, Erik Satie and Charles de Sivry, among other musicians, flanked by artists of the brush and of the written word. Indeed, from 1884 to 1900, in and out of the Chat Noir passed about everyone that Paris counted as a some-body in arts and affairs.

The Brasserie Pousset, situated at that time at the corner of the Rue de Chateaudun and the Rue Faubourg Montmartre, was another of the eating and drinking places that came to know well the soft pad of Debussy's step; and that, by no means, always an unaccompanied pad. Beside it clicked the step of Ga-brielle Dupont or Rosalie Texier, on occasion both, as there was a time when the green-eyed Gaby and the tender-lipped Lily were good friends—the time just before the one was supplanted by the other in Debussy's somewhat plastic affections. Typical of such places in the 'nineties, the Brasserie Pousset assumed a medieval aspect, with dark woodwork and stained-glass windows. It was a rather small restaurant and was frequented by journalists and others of the writers' guild. There Debussy, in the half-light and the smoke haze of a table in a corner, was like an antique medallion, as one journalist remembers him; a Macedonian coin; an Assyrian head on a carving that conceivably could have been found next to a winged bull. There, as René Peter has related, Debussy would find Catulle Mendès, his collaborator in the Wagnerian soirées that Debussy detested and the librettist of his unfinished and discarded opera, *Rodrigue et Chimène;* André Antoine, a burly buffoon of a fellow, hat askew; Paul Robert, a round-eyed painter whose jokes were loudly communicated to the entire room; and André Messager, the gifted conductor who served as midwife at the Opéra Comique for *Pelléas et Mélisande.* The Brasserie Pousset was, it seems, a veritable stock exchange of news in the after-theater hours when journalists gathered there, the night's work ended, the last "copy" dispatched on its meandrous mechanical journey to the humming presses. Père Pousset served beer from Munich. And his hard-boiled eggs were without rival. On the authority of Gabriel Astruc, at two o'clock in the morning the interior of every good journalist contained not less than five or six such hard-boiled eggs, washed down with two or three "demis" of that incomparable Munich beer. Incidentally, the admirable Pousset is said to have remembered several of his customers in his will.

Also in the parabola of these late loiterings was the Café de l'Odéon. Connected therewith is a tale about the impetuous and sharp-tongued Octave Mirbeau, who should be remembered always as one of the first public champions of *Pelléas et Mélisande;* the one who spoke up for it valiantly in advance of the first public performance, at a time when the new opera was in danger of being laughed into oblivion because of the satirical attack made upon it in the anonymous pamphlet attributed to Maeterlinck. Mirbeau, addressing a literary banquet in this café, was well embarked on a eulogy of Debussy and Cézanne. In the midst of an oratorical flight he noted approving looks and nods of the head on the part of a writer for whom he had something less than admiration or esteem. Abruptly, he paused. "What, sir?" he thundered. "You are of my way of thinking? Very well, then, I shall change that way instanter." Upon which he resumed his address, developing with skill and passion a thesis that belittled Debussy and, along with him, Cézanne.

The Chez Weber at 21 Rue Royale was another Debussy haunt. At midnight, after performances of opera or drama, Debussy would arrive in the company of one or more of his friends. In the recollection of the manager, he was a moderate eater and an equally moderate drinker, usually content with a ham sandwich and a mug of Strasbourg beer or fine, pale English ale. Though usually amiable in a retiring way, his temper would sometimes flare in arguments with his cronies and then even the waiters found him something of a trial. The authority for this little sidelight describes his appearance by saying that he looked like his pictures. He usually wore a cape and a felt hat with a large brim, in the manner of students and artists of the time. The big hat was black and creased in the middle. On his tie hung a chain. He might have posed for Julien in Charpentier's opera, *Louise*, but possibly no suggestion could have caused a more immediate flare of the temper referred to; *Louise* was, for Debussy, a very special *bête noir*. He railed bitterly at those whose tastes permitted them to applaud such claptrap. But more to the point than his resemblance to Julien or any other garreter of the Latin quarter of the opera, were the Welsh rarebits for which the restaurant was known and of which Debussy was a connoisseur. They were not everynight affairs, to be sure; more frequently foie-gras sandwiches adorned the plate set down in front of him with the English ale. Among his companions at the Chez Weber was Paul-Jean Toulet, the poet with whom Debussy collaborated in a fruitless plan to make an opera of *As You Like It*. Toulet was renowned for a dry, smileless humor. Debussy called him "the grasshopper" and, true to his name, Toulet hopped off to Indo-China just when Debussy was ready to buckle down to real work on a setting of the Shakespeare comedy. At other tables might be seen Reynaldo Hahn, Léon Daudet, Charles de Chambrun, André Tardieu, or Marcel Proust. Debussy and Hahn were supposed to be as unsympathetic toward one another as the gulf between their musical concepts might imply. Their friends formed separate groups at the Chez Weber and what was perhaps a mere matter of self-consciousness at first—each of the composers acting on the belief that the other was hostile—grew until Debussy and Hahn barely exchanged salutations. Proust, though on good terms with Debussy, whom he drove home on at least one occasion, gained the impression that he was badly listened to, and Debussy that listening to Proust was something of an ordeal because he was long-drawn-out and hard to follow. At that time, almost anyone of literary or political note was likely to be found seated in the nail-studded brown leather chairs at the Chez Weber. A small house, its tables, too, were small. Chandeliers contributed to a Louis XVI decor. Opposite the entrance was a mirror, but the fact perhaps best remembered by those who were companions of Debussy there is that the walls were tinted the color of *café au lait*.

Among Debussy's best friends in his restaurant days were Raymond Bonheur and Robert Godet. Sometimes, when the company was most congenial, he and those with him would leave the Chez Weber and go to the Reynolds next door. The bar there was of the kind known in Europe as "American." A dancing team, Foottit and Chocolat, interested him, and if there was a fracas of some sort about the bar he remained languorously unconcerned. One evening Foottit approached to ask if Debussy were an artist. "But you, too, are an artist," Debussy parried. When the man replied that he was only a clown, Debussy continued his parable with: "But that's an art, too." "Yes, the art of receiving kicks," was the rejoinder. "We musicians also get kicked," said Debussy, "but by the public." The worthy Foottit remarked upon the popularity of *Carmen.* "Do you know who wrote it?" asked Debussy. Foottit stammered. "Why—Gounod." Whereupon Debussy sagely defined the "glory" of which Foottit had spoken in envy of a composer's lot, as a state of being ignored by thirty million Frenchmen—even Englishmen—and detested by forty colleagues.

The cakewalk was then of exotic fascination to Debussy and his friends. Gabriel Astruc, who had visited New York and Chicago and observed the dance in all its strutting ascendancy at the World's Columbian Exposition, was something of an authority on a subject in which the most serious-minded artists were absorbed around midnight or thereafter. Negroes of both sexes were imported to the music halls of Paris, there to tend the sacred fire. With them came such tunes as *Whistling Rufus,* which Americans will dimly remember as a two-step of a day when the cakewalk was already a legend. But the fad was of long duration in the French capital. When Debussy wrote *Golliwog's Cakewalk* for his adored little "Chou-Chou," the child whose death was so soon to follow his own, the new century was well under way.

The Debussy of the cafés, the mature Debussy, was the Debussy of the black beard and mop of curly black hair that fell over one eyebrow. Henri Lerolle has said that he looked exactly like a Syrian. His rather delicate nose was sufficiently aquiline to comport with the Levantine swarthiness of his face. But his

huge forehead dominated his face. Of medium height, he was
short-legged and large of trunk. His shoulders were wide. His
voice was low but, as Lerolle remembered it, of a marked nasal
quality. (Elsewhere it is described as "sepulchral.") At forty,
though still not a celebrity as a composer, Debussy was a figure
to be recognized in the surroundings of his choice. Strangers
would ask who the "grand noir" was—the dark fellow with the
faunlike beard, the cowboy hat, and the Macfarlane overcoat,
the wings of which sometimes gave him a batlike appearance as
he moved among the tables or on the street. The answer to the
query, as René Peter recollects the times, might be that he was
a *Prix de Rome* winner; the one way of making him seem important to those who knew nothing of his music. But after the
première of *Pelléas et Mélisande* the "grand noir" was pointed
out by name. There were those who sought his haunts just to
have a good look at him. He was cartooned and photographed
and painted and found his celebrity irksome. But this phase of
his life was not to last long. The lingering illness which eventually claimed as forfeit the life of the whilom man of Montmartre
compelled him to seek seclusion several years before he died.
His celebrity was buried in a house that became a hospital,
though the world mistook it for an ivory tower.

André Suarès has spoken of a sort of patina over his face. It
is a choice figure to describe the peculiar pallor that others
found there—a swarthy pallor—even in the days when he was
assumed to be in the best of health. According to Henri Régnier,
Claude walked with a heavy, muffled tread. His figure was flabby
and suggested indolence. From the dull pastiness of his face
shone his keen, black, heavy-lidded eyes. Over the huge forehead with its curious bumps drooped his wayward, fuzzy hair.
He was feline in movement, and something gypsylike, with a
passionate strain discoverable under his lethargic manner. As
Suarès recalls him, there was little that was distinctive about him

at first sight. He was not tall and not short; neither was he particularly robust or delicate; in spite of a certain flabbiness, he had the look of solidity; his figure was plump and well-rounded, but he was not stout. His cheeks were full and his features heavy. Though not of the South, he was not unlike some Provençal or even Italian types. The expression was sensual and carried with it the suggestion of a capacity for violence, but there were no indices of brutality. Melancholy and obstinacy were to be read in this countenance. The brow bulged outward in a convex curve, with prominent bumps over the eyebrows. The eyes themselves were alternately caressing and mocking; the eyes, according to Suarès, of "a brilliant, imperious woman." Raymond Bonheur remarked that Debussy reminded him of a Titian portrait, and that it was easy to picture him in the sumptuous setting of a Venetian palace. For him Debussy's curious forehead was powerful and faunlike and projected like the prow of a ship. His gaze was a fixed one, straight ahead as if focused on some far-distant point. In England there were some who were struck by a resemblance to Dante Gabriel Rossetti. When Giulio Gatti-Casazza, the opera director, first visited him in pursuance of a plan to obtain new stage works by Debussy for the Metropolitan, the two took note of certain resemblances, though Mr. Gatti was considerably the taller and bulkier man.

In manner Debussy was a being of many contradictions. One description refers to him as "that very materially minded fellow," "that sleep-heavy creature," "always so taciturn unless he wanted to get good addresses for procuring caviar, for which he was on the lookout and of which he was inordinately fond." An interviewer for *Le Figaro* found that he smiled readily and spoke quietly in a soft, melodious voice (not "nasal" or "sepulchral" this time) but was almost monastic in his reserve. Raymond Bonheur noted a certain brusqueness in his speech. Often it was hesitating, "as often happens with people who are not content with commonplace remarks and who think for themselves." Moreover, he spoke with a slight lisp. Rarely on first meeting would he disclose anything of himself. While others talked, Claude would turn the leaves of a book or examine an engraving, listening but apparently not concentrating on what was said. Yet his eyes would take on a look of singular intensity when he was really interested, and it was clear that although he was master of his comportment he had difficulty controlling his emotions.

When he turned to writing his thoughts, whether in personal letters or almost equally personal music criticism, Debussy was a wit, if perforce a somewhat self-conscious one. In groping for the right word, or the one that would click its heels, so to speak, he lost readiness in conversation; but on paper he could act the ringmaster with his words—as he once said Bach did with his fugal subjects. Then, with due deliberation in the cracking of his whip, he could make his ideas leap through hoops without becoming too acutely aware of halts and hitches. Debussy made a game of writing and the outcome was often a play of ironical banter in which he was extraordinarily successful in outlawing the cliché and exiling the platitude. He wrote racily and with personality. Almost invariably he had something pertinent—or impertinent—to say, and he said it jauntily and well. He amused himself and perplexed others with pranks of handwriting, running curious lines through words or letters so as to form arabesques, with stems for ivy leaves or gulls over ocean waves, or heaven only knows what.

But writing was not the only quotidian affair of which he made a game. The virtuosity with which he rolled a cigarette in a paper always devoid of glue without spilling the slightest speck of tobacco was a source of wonder and admiration to great and humble alike among the Parisians he encountered day by day. The opera he endured—if only now and then. But the circus! There he would gladly have gone every day. He could admire Mary Garden or Maggie Teyte. But the clowns! Debussy was like a child in his relish of their time-honored slapstick. The card game he most enjoyed was called bézique—Chinese bézique. When he played, Debussy would put his pipe beside him, as a cowboy of American frontier times might have placed his six-shooter. He would cheat, more or less openly, turning down the tip of a card he might want to put in his hand later. Consultation of an English dictionary brings a reminder that bézique is a game similar to pinochle, save that it is played with piquet packs in number equal to the players. Whether, with his training, Debussy would have made an incomparable pinochle player is something not to be determined by analysis of any of his chord sequences and subtle evasions of settled tonalities.

Financially, Debussy was never out of difficulties. He went to the Conservatoire a poor man's son, a target for jibing remarks because his attire bespoke his origin. At Villa Medici, where he lived on funds supplied by the state, he borrowed, not for necessities apparently, but to indulge his fancy for art objects, a fancy that became a passion in the course of a few years. There is a tale, possibly apochryphal, of the youth tearfully asking for money needed to pay for an operation for his father. The operation was all humbug; the money was spent for some Italian figurines—at least, so runs the story. Debussy did all manner of hackwork for the sake of the petty stipends this would bring, almost up to the time of his death. Think of his arranging Raff's *Humoresque en forme de valse* for solo piano or Wagner's *Fliegende Holländer* overture for two pianos! He accepted a few distasteful commissions like that of the estimable Boston matron who had need of a fantasy, rhapsody, or something of the kind (as long as it was by Debussy) for the then-neglected saxophone. But he never cheapened his art thereby. He struggled

with compositions for which he felt no affinity, striving to create
for them music worthy of his gifts. If they proved too recalcitrant he dropped them entirely and destroyed the sketches. No
one knows how much music he may actually have put on paper
after long hours of travail for the various works on which he
was reported to be engaged but of which scarcely a scrap of a
theme has been found. Debussy published some youthful works,
which in varying degrees are only partly representative of him,
but he left no potboilers. No composer of his time preserved a
more scrupulous attitude toward his art or exacted more of himself in the matter of maintaining his own artistic ideals. Circumstances never required him to go hopelessly into debt like Richard Wagner, and there never was any reason for him to assume
a similarly arrogant or evasive attitude toward creditors, but he
knew something of the distresses that drove Mozart a supplicant
to the door of the generous Puchberg; he had similar reasons to
be grateful to his early publisher, Georges Hartmann; and not
to Hartmann alone. All things considered, he fared well in the
matter of disposing of his manuscripts. But royalties supply no
competence, even for a Debussy.

If he had possessed more of the business acumen of Richard
Strauss, and of another well-known Straussian characteristic
which may be referred to here as thrift, perhaps he would have
been a more comfortable, even a happier, man. But Debussy was
too fond of life to stint himself where his sort of modest pleasures were concerned; he could no more live primarily for money
than he could write for it. His was the art aesthetic applied to
life. Both life and art were governed by the same bent for the
sensuous, the select, the rare, the different. He was fond of books
and bibelots—fonder of possession, in the case of the former,
than he was of reading—but, as Henri Régnier said, he always
got back to music. It was there he really lived his life and, as
has been true of others who had a really seminal mission to fulfill,

he lived it largely in the music that was his own. He did not go so far as Scriabin attempted to go in a resolving to remain away from all places where music by other men might contaminate his creative soul. But he confessed as he grew older that it was his desire to hear as little music as possible—a desire ironically overridden by his acceptance of successive positions as music critic for Paris publications. He talked little about his own work, aside from an occasional letter to a close friend or a publisher, usually couched in terms of banter; but he criticized his confrères freely and often with an asperity that seemed to betray irritation over having to hear their music performed. According to Régnier, he spared almost no one except Vincent d'Indy and Ernest Chausson. The published reviews would appear to bear this out amply. His reticence and his solitariness did not mean that he was not controversial in his opinions. He has been described as the very spirit of contradiction. And it was this spirit of contradiction that upheld his musical sensibilities in their quest of new harmonic beauties, irrespective of any so-called laws. He undoubtedly had, first of all, the will to follow his own paths in the light of his vision as to what he could and must achieve; but with this pioneering impulse went, as Léon Vallas has well said, a constant, almost exaggerated determination to react against the symphonic methods and mannerisms of his day, especially against those traceable to Beethoven, Franck, and Wagner.

As an artist Debussy still merits the characterization of "très exceptionnel, très curieux, très solitaire." As an innovator he has, of course, been overtaken and left behind by neoterics bent on invalidating the old tonal system entirely. It is in his personal quality of expressiveness that Debussy remains a solitary figure, rather than as a worker in strange sonorities. The wholesale adoption and extension of his harmonic principles—an extension that has become a virtual negation of all that had been built up through centuries of adherence to the dispensation of keys and key relations—has put a new face on music, in which the recognizable features are only partly his. Still, it must be admitted that Debussy has been the determining factor in the music of the first third of the twentieth century, because of the doors he opened and the restraints he cast aside. Harmony was freed from the so-called laws of extension. The straitjacket of development was put away. Form became less a cadre for ideas than the pulsations by which those ideas ran their course. Arnold Schönberg, who had begun like other epigoni of Wagner and might have remained a mildly morbid Austrian melodist, derived from Debussy his altered orientation. Through Schönberg, Debussy saved Alban Berg from being merely the gifted representative of a school of romantic decadence. Whether the fruits have been what the tree was planted to bear is another matter. Everyone could learn from Debussy, but no one else could translate into music the visions that were peculiarly his own. Debussy was the poet of the nuances of Nature, not as the eye mirrors them, but as they are transmitted to the feelings. He was, of all composers, the most painterlike, but not in the sense of the graphic or the imitative. He dealt not with scenes but with the feelings prompted by scenes. Hence, inevitably there came the use of the term "Impressionism," without which those who must try to describe the indescribable would have a still sorrier time in dealing with Debussy's music by means of the written or the spoken word. The objections of some able French writers to the use of the designation are understandable, but not very practical. Words are arbitrary things: if one of them serves a purpose no other will quite serve, whatever its origin; nothing is more futile than to combat that one on the basis of some prior association or connotation, particularly if this has to do not with the specific need but with some parallel function. Music is music and not painting, and though obviously the use of the word "Impressionism" to characterize a musical procedure or effect was an extension of painter terminology, there is no longer any need to think of musical impressionism in terms of painting. In music the meaning applies quite specifically to technical processes that are of music and not of any sister art.

In the debates that have occupied French writers on this subject, those who have insisted that Debussy was no impressionist have been able to quote words of the composer's own, protesting against the term, which, as he caustically observed, was being wrongly applied even to his beloved Turner. Says Suarès: "He [Debussy] is not the slightest bit an impressionist. He is, on the contrary, the musician who makes use everywhere of symbols. For the landscape worthy of music, worthy of poetry, worthy of art in short, is a symbol and only a symbol." The kernel of his argument is that Debussy is a musical symbolist. One analogy is substituted for another. Instead of an art consanguinity to Monet and Renoir, the brotherhood is with Mallarmé and Verlaine. Suarès would appear to prefer poets to painters, as certainly he prefers Debussy to them. In music, he says, landscape is emotion, and the only real beauty of landscape in art will always be to make a frame, a chord, or a harmony for the passions and the thoughts of man. But, unfortunately, there is a treatment of landscape which gives importance to a theatrical void and it is fair to ruin painting. Painters, he contends, let themselves go so far as to treat the thought and the figures as elements of the landscape, while the true artist ought to paint the landscape in the style of the figure and to attempt to put into it all of the form implied by the thought. And so, painters will end by limning only still life, and that is the stage where they already have arrived "if one only considers their portraits." In declaring Debussy's *La Mer* "the greatest and most beautiful poem in French music," he continues: "Do not let us speak foolishly here of impressionist art. Music is in any case

never an affair of simple impression. The sonorous landscape itself is always closer to Rembrandt than to Claude Monet." This
sonorous landscape, he emphasizes, has a voice, "and voice is not
matter but spirit." And Time is dominant, not Space. If there
must be a comparison to some man of the brush, it is to Cézanne,
with a similar magic of color; but the true measure of Debussy
is to be found in the manner of his identification of spirit with
the ballades of François Villon. "One must have a mind without
music to compare Debussy to Claude Monet, a mind which takes
notes for sounds and colors for what they express. All true music
is, first of all, order. The painting of landscape is almost always
disorder incarnate. In Debussy all is ordered."

An ally is found for Suarès in Debussy's close personal friend,
Robert Godet. "Debussy's impressionism, Moussorgsky's realism!" Godet exclaims. "A deaf child would make a game of
writing the history of music if he employed a rubric of this
kind." He inveighs against trying to define genius in a single
word, something which Paul Landormy, defending the use of
the term, denies anyone has been so foolish as to pretend to do.
The painter image persists. "To judge by his works, and by
their titles," says René Peter, "he [Debussy] is a painter and
that is what he wants to be; he calls his compositions pictures,
sketches, engravings, arabesques, masques, studies in black and
white. Plainly it is his delight to paint in music." Thus also
Romain Rolland: "It [Debussy's orchestra] possesses the aristocratic disdain for those orgies of sound to which the art of Wagner has accustomed us; it is sober and refined, like a fine classic
eighteenth-century phrase. Not a note too many—such is the
artist's taste. Instead of amalgamating timbres for mass effects,
he either releases their personalities from one another or he delicately ties them without perverting their own distinctive nature.
Like the impressionist painters of his time he paints in pure
colors, though with a delicate sobriety. . . ." Debussy, as has

often been recalled, aspired in his youth to be a painter and to the end of her days Rosalie Texier, the first Mme. Debussy, preserved a palette on which he had daubed his colors.

But isn't this very effort to make a painter of a musician the begetter of the strife over musical impressionism? Isn't it perfectly logical for music to have an impressionism of its own? If Debussy himself disliked the term, so did the impressionist painters when it first was applied to them. Manet's seascape was styled by him "Une Impression" with no thought of creating a new category with terminology of its own. If his "impression" created a sensation, it also evoked ridicule. There was much the same history to record for the literary symbolists. The designation given them was for a time a term of hostility and derision. But in each instance the word caught on and served a purpose; the Symbolists in French literature and the Impressionists in French painting are tagged for good. The word caught on for music in precisely the same manner and for the same reason—there was need of it. When Louis Laloy wrote in 1909 that *Pelléas et Mélisande* was possibly the masterpiece of symbolism and the *Nocturnes* of impressionism he made a brave effort to draw an understandable distinction between two terms that were being used more or less interchangeably. Maeterlinck was a symbolist poet and Debussy's music for *Pelléas* was the counterpart and equivalent of his text. The *Nocturnes* were akin to Whistler's paintings of that designation, and Whistler was an impressionist. But, thinking in terms of music and not those of the sister arts, is *Pelléas* in another world, technically and expressively, than the *Nocturnes?* Paul Landormy has made some very sensible remarks on this subject. "Is a certain kind of symbolism very far removed from impressionism?" he asks. "Think of Verlaine, the most gifted representative of symbolism in France. Are we not straightway inclined to regard symbolism as simply the impressionism of literature?" Both symbolism and impressionism, in their different mediums, avoid the frank literalness of statement that is realism. Debussy resembles those poets who might have been called "Impressionists" and those painters who could have been dubbed "Symbolists," if those had been the words coined for them and if they had caught on. In literature, in painting, in music, the aim of these kindred artists was to suggest rather than to depict; to mirror not the object but the emotional reaction to the object; to interpret a fugitive impression rather than to seize upon and fix the permanent reality. As Landormy has said, there can be no such thing as absolute impressionism; it can be only a tendency— a tendency to draw near to pure sensation or pure emotion—to present illusion rather than bald fact. If there are artists who have followed that tendency—whatever their medium—they may be called "Impressionists." Claude Debussy is one of them. But there is another aspect of impressionism that is as particularly applicable to Debussy as to Monet, Sisley, Pissarro, or Renoir. Impressionism is something of technique as well as of interpretation. The impressionist painters were particularly concerned with special effects of light, hence their distinctive brushwork, their laying on of unmixed colors, side by side, in a manner to startle and offend those who had been seeking to paint objects and scenes substantially as they were. The plein-airists were technicians, first of all; theirs was a method as well as a manner; a realist at heart might paint as an impressionist and earnestly pursue the same experiments in refraction of light. Debussy's impressionism similarly had a technical as well as an interpretive basis; he achieved with chord successions much what the painters achieved when they placed color strokes side by side; and in his explanation of his purposes in the *Nocturnes* he stated that they were to be thought of, not in connection with the musical form so designated, but for "all the various impressions and the special effects of light that the word suggests."

Debussy, we have said, was a poet of the nuances of Nature.

For the most part this was Nature at its most intimate, Nature at its most atmospheric, rather than Nature in its more majestic and grandiose moods. His was not the Nature of the mountain climber, the globe-trotter, or even the round-bodied Herr who straps rucksacks on the back of every member of his considerable family and, stick in hand, goes plodding forth on a Sunday with wife and children trudging along behind. He was not a sight-seer, and Nature was not for him a vast theater set with enthralling scenes. Instead, it was the envelope of life; the nimbus, the aureole, the omnipresent shadow of the spirit of man; an all-pervasive element and no mere backdrop for the entrances and exits of strutting humankind. For him Nature was like a religion; even more was it like music. "Who will discover the secret of musical composition?" runs an interview published at the time of the première of *Le Martyre de Saint-Sébastien*. "The sound of the sea, the curve of the horizon, the wind in the leaves, the cry of a bird enregister complex impressions within us. Then suddenly, without any deliberate consent on our part, one of these memories issues forth to express itself in the language of music." In confessing that he adhered to no religion, in the sectarian or churchly sense, he said: "When I gaze at a sunset sky and spend hours contemplating its marvelous and ever-changing beauty, an extraordinary emotion overwhelms me. Nature in all its vastness is truthfully reflected in my sincere and feeble soul." The trees stretching their branches outward and upward, the grass-carpeted earth, the flowers he saw gladdening the meadows, all these, he said, moved him unconsciously to an attitude of adoration. "Nature invites her ephemeral guest"—and, Debussy observed, that was what he would call prayer. In all of his hundred and thirty-odd compositions, Debussy composed not one piece of sacred music, i. e., music that could possibly have any connection with a church service. But in how many songs, how many piano pieces, where his oneness with Nature is subtly and delicately made felt, is he the adoring pantheist, the ephemeral guest whom the eternal universe invites to reverential prayer!

He was the poet of mists and fountains, clouds and rain; of dusk and of glints of sunlight through the leaves; he was moonstruck and seastruck and a lost soul under a sky besprent with stars. All his senses were tributary to his musical inspiration. He felt faint vibrations as he heard the overtones of distant bells. He was conscious of the perfumes of a summer's day and he could scent in fancy the odors of an Andalusian night. There was touch as well as sight in these sensations, and in all a wealth of fantasy, as if he not only saw but heard the dancing of shadows on velvet feet. But there is always something more than mere sensation in what he gives back for what he has absorbed. In transmuting Nature into harmony, he has made sonorous his own emotions; never with any beating of the breast or invoking the high heavens to look down upon his agony or his transport of joy. Always there is reticence; always sobriety. Like the Symbolists, Debussy deprecated rhetoric. He could not, or would not, stamp his feet and shake his clenched fist like Beethoven. The lightnings and the tempests of Wagner were not in his world. His sensibilities were not attuned to the heroic; far from tumults and great defeats or victories, he could envisage the faun and the naiad, the dream of the moon on marble, the melancholy of the terraces, the murmurous magic of the harmonies of approaching night. For Wagner, his opposite, it has been said that there was no such thing as satiety. There are no orgies in Debussy, no bacchanales, no maddened reelings. If there is intoxication, as there is, it is gentle and, true to the code of the artist, always discreet. Sometimes in this restraint there is almost a sense of suffocation; the cry is always strangled from within. Of *Pelléas* and his compositions for the voice, it has been well said that Debussy's music does not illustrate the text, but transposes it to another order. The secret of that other order is his subtle and individual harmony. Through it glows the voluptuousness of his spirit; it is there that he searches out, and finds, the caress that is the essential of his music. The chord is the fountain; the melody—a happy phrase borrowed from Suarès—the spray of the chord. It is not always easy to distinguish between Debussy the artist and Debussy the artisan. Happily the technical aspects of his composition were so exquisitely adjusted to the creative that they seem to be one. He had no failures that could be attributed to inability to accomplish the task he set for himself, though it can be argued that he took care not to undertake to fill forms that might have taxed his architectural resources. If so, while it may narrow the scope of his genius, this very circumstance pays tribute to his taste. Debussy's music yields no evidences of strain. If he was cautious, that must be surmised rather than discerned. In *L'Après-midi d'un faune*, the *Nocturnes*, *La Mer*, and *Ibéria*, to think only of the orchestral works, he created masterpieces that have withstood the tests which in a few years serve ordinarily to determine musical vitality. In *Pelléas et Mélisande* he has done more. He has given opera a new orientation, if one that no other composer has been able to make completely and successfully his own. There is truth in the statement, though it once would have seemed wide of the mark, that *Pelléas et Mélisande* is of all lyric dramas the most objective and the most convincingly human. But it remains for all that a parable of the unreal, the most mysterious, the most baffling, the most elusive of works of its kind, a disquieting revelation of a world where, as Lawrence Gilman has written,[1] "it is not dreams, but the reflections of dreams that obsess," "where every footfall is charged with indescribable intimations," where the composer has contrived to encompass in his music "not the echoes of passional and adventurous experience, but the vibrations of the spirit underneath."

Of the era that produced *Pelléas et Mélisande* and of which

[1] *Pelléas et Mélisande, A Guide to the Opera.*

Debussy was preeminently the exemplar, Guido Pannain [2] eloquently has said:

> How fantastic were the colors and patterns of the new music that greeted the dawn of the twentieth century in Europe! It was a music that seemed to the listener at times like a mere drift of sound that stunned the senses, at times like the unearthly flower of a world yet undiscovered. The orchestra might have been a bed of exotic blooms in the garden of dreams. The strange landscape of sound was perceived rather than heard; the listener quivered as to the blows of some great bell sunk in the ocean of ineffable pleasure, where reality and its perception were fused into each other.

[2] In *Modern Composers.*

PART II

THE LIFE

CHAPTER I

THE BOY WITH THE "DOUBLE FRONT"

Birth at Saint-Germain-en-Laye—A Line of Artisans—The Sea and the First Piano Studies

FROM childhood the color green was something of an obsession for Achille-Claude Debussy. Green furnishings, green bindings, green neckties, green ribbons, and oddments of green cloth fascinated him. For him the sea was green, as all Nature was green. Parks, lawns, forests, trees, shrubs, ferns, shoots, leaves, all the greenery of the open, as he, city man that he was, knew it, had a rival for his affections in a bit of green tile or inlay; and because he loved the rich sheen of it, more than because he was an enthusiastic collector of bibelots. Midway in his life, when he was finding his true musical self and stepping over the threshold from obscurity into fame, he lost his heart to a pair of green eyes. To round out this color symphony neatly, particular mention might be made here of one of his songs, *Green*. But since the title was not of his own choosing; since, also, the song is a setting of verses by Verlaine; and since, finally, the same set of ariettes contains a setting of words from the same source with the rhyming but less alluring title of *Spleen*, this would be to labor the point too far. Sufficient is the testimony of surviving friends, who recall the composer's passion for the color as a distinguishing mark no less characteristic of the man than his partiality for broad-brimmed hats of an American cowboy design, usually a trifle too tight for his large cranium and resting a little oddly on the bulge of his famous double forehead.

Viewed from anywhere, save in its own cobblestone streets, there are few greener spots in France than Saint-Germain-en-

Laye, where Achille-Claude was born on August 22, 1862. Within sight of Paris, and only twenty or thirty minutes from the city by train or automobile, the town that nestles in the heart of the verdant Île de France has been a favorite lounging ground for painters, poets, and musicians—not without reason. Its historical associations are one thing; the beauty of its surroundings another. As the birthplace of Louis XIV, the home in exile of the Stuart pretenders, the place of death and burial of James II of England and his widow, Mary of Modena, the spot where Dumas wrote *Camille*, and the scene of the signing of the treaty of 1919 between Austria and the victors in the World War, Saint-Germain would have needed no such site above the Seine to assure it a respectable paragraph in Baedeker. Even without its famous terrace and park, the château of Francis I would stand as a reminder that for centuries before the "grand monarque" shifted his court to Versailles, this was the summer capital of France. But the château, now a museum of antiquities, suggests no such association with Debussy as does the terrace that borders the ancient, parklike forest.

Though Achille-Claude was still an infant when he was removed by his parents from Saint-Germain to Clichy, in an outlying district of Paris, and could scarcely have remembered in later years any glimpses his baby eyes may have had of the scene from a perambulator or the arms of one of his elders, he must have returned to that terrace many times in adult life and reveled in the view that is a constant refreshment, alike to villagers, Parisians, and tourists. That he did not forget the village of his nativity is illustrated by a remark he made in later life to a Viennese journalist. In mocking alike those who, on the one hand, praised him as "a man of the North, a melancholy type," and those who, on the other, acclaimed him as a representative of the South, "Provence, Daudet, tireli, tirela," he said: "And I am merely a native of Saint-Germain, half an hour from Paris."

Debussy, though much at the seacoast in his childhood and occasionally thereafter, seems never to have been on the open ocean. He was no great traveler and several crossings of the English Channel were his most extended maritime adventurings. This is a little curious, perhaps even disturbing, to those who, with no desire to be literal or factual in relating the artist's creations to his personal experience, still turn to Debussy's sea pieces, *La Mer*, for an unrivaled tonal exposition of waves and winds; an exposition none the less veracious because it was spun of sheer fantasy. What, indeed, was Debussy's sea? The visitor to the terrace at Saint-Germain-en-Laye may have need to guard against the promptings of his own imagination. As he approaches the brink of the bluff above the Seine, leaving behind him the uniform rows of tall trees, so trimmed as to suggest pantalettes, the sight before him suddenly takes on the aspect, not of a smiling countryside, but of the sea. True to Debussy's obsession, it is a green sea. Winding ribbons of river, orchards, gardens, lawns, shade trees, and hedges along the highways, all sunk far below the terrace and undulating away to the skyline of Paris, a dozen miles distant, are merged in a sweep of green, which on a summer's day will sparkle in the sunlight and dazzle the eye with an illusion of waves. Not without reason was this called Île de France. And Debussy, who never was to go to sea, was born, if the fancy of the moment is permitted to have its way in the mind of one thus surveying this scene, on the sea's marge as truly as if the place had been Cannes, or Nice, Pourville or Dieppe.

Was this panorama of verdure Debussy's sea? The answer, of course, is No; save as the stirring sight may have had some enkindling part in the play of those imaginative faculties which Debussy brought to bear on a multitude of compositions besides *La Mer*. Still, it would be easy, standing there, where it is to be assumed the poet of the sea pieces stood, eyes straining toward the towers of the church of Le Sacré Cœur on the crest above

Montmartre, to find in the prospect a visual parallel for the mysterious opening of *La Mer;* and to paraphrase in application thereto the words of an American poet of the prairies, who found, on first beholding the ocean, that before him were the same immensities he had been viewing over the cornfields ever since he was born. From Saint-Germain to Montmartre, this flight of the eye that may have left in the memory of the infant of Saint-Germain some marker for confirmation in his after years was to be the first transition of Achille-Claude's career. He who began just "a native of Saint-Germain," eleven miles from Paris, came to personify Montmartre in haunts that were not necessarily situated on its hill. But Montmartre could not hold him, nor, for that matter, could Paris. D'Annunzio acclaimed him "Claude de France." Simple, but just, was his own appellation for himself, "musicien français." But by the time he had come to apply it, he was already one of the little coterie who, whatever their pride of race and adoration of the homeland, are artists of the world. Shoreless, then, the Debussy sea; boundless, as the fantasy that retouched the autumnal colorings of music with the freshness of a springlike green.

The secret of the genius of Debussy, the composer, is not to be discovered in the simple facts of his more immediate ancestry. The Debussys before him were artisans, farmworkers, and "petits commerçants." Achille-Claude's great-great-grandfather, Pierre, divided the family's name into two parts, as did Pierre's father, Valentin; and for a time the youth from Saint-Germain affected this spelling, as if to imply that he was of noble blood. But Pierre de Bussy, the elder, was a farrier of Semur, and Valentin de Bussy, Pierre's father, a laborer on the farm at Benoisy where Pierre was born.[1] A second Pierre, the composer's great-grandfather, was a

---

[1] Valentin de Bussy was a native of Courcelles-sous-Grignon in Burgundy, only about five miles distant from Bussy-le-Grand, where the Counts de Bussy

farmer who quit Semur for Montrouge. With him the name became Debussy. At the time of the revolution, the family left Burgundy. The composer's grandfather, Claude Debussy, son of the second Pierre, was a carpenter and cabinetmaker in Paris. He married a fringemaker, Marianne-Françoise Flondeau, also of Burgundian stock. Their son, Manuel-Achille Debussy, the composer's father, born at Montrouge, May 10, 1836, for a time was a petty shopkeeper and later an accountant for a large metallurgical concern. The composer's mother, Victorine-Joséphine-Sophie Manoury, born in Paris, October 28, 1936, was the daughter of Louis-Amable Manoury and Eulalie-Sophie Delinotte, bourgeois of humble circumstance. Achille-Claude, the eldest of four children, came into the world a little less than nine months after the ceremony, performed on November 30, 1861, at the village of Levallois, near Paris, by which Mlle. Manoury became the wife of Manuel-Achille Debussy. Only five months separated the parents in age. The composer's father was twenty-six, his mother nearing that mark, when the boy was born at 38 Rue au Pain, Saint-Germain.

Manuel-Achille Debussy and his wife kept a china shop at that address. It was a small affair, representing no considerable capital or volume of trade. Today, the ground floor houses the establishment of a cleaner and dyer. Above his sign is a tablet to the composer, placed on the building in 1923 by a group of English admirers. A wooden staircase, worn and scarred, leads upstairs

---

of older times had their seat. Lockspeiser recalls that the libertine, soldier, and writer, Roger de Rabutin, Count de Bussy, better known as Bussy-Rabutin, had a prominent forehead like that which was so striking a feature of Debussy's countenance. He lived at Bussy-le-Grand during the second half of the seventeenth century. It was at the end of this period that Valentin de Bussy was born. The count was notorious for his episodes with women. It would be interesting to know something more of how the family of laborers and small landowners came to have the name of de Bussy—whether it was derived from Bussy-le-Grand or in some way from the feudal family that occupied its château. Apparently there was no tradition in the family, however, to prompt Achille-Claude's youthful small pretensions to noble lineage.

from a dingy vestibule and court, to the living quarters that for about three years were the abode of the Debussys. Rue au Pain— the street of bread, an ancient market—is narrow, noisy, and easily congested. Around a corner, two squares removed, is the church of Saint-Germain, where Achille-Claude and his sister, Adèle, were christened. A simple, but not unimposing structure, with a wooden ceiling and two rows of columns within, it dates from 1827; the exterior, with its six pillars supporting a lofty frieze, bespeaks the period. With its murals and its mausoleum in memory of James II, a gift of George IV, the Debussy pilgrim has no particular concern. Perhaps the composer's father told and retold what seems to be Saint-Germain's favorite story about James II. The exile is credited with having introduced golf to France. When his hope of regaining the throne in England was highest, and members of the French court were rejoicing over what was assumed to be his triumphal departure, King Louis is said to have murmured despondently: "No, he is not gone for good. He will come back. He has not taken his golf sticks!"

Achille-Claude Debussy was christened on July 31, 1864. Some needless mystery has been made of the circumstance, particularly as it concerned the two who stood as godparents and whose names appear on the record as Achille-Antoine Arosa and Octavie de la Ferronnière. Out of this mystery have arisen vague questionings and inferences as to Debussy's parentage, for which no sensible basis can be found.[2] Of the godparents, the man was a banker of standing; the woman the boy's aunt, a sister of his father, commonly known as Mme. Roustan. There was an attachment between them that need not be scrutinized too closely. This attachment played no small part in the early childhood of Achille-Claude; and in its breaking off, with the marriage of Arosa to another woman, is to be found the reason for Debussy's reluctance to talk about that childhood. Arosa was interested in art

[2] The report that he was an illegitimate child still finds credence, however.

AT SAINT GERMAIN-EN-LAYE

Above, the Church where Debussy was Baptized
Below, Rue au Pain, the Street of Debussy's Birthplace

and artists. He collected works of modern painters. Influenced, no doubt, by the child's aunt, he paid for Achille-Claude's first piano lessons with an elderly Italian named Cerutti. The couple took the boy to the seacoast and otherwise favored him with pleasures and experiences his parents could not afford. Then, as later, he was much away from home; so much, indeed, that his surviving sister, Adèle, who was only a year and a half his junior, can recall little of his life in the days when the two children might have been expected to be playmates. With Arosa's marriage, the financier's interest in the boy lapsed. Out of respect for his aunt, the adult Debussy quite understandably drew a curtain between his friends and his early memories. We know from his sister that he was a shy, sweet, undemonstrative child who watched others play, more than he played; moody and a little aloof, but not unfriendly; favored over others by his mother, who kept him much to herself, but neither abnormal nor spoiled. There is a photograph of the boy on a tricycle, taken in 1867, when he was five, that clearly suggests the Debussy of later years, though a narrow-brimmed little hat hides the "double front" that from babyhood was the most distinguishing feature of his face and head. This photograph was taken, of course, after the Debussys had left Saint-Germain. Achille-Claude was in his third year when his parents gave up the china shop and moved to Clichy, adjoining Paris, where the father seems to have engaged in odd jobs until, in 1873, he became an employee of the Compagnie Fives-Lille, with which he remained until his death in 1906.

Three other children, Alfred, Emmanuel, and Eugène, were born after the removal to Clichy. Eugène died of meningitis in infancy. Alfred and Emmanuel survived their celebrated elder brother and at this writing are living, one in southern France, the other, like the sister, Adèle, in Paris. Only Achille-Claude of the children was musical or otherwise inclined to the arts, and so the others have remained almost without mention in the chronicles of the life and work of the "musicien français." Debussy's father was moderately fond of comic opera and took the boy to hear works by Offenbach and Lecocq. Donizetti and Hérold, as represented by *The Daughter of the Regiment* and *Le Pré aux clercs*, also came within his range of enjoyment. How much Manuel-Achille Debussy believed in the possibility of a musical career for his son before he attracted attention outside the family is conjectural. There is nothing to indicate that he opposed musical study or that he particularly recognized in the boy any unusual talent. Debussy himself has said that it was intended that he should become a sailor. His father considered sending him to a nautical school, with a high hope for the navy. The boy, himself, quite probably as the result of his childhood association with Arosa, had aspirations to become a painter. But his early piano studies with Cerutti bore fruit. The twig was inclined toward music. Mme. Debussy, who seems to have left much of the care of the household to Mme. Roustan, was sympathetic. She is assumed to have taught him the French equivalent of the "three R's." The accepted story is that the lad never went to school. Summers at Cannes had their hours at the keyboard for the boy of nine and ten years old, still the pet of Arosa. It can be assumed that even then he was not content slavishly to practice scales, for within a year or two he was to be found experimenting boldly with harmonies not of an order to be learned through elementary piano instruction.

The year 1871 brought a fortunate meeting with a musician able to do more for the nine-year-old boy than the old Italian who had initiated him into the fascinations of the white and black keys. His new friend and mentor was Mme. Mauté de Fleurville, who had been a pupil of Chopin. She was the mother-in-law of the poet, Paul Verlaine, one of the literary voices to which the later Debussy gave eager ear, and mother of Charles de Sivry, an operetta composer of taste and success in his limited field. Mme. de

Fleurville was quick to recognize the unusual talent of the shy, dark-haired, dark-eyed boy. She suggested or fell in with a plan to get him ready for the Paris Conservatoire, and herself gave him piano lessons without charge. How much of Debussy's later piano style was founded on her teaching can only be surmised, since he was to pass through the classes of other and perhaps more assertive teachers. But if something of Chopin's technique was, indeed, characteristic of Debussy's very personal and individual playing, the assumption well may be that this gifted and cultured woman, toward whom Debussy always manifested feelings of affection and gratitude, was the one who imparted to him its fundamental touch and spirit. In later life, when he was to prepare an edition of Chopin's works, primarily because he needed funds, Debussy approached the task as a grand-pupil, so to speak, of Chopin. He often spoke and wrote of his high regard for the woman who had brought him close to the Polish master and whose death had been a personal loss. This loss he continued to feel after the creative aspects of his career had completely submerged those of the keyboard artist.

It was due almost solely to Mme. de Fleurville that in a few months the boy was ready to take and to pass the entrance examinations of the Paris Conservatoire, after which all thought of the sea must have vanished from his father's mind, as reports of his son's progress confirmed Mme. de Fleurville's conviction that here was an unusual, if even then not altogether orthodox, talent. When Achille-Claude reported at the Conservatoire, his classmates have recalled, he wore a sailor's cap with a tassel. But the dream of the cockade and epaulettes of an admiral was gone.

CHAPTER II

AT THE CONSERVATOIRE

A Prize for Solfège, with Ups and Downs in Piano Tests—
Mentors and Revolts against the Sacred Rules

For eleven contention-filled years Achille-Claude Debussy alternately toiled and slacked at the Conservatoire, his immediate goal the *Prix de Rome*. As a student, he knew success and failure, friendship and hostility. He irritated and antagonized his mentors, the while he aroused their curiosity and in some noteworthy instances won their respect. It was said of him by one of his teachers that he was more disputatious than he was industrious. At first, faculty opinions as to his gifts were formed largely on his piano playing, which had its good points, as was demonstrated in successive competitions. But relatively early in his Conservatoire studentship it was said of young Debussy that he was more fond of music than of the piano. What form of expression this musicality would take baffled those of his elders who watched him growing more and more stubborn in his reluctance to accept the musical principles and rules of procedure then dogmatically laid down. At first, his record as a pianist was one of progress, with clear indications of exceptional ability. But he subsequently lagged behind and his was not the orderly and systematic march from achievement to achievement credited to some of his less gifted classmates.

Within a year of his entering the boy was awarded third medal for solfège. This was at his first examination, held in the summer of 1874. He also won second honorable mention at that time in a piano competition.

38

The next year, 1875, he won second medal for solfège and first honorable mention in the piano contest.

In 1876, his third year, first prize for solfège came to him, but no mention for piano playing. In 1877 he shared second prize in the piano competition with the future critic, Camille Bellaigue, who in 1878 won first prize, with none for Debussy. Again there was no mention for Debussy in the contest of 1879 and so far as conservatory success could indicate he was distanced by the more promising of his fellows, and had less and less prospect of a career as a concert pianist.

What part the music chosen for performance in these successive competitions played in this apparent retrogression can only be surmised. At his first trial, when he was barely twelve years old, the boy gave his attention to Chopin's F Minor Concerto; at the second, to the same composer's second Ballade. This was familiar ground. Only recently, he had been under the tutelage of Chopin's pupil, Mme. de Fleurville. Already was exhibited something of the kinship existing between the French artist and the Polish genius. Then, as later, there was an affinity in the spirit as well as the manner of their playing. If high predictions made for Debussy after his second piano competition were not fulfilled at the third, the reason for this may be found, partly at least, in the substitution of Beethoven for Chopin in the choice of composer drawn upon for the contest number. Achille-Claude played the first movement of Beethoven's Sonata, Opus 111, which, understandable enough, was not his meat. He fared better the next year with the first movement of Schumann's G Minor Sonata, but got nowhere with his trial piece of 1878, the allegro from Weber's A-Flat Sonata. Yet, before he was to make any headway as a composer, even at the Conservatoire, Debussy was to put his piano talent to practical uses that must have elicited the envy of some of his youthful associates, particularly those who regarded him as offish and difficult, even something of a monstrosity at times.

Achille-Claude was eleven years old when he entered the Conservatoire, in October, 1873. Thickset and ill at ease, his shyness had about it a clumsiness that caused him to appear surly. He was at a disadvantage, moreover, because he dressed like a workman's son and neither spoke nor wrote correctly. Conceivably, too much has been made of faults of orthography, as indicating a lack of ordinary schooling. The world has its liberal number of university graduates who never learned to spell. When it is remembered that from his twelfth year to his twenty-third Debussy was at the Conservatoire, where he was occupied almost solely with music, there may be less reason to blame elementary educational deficiencies of earlier years for such lack of literary and general culture as he occasionally betrayed. The Conservatoire was not a university, nor yet a high school. The boy of the "double front" gave himself up to music, though not always in a manner to gratify the martinets and traditionalists under whose pedagogical scrutiny he came.

At the time of Debussy's admittance, Ambroise Thomas, the composer of *Mignon,* was director of the Conservatoire. Although the boy had no such cause for personal complaint against Thomas as the fiery Berlioz had against Cherubini, as time went on Thomas was to indicate that Achille-Claude was not one of those who stood highest in his favor. Nor is this beyond understanding, in the light of Thomas's own career, his personality, and his musical predilections. A winner of the *Prix de Rome* as a conservatory student in 1832, a teacher of composition there since 1852, and fated to direct the destinies of the institution for nearly a quarter of a century, he was neither a classicist who could maintain the sacred standards of a noble past, nor an innovator who could discover new vistas for music's future. Refined and sensitive, even overgentle by nature, he reflected in his own compositions the popular trends of his time, presenting less a product of his own than a compound of Auber and Gounod. If, in 1873, he could have envisioned a composer of the future, that composer would have been Jules Massenet, whose early *Don César de Bazan* had been brought out at the Opéra Comique the year before. Thomas was an apostle of the well-ordered, the well-sugared, and the commonplace.

If thus unlikely to gain the personal sympathy of the director, the youth who subsequently was to disclose gifts far transcending those of both Thomas and Massenet was fortunate in being placed in the solfège class of a professor young in outlook, as in years. The English-speaking and reading world recognizes the name of Albert Lavignac chiefly as the author of a book on Richard Wagner that contains a useful analysis of the music-dramas and a handy record of Bayreuth casts. As a compendium of the *leit motifs* it has remained one of the most serviceable volumes of its kind, though its biographical data will scarcely stand the test of twentieth-century common knowledge. Frenchmen who could penetrate to the essence of Wagner's music as Lavignac did were none too common in his time; the factual mistakes or evasions of the book he wrote in 1897 can scarcely be viewed as of any consequence in considering the instruction and counsel he gave to young Debussy in 1873 and the four years immediately thereafter. Lavignac was not yet twenty-seven years old when he was called upon to initiate his awkward, swarthy pupil into the fundamentals of musical science, of which Debussy had acquired only a smattering in his two periods of piano study, first with Cerutti, then with Mme. de Fleurville. Recognizing in the boy something out of the usual, Lavignac soon became attached to Debussy; and the boy, less consciously, to him. By no means an ordinary schoolteacher, Lavignac went over new works with his pupil after school hours, including besides others the Overture to Wagner's *Tannhäuser*, which had been hissed in Paris fifteen years before. Both became so completely absorbed in these extracurricular studies that on one occasion they had to grope their way out through the dark corridors of the Conservatoire, which had been closed several hours earlier.

Thanks to Lavignac, young Debussy developed rapidly, but it seems that the pupil also developed the teacher, for Lavignac was forced to answer surprising, at times malicious, questions put to him by the boy. From the first, Debussy fought passionately against the rigidity of rules. He was still far from the point of understanding how they came to be and their necessity for the profession. He characterized them as something Chinese, and he ridiculed not the teacher, but the teaching. Frequently Lavignac had to agree with him in secret. The teacher realized that there was much musical erudition which served the eye more than it served the ear. On many points he had to satisfy the boy, still inclined to resistance, with proofs which lay outside the sacrosanct methods of the Conservatoire. Lavignac even declared that the opposition of the passionate pupil was a stimulus to him, since the boy's questions compelled him to reflect on things that had appeared to be fixed for all time and which suddenly became problematical. At any rate, Achille-Claude proved to be a grateful pupil. As we have seen, he distinguished himself in the solfège competitions. Lavignac was proud of him.

In the upper piano class, which the boy entered in the fall of 1875, things did not go so smoothly. His teacher, Marmontel, was no longer a young man and, having been active for thirty years at the Conservatoire, was not as readily "teachable" as Lavignac. Marmontel stood upon his dignity, declined discussions and frequently reprimanded his pupil, not without cause. Achille-Claude showed little inclination for the athletics of the piano and, instead of practicing the technical exercises set before him, preferred to play the quartets of Haydn and Mozart from score. He also irritated the old gentleman by improvising bizarre preludes for the études assigned to him and interpolated all

manner of eccentric modulations. Although he seemed to be
more interested in music in general than in perfecting his keyboard technique, he surprised his teacher at the first half-year
examinations. Marmontel had him play the F Minor Prelude
from volume two of Bach's *Well-Tempered Clavier*, and the
pupil put so much feeling into the execution that the teacher was
much impressed. Director Thomas was not to be won over so
easily. He looked upon the *Well-Tempered Clavier* as a polyphonic school of practice in which "feelings" were not permissible. Marmontel, however, took more notice of his pupil from
that day on, and eventually became his champion. Yes, the
boy's playing was eccentric, his own preludes more so, and he
scarcely knew how to get at the essence of Beethoven; but he
played Chopin as one obviously absorbed, even intoxicated by
the music. So Marmontel, who sensed in the boy a mind in the
making, excused many a whim and even some recalcitrance on
the part of his peculiar pupil. The boy's playing seemed grotesque to other students. Gabriel Pierné had the impression that
Achille-Claude puffed and blew at the difficult passages like an
unskilled rider. Paul Vidal recalled his awkwardness in playing
trills. Not until he was placed in the accompaniment class of
Bazille was it admitted by his companions that something more
than eccentricity gave individuality to Debussy's playing.

To his harmony teacher, Émile Durand, Debussy's battle
against rules for rules' sake appeared at first to be out-and-out
mischief. Himself a routine musician whose reputation rested on
two unimportant operas which once had been performed in
Paris, Durand found little pleasure in his calling or in his pupils,
least of all in the argumentative Debussy. Scarcely was a lesson
at an end when Achille would be sitting at the piano improvising unorthodox harmonies, whereupon the infuriated professor
would slam down the cover of the piano and exclaim: "You had
better do your lessons!" The lack of respect with which this

pupil treated his cadence formulas exasperated the pedagogue, yet interested him, too. After Durand had examined and duly rated everyone else in the class, he applied himself to Achille-Claude's exercise book with the satisfaction of righteous indignation. Strokes of his pencil rained down, corrections fell like hail. But he was a musician and he was curious. How could a lad in his early 'teens think of such oddities? Whence came the feeling for such indefensible combinations? What he did was absolutely contrary to all the laws of composition. But surely he was talented! Eventually, teacher and pupil became accustomed to one another. As an ostent of the half-hostile sympathy that grew up between them may be instanced a youthful trio in G, for piano, violin, and violoncello, which Debussy dedicated to Durand in cordial terms. Extant are some exercise books of the pupils in harmony of the years 1878–80, among them Debussy's. They are concerned with the harmonizing of melodies and given basses. Léon Vallas has said of them that they evince a certain charm which could not leave the examining officials untouched. But plain to be seen were many offenses against syntax which made it impossible for them to reward this charm with a prize. A quarter of a century later Debussy himself saw these first exercise books again. He was then a famous composer, a critic, and a member of the *conseil supérieur* in the Conservatoire. Debussy the celebrity acknowledged unblushingly the waywardness of Debussy the pupil. One suspects he was more than a little proud.

CHAPTER III

ADVENTURE IN MUSCOVY

The Young Debussy's Several Visits to Russia as Household
Pianist for Mme. von Meck—A Proposal of Marriage

IT is the time of the divided name. Achille-Claude Debussy has
become Achille de Bussy. He has composed some songs, *Nuit
d'étoiles, Beau soir, Fleur des blés*, dated 1876–78. At least two
others of the period, *Ballade à la lune* and *Madrid, princesse des
Espagnes*, unfortunately, are lost. Not yet eighteen, he is to become the protege of a wealthy woman and to pay court to one
of her daughters. But concurrently his heart is to be lost elsewhere, to the young wife of an elderly friend. Other interests,
the feminine not to be excluded, compete with the young man's
studies at the Conservatoire. His own family circle has less and
less to hold him. Already he has had a few days in England.
There he has heard *Pinafore*. Now is to come a visit—or several
visits—to Russia, the details of which Debussy seems never to
have imparted to his friends of later years. Only a little light has
been shed on the circumstances of Debussy's adventure of 1880,
by the publication in 1935 and 1936 of letters written by the
woman who was responsible for his early travel on the Conti-
nent.

This woman was Mme. Nadejda Filaretovna von Meck, the
same Mme. von Meck who was the mysterious correspondent
and patron of Tchaikovsky. The letters that have disclosed
something, if only a provocative little, of Debussy's journeys in
her company, were written to Tchaikovsky. She called him "my
little Frenchman" and "Bussy," without the "de." Mme. von
Meck, the widow of a Russian engineer, was supposed to be very

wealthy. Part of her time she spent in France, part in Switzerland, part in travel, part in Russia. At the celebrated château of Chenonceaux, where she made her abode betimes with Mme. Pelouse-Wilson, she maintained a trio of the orthodox order—violin, 'cello, and piano. A Conservatoire student, Jiménez by name, was for a time pianist of this trio. Debussy succeeded him. A letter from Mme. von Meck to Tchaikovsky, written on July 10, 1880, and dated from Interlaken, tells of Debussy's arrival two days before, to give lessons to Mme. von Meck's children, who were eleven in number when their millionaire father died in 1876. Debussy's duties included playing piano music, four hands, with his employer. He had also to accompany the singing of a daughter, Julia. Before many months had passed, he asked another daughter, Sonia,[1] to marry him. She refused. Nothing is known of any permanent damage thereby to Debussy's heart. The youth had just won a prize in Bazille's sight-reading class at the Conservatoire. Mme. von Meck reported to Tchaikovsky that he was quick in reading, played well, and was the possessor of a brilliant technique, but lacked any personal expression. Though he told her he was twenty, she remarked that he looked sixteen.

The widow was then at the height of her strange infatuation for Tchaikovsky and his music—an infatuation that led her to pension him, as well as to carry on the most sympathetic and personal correspondence with him over a period of sixteen years, though she made it a point of honor that they were never to meet. Debussy's first musical experiences outside of the Conservatoire thus brought him into an atmosphere of adoration for a composer whose personality and methods were the precise opposite of his own, as later established. He was immersed in a passionate cult, of which Mme. von Meck was high priestess and evangelist. That the association left so little impress upon

[1] Lockspeiser gives the name as Sophie.

MME. VON MECK

ACHILLE-CLAUDE AT SIX

DEBUSSY OF THE COWBOY HATS

him is remarkable. His employer regarded him as a pupil and follower of Massenet. When she played a four-hand piano arrangement of Tchaikovsky's Fourth Symphony with him, she was not satisfied with his part of the performance, though she confessed that he read it splendidly. Possibly her little Frenchman displeased her by not sharing in the "fever" which, she wrote Tchaikovsky, so penetrated all the fibers of her being that for a whole day she was in a terrible state of nerves. Bussy, as she styled him, did praise the fugue of another Tchaikovsky work—referred to as "your suite" in a letter from Arcachon on the East coast of France. Of course, Mme. von Meck passed the praise on to Tchaikovsky, though Bussy could have meant nothing to him. But as she had already "graduated" the youth from the conservatory with the "first prize," which, in point of fact, he was not to win until four more laborious years had brought him cruel disappointments and defeats, there may be reason for caution in relating Debussy to Tchaikovsky in the precise terms of these worshipful letters. The passionate widow liked the youth's accompanying, even describing it as "perfect"; she said he composed very nicely; and she pictured him as a typical product of the boulevards of Paris.[2] By way of pointing up her adulation of Tchaikovsky, she expressed herself as afraid of "those French charlatans—composers like Massenet, Delibes, Godard, etc."—and, apparently in concern over possible plagiarism, informed Tchaikovsky that on second thought she had decided not to show her little Frenchman the score of the Russian's *Jeanne d'Arc*. She told Tchaikovsky that Debussy did not care for the German composers, a statement which might have been true enough of the "musicien français" of later years but would appear at variance with what is known of his early obsession for Wagner, reaching back to his study of solfège with Lavignac in

[2] "Parisian from tip to toe, a typical *gamin de Paris*, very witty and an excellent mimic," she wrote on August 28, 1882. "His imitations of Gounod and Ambroise Thomas are perfect and most amusing."

his first year at the Conservatoire. That the full-blown Debussy was to resist the world dominance of Bayreuth, after some hearty adult prostrations on his part at its shrine, could scarcely have been foreseen by Tchaikovsky's idolater.

From France, the von Mecks, six or seven of them, moved on to Naples, then to Florence. At Fiesole they occupied and made music in the Villa Oppenheim, out among the hills. "My little pianist, Bussy," was with them, as Mme. von Meck particularized in a letter written early in September, 1880. Tchaikovsky is told of the youth's desire to be a composer, of the echoes of Massenet in "the very nice things" he writes, particularly a trio —the work that was dedicated to Durand. The widow sent one of Achille's youthful efforts to the symphonist in Russia for the master's opinion. It was the recently rediscovered *Danse bohémienne*. Tchaikovsky gave it tepid praise as "a nice little thing," but found it too short, lacking in unity, bungled as to form, and without a single thought developed to the end. Whether Mme. von Meck ever communicated Tchaikovsky's criticism to Debussy is not known. The trio of which the widow wrote was finished shortly thereafter and no doubt was played forthwith by the household ensemble consisting of Achille, pianist, Pachulsky, violinist (the future husband of Julia von Meck), and Danilchenko, 'cellist. It was in Florence that Debussy proposed to Sonia von Meck and was told to look elsewhere. The dedication of the song, *Rondeau,* written in 1882, "Pour mon ami Alexandre de Meck," brother of Julia and Sonia, bears witness to the close relations between the little Frenchman and the children of Madame, who was then about fifty years old. A photograph of the Pachulsky-Danilchenko-Debussy trio, sent to Tchaikovsky at about this time, caused him to write back to Mme. von Meck that there was something in Bussy's face and hands that vaguely recalled Anton Rubinstein in his youth. Tchaikovsky was so generous as to express the hope that it might be the young man's lot to be as happy as the "king of pianists," but left unsaid whatever he may have thought on the subject of a king of composers. Debussy, meanwhile, had arranged for keyboard duet some of the dances from Tchaikovsky's Ballet, *Le Lac des Cygnes*. In due course the arrangement was forwarded to the composer for publication with his consent, accompanied by the request that Debussy's name should not be used, as it might come to the knowledge of Massenet and bring on the student "a severe rating." As there is nothing to show that Massenet had any hand in Debussy's education at the Conservatoire, the widow's references to him are puzzling. Bussy was now "Bussik"; also, on occasion, "Petrouschka," in the familiar speech of the von Meck household, where nicknames were bestowed with a prodigality commensurate with the size of the family. Nicholas has related that Debussy styled the children's plump teacher "petit hippopotame en vacances" and that they in turn called him "le bouillant Achille." To Mme. von Meck's son, Debussy was a "sarcastic fellow," though his mother described him as good-humored, pleased with everything, and enormously entertaining. Debussy wept bitterly, she told Tchaikovsky, when the time came for him to return to Paris and his lessons.

In the autumn Debussy reentered the Conservatoire, to become a composition pupil of Ernest Guiraud. Whether he met Wagner [3] in Venice in this year, or heard *Tristan und Isolde* in Vienna in the course of his travels with the von Mecks, as has been stated in the reminiscences of friends, is still to be established. *Tristan* was not given at the Vienna opera before 1883. But the travels of 1880 were only the beginning of Debussy's attendance upon Mme. von Meck. The summer of 1881 found him in Moscow, after an exchange of letters with the widow, who was then at Brailov in the Ukraine. Sojourning in Moscow

[3] According to Jean Lépine, Mme. von Meck introduced Debussy to Wagner.

from July until September, Debussy is supposed to have met Rimsky-Korsakoff and Borodin of the so-called Russian "Cabinet," but not Moussorgsky; to have come under the spell of gypsy music in the cabarets and to have absorbed much that was to influence his own compositions of succeeding years. With Nicholas, another of the von Mecks, he went to Gourievo, near Moscow, to play—again the Tchaikovsky First Symphony in its four-hand reduction—at the villa of Alexandra von Meck, by marriage Countess Bennigsen. There is no record or mention of any meeting with Tchaikovsky, though there is a reference in a letter to show that Debussy had come into possession of the score of the *Romeo and Juliet* Overture-Fantasy as well as the *Jeanne d'Arc* music previously withheld from him. If, as a member of the von Meck family informed an English writer,[4] Debussy spent three summers in Russia, the harvest was amazingly small. A few songs, *Jet d'eau, Paysage sentimental, Voici que le printemps,* and *Belle au bois dormant* have been found to suggest Borodin. And if, as some have contended, Moussorgsky's music-drama, *Boris Godounoff,* has some echoes in *Pelléas et Mélisande,* they must be attributed to Debussy's much later discovery of the Russian masterpiece, made not in Moscow, but in Paris. Moussorgsky may have figured in Debussy's Russian sojourns, but nothing to indicate either personal contact or knowledge of his music at that time has come to light.

As for Tchaikovsky, one perhaps far-fetched association may be found in the lament of an interlude in *Pelléas et Mélisande,* that which follows the scene of Golaud's brutal seizing of Mélisande by the hair, before the eyes of the helpless old Arkel. But, if any such momentary affinity is to be found, it is with a much later and more characteristic Tchaikovsky than the composer of the First Symphony and *Jeanne d'Arc.* "Pourquoi Monsieur Tchaikovsky a-t-il changé son style?" the youth asked Mme.

[4] Edward Lockspeiser, *Musical Quarterly.*

von Meck, as mentioned in a letter which she wrote to Tchaikovsky in 1883, telling of the youth's admiration for the early
symphony. Certainly, there is nothing of Tchaikovsky—if perhaps not much of the real Debussy—in Debussy's own attempt
to write a symphony at this time. The recent publication in
Russia [5] in two-piano form of a single movement of the projected
symphony supplies in the notes themselves about all that is known
of this work, which is dedicated to Debussy's hostess. The manuscript was discovered in a Moscow market.

At any rate, Debussy was no favor seeker, then or later, and
he did nothing to ingratiate himself with Mme. von Meck's adored
celebrity. This is the more to his credit when it is noted that Pachulsky, another of the von Meck family's group of musicians,
flattered Tchaikovsky in the most obsequious way, in endeavoring to reach his good graces through Mme. von Meck. She quotes
him as saying, "How can such a luminary, such a colossus, stoop
to a worm like myself" and "God! what a man"—all over a bit
of gloved criticism of Pachulsky's music which Tchaikovsky had
sent on in answer to a request from his benefactor. Elsewhere, in
letters to his brother, Modeste, Tchaikovsky described Pachulsky's music as "indigestible rubbish" which was "poisoning" his
life; appending, however, that for "Mamma's" sake, there was
"nothing to do but to pretend that Pachulsky's filthy music is
serious."

Some few facts and dates are available for 1882, as gleaned from
Mme. von Meck's letters. Debussy joined the family at Plecht-
chevo, a small estate near Poldolsk, about thirty miles from Moscow, on August 27 of that year. During the month of September
he was with the von Mecks in Moscow. On October 1 they were
in Vienna and again on November 7, with a trip to Paris interven-
ing. The final parting took place in the latter part of this year.

In one of her letters (dated October 25, 1880) dealing with an

[5] By the Soviet State Publishing Company.

earlier adieu, Mme. von Meck speaks of her regret that he is leaving. "Musically," she wrote, "he gave me much pleasure, and, all in all, he is a boy with a good heart." But she didn't like some of his ways. "As I should have foreseen," she added, "his friendship with our Russian tutor has had a bad influence on him. That youth, for some unknown reason, set himself up as an aristocrat, and Bussy, still quite a child, caught the contagion and succeeded only in making us laugh at his airs." But the tutor left, and to the Madame's apparent relief, "Bussy is his old self again." That "old self" returned to the Conservatoire and to something he prized more than any of the fruits of his early travels, the charms of the woman he was to describe as "the melodious fay."

CHAPTER IV

THE VASNIER IDYL

An Elderly Friend and His Singing Wife—Compositions at Twenty for "the Melodious Fay"

His first proposal of marriage rejected, young Achille was to substitute for the image of the childish Sonia von Meck that of Mme. Vasnier, the mature, if still young wife of an also mature, but not so young, Paris architect. Of the four affairs of the heart that played any real part in Debussy's life this was the first, one-sided though it probably was in any real depth of feeling.[1] Mme. Vasnier was his friend, as was her husband; Gaby, of the green eyes, his mistress; Rosalie Texier and Mme. Bardac he married. With the light-o'-loves of his café days and nights there need be no concern.

Debussy was eighteen or nineteen when he was taken into the lives of the Vasniers. Besides his studies with Lavignac and Marmontel, the first in solfège, the second in piano, he had attended for a time a course in organ given by César Franck and he had distinguished himself in the accompanying class of Auguste Bazille. His ability to play well at sight, even more than his talent as a pianist, had been of service to him in his association with Mme. von Meck. Now he was to seek and find professional work as an accompanist, chiefly because he needed funds to play the role he was assuming for himself as Monsieur de Bussy. Through Paul Vidal, then a fellow student at the Conservatoire, Achille obtained a studio post with Mme. Moreau-Sainti, a singing teacher, to whom he dedicated his *Nuit d'étoiles* in 1882. Soon he was ac-

---

[1] Lockspeiser says bluntly that Mme. Vasnier became Debussy's mistress. Prunières has spoken of her as Debussy's "first great love."

companist for the Société Concordia, of which Charles Gounod was president and Charles Widor conductor. Among young singers who were pupils or friends of Moreau-Sainti, Mme. Vasnier came to mean something more than just a voice and tiresome arpeggios for the young accompanist. He admired her sweet but fragile soprano, but chiefly as it expressed for him her very winning personality. She found him agreeable and helpful, with something of strangeness, even a suggestion of the medieval, in his looks and manner. The Vasnier home soon was open to him; he spent as much of his time there as with his parents at Clichy; but it may be doubted whether he left his father's house and lived as one of the family at the Vasniers', as it has been said he did.

In a retrospective article in the *Revue Musicale*, Marguerite Vasnier, the daughter of the family, speaks of Debussy's coming to see them every day and of going home every night on the last train during the summer when they had a villa at Ville-d'Avray. In the winter he had permission to study and compose at the Vasniers', when he was not attending classes at the Conservatoire. That does not mean that he lived there, and that he left his home entirely. Marguerite Vasnier describes him as "coming almost every evening, sometimes in the afternoon, leaving pages begun, which, as soon as he would arrive, would take their place on a little table." Much has been said of the cultural poverty of Debussy's home, with references to Debussy's father as "pretentious" and his mother as a woman of the most commonplace type. But according to Paul Vidal,[2] a classmate of Debussy at the conservatoire:

> Mme. Debussy was a mother passionately attached to her son, and very "exalted"; each letter that she received from him during his voyage [in Russia] was a veritable event in her life. She was of great kindness and spoiled me a great

[2] Article in *Revue Musical*, 1926.

deal; she was an excellent cook, and liked to make delicious desserts which also flattered the well-developed gastronomical tastes of Debussy.

This couple belonged to a very modest class, but was not "peuple," inasmuch as they were interested in everything, and were abreast of the times; one finds only in Paris people of this sort—this was the household of a petty employee who went to hear all the novelties that were given in the theaters and liked to discuss them. . . .

[And later:] At the end of the year 1883 I carried off the first prize of Rome while Debussy obtained the second with the cantata "Le Gladiateur"; this event was celebrated in the Debussy family by a repast of which I have kept a moving souvenir. I was treated like a child of the house. Ernest Guiraud [teacher of composition at the Conservatoire] presided over this little family fete.

Others have said that Debussy's father insisted on his practicing faithfully and had high hopes for him as a pianist.

At the Vasniers', however, the youth apparently felt more a man; he was free of the petty distractions of family squabbles; he had what he most hungered and thirsted for, artistic surroundings, as well as the affectionate companionship of the woman who seems to have awakened in him the first adult passion of his life.

Debussy's Viennese biographer, Ernst Decsey, pauses to consider the young musician's earliest innamorata.

One looks again at the portrait of Mme. Vasnier by Baudry [he writes], regards the Juno-like shapeliness of her figure, the expressive dark eyes, a combination which even he admires who is not a temperamental musician of twenty years. In this picture, moreover, one can see a certain womanly kindness while one reads in the features of Monsieur Vasnier, her husband, a wise and fatherly goodness . . . and one can imagine that Achille felt well content in this house.

But there was restlessness, with a streak of the quarrelsome, to vary this content. Achille could be very cheerful and when he was in the mood he amused the Vasniers as he had amused the von Mecks. Pretending, operetta fashion, that his cane was a guitar, he improvised Southern serenades and parodied Italian music in a manner to provoke hilarity in the fifth-floor flat in the Rue de Constantinople that was for the time his real home. He devoured book after book, among them the schoolbooks of the daughter of the house, with frequent assaults upon an encyclopaedia to attest his eagerness for knowledge. He tried to give little Marguerite piano lessons, but he was a poor teacher and the child's mistakes irritated him so much that little progress was made. He smoked cigarettes incessantly and liked to pace about. He composed anywhere and everywhere, on the walk as well as at the piano, often singing the phrases he had conceived, without removing the eternal cigarette, before he jotted his ideas down on paper.

These and other impressions of Debussy in his early manhood have been passed on to posterity by Mlle. Vasnier. As she has described him, he was a big, beardless boy, with clearly marked features and thick, black curly hair which he wore flat on his forehead. It was this manner of wearing the hair, as much as anything else, that gave Debussy something of the appearance (as Mlle. Vasnier described it) of a medieval Florentine. She recalled that his eyes were particularly striking and that his personality made itself felt. She especially remembered that he had strong and bony hands and that his fingers were square. Among contradictory things reported of his piano playing, she said that it was powerful but on occasion very tender. He was a creature of moods, easily put in good humor and as easily put out of it. He would take offense at trifling remarks and would have sullen spells, when it was best to leave him alone. He was shy if the Vasniers had company and often sulked because of the presence

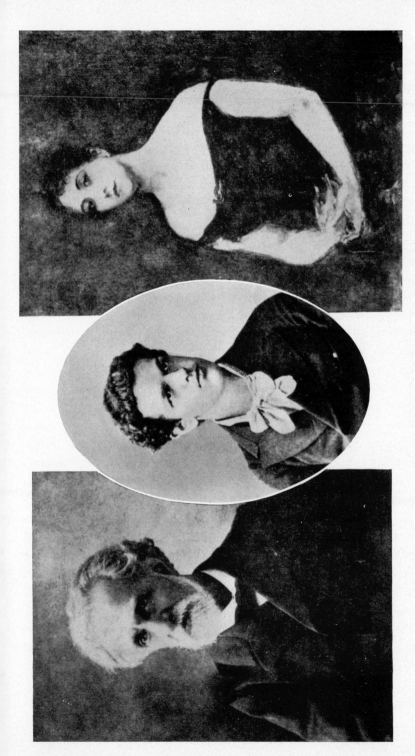

THE VASNIERS AND DEBUSSY AT EIGHTEEN
(Portrait of Mme. Vasnier by Paul Baudry)

of unexpected or undesired visitors. Though he showed this displeasure openly, he could be amiable with strangers if they happened to please him, even to the extent of playing and singing parts of the Wagner music-dramas or indulging his bent for musical caricature. He was sometimes rather loutish and never was what would be called polished. But his native charm asserted itself when he was pleased or interested.

At cards he was a bad loser, just as he was a bad player. Mlle. Vasnier explained that he really needed the stakes to pay his way home, particularly when he was a daily visitor at the family's suburban place at Ville-d'Avray. To restore his spirits, his hostess would put a packet of tobacco under his serviette at the table and then he was pleased. Accompanied by the budding composer, Mme. Vasnier sang the earliest Debussy songs. In a private collection is an album of them, dedicated to her by "the eternally grateful author." She alone has made them live, the dedication says; and they will lose their enchanting grace if they are never again to come from "her singing fairy lips." Verlaine and Mallarmé were poets who came into the young Debussy's ken largely as the result of his browsings in the Vasnier library. To this period belong the *Fêtes galantes* in their original version, on the poems of Verlaine—*Pantomime, En sourdine, Mandoline, Clair de lune*, and *Fantoches*. Also of this time, a *Chanson espagnole* for two voices was sung at a fancy dress ball by Mme. Vasnier and Debussy. A *Rondel chinois* and a *Nocturne* and *Scherzo* for piano and violin, which have disappeared, were composed in these years. Mme. Vasnier and Debussy participated in a program given by the violinist, Maurice Thiéberg, at which the *Nocturne* and *Scherzo* were played.

The next milestone in Debussy's career, the winning of the *Prix de Rome*, was to mean his departure from the Vasnier home and the waning of his adoration for the mistress of the household. There were at first many letters, but once Debussy had gone forth from the spell of the singing matron's indulgences, he was never to return to them. The daughter has told of her intention to write to him, a short time before the war, under the pretext that she would have liked to see his *Pelléas*.

> But it got no further than the intention [she wrote], and with deep regret I then heard of his death. . . . I believe he would have been glad to see again another witness of those beautiful years which he could not forget, for they were the years of his youth, of his hopes, of his well-being. . . . Now all three are dead, my parents and he, and nobody can ever hear again mother sing Debussy's songs, accompanied by Debussy. . . .

It has a pretty and a melancholy ring. But there were to be other singers and other songs. Debussy was by no means so inconsolable as his first letters from the Villa Medici may have made him out to be; half-boy that he was, and with artistic gifts that found their contemporary peak in the dramatic aspirations of *L'Enfant prodigue;* a work full of character for the product of a youth not yet twenty-two, but in its essential spirit as well as in its technical dress showing how far he was from being ripe for the full-blown sensualism of *The Afternoon of a Faun* of only ten years later.

CHAPTER V

THE *PRIX DE ROME*

Trials and Rebuffs at the Conservatoire—Failure in the Harmony Class—*L'Enfant prodigue*

"All this is very interesting but you must keep it for later. You will never get the Rome prize with that."

THIS was what Debussy's teacher of composition at the Conservatoire, Ernest Guiraud,[1] then a man in the late forties, said to Achille when the youth took to his mentor the music which, as a student, he had composed under the title of *Diane au bois*, a choral setting of words by Théodore de Banville, just then the favorite among French poets with the impressionable young musician.

So Debussy, rebel though he was against the dictums of his masters, put *Diane* away, masking his resentment against being required to compose by formula and according to the prevailing traditions of the school. He saw that in the Academy of Fine Arts, which awarded the *Prix de Rome*, there was little sympathy for the nonconformist. Gounod liked him and considered that he had exceptional talent. But it was at about this time that the composer of *Faust* delivered himself of these portentous words by way of advice to the younger generation:

Don't permit yourself to be snared by big, hollow-sounding words, like realism, idealism, impressionism—who knows, one of these days we shall have intentionism! All these catchwords are taken from the dictionary of that nihilism which is called *modern art* today!

[1] Ernest Guiraud was born in 1837 and died in 1892. He composed the operas *Le Kobold, Mme. Turlupin, Piccolino,* and *La galante aventure.*

59

Guiraud and Gounod may be considered the liberals of the circle Debussy had to satisfy in his progress at the Conservatoire. Plainly, as he might have told himself at any moment in the days of his studentship, the road to Rome was going to be a bumpy one. That he eventually traversed it successfully was due partly to the concessions he made, reluctantly, even sullenly, to the tastes of adjudicators who would never have stomached in the trial composition of a Conservatory fledgling such music as Debussy was later to write when he had only himself to please.

But it is not to be assumed that Debussy was at that time the master of innovation he subsequently became. Neither in the Conservatoire nor at Rome was he free of doubts as to his ability to achieve what he had in mind. Discouraged in his particular bent, with the thought continually impressed upon him that he had talent that might carry him far if only he would buckle down to the proper sort of composer-discipline, which meant putting out of mind his objections to accepted principles of harmonic relations, the wonder is that he was not more uncertain of himself than he was. He was young and he found pleasure, of course, in other men's music—including much music that could scarcely be regarded as in any sense revolutionary or in consonance with his own conceptions of harmonic freedom.

There was Lalo, for whom Debussy spoke a good word until the end of his days. The composer of the *Symphonie espagnole* and of *Le Roi d'Ys*, the latter not brought out until after Debussy had left the Conservatoire, was regarded as a rather uncouth adventurer by the classicists of the time, though his music is polished enough, in all conscience, for our later day. In his operatic writing he was oversymphonic for his contemporaries and it was on this score that he had difficulty in getting his stage works accepted for performance. There are those who regard Lalo as a true precursor of the modern French school and they find in the texture of his writing foreshadowings of Debussy, as well as of d'Indy and Dukas, on whom his influence is more obvious. That he contributed to Debussy's harmonies as he did to Dukas's orchestration is conceivable, but not quite so in-dubitable as some French writers have contended. At any rate, the student Achille was one of a number of young musicians who could scarcely contain their enthusiasm for the pantomime, *Namouna*, which had its première at the Opéra on March 6, 1882.

For the young Debussy this première was a scandal. It seems that the ballet dancer, Mlle. Sangalli, a favorite of the sub-scribers, did not like the music. Because it did not please her, it did not please her devotees. Leaving their seats, they conversed among themselves in a manner and to an extent to disturb others. From his place in the conservatory box, the indignant Debussy protested, shouting bravos and otherwise making such a com-motion of his own in favor of Lalo's music that he was put out of the box and out of the opera house. For some time he nursed a fury against the director, the ordinarily gentle Vaucorbeil, for having him ejected. Though in an article in *Gil Blas* some twenty-one years later he said that the old anger had melted away, the enthusiasm for Lalo remained. Nearly forty years his senior, Lalo (1823–92) died in the year that Debussy began work on *The Afternoon of a Faun* and made his initial sketches for *Pelléas et Mélisande* as the result of his first contact with Maeterlinck's play.

That Debussy was not expelled from the Conservatoire before he finally succeeded in winning the *Prix de Rome* may be put down as something of a miracle in view of what happened to two musicians whose names have been associated with his. A fellow composer, Maurice Emmanuel, who subsequently was to write a scholarly and penetrating analysis of *Pelléas* and who today is professor of the history of music at the Conservatoire, was expelled from that institution in 1886 because of contending emphatically in an argument with his teacher, Delibes, that it was possible to get out of medieval church chorales "new, *not yet exhausted* means of expression." A lustrum later, the future critic, Émile Vuillermoz, whose first love had been composition, was expelled because, contrary to the orders of his teacher, Antoine Taudou—who, it seems, was merely the mouthpiece of the director, Ambroise Thomas—he went to hear *Pelléas*, thereby submitting himself to an infection for which his instructors had no efficient prophylactic to prescribe. Within Achille was a demon that prompted him to vaunt his independence and his disdain of the professors before his fellow students. If he had been so unlucky as to get caught in the act, when indulging in one of his pranks of sarcasm, his conservatory career might have ended then and there. It is related how the youth, waiting for the kindly Guiraud to arrive for the beginning of class, amused his fellows by imitating on the piano the sound of an omnibus rattling down the Faubourg Poissonière, employing chromatic passages that were subsequently to find an honorable place in music but which then sounded forced and outlandish. Noting the reception of his musical mimicry, he suggested that in case his listeners had not understood the harmonies it might be advisable for them to have their ears cleaned out by the director.

Achille failed in Émile Durand's harmony class, partly because of his use of consecutive fifths and octaves. Yet he had already composed the songs *Nuit d'étoiles*, *Beau soir* and *Fleur des blés*, dated 1876–78; and to the period of his struggles at the Conservatoire are to be credited *Paysage sentimental*, *Voici que le printemps* and *La Belle au bois dormant*, dated 1880, though not published until 1903. Also of this period is the favorite *Mandoline*. It is not altogether surprising that a youth who could write songs of this quality should presume to pit his own notions about composition against rules for which he could find neither rhyme nor reason. "A feast for the ear" he called a parade of all manner of unorthodox successions of chords with which he once held the attention of the fascinated but possibly horrified students of Delibes's class, of whom he asked why parallel movements in fifths and eighths should be forbidden whereas counter movements were supposed to be sacred. Imperiously playing the role of teacher, the young rebel summoned fellow pupils to the piano, called upon them to accomplish a modulation, and muttering either in approval or disapproval, shook his mass of black hair at any pupil who, as the expression went, "fell into the arms of the old lady," otherwise a traditional cadence. Guiraud, who made something of a companion of the youth, both being fond of billiards, cigarettes, and noctambulation, clearly was interested in his harmonic ideas. But Guiraud was then only newly appointed to the Conservatoire. To advance along the road to Rome, Debussy must please other ears than those of his friendly composition teacher.

In 1881, at the time when he was first discovering new horizons at the Vasniers', Achille wrote a fugue that won him honorable mention in competition with his fellow students. It was at about this time that he studied organ with César Franck, whom he is said to have described as "a modulating machine," but it is to be doubted that he had any lessons in composition from that master. Heeding the advice of Guiraud, and conforming as best he could to what was expected of him, he contrived to gain a "second accessit" the next year (1882) in the conservatory contests in counterpoint and fugue, the subject being one supplied by Gounod. The manuscript of his entry is now in the conservatory library. He then made his first effort to attain the Rome prize. This took the form of a chorus for women's voices, based on a poem by Comte de Ségur. Originally entitled *Printemps*, it was published in 1928, ten years after Debussy's death, as *Salut, Printemps* because of other works bearing the former name. It illustrates Debussy's fondness for the harp, but there can be no particular quarrel, today, with those who sat in judgment on the student compositions of this year and failed to find in the work an originality to offset its immaturity. Commentators have gone to some pains to point out the misspelling in three places of the word *couronne*, in which Debussy doubled the *r*. Orthography was not his long suit.

With the next year's contest in mind, Debussy almost immediately composed *Intermezzo*, described as an interpretation of a passage in Heine's atmospheric work of that name. It survives both as a piano duet and an orchestral score in the Legouix collection, with some more misspellings in the copying of words. The signature shows that Achille had not as yet become Claude Debussy. But it was not *Intermezzo* that was to mark him as still a contender rather than a victor in the *Prix de Rome* contests. For his second preliminary examination in 1883 he submitted a chorus, *Invocation*, for men's voices, to text by Lamartine, along with the required fugue. The manuscript of the fugue is missing, though the chorus has been preserved at the Conservatoire. Debussy is said to have told his comrades that he lacked the religious feeling to deal adequately with the subject. At any rate, to him was awarded fourth place; with Paul Vidal, Charles René, and Xavier Leroux getting higher ratings. Not yet twenty-one, Achille made a brave try for the prize in the contest itself, composing to text by Émile Moreau, a cantata, *The Gladiator*. Gounod presided at its trial performances on June 22 and 23, before the Académie des Beaux-Arts. Soloists were Gabriele Krauss, Taskin, and Muratet. Vidal won the prize; Debussy took second place. Both works were commented upon in the press. Though Vidal was conceded to have evolved the smoother and more skilled composition, technically, Debussy was recognized as having the more personal, temperamental, and individual talent. Debussy was still in the piano stage so far as orchestration was concerned, but he could not conceal the individuality of his harmonic personality. Neither could he escape the influences of the music, particularly the newer music, that was admired at this time. Massenet's *Manon* and *Herodiade,* as well as Lalo's *Namouna* left their mark upon him.

Returning to the battle in 1884, he entered the preliminary examination with a chorus and fugue, the one based on verses of Jules Barbier (again a Spring poem) the other on a theme that originated with Massenet. As Debussy rediscovered for himself in later years, when he examined and corrected the manuscript, he made mistakes that were to prove him no lineal descendent of Johann Sebastian Bach in the art of fugue. But he again received fourth place, with Leroux and René once more among the leaders. Though Leroux was subsequently to achieve a measure of fame as the composer of *La Reine Fiamette, Le Chemineau,* and other operas akin to those of his teacher, Massenet, neither his talent nor that of René was of an order to justify for posterity any assumption that either rightly could stand as a rival to one who already had about him something of genius. But his colleagues had one great advantage. There was no conflict between their talents and their training. What they were taught served to discipline and make serviceable such native endowment as they possessed, whereas Debussy was torn by an inner struggle in which the best and the most essential of his gifts was in conflict with much of his instruction.

Out of this struggle, and with not only Guiraud at his elbow but Lalo and Massenet in his ears, Debussy evolved his *L'Enfant prodigue,* which was finally to win for him the coveted *Prix de Rome* in the contest of 1884. A setting of a poem by Édouard Guinand, the lyric scene (or cantata as it is more commonly known) called into play the latent dramatic gifts of the young man of twenty-two. Debussy did not conceive *L'Enfant prodigue* as a stage work.[2] But like Berlioz, if the stage was to be denied to him, that aspect of his musical genius must inevitably assert itself in music devised for other ends. The setting was neither flaccidly sentimental nor assertively emotional. To the contrary, it possessed a surprising poise and sobriety. Gounod probably saw further than the work itself when he took the young composer aside and whispered to him: "Toi, tu as du génie."

At the public performance, Debussy played the piano part himself, with the assistance of his friend René Chansarel. The soloists were Rose Caron, Ernst van Dyck, and Taskin. Twenty-two of the twenty-eight judges gave him their votes. He had won the *Prix de Rome*. Though he revised parts of the score after a lapse of a quarter of a century, friends of the later years have said that the mature Debussy was often annoyed by the enthusiasm manifested for it, and more particularly for the too-popular air of Lia. Perhaps it reminded him of Romain Rolland's sly observation that something of Massenet is lodged in every Frenchman. But even bits of *Pelléas* could be singled out as corroboration of that. *L'Enfant prodigue* has stood on its own feet as music of respectable quality and a fair measure of appeal, irrespective of "influences," and possibly just as independent of those fifths and fourths, and prefigurements of the later use of the whole-tone scale, which enthusiasts like to point to as the beginnings of the Debussy style. With equal justice, those beginnings can be traced further back, to the songs of the earliest 'eighties.

It was not while the music of the performance was chiming in his ears, however, that Debussy was to learn of his success. He was in love and in no particular mood for Rome. Such pil-

[2] On December 10, 1919, it was produced as a "lyrical drama in one act" at the Théâtre Lyrique de Vaudeville.

grimage as there was in his heart was to Ville-d'Avray where the kindly Vasniers had left the latch open for him. As he has related in his *Monsieur Croche* [3] he had gone to the Pont des Arts, one of the bridges spanning the Seine, and like other idlers there was watching the play of light at sunset, with the little steamers scurrying by, beneath him. Placidly enjoying the scene, he had put from his mind everything pertaining to the Rome competition. Someone tapped him on the shoulder and breathlessly told him that he had won the prize.

"Believe me or not," he said, in recalling the emotions of the moment, "I can assure you that all my pleasure vanished! I saw in a flash the boredom, the vexations inevitably incident to the slightest official recognition. Besides, I felt no longer free!"

He was no longer free to do as he pleased at the Vasniers', to sing Italian serenades with a cane as his guitar, to sulk if that was his mood when unwelcome guests arrived, to bask in the smiles of the woman who had converted an adolescent into a man, to play the clown and relish the laughter of his chosen friends. Those delightful idlers on the bridges of Paris, as he saw them in that hour, were properly the envy of all Europe. He did not know it, but he was now to figure for the last time in the correspondence of Mme. von Meck and Tchaikovsky, that Madame might have her moment of reflected glory.

> Did you happen to read in *Le Figaro* [she writes her idol] that the little Frenchman, Achille Debussy, who spent several seasons with me, won the *Prix de Rome* with a composition on the text of *L'Enfant prodigue?* It is being very highly praised. I am not surprised, for he is a very gifted boy, and having spent much time with me, he was able to widen his outlook and improve his taste by becoming acquainted with music in other countries. This wider knowledge has served him very well.

[3] A book of collected critical essays.

There is nothing to indicate that Tchaikovsky, who was then at work on his *Mazeppa* or his *Manfred*, made any readjustments of his life on receipt of the news.

CHAPTER VI

ROME AND THE VILLA MEDICI

In the Footsteps of Berlioz—Homesickness and Wagner—Flight
and *La Damoiselle élue*

"A ROMAN against his will," Debussy spent a little more than
two of the prescribed three years at the Villa Medici, protesting
the while in his letters to the Vasniers that he was in prison, or,
if a little less disconsolate, in barracks like a noncommissioned
officer. Seven months to the day after he had won the Rome
prize, he set out on January 27, 1885, for the Eternal City and
its little band of French youths who were furthering their bent
for painting, sculpture, music, architecture, or engraving at the
expense of their government. He knew well Gabriel Pierné,
Georges Marty, and Paul Vidal, prize winners of preceding
years. With others at the Villa Medici was the architect Gaston
Rédon, who played the flute, the sculptor Lombard, whose
musical friendships included a close tie with Chausson, and Marcel Baschet, a painter with literary appetites similar to those Debussy was to develop, as he became better acquainted with Verlaine, Baudelaire, Rossetti, and Shakespeare.

But Achille approached Rome in no mood for companionship. According to custom, several of his fellow laureates met
him at Monte Rotonde, and, as he complained in a lengthy letter
to M. Vasnier, six of them slept in one dirty room. He found,
or fancied, that the others had changed since he had known
them in Paris, and he lamented the loss of the good-hearted,
friendly ways that were theirs as conservatory students. They
were stiff and impressed with their own importance, he said—
"too much *Prix de Rome* about them!" Once arrived at the

Villa Medici, he found no such artistic atmosphere and camaraderie as would agree with what he had heard about the life there. The Villa itself he described as "abominable." Moreover the weather was "awful"—rainy and windy. There was no need to journey to Rome for such weather; he could have it in Paris. He had a grudge against the place, even before there was opportunity to look it over. What he most wanted was an old-time chat with the Vasniers. Instead, he had to listen to egoistic musicians demolishing one another—Marty and Pierné against Vidal; Pierné and Vidal against Marty—the while Achille-Claude pined for his "melodious fay." If he did not write quite these words to Vasnier, he may have penned more impassioned ones to Madame. Achille's letters to his singing fairy have been destroyed.

Berlioz had indulged in no such fulminations against the Villa Medici. Indeed, he had felt himself as in a dream when the carriage set him down "in front of a palace of noble, severe architecture," after his first glimpse of the imposing majesty of the Piazza del Popolo. But both were fantasts, in their different ways, and the purpose of Debussy's letters to the Vasniers was a very different one from Berlioz's in his memoirs. Berlioz indulged his penchant for rhetoric. Debussy sought sympathy. The later Frenchman saw everything through glasses of gloom. Even at Marseilles, only well started on the journey to Rome, he had written to Vasnier to say that he was very sad and was trying to keep up his courage.

Still, one wonders if he was really so insensate to the charms of the spot to which he had been transported. The Villa Medici, the property of the French government since 1803, occupies a superb site on the slope of Monte Pincio, the northernmost height in Rome, with its great gardens laid out in the Napoleonic era; to the right, the Pincian Way, to which Berlioz referred as "the Champs-Élysées of Rome"; to the left the church of

Trinita del Monte with the obelisk, from which descends the famous marble stair leading down to the Piazza d'Ispagna. Built in 1557 by Annibale Lippi, the villa was later enlarged and ornamented by Michelangelo. Surrounding it is a spacious, fragrant park. From here, among pines, laurels, palms, and statues, said Berlioz, the outlook is one of the most beautiful in the world. Below, St. Peter's lifts its huge dome, with the Vatican adjoining, the Tiber near by. In the sweep of the eye is revealed also the spire of the church of Lourdes, a portion of the Leonine Wall, the castle of Sant' Angelo, crowned with its bronzed angel; the cypresses of Monte Mario and the pines on the Janiculum, which a later composer was to celebrate along with those of the Appian Way.[1]

But the cellular studios within had a quiet that was more than monastic for Achille. They were the cells of a jail. His first room, with walls painted green, was termed "the Etruscan tomb." Debussy described it to the Vasniers as enormous; the walls, he said, seemed to recede as he went toward them; he had to walk a league from one piece of furniture to another. In these quarters, he felt so lonely that he wept. Later, he had a room that was decorated with frescoes by Besnard. But in one room or another, the Villa Medici impressed him as "a cosmopolitan hotel, a private college and a compulsory civilian barracks." He was annoyed by the table talk. There were deficiencies in the housing arrangements—deficiencies that remained so acutely and stubbornly in mind that many years later—in 1903, when the centenary of the Académie de France in Rome was celebrated—he wrote some trenchant comment to the effect that it would have been fitting if in honor of the occasion some improvements had been made in the meals supplied to the *Prix de Rome* students. "We narrowly escaped poisoning," he said, "and dyspepsia is not a necessary part of an artist's equipment." He

[1] Respighi, *The Pines of Rome*.

was then critic for *Gil Blas,* and eighteen years had elapsed since he had acquired in Rome the sobriquet of "The Prince of Darkness."

It is recorded that the first winner of the Rome prize for music, young Andrôt, who arrived at the Villa Medici in 1804, died within six months, taken by a violent fever. In Debussy's day, as in Andrôt's and Berlioz's, there was among Romans and informed visitors alike an almost superstitious dread of "l'aria cattiva" from the Campagna, which caused the pedestrians, equestrians, and carriage riders on the Pincian Way to disperse (as Berlioz described it) like a swarm of flies on the stroke of seven in the evening, leaving to rash strangers all thoughts of lingering to admire the gorgeous sunset behind Monte Mario.

Of the many noted French musicians who had preceded Debussy to the Villa Medici, one of the earliest was Hérold, who (along with *Zampa* and various other operas all but forgotten today) composed *Le Pré aux clercs* of which Achille's father was so fond. Hérold was sent to Rome in 1812. Benoist was a prize winner of 1815; Halévy, whose *La Juive* has lingered on, followed in 1819; Leborne in 1820; Berlioz, 1830; Prévost, 1831; Thomas, 1832; Elwart, 1834; Gounod, 1839; Bazin, 1840; Massé, 1843; Gastinel, 1845; Bizet, 1857; Paladilhé, 1860; Massenet, 1863; Passard, 1866; Serpette, 1871; Salvare, 1872; S. Rousseau, 1878; Bruneau, 1881; Pierné, 1882. These were outstanding among Debussy's predecessors, though some of them have ceased to be even names for the ordinarily well-informed musical devotee of today.

The *Prix de Rome* was not discontinued, to be sure, with Debussy's winning of it in 1884. Charpentier, whose *Louise* the composer of *Pelléas* was to attack in the most scathing terms a decade and a half later, arrived in 1887, the year that Debussy returned finally to Paris. Rabaud was the winner in 1894, Florent Schmidt in 1900, Caplet in 1901, Laparra in 1903, Gaubert in

1905, Lili Boulanger in 1913, Dupré in 1914. Since Debussy's death in 1918, young men from the Conservatoire have blithely or solemnly taken their place at the table about which he complained. The small talk—with, let us hope, the high aspiration—goes on.

Amusing is the word picture which the Debussy of later years left us of the dining room, with its portraits of previous laureates reaching to the ceiling. Each, he says, wears the same rather dejected expression; and the multiplicity of the frames, with their fixed dimensions, causes the beholder to feel that the same prize winner is repeated to infinity!

The director in charge when Debussy arrived at the Villa Medici was Louis-Nicolas Cabat, an elderly landscape painter who impressed the young musician as first of all a distinguished man of the world. But, for all his distinction, he was head jailor until superseded by M. E. Hébert, another painter, and one more Roman than the Romans. To Hébert, Debussy complained about "the Etruscan tomb," only to be told that if necessity so required an artist could sleep in the Colosseum, where grandeur and awe would amply atone for any hygienic or other inconvenience. No doubt Debussy was aware that the villa actually had served as a prison for Galileo Galilei.[2] Now the martyrs had been increased to two. As he had foreseen on the bridge in Paris, his freedom was gone. He had been caught up in the net of petty officialdom. Life was precisely the bore he had predicted it would be.

Yet on the very night of his arrival at his Roman prison, he had played through his *L'Enfant prodigue* for his colleagues and had heard them praise it. There were trips with some of them to

[2] Galileo was confined in the Villa Medici, from 1630 to 1633, at the instance of the Inquisition, for the criminal offense of "having seen the earth go around the sun." The Villa takes its name from Cardinal Alessandro de Medici, who came into possession of it in 1605, and who became Pope Leo XI. It was built for Cardinal Ricci da Montepulciano and was long the property of the Grand Dukes of Tuscany.

various landmarks and charming sights almost immediately. He read Shakespeare with the poet Maurice Vaucaire and his fellow musicians Xavier Leroux and Paul Vidal; he shared his expanding literary enthusiasms with Marcel Baschet, who painted a Florentinelike portrait of him; and he played Mozart sonatas with the director himself, Hébert having turned out to be quite a fair violinist. If there was little music to interest him in the Italian theaters or concert halls, the former being occupied chiefly with Donizetti and early Verdi, aria operas of a type for which Debussy had no liking, there was Wagner to explore in the privacy of a music room or in company with other novitiates. Hours of the day and night were devoted to the study of *Tristan und Isolde*.

For the young Debussy it was Hébert's misfortune to dislike Wagner as heartily as he adored Mozart. Moreover, as Achille described himself in his emancipated later years, the young laureate was at that time a Wagnerian "to the point of forgetting the most common principles of politeness." Little did he dream, as he was subsequently to confess, that the time would come when he would share the anti-Wagnerism of "that clairvoyant old man." It is of record that he heard a performance of *Lohengrin* with Vidal. Later he was to dispute with Gounod about its merits.

If the Italian opera had little to attract him, he contrived to find stimulating entertainment in the typically Italian *Pulichinelle*. Moreover, the musician and the artist within him was stirred by the great works of Palestrina and Orlando di Lasso, which he heard in the church of San Maria dell' Anima, tucked away "among some awful little streets." It was only in such a place, he wrote the Vasniers, that such music should be heard; and it was the only church music for him. Comparing a mass by di Lasso with one by Palestrina, he liked the former better; Orlando, he felt, was the more decorative and human. The scroll-

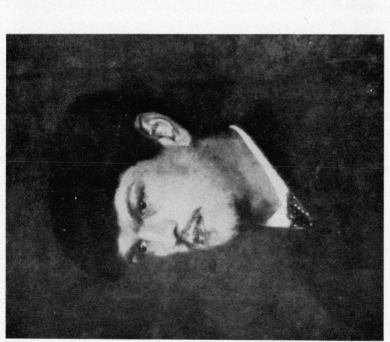

TWO PORTRAITS OF DEBUSSY AT THE VILLA MEDICI

(Left, by Marcel Baschet; right, by Henri Pinta)

like melodic outlines of this music fascinated him; and its counterpoint—even though counterpoint could be the most forbidding thing in the world—was something exquisite, bringing out the meaning of words in a way to evoke wonder. Though never himself a contrapuntist in the formal sense, the majestic polyphony of sixteenth-century liturgical music was to shake Debussy's spirit in later days as it did in Rome; witness the story of a colleague [3] who met him as he came out of the Church of Saint-Gervais with his eyes aflame and the fervid words "Voilà la musique!" But it was not the music for his own pen. He knew that he was a harmonist, not a master of the mass or of fugue. Within his mind was a continual clarifying of his desires; more and more, he knew what he wanted to do. "But am I big enough?" he asked himself and the Vasniers. What worried him most was that he was unproductive. Leaving his "barracks" for a short time in 1885, he sojourned pleasantly enough at the villa of Count Josef Primoli on the seaside at Fiumicino. There he had everything to himself; he did not need to talk to anyone, except to order his meals. To the Vasniers he wrote that he worked "almost well." But, confronted with the necessity of writing the first of the *Envois de Rome* that were expected of the laureates by those in Paris who were taking official note of their progress, he apparently made no more real headway than at the barracks.

As time went on several celebrities were added to the list of acquaintances among world figures in music that had been mounting since the boy's peregrinations with Mme. von Meck. Though Ruggiero Leoncavallo was at the time more journalist than composer, he was important to Debussy as the means of an introduction to Arrigo Boïto, who, in turn, paved the way for the young Frenchman to call on Verdi. Boïto impressed Debussy as much more a literary man than a musician. His abode was littered with books, newspapers, magazines, clippings,

[3] Julien Tiersot, in the Rivista Musicale Italiana.

proofs, and manuscripts. On his mind at the time of the meeting was a lecture he had prepared on "The Lake Poets." Verdi was in his shirtsleeves, working in his garden at Sant' Agatha when Debussy arrived, and after they had dined together, went back to his flowers. The old man—for he was in his seventies; it was the time of *Otello*, with *Falstaff* still to come—was chary of discussing his contemporaries. There were a few remarks about Wagner, Gounod, and Ambroise Thomas, but nothing that Debussy himself regarded as worth recalling in print in the days when he was writing articles on music for publications in Paris.

More exciting for the young composer from the Conservatoire were meetings with Franz Liszt, brought about through his pupil, the pianist Sgambati. As narrated by the English journalist André de Ternant, it was at the home of Sgambati, a frequent visitor at the Villa Medici, that Debussy met the venerable Abbé, who called there with his friend Cardinal Hohenlohe. At the request of the cardinal, Liszt consented to play with Sgambati the Saint-Saëns *Variations on a Theme of Beethoven*, the two pianos resounding with what may have been intended as a particular mark of recognition of French genius. The impression made on Debussy, the pianist, by Liszt's command of keyboard resource was an abiding one; more than a quarter of a century later he wrote that Liszt "seemed to make the pedal breathe." With Liszt as listener, Debussy and Vidal on another occasion played on two pianos the *Valses romantiques* of Chabrier. When Liszt left Rome soon thereafter, it was never to return. Ternant is authority for the statement that Debussy heard Liszt the last time the old virtuoso played in Italy. Divergent as were the paths of Debussy and Saint-Saëns in the years that followed, they are reported to have embraced one another—true Frenchmen that they were—when Debussy narrated the experience to his older compatriot. Saint-Saëns, the fanatical admirer of Liszt, was one thing; Saint-Saëns, the defender of the orthodox in art in the

Académie des Beaux-Arts, was quite another, as Debussy was to learn in the course of his several efforts to fulfill the requirements in the matter of the *Envois de Rome*.

Oppressed by "an indescribable feeling of being out of his proper atmosphere," as he wrote to his old friends in Paris, and nourishing an antipathy, real or fancied, against his companions, of which some of them seem to have been aware, Debussy worked at composition in desultory fashion. So ill-contented that he planned to quit Rome at the end of the first year—"I really believe that to remain here a second year would do me no good whatever," he wrote to Vasnier—he still could not escape the work that the laureates were expected to do. At the time that he was considering a speedy return to Paris and was imploring his friends not to think harshly of him—since he would only be doing this for the sake of his future, and to remain in Rome would only make him hate the place the more—he was clarifying his mind concerning what he really hoped to achieve. On June 4, 1885, he wrote of his desire to produce something original and not always follow the same paths that others had trod. "I am sure the Institut would not approve, for, naturally, it regards the path which it ordains as the only right one. But there is no help for it! I am too enamored of my freedom, too fond of my own ideas." This, he said, was the only kind of music he could write. The question was, as he put it to the Vasniers, whether he was capable of achieving it. But if he could satisfy only a few people, he would not care what all the others might think.

For his first *envoi*, he took up the composition of *Zuleima*, a work for chorus and orchestra, with text by Georges Boyer that was an adaptation of Heine's *Almanzor*. After the first flush of enthusiasm he gave it up, finding the great, heavy verses—"great only in their length"—oppressive and stupid. "My music," he said, "would be submerged by their weight." He began to see the need for an emotional or soul state in music, rather than action. He wanted a subject which would be more human, in that it would deal primarily with feelings rather than events. Already the future composer of *Pelléas* was thinking of drama as primarily something of the spirit. But he was not, in fact, through with *Zuleima*. It was one of several works that were to be taken up again after they had been laid aside.

Diane au bois, which Guiraud had told him at the Conservatoire to keep until later, came back to mind. He wrote to the poet's godson for permission to use de Banville's comedy as the basis of a musical stage work. He was weary of cantatas. It was in connection with the resumption of work on this subject that he wrote of his desire to do "something original," even though he knew he would not be following the path prescribed by the Immortals of the Institut. "I may have undertaken a work beyond my powers," he wrote at this time. "As there are no precedents, I must create new forms." In another letter he expressed his inability to put music into a strict mold, going on to explain that he did not mean a musical mold. "It's a literary question." Much as he then adored Wagner, he regarded it as ridiculous that he should seek help in that direction. He did not want the orchestra to predominate. Instead, he sought to maintain a lyrical atmosphere. One day he felt that he had found what he was seeking; the next he was doubtful and feared he was on the wrong track. Diane herself caused him much anxiety. "How difficult it is," he wrote the Vasniers, "to express the thousand and one sensations of a character" while still seeking to retain clarity of form. He feared that the scenes, which the poet had not planned with the thought of musical investiture, would seem too long; to keep up the interest so that the public would not be bored to tears—that was "the very mischief."

Nine months later on, *Diane au bois* stood with only one scene completed and that one not to Debussy's satisfaction.

From it, Achille turned to a rough sketch for a work to be called *Salammbô*, in turn put aside for possible future consideration in Paris. Ideas for songs occupied some of his attention. But although he again had Paul Bourget (whose verses he had used for the *Beau soir*, *Voici que la printemps* and *Paysage sentimental* of his Conservatoire days) as his inspiration, his muse remained recalcitrant. He visited museums and galleries in a distracted way and found more pleasure in playing through Beethoven's Ninth Symphony or Chabrier's *Valses romantiques* with Vidal than indulging his own gift for composition. But as something had to be done to meet the requirements, he went back to *Zuleima* and, finishing the first part of it, sent that much on to the Académie des Beaux-Arts in Paris as a "symphonic ode." So little was Debussy pleased with this effort, that he subsequently destroyed the manuscript. It made no appeal to the Academicians of Paris, who took occasion to praise works sent in by Pierné and Vidal, while branding as "bizarre, incomprehensible, and impossible to execute" the truncated *Zuleima*. As published in the *Journal officiel* of December 31, 1886, the view of the judges was that the vocal part of the work was uninteresting, both as to melody and declamation, though it was grudgingly admitted that here and there was a passage that showed individuality. Achille was regarded as a backslider. The Académie, according to the report, had had reason to expect that this young artist, described as "remarkably talented," would exhibit further the dramatic and melodic gifts noted in *L'Enfant prodigue*. It could only record the opposite. Still, the hope was expressed that the young man, given more time and further experience, would see the light and modify the extravagance of his writing. Saint-Saëns is presumed to have been a leading spirit in the preparation of this report. If so, this was the beginning of a gloved warfare on his part against the eccentricities, as he seems at first to have viewed them, of the French genius whose star was to burn brighter than his own.

Meanwhile, Debussy had contrived to get away from the "barracks" and in February, 1886, descended upon the Vasniers in Paris. To accomplish this, he was said to have thrown himself, weeping, before Hébert and to have threatened suicide if he could not get away. Doubt has been cast upon the seriousness of the incident. The laureate had not lost his gift of play-acting, and fellow students have spoken of his ability to give them a bit of hysterical tragedy on demand. Presumably the Vasniers persuaded him to return to Rome, though possibly he was never so wholeheartedly convinced that he should toss overboard the fellowship as his letters have seemed to indicate. For one thing, so far as is known, he had no other source of income. At Rome he was supported by the state. Back in the Villa Medici for the remainder of 1886, certain of his letters—addressed not to the Vasniers but to Émile Baron, a Paris bookseller—were of a less complaining and self-pitying character. He tells of processions of priests in red and black, suggesting radishes and pimentos. When an unusual cold snap came, he wrote of the inability of the Romans to dress properly for it; their coats were too short. Paradoxical as he confesses it to be, he even expresses a desire to hear some Offenbach! Whether there had come some cooling of his long-distance relations with the Vasniers, possibly because of his having been persuaded to return to Rome, or whether he was merely enlarging his appeal for sympathy, it is now to Baron that he turns, as the only one to whom he can speak of such things as his inability to compose music to order, an obvious reference to the *Envois de Rome*.

But since *Envois* there must be, he returns to the subject of "Spring." For the third time, a composition comes from his pen entitled *Le Printemps*. This time a painting supplies the inspiration, the *Primavera* of Botticelli. The composition is described as a symphonic suite in two parts, for orchestra and wordless chorus. It bears the date of February, 1887, and has no connection with the choruses written in 1882 and 1884 when Debussy was a contestant at the Conservatoire for the *Prix de Rome*. Debussy wrote to Baron that it had caused him a lot of trouble. Indeed, compared to the travail of its composition, the life of a convict was to be regarded as altogether leisurely. It was not his object, he said, to write a descriptive *Printemps*, but an essentially human one, in which he could express the gradual blossoming, as it were, of the joy of living from miserable beginnings in Nature. He added that this was in no sense a program, as he then despised music that was hitched to a literary idea. What he sought was music that would be "suggestive" by virtue of a special color and which would embrace a wide play of the feelings. The last work actually to be finished during Debussy's stay in Rome, *Printemps* was played as a piano duet by Debussy and Augustin Savard (*Prix de Rome* winner of 1886) at a reception given by the director. In Paris it was received with less hostility than was *Zuleima*, but not without reservations. The employment of humming voices as if they were instruments was a source of criticism. There was unfavorable comment on the use of the key of F-sharp major, which was considered a poor one for orchestral writing, as César Franck had learned a decade or so earlier in connection with *The Redemption*.

By some accident the orchestral *partitur* sent in by Debussy had been burned at the bookbinders, so that the *envoi* had to be judged from the piano score, with the exception of a few passages which he had hastily rescored. The official report conceded that he did not transgress through dullness or triteness. To the contrary, the laureate was again found to be "courting the unusual" and indulging in color to the extent of sacrificing line and form. That troublesome word "impressionism," which was to dog Debussy's music in later days—much to the irritation of wholehearted Debussyists like Suarès, who maintain that there was nothing of impressionism about him; that he was, in fact, a symbolist—finds place in the report. Debussy is told that he should beware of this vague mannerism; in his opening adagio his dreamy atmosphere only leads to confusion. At any rate, the Academy continues to wait for something better from so gifted a musician. "He is an enigma," was Massenet's summation of him.

The "something better" was not to come out of Rome. In the early spring of 1887 Debussy returned to Paris, and this time no persuasion could cause him to return to Italy, though there remained a year of his fellowship. His final *Envoi de Rome* was properly an *Envoi de Paris*, for it was from Paris, to Paris, that he sent his last offering to the Academicians, *La Demoiselle élue*. The work, however, had its roots in Rome, for it was there that he had come under the spell of the pre-Raphaelites and had made the acquaintance of the poems of Dante Gabriel Rossetti. *The Blessed Damozel* was then forty years old. Not Rossetti's English original, but Sarrazin's translation of it, had attracted Debussy to the subject and it was this translation he set to music. The adjudicators found good qualities in the score, though they did not proclaim it a masterpiece or, for that matter, a full realization of all that had been expected of the laureate they had described as "gifted" and "remarkably talented." The report of January 29, 1889, recognized that the lyric poem (for solo voices and chorus, with orchestra) was not lacking in poetry or charm; the prose text they found somewhat obscure and on this basis they justified a certain tendency toward vagueness—a vagueness, described as "systematic," which served to recall previous complaints against Debussy's treatment of form and expression. The indefinite nature of the subject was found to exculpate, in some degree at least, the indefiniteness of the music.

Debussy now was through with *envois*, through with laureates, and through with academicians, as he was through with studies except those which were self-imposed. Though he did not at first realize it, he was about through with the Vasniers as well. For a time he resumed his former visits, playing the music he had composed in the time he had been away, and, when hard pressed, seeking and obtaining material help from his old friends. Apparently there was no open rupture; as Marguerite Vasnier said, he drifted away; they had moved and everyone had changed with the passing of time and the acquiring of new friends. Probably among the works that Debussy brought to the attention of the Vasniers in this period was his *Fantaisie* for piano and orchestra, dedicated to the pianist René Chansarel. It was begun in Rome and completed in Paris, but never publicly performed until after Debussy's death. The composer was now twenty-five years old. *La Demoiselle élue* and *L'Enfant prodigue* were the chief works of a list that included also the cantatas *Daniel* and *Le Gladiateur*, the suite *Printemps* (as distinguished from the two earlier choruses of the same name, one later called *Salut, Printemps*); the choral *Invocation*, the unpublished trio in G for piano, violin, and 'cello; a score of songs, including *Nuit d'étoiles, Beau soir, Fleur de blés, Mandoline, La Belle au bois domrant Voici que le printemps, Paysage sentimental, Zephyr, Rondeau, Pantomime, Clair de lune, Pierrot*, and *Apparition*, of which the last four and *Mandoline* were dedicated to the soon-forsaken "melodious fay."

CHAPTER VII

PARIS AND BAYREUTH

Adoration of Wagner and the Breaking of the Spell—The
Baudelaire Songs—Moussorgsky and the Gamelang—Gaby of the
Green Eyes

In Paris it was the era of the symbolist poets, the impressionist
painters, the Wagner delirium and, still more particularly for the
homecoming Debussy, of "La demoiselle aux yeux verts." The
years immediately following the return from Rome were not
years of fame. The young composer of the late eighteen eighties
remained a relatively obscure figure, as did the mature artist of
the 'nineties. Not until the turn of the century was Debussy to
win any real public success, though here and there were individuals who held his gifts in high esteem. When he was thirty-
one, Claude wrote to the friendly Chausson in a manner to indicate that he was not yet quite sure of his aesthetic. He confesses
that there are two things he still is unable to do—"create masterpieces" and "be really responsible." Songs and piano *morceaux*
of engaging quality, if scarcely of a magnitude to prefigure the
masterpieces that are still to come, occupy the next few years
after *La Demoiselle élue*. As for being "really responsible," there
is evidence that Claude worked methodically at his composition,
though he acquired the reputation of being a Bohemian because
of the time he spent in cafés, with or without the companionship
of Gaby of the green eyes, and because of the circles in which
he moved. For Debussy it was a time of assimilation and gesta-
tion, of finding himself in a world which was awaiting the
flowering of just such musical individuality as was his, an individuality that paralleled in ways not at first apparent the art

84

personalities of men who already were giving a new direction to poetry and painting.

Factually, the period is rather a barren one for the chronicler of Debussy's life. Soon after his return to Paris in the spring of 1887 he made his second journey to England, and there is a still debatable account of an excursion to Vienna and a call upon Brahms. The English visit seems to have been made primarily in the hope of negotiating some profitable arrangement for disposal of the rights to *La Demoiselle élue*. Referred to Franz Hueffler, then music critic of the London *Times*, as well as publisher of the *Musical World*, Debussy was introduced by that gentleman to Berthold Tours, at the time a reader for the publishing house of Novello. Tours regarded Debussy's music as "remarkable" but was of the opinion that no London firm would publish it. The expedition, therefore, came to nought. After a week Debussy returned to Paris. There is not even a record of a compensatory *Pinafore*, such as Debussy recalled from his visit of nine years earlier, when he was a youth of sixteen.

The one authority for the purported meeting with Brahms in the same year as the second London sortie (1887) is André Ternant, a French-born English journalist whose information, he said, was derived from Debussy himself.[1] No biographer of Brahms makes any reference to it, and Debussy's Viennese biographer, Decsey, is plainly if politely skeptical. As related, the tale is that, before or after his arrival in Vienna, Debussy wrote several letters to Brahms which remained unanswered. Finally, through one of the secretaries of the French embassy, a woman of Hungarian birth married to a French diplomat, a luncheon was arranged. Brahms, in growling mood, asked if Debussy was the young Frenchman who had been importuning him with letters. When Claude answered in the affirmative, the Holsteiner gruffly forgave him but added: "Don't let it happen again."

---

[1] Article, "Debussy and Brahms," in London *Musical Times*, June, 1924.

French champagne and a common interest in the music of Bizet brought about a happier relationship. Brahms, in his enthusiasm for *Carmen*, which he said he had seen twenty times, became so companionable that the next day he invited the twenty-five-year-old stranger to dine with him and to attend a performance of Bizet's opera. Together, they visited the Conservatorium and the graves of Beethoven and Schubert. Brahms is quoted as having said of Bizet, then dead for twelve years, that he would have gone to the ends of the earth to embrace him.[2] The event, of course, would have been one much more important and memorable for Debussy at twenty-five than for Brahms at fifty-four. But is it likely that it could have escaped such mention in Vienna as would have brought it to the attention of those concerned subsequently with the life story of Brahms? Dr. Karl Geiringer, one of the most thorough of Brahms scholars, thinks not.

Debussy's two visits to Bayreuth to attend the Wagner festivals of 1888 and 1889, are duly authenticated. The first pilgrimage was made in the company of a well-to-do friend, Étienne Dupin, at a time when Debussy was in such financial straits that he considered going on foot. He was enchanted by *Parsifal*, as French musicians continue to be, sometimes in a manner and to a degree so rapturous as to bewilder their fellow Wagnerians in other lands. He heard *Meistersinger* also at the 1888 festival. After a further *Parsifal* and another *Meistersinger*, he was deeply moved by his first *Tristan* when he returned the next summer. The conductors at these two festivals were Hermann Levi, Felix Mottl, and Hans Richter. Singers included Ernst van Dyck, Theresa Malten, Amalie Materna, Rosa Sucher,

---

[2] When the Debussy of later years, writing as M. Croche, "dilettante hater," turned his pen to a discussion of the symphony since Beethoven, he contrived the masterly feat of doing this without so much as mentioning Brahms. Elsewhere in his critiques he dealt little with the music of the German master. The violin concerto he described as "very tiresome."

Gisela Staudigl, Heinrich Vogl, Eugen Gura, Franz Betz, Theodor Reichmann, Anton Fuchs, and, in the small role of the sailor in *Tristan*, Andreas Dippel.

To understand Debussy's adoration of Wagner, and the manner in which he eventually became anti-Wagnerian, stock should be taken of the situation in which he found French music on his return to Paris, particularly as related to the other arts. A rapid glance over the entire panorama of music in Europe at that time brings into view these markers: Wagner and Liszt were recently dead (Wagner, 1883; Liszt, 1886). Brahms had written his fourth and last symphony (1886). César Franck's only symphony was contemporaneous (1888). Bruckner had written seven of his eight completed symphonies and Mahler one of his nine. Richard Strauss, not yet the paladin of the tone-poems, had composed his *Burleske*. Hugo Wolf, in his capacity of music critic, was attacking Brahms. Russians were having their first experience with Tchaikovsky's Fifth Symphony and Rimsky-Korsakoff's *Capriccio espagnol*, soon to be followed by *Shéhérazade*. In the world of opera, the *Otello* of Verdi had been brought out in Milan; Massenet was writing *Esclarmonde* for the "Eiffel Tower notes" of Sybil Sanderson; and a promising young Italian, four years older than Debussy, Giacomo Puccini, had produced his now forgotten *Edgardo* in succession to the early *Le Villi* of 1884. In England it was the time of Sullivan's *Ruddigore* and *Yeomen of the Guard*. In America Charles Martin Loeffler had just become a citizen and Edward MacDowell [3] had returned to the homeland from his studies with Raff in Germany. In Paris French opera held the boards preponderantly at both the Opéra and the Opéra Comique, with rounds of *Fausts*, *Roméos*, *Carmens*, *Manons*, and *Mignons*. There were revenants, also, of Meyerbeer, Halévy, Auber, and others of an era which led back to Spontini,

---

[3] MacDowell had been a fellow pupil of Debussy in Marmontel's piano class at the Paris Conservatoire.

with some lingering smoke still of the battles fought over Berlioz and Cherubini as the opposite poles of French musical culture. Even as Spontini and Cherubini had represented an Italian orientation for French music, the far more powerful and domineering genius of Wagner was to quicken and bedevil it from across the Rhine. Gounod and Ambroise Thomas were not composers of the strength of character to resist this domination—Gounod, who presented Wagner with a beautifully engraved score of *Tristan und Isolde*—the more remarkable, commented Wagner, since nothing under the sun could prevail upon him ever to listen to Gounod's *Faust*. Franck, Saint-Saëns, d'Indy, Chabrier, and lesser lights were accused, each in turn, of resorting to a tincture of Wagnerism in their own music. To Massenet was applied the not very complimentary sobriquet of "Mlle. Wagner" and Paris found itself described as "Le Petit Bayreuth," a term originally applied to certain composers conveniently grouped together. Not all of this came about in a lustrum or a decade; some of it was still to develop after Debussy's return from the second of his Bayreuth visits. He had gone to the Villa Medici with Wagner in his blood. When he returned from Italy, he found Wagner in the blood of most of those with whom he associated. France was in the clutch of a Wagner cult that was to grow rather than diminish in the years leading onward to the World War. Today, French writers speak of the yoke of Wagner. In the eighteen eighties that yoke was a beacon, a flaming torch, the most powerful of all incentives—though, here and there, even an ardent Wagnerian like the poet Baudelaire thought of this music as a variety of drug, an opiate; hashish for those who gave themselves up to satiation of the senses.

Debussy, particularly susceptible to the ceremonial atmosphere of *Parsifal*, had been swept off his feet by the drama of the Grail at the festival of 1888. *Tristan*, in the succeeding year, had greatly stirred his emotions but had left him in some way disillusioned.

On his return to Paris, it is said that he criticized Wagner to Guiraud, not so much on the musical side, but as a dramatist and man
of the theater. This is the more noteworthy in view of another
tale, having to do with an ambulatory argument between Debussy and Gounod over *Lohengrin*, which Gounod berated and
Debussy defended; and ending when Gounod coldly turned
away from his companion and said: "Your path lies that way,
mine this way." Debussy had read Nietzsche's *Der Fall Wagner*
and was by now agreed with the philosopher that there was nothing in the German giant's music-dramas so moving as the closing
cry of Don José in *Carmen*. It is related that when he sang and
played the last pages of the Bizet opera to his friend, René Peter,
he was completely overcome by the emotion it induced. As related by Maurice Emmanuel, Debussy told Guiraud that he did
not feel tempted to imitate what he admired in Wagner. Music,
for him, was intended to express the otherwise inexpressible. He
liked to think of Euterpe "as if emerging from the shadowy
regions to which she would from time to time return." He would
have her "always discreet." The very boldness and bigness of
Wagnerian utterance, as he was beginning to find, was antithet-
ical to his own reticence and his craving for subtlety in the expression of the emotions. But he could no more escape Wagnerian
influences, in the purely musical aspects of his creative work, than
could the men about him. He responded to Wagner's sensuousness, the while he built up a feeling that the French needed a
different order of lyrical clarity. Still he was ready and eager to
defend Wagner, the technician, when argument arose as to some
detail such as the English-horn solo at the opening of the last act
of *Tristan;* an episode which apparently irritated the worthy
Guiraud, possibly because, as Debussy contended, he failed to
grasp the unheard harmony that was later developed in the score.

It has been argued that each of the successive *Envois de Rome*
reflected Wagnerian influences. So, too, one of the chief pro-

ductions of the final 'eighties in Paris, the *Cinq Poèmes de Baudelaire*, which were put on paper between 1887 and 1890 and published in the latter year. In December of 1887 was written the first song of the set, *La Mort des amantes*, followed in January, 1888, by *Le Balcon*, with its motif taken from *La Demoiselle élue*. In 1889 were composed *Harmonie du soir*, *Jet d'eau*, and *Receuillement*. To this period belong also the *Ariettes oubliées*—originally merely *Ariettes*—dedicated at a later time to Mary Garden, the "inoubliée" of the inscription. Settings of Verlaine, the six songs of this group, *C'est l'extase*, *Il pleure dans mon cœur*, *L'ombre des arbres*, *Chevaux de bois*, *Green* and *Spleen*, were published separately in 1888 and it was not until 1903, after the success of *Pelléas et Mélisande*, that the "forgotten" ariettes appeared together with their tribute to the "unforgettable" Mélisande. Many will feel that there is much more of the essence of Debussy, irrespective of the debatable patches of Wagnerism in the Baudelaire settings, in this second group. The use of the English titles, *Green* and *Spleen*, a never-ending source of questions on the part of Debussy singers, goes back to Verlaine, who at one time was domiciled as a teacher in the south of England.

Other compositions of the late 'eighties were the *Deux arabesques* for piano (1888) and the *Petite suite* (1889), consisting of *En Bateau*, *Cortège*, *Menuet*, and *Ballet*, written for two pianos but best known today in its orchestration by Henri Büsser, who also provided the instrumental dress for the *Printemps* of 1887. It is an interesting commentary on Debussy's subsequent attitude toward these early compositions that he would bother to orchestrate two of Erik Satie's three *Gymnopédies*, the while he was content to let his own music live or languish as originally written.

Dedicated to Dupin, the rich young friend who had accompanied him to Bayreuth, a de luxe edition of the *Cinq Poèmes de Baudelaire*, limited to one hundred and fifty copies, one-third of which were on handmade paper, was published in 1889 by Hamelle. Dupin probably aided in the financing, which otherwise was cared for by subscriptions collected by Gaston Choisnel, a Conservatoire laureate who had taken employment with the publishing house of Durand. When the songs were republished in 1912, it was by Durand.

At about this time, though there is some conflict of memory among those who have endeavored to recall the circumstances, Debussy came into possession of a piano score of Moussorgsky's *Boris Godounoff*. This score was originally the property of Saint-Saëns, and was brought back by him from a concert tour in Russia in 1874. The composer of *Samson et Dalila* was said to have found little that was congenial or interesting in the work and so to have passed the script on to Jules de Brayer, manager of the Lamoureaux concerts and one-time organist at Chartres Cathedral. Apparently it was not until 1893, some four years after he got the de Brayer score, that Debussy discovered in Moussorgsky a kindred spirit. That was the year when he was photographed, coatless, in the act of playing the score of *Boris* for an assembly of six, including Chausson and Raymond Bonheur, in the abode of Chausson. It may be well to remember, along with accounts of Debussy's enthusiasm for Moussorgsky, that he wrote a letter in 1911 which shows that he was far from taking the Russian composer as a model; he did not consider the patchwork (*placage*) of *Boris* any more satisfactory, he said, than the "persistent counterpoint" in the *Meistersinger* finale. But it was not Moussorgsky who dogged him in his efforts to escape the yoke of Wagner in these final 'eighties. It was Massenet, abetted a little by Grieg.

New musical vistas were opened for him, not by the printed pages of imported or domestic scores, but by unfamiliar sounds that attracted his sensitive ear at the Exposition Universelle of 1889–90. In company with Paul Dukas and Robert Godet he

turned musical explorer along the Champs de Mars and the Espla-
nade des Invalides, where in open air, or in tents or booths, native
musicians from the Far East brought to Paris a medley of the
exotic. For most visitors, this was merely "atmosphere." For Debussy, some of it, at least, was a revelation. Javanese and Annam-
ite orchestras chiefly fascinated him. He was won over by the
Gamelang, the group of instruments which accompanied the undulatory dancing of the Bedayas. This was a little orchestra entirely of percussion, save for a two-string instrument resembling
in appearance the viola. Clappers, rattles, tiny bells, and a variety
of gongs gave to this music timbres then unfamiliar in occidental
ensembles. The tuned drums of the East were a new source of
rhythmic subtlety and excitement. The persistent use of the pentatonic scale altered and, for the moment, freshened melodic
utterance. In long-drawn tremolos of the percussion instruments,
with their peculiar tuning, were promptings for those successions
of ninths that subsequently were to become fingerprints on Debussy's manuscripts. In the minor pulsations of the Gamelang,
Debussy found an antidote for the great surges of the Wagnerian
orchestra. In a more formal sphere, he attended two concerts of
Russian music at the Trocadéro, arranged by the publisher, Be-
laief, and conducted by Rimsky-Korsakoff. Included among the
works performed were Rimsky's own *Antar* and *Caprice espagnol;* Moussorgsky's *Night on the Bald Mountain*, Borodin's
Polovetzian Dances and *On the Steppes of Central Asia*, with
other works by Glinka, Dargomijsky, Balakireff, Cui, and Gla-
zounoff. The globe-trotting Rimsky, always with an ear cocked
for the exotic, recorded in his own memoirs his interest in some
of the native orchestras he heard at the exposition, notably those
from Algeria and Hungary, but found nothing in the new French
music of the day to leave any indelible impression on his musical
consciousness. Before he died in 1908 he was to take note of harmonic innovations and details of orchestral coloring in the art of

the Frenchman who had heard his exegesis of the Russian "Cabinet." Debussy at the time of this visit by Rimsky was crystallizing the aesthetic and the technique that within three years he was to apply in the writing of *L'Après-midi d'un faune* and the first pages of *Pelléas et Mélisande* and with which, thereafter, he was to open the eyes of the Rimskys of the world.

Perhaps the first complete convert for Debussy's music in Paris, the first prophet, even, was Edmond Bailly, a man with a modern bias, who was the manager of the bookshop of the "Art Indépendant," where Debussy was a frequent caller. Bailly admired Régnier, Pierre Louÿs, and Gide, whose works he seemed to wrest from his bosom when he sold them, but above all Debussy. He spoke his name with a radiant countenance and said to René Peter one day: "This wonderful young artist, who honors me with his friendship, is the greatest and noblest and will one day be the most famous of all. You shall see. As one spoke in the last century of the Piccinis and the Glucks, so one shall speak one day of the d'Indys and the Debussys. . . ."

The beginnings of Debussy's friendship with Erik Satie have been variously described. One version is that Satie heard Debussy playing a piano in a café, whereas another has it that Satie was the one who played and Debussy he who heard. The latter would seem more probable, as Satie was employed for a time as a musician in Montmartre cabarets. The son of a Scotch mother and a French father, he had studied first with Guilmant, then at the Conservatoire, but he was not a shining light as a pupil. Carl van Vechten has characterized him as a "shy and genial fantasist, part-child, part-devil, part-faun," "played on by Impressionism, Catholicism, Rosecrucianism, Pre-Raphaelitism, Theosophy, the *camaraderie* of the cabaret." He produced music voluminously, chiefly for the piano, most or all of which would now be forgotten entirely but for two circumstances. One was that two of his three *Gymnopédies*—the first and third—were orchestrated by

Debussy and have occasional performance in the concert room, thanks to this act of friendship on the part of a composer who passed on to others orchestrations for some works of his own. The other circumstance was that the eccentric Satie invented absurd titles for some of his works and supplied equally absurd directions for the performer. Thus there are among his piano trifles *Three Pieces in the Form of a Pear*, *The Dreamy Fish*, and *Airs to Make You Run*. Pianists are told to play "on yellow velvet, dry as a cuckoo, light as an egg," or "in the most profound silence," "with hands in the pockets," "like a nightingale with a toothache." Or they must endeavor to conform to a program like the following: "This is a hunt after a lobster; the hunters descend to the bottom of the water. They run. The sound of a horn is heard at the bottom of the sea. The lobster is tracked. The lobster weeps."

A deal of ink has been spilled about Satie's supposed influence on Debussy. But in the light of what is known of Debussy's own early attraction to just such harmonic processes as he afterward was to bring to fruition, and the painterlike quality suggested by some of his early songs, it seems fair to assume that Satie amused Debussy more than he shaped him. A droll and delightful comrade, he may very well have encouraged Debussy by his opinions as well as by the lawlessness of his own inconsequential music. But he remained a gamin, a parodist, a farceur, and his tonal pathbreaking had no such serious purpose as had Debussy's, even in his Conservatoire days. Debussy was ever an artist. About Satie was more than a touch of the poseur. Some small resemblances have been found between the early *Sarabande* by Satie and the later one of Debussy's *Pour le piano*. But these and certain parallel departures from the traditional harmonies of the academicians of his time do not justify the notion that Satie was a precursor or other really important factor in Debussy's career. Satie's satellites, to be sure, thought, wrote, and talked otherwise.

Though legally his was a state of single blessedness, Debussy was not to go through these years companionless and alone. About 1888 he met Gabrielle Dupont, she of the green eyes, who for something like ten years was to manage his household, such as it was, and to stand guard over him while he worked regularly at composition. Gaby, as she was known to him and to those with whom he associated in these years, was a blonde, strongly built and with a forceful chin. According to René Peter, she looked at a visitor as resolutely and steadily as a cat. And Debussy, whose own nature was often described as having something feline in it, had a lifelong fondness for cats, even those of porcelain. The circumstances of the meeting of these apparently sympathetic and complementary spirits, have been the basis of unprovable tales that trail off to the demimonde. It is perhaps enough to know that for some years all went well with them, so far as their acquaintances could observe, both in the Rue de Londres, where they first had their domicile, and later in the Rue Gustave-Doré. It was at No. 10 in the latter street that Debussy composed most of *Pelléas*, presumably while Gaby busied herself with the routine of their little establishment or with looking after the creature comforts of the man at the piano. There he toiled for long hours, sometimes in the clouds, no doubt; and perhaps quite as often in the doldrums or the dumps, as he encountered the inevitable setbacks of artistic creation. A stagework on which Debussy embarked before his genius led him to *Pelléas*, the unfinished *Rodrique et Chimène*, was inscribed to the green-eyed Gabrielle.[4] So was a sketch for *L'Après-midi d'un faune*. At this time, Debussy gave both piano and singing lessons to keep afloat and took odd jobs as an accompanist. The sarcastic wit that grew with his mastery of musical technique was often directed Gaby's way and she was the victim of pranks and innuendoes in the presence of friends. There are tales of improvisations at the piano especially

[4] The inscribed manuscript is in the possession of Alfred Cortot.

for her benefit, the composer relishing the joke when some expression of delight or commendation was drawn from her by what was an obvious parody of Offenbach or some cheap ballad of the day. But Gaby apparently was not easily fussed or humiliated. It was not until other women crossed her path that serious trouble arose in the Debussy-Dupont ménage. In what may appear to be a rather heartless letter,[5] Debussy was to tell of Gaby's discovery in his pocket of a missive which left no doubt as to the rather advanced state of another love affair. (For him, her green eyes are now to be described as "steely.") "Whereupon," he continues, "tears, drama, a real revolver and a report in the *Petit Journal!*" And "on top of it all, poor little Gaby lost her father." But he confesses to feeling very sad and upset—"sometimes I am as sentimental as a modiste who might have been Chopin's mistress"—the while he observes that his heart is "still capable of fluttering." Debussy could scarcely write without banter; he talks here of an eraser for kisses and caresses to be called "The Adulterer's India-Rubber." With the passing of years, the strong-chinned, green-eyed Gaby is replaced by the gentle, small-mouthed Lily, but that is a story that belongs properly in a later chapter.

[5] To Pierre Louÿs, February 9, 1897.

CHAPTER VIII

IN STEP WITH THE SYMBOLISTS

Mallarmé, Verlaine, and Poe—Music as Poetry and Poetry as Music—Debussy Formulates an Aesthetic

THÉOPHILE GAUTIER dubbed music "the most costly of all noises." Stéphane Mallarmé, defining Symbolism, adjured the poets of his later era to seek their salvation in music and—"reprendre à la musique leur bien"—to take back from music what they had given to it.

Between the respective attitudes toward music of the French writers of Gautier's time and those of Mallarmé's [1] was a great gulf which needs to be seen and understood if we are to comprehend the flowering of that Claude Debussy who, in the Paris of the eighteen nineties, succeeded the Achille Debussy we have known thus far as student and laureate. More than of the Conservatoire, more than of Rome, more than of Moussorgsky, more than of the Gamelang, the rising composer with whom we now have to deal was the product, spiritually and aesthetically, of the literary movement called "Symbolism," which had in Mallarmé one of its most characteristic and influential spokesmen. Of those who had sown the seed, perhaps none was more truly a precursor of this movement than the American, Edgar Allan Poe, whose poetry, as translated by Baudelaire, had an effect upon French literature in the succeeding epoch, technically and in choice of subject matter, that perhaps still is underestimated in Poe's own country.

Significant, therefore, is Debussy's abortive effort to follow *Pelléas et Mélisande* with one or more operas based upon Poe,

[1] Gautier, 1811-72; Mallarmé, 1842-98.

to be dealt with in its proper place in this narrative. From the verbal music of Poe—not excluding the tintinnabulations of the bells, bells, bells—was derived an incentive to the writing of verse that of itself was sonorous and musical; in the end it was carried so far that certain vowels were regarded as having the sound of individual instruments of the symphonic ensemble and there was something akin to conscious "orchestration" in their use.

This development, by which music became the afflatus of poetry, was the exact opposite of that of the earlier part of the century, wherein the Romantic movement in music had been fertilized by literature. If any clear line of demarcation can be drawn between the classicists and the romantics in the tonal art, it is to be found in the substitution, for the more purely musical conceptions of the elder era, of those other and more personal conceptions which composers drew from, or shared with, the poets, the novelists, and the philosophers of their time. Dante, Shakespeare, Byron, Goethe, and Lamartine were but some of the men of letters whose works gave inspiration to a sister art no longer content with mere beauty of line and grace of form—granting, of course, that "pure" music was never quite so innocent of the romantic type of expression as the definition maker might have us believe. For Liszt, Berlioz, and Wagner, voracious readers all, literature was what might be termed a direct generative force. The evolution of the symphony toward the symphonic poem and the growing tendency toward program music were manifestations of a trend which attracted to it virtually all the composers of the romantic upswing, whether bookish or not. On the literary side, no such widespread, kindred interest was to be found in music. If not exactly tone-deaf, most writers of eminence were much more concerned with the picturesque trappings of a troubadour serenading a lady in a tower than they were with the almost miraculous growth, under their very noses, of the modern symphony orchestra. Of course there were distinguished exceptions; but it could not be said that the literary men of the Romantic exfoliation felt toward music as composers felt toward literature: that it was an endless font of incentive and inspiration. Particularly in France, outstanding littérateurs of the Romantic movement during the first three quarters of the nineteenth century were inclined to view music with indifference or apathy. Liszt went to Lamartine for the poetic basis of *Les Préludes*, but Lamartine cared not a whit for Liszt. Sundry composers turned to Victor Hugo's poems for their lyrics, the while Hugo left music to the musicians. Baudelaire,[2] whom the eloquent James Huneker fondly described as "the saddest and profoundest of poets," was one of the really notable exceptions. It was Baudelaire who discovered Poe for the French. It was Baudelaire who saw in music, and particularly the music of Richard Wagner, an expressive medium that was a transcendant form of poetry. With Poe, Baudelaire was a true precursor of the new era in French literature; the era which was to bring about, in turn, the flowering in music of Claude Debussy, as it was to influence strongly certain other composers who, more than Debussy, were admixtures of the new and the old.

Without this flowering of Debussy as part of what was in fact an aesthetic revolution, the music of France in the last quarter of the nineteenth century might well have gone from sterility to sterility, insipidity to insipidity, in spite of the high qualities of César Franck and the virtues of some of his pupils. For the greater part of the century, the opera was the thing. All music was in some measure subservient to the theater. Even Berlioz was driven to writing theatrical music for the concert room. The Meyerbeerian tradition held on. Auber, Adam, David, and Thomas were succeeded by Gounod, Reyer, Delibes, Massenet, and Saint-Saëns. In the words of Landormy, the whole tendency of the times—striking and admirable as might be some prosilient work like Bizet's *Carmen*—was toward "un art sans elévation, sans

[2] Charles Baudelaire, 1821-67.

poésie et sans nuances." It is not necessary for us to decry a *Faust* or, for that matter, even a *Dumb Girl of Portici*—inhabitants, of course, of quite another world than the progeny of the symphonists and some few masters of the loftier type of music drama— to see the aptness of this description.

Two composers of the era which preceded the rise of Debussy must be considered as apart from the main current of conformity to the theatrical tradition. These were Hector Berlioz and César Franck, the one still a controversial and somewhat isolated figure; the other an artist of such gifts, and so strongly in sympathy with the symphonic ideal, as to place him on the threshold of the new era; and, through the work of his pupils, to enable him to participate vicariously in the great revival of French music which was to come after his own career was closed. With these pupils— Chausson, Duparc, d'Indy, Pierné, and Bordes—and with Debussy, stood Dukas and Fauré, the while Berlioz achieved an amazing posthumous popularity in the concert halls. Eventually, their battle was with Wagner, whose music provided the main sustenance of the programs of the concerts of Lamoureaux, Pasdeloup, and Colonne.

With mention of Wagner, we are led back to the beginnings of the Symbolist movement. The Wagner cult extended far beyond the confines of music. Particularly did it permeate that of literature. In 1885, at about the time Debussy, the student, was discovering for himself the intoxications of *Tristan*, there was founded in Paris the *Revue Wagnerienne* and within the next year were published therein six sonnets in praise of Wagner by such poets as Mallarmé, Verlaine, and René Ghil. Wagner—"his path to heaven with his own radiance strewn," to quote Mallarmé —was a god in that world to which Debussy returned from Rome. Victor Hugo, who had epitomized for France the Romantic movement in literature, was gone from the scene, and with him the overwhelming eloquence and virtuosity of his utterance in both poetry and prose. Under the leadership of Leconte de Lisle a group called the Parnassians had enlisted, for the time being, the allegiance of Baudelaire, the essentially personal quality of whose writing was to separate him from the materialism and the objectivity of attitude which governed others of the group. Théodore de Banville, the favorite poet of Debussy's student days, and Gerard de Nerval were imitating folk-song patterns and in some small measure foreshadowing what was to come by a technique of implication and suggestion rather than direct statement. Verlaine, Rimbaud, and Tristan Corbière were more strongly bent in this direction, and to Verlaine [3] is attributed, a posteriori, the conversion of the Parnassian outlook to the ideals of Symbolism. His *Poèmes saturniens*, published in 1866, were a Parnassian production. Today, they can be regarded as among the first fruits of the Symbolist tree; though ordinarily the Symbolist movement is considered as not coming into being until about 1885, some nineteen years later. The Symbolist poets were never a unified group or school. Among them were adherents of free verse who had a special cause to promulgate. Some were called "Romans," some "Decadents," the latter a term applied derisively to the entire movement. In Debussy's lifetime, Mallarmé came to be recognized as the Symbolist leader and it is illuminating to note how some of his elucidations of the purposes of the movement conform to qualities the world has attributed to Debussy's music. As, for instance, the dictum that poetry should "evoke in a deliberate shadow the unmentioned object by illusive words." Mallarmé was twenty years older than Debussy, and died just twenty years before him. He was a man of forty-five when Debussy returned from Rome. The composer was among those attracted to the Tuesday evenings at Mallarmé's home, though he was never one of the regular frequenters of these famous gatherings. At Mallarmé's, Debussy met Verlaine, one of

[3] Paul Verlaine, 1844–96.

those who thought of music as "colored hearing" and of "or-chestrated verse." Among the well-known Symbolists with whom he was brought in contact were, presumably (in some instances, certainly) Jean Moréas, Jules Laforgue, Gustave Kahn, Henri de Régnier, Charles Morice, Francis Jammes, and Remy de Gour-mont. Kindred spirits were the Belgians, Émile Verharen and Maurice Maeterlinck.

In painting, the Symbolists were attracted by the English pre-Raphaelite school: Watts, Burne-Jones, and Rossetti whose *Blessed Damozel* in Sarrazin's translation had been set by Debussy as his final *Envoi de Rome*. Among French artists, they were in-terested in Puvis de Chavannes, and in the Impressionists Édouard Manet, Claude Monet, Pissarro, Sisley, and Renoir, and also in Van Gogh, Degas, Gauguin, and Whistler, the American having an especial appeal for Debussy. Of sculptors, Rodin was their man. With their obsession for Wagner, those French composers who were most obviously influenced from across the Rhine stood perhaps the best chance of winning the Symbolists' approval. Yet the whole movement was so essentially French in spirit that in-evitably it was to lead to a music that was in conflict with Teu-tonic vehemence and muscularity.

Debussy, the once ardent Wagnerian, was to hear much adu-latory talk about the mighty Richard and his music, at Mallarmé's and elsewhere among the Symbolists. He was not always to acquiesce. In *Mes Souvenirs du Symbolisme*, André Fontainas pictures a scene at the abode of Pierre Louÿs, where the Symbol-ists were thoroughly at home and where the atmosphere was musical as well as literary. His fingers gliding over the keyboard, Debussy seemed more absorbed in his thoughts than in the con-versation about him. There was the usual discussion of Wagner. "Suddenly, from a hand released as by a spring, there sprang forth an ingenious and impromptu arabesque." Under the dark, rebellious locks of the man at the piano, "the unfathomable,

dream-haunted eyes were alight with calm audacity and irony."
From memory, without the slightest hesitation, Debussy began to
elaborate a pattern of Wagnerian motives, but not as an idolatrous
Wagnerian.

"What!" he exclaimed. "Don't you see that Wagner, with all
his formidable power—yes, in spite of his power—has led music
astray into sterile and pernicious paths? He has accepted from
Beethoven a fearful heritage. Already for Beethoven the art of
development consists in repetition, in the incessant restatement
of identical themes. Listen!"

Whereupon he played a passage from a sonata by Beethoven.

"And Wagner," he continued, "has exaggerated this procedure
to the point of caricature. I hate the *leit motif*, not only when it is
abused, but even when it is used with taste and discernment. Do
you think that in composition the same emotion can be expressed
twice? In that case, one has either not reflected, or it is simply an
effect of laziness."

He warned his listeners against permitting themselves to be
fooled by shifts of rhythm or tonality, which he described as
nothing but trickery. Then he expressed something of his own
credo.

"I should like to see the creation—I, myself, shall achieve it—of
a kind of music free from themes and motives, or formed on a
single continuous theme, which nothing interrupts and which
never returns upon itself. Then there will be a logical, compact,
deductive development. There will not be, between two re-
statements of the same characteristic theme, a hasty and superfluous 'filling in'! The development will no longer be that am-
plification of material, that professional rhetoric which is the
badge of excellent training, but it will be given a more universal
and essential psychic conception."

Fontainas, who jotted down in his notebook all that he could
recall of Debussy's harangue, adds that such speeches did not

diminish the Wagnerism of these Symbolist soirées, attended, on occasion, by various of Debussy's musical contemporaries, including Vincent d'Indy, Gabriel Fauré, Ernest Chausson, Henri Duparc, Alexis de Castillon, Pierre de Bréville, Guy Ropartz, Déodat de Sévérac, mostly pupils of César Franck. Says Fontainas: "The movement of musical renovation confirmed our aspirations and our experiments as poets."

Mallarmé did most of the talking at his "Tuesdays." In his *Divagation Première, Relativement au Vers,* he gives us a glimpse into his feeling for music such as undoubtedly was disclosed also in his less formal discussions. Comparing the new freedom acquired by verse to "the multiplicity of voices of an orchestra," he declares that whenever he attends a concert "he perceives in the obscure sublimity the outline of one of the poems immanent to humanity." Music, for him, is poetry in a latent state. With the essential bias of the poet, he further expresses the view that ideal music results not from the "elementary sonorities of the brass, the wood, the strings, but from the intellectual word at its apogee." This was the man who, taking back from music that which poetry had given it, orchestrated in words the verbal magic of the literary *Après-midi d'un faune,* which Debussy, with a no less magical touch, restored to the orchestra of klang-tints and timbres. In an era that buzzed with talk of a unification of the arts, France having taken over the Wagnerian ideal of a synthesis in which all the arts would play a collaborating part, this was a memorable marker. Beyond that it was a signpost pointing ahead on the road that was leading straight to *Pelléas.* Debussy at that time was strongly attracted to the idea of some such fusion as later was to fascinate Scriabin. For the Frenchman, as for the Russian, "perfumes, colors and sounds correspond to each other." As he went on with composition, he was to borrow titles for his works from the visual arts, as Whistler borrowed titles for paintings from music. Painterlike, he was to be drawn especially to clouds and waves, and was to reflect them in his music, not as specific images, but in the nebulous and at the same time fluid character of many of his most characteristic compositions. There was to be much polishing of his technique in relatively minor works that reflected the influence of the Symbolists, before Debussy was ready for that large-scale impressionism—protested though the word may be—of the dream-haunted *Nuages* and the chameleonic, windswept *La Mer*.

CHAPTER IX

THE *FAUN* AND FRUITFUL YEARS

From *L'Après-midi* to the *Nocturnes*—The Appearance of the
String Quartet—A Decade Particularly Rich in Songs

THOUGH not until after the dawn of a new century was Debussy
to achieve any resounding success, the eighteen nineties, when he
was between the ages of twenty-eight and thirty-eight, were
among the most productive years of his life; years when it could
no longer be said of him—as he had said of himself in the late
'eighties—that he could not write masterpieces. For in this period
he composed the String Quartet, *L'Après-midi d'un faune*, the
Nocturnes, virtually all of *Pelléas et Mélisande*, and many of the
best-known songs and piano pieces. The *Nocturnes*, originally
intended for solo violin and orchestra, occupied Debussy for six
years, *Pelléas* for ten. Both were brought to first public performance after 1900. But they belong to the 'nineties. Even without
them, the quartet, *Fêtes galantes*, *Proses lyriques*, and *Chansons
de Bilitis*, together with the earlier pieces of the *Suite bergamasque*
and *Pour le piano* (also carried over into the nineteen hundreds),
would stamp this as a memorable decade.

An early incident of 1890 led to Debussy's severing his connection with the Institut. It reminds us that in the years since he
returned from Rome Debussy was still a dependent of the Académie des Beaux-Arts. This is perhaps as good a place as any to clear
up the confusion that may exist in the ordinarily well-informed
reader's mind regarding these institutions. The Académie des
Beaux-Arts, which annually offers the *Prix de Rome* competed
for by students of the Conservatoire, is one of five academies embraced within the Institut de France. They are the Académie

Française, the Academy of Inscriptions and Belle-Lettres, the Academy of Moral and Political Sciences, the Academy of Sciences, and the Académie des Beaux-Arts. The last of these, with which we have been particularly concerned, is composed of forty members, painters, sculptors, engravers, and musicians, plus a permanent secretary. The musical section has six members. The Institut de France occupies a building on the left bank of the Seine—the Palais d'Institut—built in the seventeenth century by Cardinal Mazarin and since 1806 used for its meetings. It is there that the winning *Prix de Rome* cantata is performed.

According to tradition, each returning laureate was required to compose an overture, and thereafter a concert devoted to his Roman *envois* was performed. Debussy balked at composing this overture. Moreover, those in authority declined to permit the too adventurous *Printemps* a place on the program with *La Demoiselle élue*. Either because of the refusal to write the overture, or because of the composer's insistence on the inclusion of *Printemps*, which the judges had condemned three years before, there was no concert—or, as the composer ironically referred to it, no "Debussy festival"—and *La Demoiselle élue* waited another three years for its first performance in Paris. Nor was this the only curious episode that was to result in the withdrawal of music by Debussy from public performance. In 1900 the *Fantaisie* for piano and orchestra, which Debussy had composed after his return to Paris for his friend René Chansarel, was scheduled for one of the concerts of the Société Nationale. Vincent d'Indy was to conduct it, along with other new works on a program of generous length. Debussy appeared at one of the rehearsals and quietly removed his music from the stands. Two explanations of Debussy's act have been made: one, that he felt the work was not being adequately rehearsed; the other, that he was not satisfied with his own score. Curiously enough, the *Fantaisie*, which was not published until after Debussy's death and which even today is little known, has prompted some commentators to liken it to d'Indy's *Symphonie sur un thème montagnard français*, composed in 1886. Did Debussy, perhaps, discover the dubious resemblance? Though he did not publish it, Choudens engraved the *Fantaisie* in 1890, at a time when Debussy was selling any and all of his manuscripts, wherever he could find a publisher. Hartmann, Durand, Hamelle, Dupont, and Girod, the last-named bought out by Fromont, came to know the conspicuously neat notation of a man continually in need of funds. Debussy sold in 1890 the piano pieces, *Reverie, Ballade slave, Tarantelle Styrienne, Valse romantique*, and *Nocturne*, commonly credited to this year, although there is evidence that at least some of them had been composed earlier. To 1891 are attributed a studentlike *Mazurka* and the *Marche écossaise sur un thème populaire*, otherwise "The Earl of Ross March," a piano duet written under circumstances tending to corroborate the composer's state of impecuniosity at the time. The march was written to order for a Scotch officer, General Meredith Read, a descendent of the Earls of Ross, who supplied the theme. Debussy thought enough of it to orchestrate it, about eight years later; and when he first heard it performed, after still another seven years, he exclaimed: "Mais c'est joli." Léon Vallas is of the opinion that the *Mazurka* is much older, probably dating back to the days of the Russian excursions with Mme. von Meck. In his need, Debussy prepared a solo piano arrangement of Raff's *Humoresque en forme de valse* and offered to write easy pieces for children and even to prepare a piano method for Hamelle. Apparently he got the money he needed in some other way or went without, as no such easy pieces and no such piano method appeared.

The decade is one rich in songs of a character not only individual and Debussyan, but prophetic of the vocal writing of *Pelléas*, which, as a matter of fact, was largely contemporaneous. In 1891 emerged *Deux Romances—Romance* and *Les Cloches—*to text by Paul Bourget, which suggest an earlier period; *Les Angélus*

(G. le Roy), *Dans le jardin* (Paul Gravelot), *Trois Mélodies* (Verlaine)—*La mer est plus belle, Le son du cor s'afflige,* and *L'échelonnement des baies.* Save the two romances, these are songs of an atmosphere unmistakably that of the creator of Mélisande. Dedications to the composer, Ernest Chausson, and the Swiss journalist, Robert Godet, are reminders of close friendships cemented in these days: that with Chausson terminated by death in 1899 when the composer of the celebrated *Poème* for violin and orchestra was killed in a bicycle accident; that with Godet continued until Debussy's own death in 1918, one of the few that survived the strained relations brought about by Claude's marital difficulties in 1904-05. Verlaine was by now much in Debussy's consciousness, and in 1891 he took to Hamelle a book of the Symbolist's poems, asking the publisher to select therefrom texts for songs which Debussy would write. The book remained there, with no action taken on the composer's proposal.

Verlaine was the poet drawn upon in 1892, when were written, or rewritten, the three songs which subsequently were to make up the first set of *Fêtes galantes—En Sourdine, Fantoches,* and *Clair de lune.*[1] There are suggestions in these songs of *L'Après-midi d'un faune* and the String Quartet, products of the same period. All give a clear clue to the Debussy of the larger masterpieces in store, but they were not to be printed (though two publishers had the manuscripts in hand) for a dozen years, after *Pelléas* had made Debussy's name the large and small change of Paris.

In his next set of songs, the *Proses lyriques,* credited to 1892–93, Debussy appears as the author of the texts set by him. In addition to the four songs of the group, *De Rêve, De Grève, De Fleurs,* and *De Soir,* it is understood that the composer had planned four or five more, all to be included under the title of *Nuits*

---

[1] *Fantoches* has been shown to date back to ten years earlier. *Clair de lune* was Debussy's second setting of this poem.

blanches. Debussy had taken Mallarmé and Laforgue as his models and his alliterative, ultrapoetical texts were a handicap rather than a first recommendation for the songs, so far as their early reception was concerned. In spite of many details that were audacious for the time, these are songs less independent than some others of the period. Old Klingsor, otherwise Richard Wagner, of whom Debussy was to complain in the course of his first labors with *Pelléas*, was at his elbow, even to the extent of prompting the use of phrases that a watchful enemy might have seized upon as nothing very different from the detested leading motive.

Four years after the *Proses lyriques* came the *Chansons de Bilitis* (1897) to texts by Pierre Louÿs,[2] author of *Aphrodite*, who has been credited with being the director of Debussy's literary conscience and one of the chief factors in the development of his cultural background. *La Flute de Pan*, *La Chevelure*, and *Le Tombeau des naïades*, the three songs of the set, gave play to that deep-seated sensualism, that love of the voluptuous, which stamped Debussy as a hedonist and a sybarite. In the opening bars of the first of these songs, redolent of the incense and myrrh of a world where there was little to choose between priestess and courtesan, where the cult of love was, in truth, a religion, and where the spirit was enamored of the seductions of the flesh, is an example of that whole-tone scale which was to be regarded as the personal signature of Debussy, though he was never persistent or lavish in its use—at least in the bald way which everyday report would credit to him. The fair Bilitis, of course, was pure fiction, though so well did Louÿs body her forth, that she became a literary hoax like Ossian. A party of German antiquarians even formed an expedition to the Greek East in an effort to collect authoritative data about her. Again, there are details in which we are not far from *Pelléas* and very close, indeed, to *The Afternoon of a Faun*, the latter completed about three years before the

[2] Pierre Louÿs, 1870–1925.

Chansons de Bilitis appeared.

Of more immediate significance in the world wherein Debussy lived and worked than either the songs or the piano pieces was the String Quartet of 1893. That it continued to bear the designation "Première quatuor," indicated that the composer had a second in mind. As corroboratory of this a Brussels paper mentioned that a movement of a new quartet had been written. Moreover, in a letter to Chausson, who seems not to have shared the enthusiasm of some of his associates, Debussy said he would write, solely for Chausson, another quartet in which, he promised, "I shall try to give dignity to my forms."

When the Quartet was published by Durand, Paul Dukas hailed Debussy as "one of the most gifted and original artists of the young generation of musicians" and praised him as "a lyricist in the full sense of the term." On December 29, 1893, the work was performed by Ysaÿe, Crickboom, Van Hout, and Jacob at the Société Nationale before an audience that included many devotees of the chamber music of Haydn, Mozart, Schubert, and Beethoven. Some of these were nonplussed, others irritated, even scandalized. The part writing was regarded as too orchestral; there were objections to the persistent pizzicato, to the mandolin and guitar suggestions. One reviewer spoke of "orgies of modulation"; the composer was credited with being "rotten with talent." Not until after *Pelléas* was the Quartet to achieve any such measure of recognition and understanding as to make it other than dubious material for the program makers of Paris. The one undoubted success among those compositions in which the composer can be said to have adhered to classical modes and to the principles of absolute music, its enduring place in the répertoire of chamber musicians may be attributed today largely to those individual qualities which were furthest from the models of the old masters and which enabled it to add something that was Debussy's own. The musical content and, more particularly, the coloring of that content, asserts a continuing appeal in which there is only a modicum of concern with questions of orthodox form.

Between 1892 and 1894, contemporaneously with his evolution of the Quartet, Debussy composed *L'Après-midi d'un faune,* a masterpiece so personal, so free of the ordinary indices of derivation, so distinctive in feeling and coloring, so unlike any music of the past or of its own era—Debussy's other compositions alone excepted—as to strike us today, after more than forty years of currency and familiarity, as one of the major miracles of musical history. Originally intended as a triptych, the work was begun according to a plan for Prélude, Interlude, and Paraphrase finale. In this form it was announced for performance in Brussels on March 1, 1894, but could not be given for the simple reason that only the Prélude had taken definite shape, the other sections having been carried no further than the barest sketches. Near the year's end, Debussy completed a revision of the Prélude, having dropped entirely the Interlude and Finale. On December 22, 1894, some months before the score was engraved, and precisely a year after the first public performance of the Quartet, *L'Après-midi d'un faune*—or, to give it the full and correct title, *Prélude à l'Après-midi d'un faune*—was brought to a first hearing. The concert, like that at which the Quartet had been introduced, was under the auspices of the Société Nationale, and took place in the Salle d'Harcourt, 40 Rue Rochechouart. The conductor was Gustave Doret. There are conflicting reports as to its reception, Vallas speaking of it as having met with "a brilliant and immediate success," with the result that it was given again on the next day; and Lockspieser noting that there was no enthusiasm in the press, either then or at a subsequent performance at the Concerts Colonne in the following year.

Let us give place here to the account of one who is qualified to pass on to us the report of his own eyes and ears. We quote Camille Mauclair, the poet; his testimony forms part of an article on Claude Debussy and the poets, which was published at the time of the dedication of the Debussy monument in the Bois de Boulogne in 1932.

> I was present [he says] near Mallarmé, who was my initiator and my teacher, and whose indulgent affection and infinite kindness toward me in the beginnings of my career will remain the honor of my life. And we returned struck with consternation by the hisses of a public which denounced this music as lacerating the ears, this music so volatile that one scarcely hears its adorable murmuring! . . .
>
> And what a revenge, afterwards [continues Mauclair], when the ovations given *L'Après-midi* in all the concerts of the world are numberless. Through them the name of Mallarmé will remain inseparable from that of the musician who so marvelously understood his mystic and sensuous vision of the Ancient World.

There is extant a letter [3] about *L'Après-midi*, written by Debussy to Henry Gauthier-Villars, the caustic and humorous critic familiarly and sometimes derisively known as "Willy," who contributed to the *Echo de Paris* articles headed *L'Ouvreuse du Cirque d'Été* (and who, incidentally, became the husband of Colette). It illustrates Debussy's way of relying on banter and irony when forced to defend or elucidate his art before the public. Under date of Thursday, October 10, 1896, and with the address given as 10 Rue Gustave-Doré, where the green-eyed Gaby may have sat sentinel while he wrote, he penned this characteristic bit of mockery:

> The *Prélude à l'Après-midi d'un faune*, dear sir, is perhaps what remained of the dream in the recesses of the flute of the faun. More precisely, it is the general impression of the poem, for in following it more closely the music would

[3] In the possession of Colette, the novelist and librettist of Ravel's *L'Enfant et les sortilèges.*

puff like a cab horse running for the Grand Prix against a thoroughbred. It is also disdain for that "science of the beavers" which makes our proudest minds top-heavy; then! it is without respect for good breeding! and rather in a mode which tries to embrace all the nuances, which is very logically demonstrable.

Now that follows, all the same, the ascendant movement of the poem, and it is the scene marvelously described in the text, with, moreover, the humanity introduced by thirty-two violinists who got up too early! The end is the last verse prolonged:

> Couple, adieu! je vais voir l'ombre tu devins.

I see that the care in responding to your so gently urgent letter is going to deprive me of all that you could say without me, and I do not wish to restrict your liberty in any way.

In all sympathy,
Claude Debussy

P.S.—A whim: I prefer "Debussy" and not "de Bussy"!—

Eight years before his death, Debussy recalled in a letter to G. Jean-Aubry (dated March 25, 1910) that Mallarmé came to him in his flat, "with his air of a prophet" and his Scotch plaid wrapped around him, and listened to the composer play the Prélude on the piano. Silent for a time, Mallarmé finally said: "I had not expected anything like that. The music brings forth the emotion of the poem and gives it a background of warmer color." And Debussy quoted a verse which Mallarmé had written on a copy of the score:

> Sylvain d'haleine première,
>   Si ta flute a réussi,
> Qouïs toute la lumière
>   Qu'y soufflera Debussy.

Public performances were accruing to other Debussy works, not always to the advantage of the composer, if such attention as they gained from the press was at all determinative. *La Demoiselle élue* was finally brought to hearing by the Société Nationale on April 8, 1893, at a concert conducted by Gabriel Marie and given in the Salle Érard. Other composers represented were Dukas, Bonheur, Fournier, de Bréville, and Duparc. Soloists for the Debussy cantata were Thérèse Roger and Julia Robert. The former will be met with again in these pages and for a reason not likely to have brought peace to the possessive spirit of Gabrielle Dupont. Of those who wrote of the work, Charles Darcours and Julien Tiersot rated it an original and even exquisite score, both referring to it as highly "modern." Vincent d'Indy championed it and did much to obtain additional performances for it. But the witty "Willy" described the cantata as "a symphonic stained-glass window" somewhat perversely contrived by "Fra Angelico Debussy," with a further allusion to it as the "damoiseau élu." Debussy was said to have "fertilized" Baudelaire's flowers with his music and on another occasion to be "more fleur-du-mal than ever." This last was when he was caught in the act of listening to Liszt's *Valse de Méphisto* at the Concerts Lamoureux with "disdainful pity." By way of correction for not adoring Liszt, it was recommended that he consult Saint-Saëns and his *Danse macabre.*

At about the time of its first performance, a de luxe edition of *La Demoiselle élue,* with cover in colors by the painter Maurice Denis, and limited to one hundred and sixty copies, was published by Bailly at the Librairie de l'Art Indépendant. Presumably it conformed to the composer's wish that the work be issued in "a rare and exquisite manner." This was but one of several instances in which luxury of format entered into Debussy's publication arrangements to attest in a not altogether practicable way his sybaritic tastes and inclinations.

In February, 1894, the same Thérèse Roger who had been one
of the soloists in the first performance of *La Demoiselle élue* sang
two of the *Proses lyriques—De Fleurs* and *De Soir*—at the Sociéte
Nationale, with Debussy as her accompanist. One critic, J. Guy
Ropartz, described them as "exquisite," with a "rare distinction
of feeling" and a very individual treatment of the piano part,
which he credited the composer with playing to perfection.

Debussy and Mlle. Roger were by now engaged. But not for
long. Neither she nor a young society woman to whom Debussy
also was said at one time to be betrothed was to become his
wedded wife. The tale of Gaby was not yet done, though, as he
wrote to Pierre Louÿs, the heart of the man of Saint-Germain and
Montmartre was still capable of fluttering.

Debussy paid two visits to Belgium at about this time. Specific
mention of the journey made especially to see Maurice Maeterlinck may be left to the chapter dealing with the inception and
maturation of *Pelléas et Mélisande*. On the other trip he was accompanied by Mlle. Roger, who appeared as soloist in *La Demoiselle élue*. She also sang two of the *Proses lyriques* in substitution for two of the *Cinq Poèmes de Baudelaire*, which were to
have been given by another singer. The program constituted a
first foreign "Debussy festival," the Brussels Libre Esthétique,
of which Octave Maus was director, having arranged an entire
concert of Debussy's music. This was the concert for which the
Prélude, Interlude, and Paraphrase (afterward contracted to the
Prélude à l'Aprés-midi d'un faune) was prematurely announced.
The String Quartet completed the list of Debussy compositions,
and again had as its performers the members of the Ysaÿe quartet.
Eugène Ysaÿe was the presiding spirit of the festival, though to
Vincent d'Indy was due the inclusion of *La Demoiselle élue*. It is
of record that the first movement of the Quartet was begun twice
because of the late arrival of a guest of honor, F. A. Gevaert, Director of the Brussels Conservatory and author of a widely known

treatise on instrumentation. For at least one of the Brussels reviewers the Quartet was strange and bizarre, with too many echoes of the streets of Cairo and the Gamelang. Others admired its attractive tone coloring. Again is to be found resort to the word "impressionism" in the effort to deal with the work's harmonic novelty. Not all were agreed as to the composer's individuality of utterance; one writer found suggestions of Grieg, Borodin, and Wagner, as well as the "influence" of Debussy's compatriot, Alfred Bruneau, pupil of Massenet and bosom friend of the novelist, Zola.[4]

In 1895, the year following the Brussels visit, Debussy went to England for the third time. Crossing the Channel, he met Saint-Saëns and that globe-trotting celebrity took the trouble to introduce his younger colleague to Sir Hubert Parry at the Royal College of Music. Nothing came of Debussy's efforts to arrange for publication of his works in England and after three weeks spent in the home of a French professor near Belsize he returned to Paris, as empty-handed as he had been eight years before. In these lean years, when his royalties would not have kept him in shoes, Debussy cast about for a position as conductor in some secondary place. But when a post as an assistant was proffered him at Royan, with a salary that promised only the most meager living in return for hours of rehearsal drudgery at the piano, he shrank from it, confessing that his only hope was in *Pelléas*.

By now he was deep in the *Nocturnes*. These were to occupy him, in conjunction with *Pelléas* and other works, between 1893 and 1899. He conceived them originally for violin and orchestra; they were designed for Ysaÿe, to whom Debussy wrote in 1896, begging him to accept them as a work to be played only by him. There were to have been three movements, but it is almost inconceivable, considering the medium for which they were in-

---

[4] For extended digests of these and other contemporary criticisms of early performances of Debussy's works, see Vallas, *Claude Debussy: His Life and Works*.

tended, that one could have paralleled the choral *Sirènes* of the final form.

In a letter to Henri Lerolle, dated August 28, 1894, Debussy makes the following reference to the *Nocturnes*.

> I have begun some pieces for violin and orchestra which will be called *Nocturnes* and in which I will employ groups of the orchestra separately, so as to try to discover nuances for these single groups; for people truly do not dare to do enough in music, fearing that sort of divinity which they call "common sense," which is indeed the most wretched thing I know. For it is, after all, only a religion founded to excuse the fools for being so numerous! . . . Let us cultivate only the garden of our own instincts, and let us walk without concern over the flower beds where ideas in white neckties are symmetrically aligned.

As originally planned, Debussy likened the projected score to a study in gray in painting, and there have been conjectures that the title may have been derived from the *Nocturnes* of Whistler. But whatever Debussy had in mind, it must have been materially altered in the orchestral recasting, and the fresh conception of the concluding movement as for a wordless women's chorus. The completion and the success of this work—the first really great success of Debussy's career—carry us on to another decade. It is the decade made unforgettable by the triumph of *Pelléas,* and the decade which brings to its sorry conclusion the still untold tale of Rosalie Texier, the "Lily-Lilo" of the affectionate inscription on the manuscript of the *Nocturnes;* dedicated, however, in their printed form, to the publisher, Georges Hartmann.

CHAPTER X

THE GROWTH OF *PELLÉAS*

Rodrigue et Chimène and Other Changes of Heart—Wagner
Lectures with Debussy as Pianist—A Score That Wouldn't Stay
Finished

It was in the furnished flat he shared with Gaby in the Rue de
Londres that Debussy began *Pelléas et Mélisande* in 1892. Two
years earlier he had composed or sketched a considerable part
of *Rodrigue et Chimène*, the uncompleted manuscript of which
is inscribed to his green-eyed mistress. Planned as an opera in
three acts, the text for *Rodrigue* was adapted by Catulle Mendès,
who wrote the libretto for Chabrier's very Wagnerian *Gwendoline* and who served Massenet and Pessard in a similar capacity.
In 1892, at the time of the inception of *Pelléas*, the work on
Rodrigue had progressed to the extent of two acts committed to
ruled paper and Debussy had expressed to Robert Godet a desire
that his friend should hear what he had written. The composer's
abandonment of the project soon afterward led to strained relations with Mendès, one of several literary figures whose labors
were to prove fruitless because of the musician's changes of heart
about the suitability of dramatic subjects to his purposes. The
accepted explanation in this instance is that Debussy again found
himself in the toils of Klingsor; the music, according to some
who have seen the manuscript, is palpably Wagnerian.

In the course of the next four or five years three other stage-
works were considered by Debussy, deeply immersed though he
was in *Pelléas*. To a libretto by Pierre Louÿs he planned an opera
to be called *Cendrelune*. Little headway was made, Debussy asking for so many changes in the original scheme that Louÿs finally

told him to write his own text. Louÿs also figured as translator of Rossetti in a work to be called *La Saulaire* and derived from the English poet's *Wildwood*. Claude wrote to Ysaÿe at the time of his "latest discoveries in musical chemistry," but the work in which these were to be revealed never came into being. In 1806 a proposal came from Houston Stewart Chamberlain, the English music critic who had acquired his education in France and after his marriage to Eva Wagner had become more German than the Germans. It was for a ballet on the subject of Daphnis and Chloe, a theme which fifteen years later was to supply Maurice Ravel with the inspiration for one of the most scintillating scores of the first quarter of the new century. Debussy was inclined to be ironical about Chamberlain's proposal from the start, scoffing at his belief "in the recipes of that old poisoner"—Wagner—and asking Louÿs whether this was to be a work for "xylophone, banjo or Russian bassoon." Later he reported having done some work on the score but referred to Daphnis as "not getting on," the while Chloe, he said, "takes after him."

His accumulated and accentuated anti-Wagnerism did not debar Debussy from appearing in public as a Wagnerian pianist. In May, 1893, he and Raoul Pugno, later to become widely known as a concert virtuoso, supplied at two pianos the musical illustrations for a lecture on *Rheingold* delivered by Catulle Mendès. Debussy wrote sarcastically of the event, which he described as "a terrible bore." He told of mothers who naïvely had brought their daughters to learn about the Ring being frightened away by Mendès's fiery description of *Walküre* and declined to subscribe to the belief of "some simple-minded people"—for whom "the month of May, it would seem, is henceforth to be the month of the *Walküre*" and for whom that score heralds "the spring of a new music and the death of the old worn-out formulae." There were engagements, also, to play *Parsifal* and *Tristan* in piano reductions, which Debussy accepted and fulfilled because

of his need of funds. As Henri Lerolle described it, he did this
playing for the same reason that a porter carries trunks—"to earn
a few coppers." Involved, apparently, was something like a thousand francs. His friends praised his playing; apparently his aversion to Wagner did not interfere with his ability to enucleate
and project the warm essence of Wagner's musical thought. But
instead of airing any vanity, he was inclined to deprecate his keyboard prowess. To Pierre Louÿs he wrote of what he described
as a wretched habit of scattering whole handfuls of wrong notes
about whenever he played before an audience of more than two
persons. Lerolle has recounted that at a *Parsifal* soirée Debussy
was near collapse because of the energy with which he played
and sang—though apparently he bothered little about the words.
The next time, added Lerolle, time out would be taken for a
cigarette in the middle of the second act, and then all would be
well. But for the presence of Lerolle to turn the pages, Debussy
said he would have closed the score and run off.

With the crystallization of his musical aesthetic, Debussy was
clarifying his mind as to what he wanted as a literary basis for
his music. Soon after his return from Rome, he developed in conversations with Guiraud, as noted down by Maurice Emmanuel,
their companion at the luncheon table, a theoretical basis for his
experiments in sonority; he argued for the use of scales of all
kinds, with a liberal utilization of the enharmonic; he discussed the
effectiveness of swaying between major and minor by the use
of ambiguous chords and modal devices such as came to be characteristic of his music. Not long after this—at about the time he
had returned disillusioned from Bayreuth—he described as the
poet of his choice "one who will only hint at things and thus enable me to graft my thought on his." His great desire, he said,
was to find poems that would not condemn him to long ponderous acts—"poems that will provide me with changing scenes,
varied as regards place and atmosphere, in which the characters

will not argue, but live their lives and work out their destinies."
He sought a poet who would not "tyrannically impose his will"
upon him but would permit him on occasion even "to outdo him
in artistry" and thus "perfect his work." And he, in turn, would
have a boon for the poet, in that he would not follow the usual
plan of the lyric drama, "in which the music arrogantly predomi-
nates," thus obscuring and smothering with its trappings the
words of the poet. "Nothing should retard the progress of the
action." Again, "there is too much singing in musical dramas."
The characters, he held, should sing only when the scene was
lyrical. The pathetic note should be held in reserve. There should
be variations in intensity. At times it was preferable to paint in
gray monochrome. Since all musical development must be essential to the text, any such development as assumed the protracted character of symphonic music could not possibly conform
to the mobility of words. These opinions were expressed in 1889,
three years before *Pelléas et Mélisande* came to Debussy's attention as a possible subject for his music. They are prophetic of the
satisfaction and the eagerness with which he must have turned to
Maeterlinck's poetic drama as the suitable text, at long last, for
the stagework of which he had dreamed. Here was opportunity
for that music which "begins where speech fails," music "intended to express the inexpressible," music that would "appear as
if emerging from the shadowy regions to which she would from
time to time return," music that would be "always discreet."

The ten years of *Pelléas* began with a day in the summer of
1892 when Debussy, strolling among the shops on the Boulevard
des Italiens, came upon a copy of Maeterlinck's play, published in
May of that year. He bought it and seems to have read it through
at a single sitting. Then and there he wrote down some sketches
and themes which he sent to Godet.[1] In the following May he

---

[1] Vallas has identified some of these as preserved in the final version, including: Golaud's rhythm, the five-note arabesque which describes Mélisande;

attended a performance of the play at the Théâtre des Bouffes-Parisiens and this confirmed him in his desire to write an opera to the Maeterlinck text, though the drama had not been favorably received by some of the critics, and Debussy's own literary mentor, Pierre Louÿs, had not been greatly impressed. Debussy was thirty when the opera was begun; forty when it was finished. A first step was to obtain Maeterlinck's permission to use the play for musical purposes. Henri de Régnier, the novelist, who became Debussy's friend through Pierre Louÿs, wrote to the Belgian poet in behalf of Debussy, whom he described as "a musician of the most clever and delicate talent" and—referring to the preliminary sketches—one who already had written music which "garlands the text."

Camille Mauclair, the poet, who met Debussy through Louÿs, has told of a letter from Maeterlinck,[2] in which he said that he had received a request for authorization to use the play from one M. Debussy, "of whom I know nothing." Continuing, Maeterlinck wrote:

> You know that I, unfortunately, am not only incompetent to judge, but that music is as unintelligible to me as if I were deaf. You, who are a fervent melomaniac, do me the favor of going to listen to this score, and if you judge it good, I shall authorize it.

With Louÿs, Mauclair went to Debussy's apartment [3] and there Debussy played and sang his score for them. The poet relates:

> Louÿs and I were pale with emotion. When it was finished, Debussy said to me with his sarcastic smile:

---

the theme in 6/4 time which accompanies Pelléas's "On dirait que ta voix a passé sur la mer au printemps!"

[2] Mauclair places the letter in 1895. His account was published in the souvenir program for the Debussy festival at the time of the dedication of the monument in the Bois de Boulogne.

[3] He refers to the address in Rue Cardinet, No. 58, which bears out the reference to 1895 as the time.

"What are you going to say to M. Maeterlinck?"

"This," I answered, taking a sheet of paper on which I wrote this dispatch: "I have just heard one of the most beautiful masterpieces in all music; be proud and happy to have inspired it; send your authorization immediately."

This incident would appear to have followed rather than preceded a visit to Maeterlinck which Debussy, accompanied by Louÿs, made in 1893. The pair found the poet in Ghent, and there spent a day with him. In Debussy's words, Maeterlinck "behaved like a young girl meeting an eligible young man," but he not only authorized Debussy to proceed with his project but also to make such cuts as he considered necessary, even suggesting some of his own accord. He confessed that, with music, he was "like a blind man in a museum." The cordiality of this meeting, and the poet's willingness to have his text sacrificed, where advisable, to the exigencies of musical performance, are strangely in conflict with the open hostility and the denunciation of any and all textual elisions which provoked a scandal at the first performance of *Pelléas* nine years later.

En route Debussy stopped in Brussels to see Ysaÿe. The violinist received him, the composer said, like a "little brother." They played together for hours, going over parts of *Pelléas* as well as the *Cinq Poèmes de Baudelaire* and *La Demoiselle élue*. It was at about this time that the composer informed Chausson that he was finishing the fourth scene of the fourth act, that of the fountain in the park. In October of the same year (1893) he confessed that he was not so satisfied as he had thought he was. Klingsor had turned up. So he tore up the manuscript of the scene. He was trying, he said, "to be as Pelléas as Mélisande" and he was off on a new line. He spoke of having used "silence as a means of expression." "Don't laugh," he added in parenthesis. "It is perhaps the only way of bringing into relief the emotional value of the phrase." How right he was has long since been corroborated by the wonder and the poignance of that simple declaration which discloses the love of Pelléas for Mélisande and hers for him—a declaration made not on the tumultuous wings of a soaring orchestra but with the instrumental choirs all silent and the voice speaking alone.

On a little melodeon that was in the possession of Louÿs—described by J. E. Blanche as "a wretched instrument"—Debussy would play for his friends the music as he composed it, singing the parts, or, rather, murmuring them, in his "curious, timbreless voice." Robert Godet, René Peter, Henri de Régnier, and Camille Mauclair heard snatches of the opera in this way, as it progressed through the middle 'nineties. Though other scores occupied his attention—the *Nocturnes* among them—Debussy could write to Ysaÿe that he was not forgetting *Pelléas*. Progress was slow, sometimes halting. In a letter of 1894 to Chausson Debussy dwelt upon his difficulties and told of "a vague desire to weep" as he contemplated the fate of his own musical personages. At the moment he was troubled by old Arkel, who, as he expressed it, "belongs to a world beyond the grave"—he is "disinterested and has a far-seeing affection for those who are about to pass away. . . . And one has to express all this with *do, re, mi, fa, sol, la, si, do!*" In another letter he expressed the fear that all will "end in smoke."

In the spring of 1895 Debussy told Godet that *Pelléas* was completed in its first form and that he was setting about immediately to revise it. From Brussels came a request from Ysaÿe, for permission to perform excerpts. This Debussy opposed, writing in his customary ironical vein that he couldn't face "the American riches of Wagner" and that he didn't want to "be placed in the position of some poor fellow who couldn't afford a contra-bass tuba."

In his *Henri Lerolle et ses amis*, Maurice Denis prints a letter from Debussy to Lerolle (dated "Samedi," without month or

year) in which Debussy, accepting an invitation for the following Tuesday, says: "As for the second act of *Pelléas*, I do not
think it is presentable enough for Tuesday; it is a little concoc-
tion that may interest both of us, but which, like all laboratory
work, is not done in public."

Mailed to Lerolle through the "pneumatique" on June 20,
1895, was the sketch reproduced here from the booklet referred to above.

Two letters to Lerolle, written by Debussy in August, 1894,
tell of progress with *Pelléas* and afford significant glimpses into

the composer's feeling for the characters of his opera. On the 17th he wrote:

Mon Dieu, my dear Lerolle, I have found myself sadly obliged to finish *Pelléas* while you are so far from me. Moreover, that has not been done without some foot-stamping; the scene between Golaud and Mélisande, above all! For it is there that one begins to have a premonition of catastrophes, there where Mélisande begins to lie to Golaud and to become enlightened about herself, aided therein by this Golaud, a fine man all the same, who shows that it is not necessary to be entirely frank, even with little girls! I believe that the scene before the grotto will please you. It tries to be all the mysteriousness of the night, where, amid so much silence, a blade of grass stirred from its sleep makes a really disquieting noise; then, it is the near-by sea which sings its sorrows to the moon, and it is Pelléas and Mélisande who are a little afraid to speak amid so much mystery. . . .

Now, all my worry is beginning; how will the world get along with these two poor little beings? (I hate crowds, universal suffrage and tri-colored phrases! . . .) Wait, there is Hartmann, who is certainly a representative of a good, medium intelligence. Ah well! the death of Mélisande, such as it is, does not move him more than a trifle. On him, it has no effect. For the rest, in France, every time a woman dies in the theater, it must be like the "Dame aux Camélias"; it suffices to replace the camelias with other flowers and the woman with a princess in a bazaar! People cannot concede that one leaves discreetly, like one who has had enough of this planet, the Earth, and is going away where the flowers of tranquility blossom! . . .

What you tell me of Nature is wholly true. Do you not believe, at first, that in order to become interested in Nature, one must be either an old oak which has seen her in all her guises, and which does not have to take refuge, when it rains, under a ridiculous instrument called umbrella, since it is always its own umbrella; or mayhap a shepherd who has never conversed except with his sheep, a conversation fully as interesting as that of a member of the Jockey-Club! . . .

Eleven days later, on the 28th, Debussy again writes to Lerolle, likening him to "a big brother" and prefacing his further discussion of Pelléas with a tribute of affection. He asks that this be interpreted not as sentimentality—"although sentimentality is not what M. C. Périer thinks it is." Turning to his work, he touches lightly on the difficulties he continues to encounter.

Pelléas and Mélisande began to sulk and no longer wanted to come down from their tapestry. I have therefore been obliged to play with other ideas. Then, a little jealous, they returned to bend over me, and Mélisande, with the soft, silky voice which you know she has, said to me: "Drop these little follies, the longing favorites of the cosmopolitan public, and keep your dreams for my hair; you know well that no other tenderness is like yours."

And the scene in the underground caverns was done, filled with subtle terror and mysterious enough to give vertigo to the best inured souls! And also the scene on leaving those same caverns, filled with sunlight, but with sunlight bathed by our good mother the sea. . . .

I have also completed the scene with the little sheep,[4] in which I have tried to put something of the compassion of a child to whom one of the sheep first gives the conception of the game in which he cannot take part; and also of the pity which people eager to be comfortable no longer feel. Now I am working on the scene between the father and son, and I am afraid, I must have such profound and sure things at my command! There is a "little father" in it that gives me nightmares.

Debussy then asks his friend's opinion of an idea which he said had come to him for the death of Mélisande, "which is to put an orchestral group on the stage, in order to have in some

---

[4] Commonly omitted in performances of the music drama.

sense a death in all sonorousness." Whatever Lerolle's reaction may have been, the composer left his players in the pit.

Camille Mauclair tells of having asked Debussy where he expected to have his work performed.

> "I do not know anything about that," was the reply. "I wrote it out of admiration of M. Maeterlinck. It is no slight work. I should like to find a place for it, but you know that I am badly received everywhere. But I do hope that Robert de Montesquiou will be good enough to give two auditions at his Pavillon des Muses. . . ."

Debussy here was thinking of a private performance, with the Comte de Montesquiou, a rich dilettante, as his most likely sponsor or entrepreneur.

The revision launched upon as soon as Debussy had completed the first version of the score in 1895 was completed in 1897, and it is said that Pierre Louÿs had to persuade his friend not to destroy the new version forthwith. Through André Messager, the work was submitted to Albert Carré and was accepted in principle for performance by the Opéra Comique. The circumstance that it did not achieve its première until five years had elapsed seems attributable not to procrastination on the part of Carré or his organization but to the composer's course in continually taking back the score to revise it further. This continued even after the conductor, Messager, had put it in rehearsal. As submitted, the manuscript was in the form of a big piano and vocal score, with notes on the orchestration, the parts for the latter occupying Debussy until the beginning of 1902. The orchestral interludes were an afterthought, of practical advantage in bridging over the various changes of scene, besides adding to the score some pages of extraordinary effectiveness and beauty. Messager, who had performed *L'Après-midi* almost immediately after it had been presented for the first time at the Société Nationale, was altogether sympathetic from the first, though Carré began by demurring to some of the apparently unorthodox details of a work neither symphonic in the Wagnerian sense nor essentially vocal in character, like the Italian and French aria operas. Messager's enthusiasm grew as he studied the score for production. Debussy was indeed fortunate in having the destinies of *Pelléas* entrusted to one of the few leading musicians of the day who were not weightily Wagnerian and one whose instincts as well as training qualified him for a sensitive comprehension and appreciation of the highly individual character of the task in hand. A letter from Debussy to the conductor, written somewhat later, after referring to "a splendid house, including Jean de Reszke," pays Messager this tribute:

> I make myself plain. You knew how to evoke the sonorous life of *Pelléas* with a tender delicacy which one might as well not try to recover, for it is certain beyond question that the interior rhythm of all music depends on him who evokes it, just as any word depends on the mouth that pronounces it. . . . Thus each impression in *Pelléas* was doubled by what your personal emotion had found in it, and had given it thereby a marvelous sense of appropriateness. This is surely something beyond the discoverable. You know as well as I . . ."

The score of *Pelléas* is dedicated to Messager and to the memory of the publisher, Hartmann, the generous publisher who repeatedly had advanced Debussy money, expecting scores that the composer was not prepared to deliver. Hartmann's heir, General Bourgeat, was in a hurry to square accounts and just at the time *Pelléas* was to be produced sent a bailiff to collect the sums alleged to be due. Subsequently "le général" sold to another publisher, Fromont, all the rights inherited from Hartmann. Meanwhile, Debussy, hard-pressed though he was, guarded his rights to *Pelléas*, which was not sold to his friend, Durand, until 1905.

CHAPTER XI

THE SUCCESS OF *PELLÉAS*

Enter Lily-Lilo, a Little too Late to Be Mélisande—The Breach
with Maeterlinck—Some Critical Reactions of the Day

THE time is no longer that of Gaby of the green eyes. In 1899,
three years before he completed *Pelléas*, Debussy married Rosalie Texier, the Lily-Lilo to whom the manuscript of the
Nocturnes is inscribed. Certain French writers have sought to
glorify this pretty and rather meek midinette as Debussy's Mélisande, though the opera had been conceived and all but the
orchestration and the interludes had been put on paper before
he met her. She was to share his life through five or six eventful
years—years that saw the première and the subsequent establishment in the repertoire of *Pelléas;* also the first performance
and the success of the *Nocturnes* and the beginnings of *La Mer;*
but the inspiration of *Pelléas* belongs as properly to the era of
her predecessor as that of *Ibéria* and *Le Martyre de Saint-
Sébastien* does to that of her successor.

The beginnings of the "Lily affair"—for so it was to be described in its early stages—have been left in an obscurity only
a little less concealing than that of the meeting of Debussy and
Gaby Dupont. Rosalie Texier came of solid bourgeois stock,
her father being a *chef de gare* in the employ of a railway in
Burgundy, and Rosalie had come from Yonne to Paris to make
an honest living as a dressmaker. She became friendly with
Gaby, who apparently liked her very much at a time when Debussy only poked fun at her. Rosalie accepted his mimicry of
her speech and her mannerisms good-naturedly and it was not
long before she had replaced Gaby, from whom, as we have

seen, Debussy already was straying. She became his companion in his nocturnal adventures and his long hours at cafés, and, more than any other of the several women who come within the scope of this narrative, she won and held the friendship of the musicians, writers, and painters who were close to Debussy in his most fruitful years.

Rosalie had chestnut hair, shading into a darker brown, a pale, fair complexion, regular features, and a small, tender mouth. She gave the impression of being rather delicate, but was above average height. One not very attractive detail was her voice, the sound of which eventually came to annoy the composer, though at first he made sport of it, along with his aping of her mannerisms. When Debussy first transferred to her the affections he had bestowed on Gaby, she accepted the situation without thought of marriage. Indeed, she held out against a formal union when Debussy first proposed it, arguing that it would not work out for the best for him as an artist. He is said to have threatened suicide—perhaps only a repetition of the Roman histrionics—and one day she consented. Debussy was without funds and gave a piano lesson to earn the wherewithal for the marriage breakfast. Then, with two or three friends, the newly wedded pair went to a circus—a favorite entertainment for the Debussy of this period. Counting up what was left, they dined together in one of Claude's restaurant haunts, ordering precisely what their remaining funds would pay for, the tip included, so that they could say that they were starting their married life without a sou. The day was October 19, 1899.

In a letter to Robert Godet, written under date of January 5, 1900, Debussy has left confirmation of what some of his friends have said about Lily, as scarcely a musical companion for the man who then was revising *Pelléas:*

> I give you at once the anecdotal side of my life. Two events have crossed it: the first my house-moving, the sec-

ond my marriage. . . . Miss Lily Texier has changed her
unharmonious name for that of Lily Debussy, much more
euphonious, everyone will agree! She is incredibly fair;
pretty as a legend. To these gifts she adds that of being not
in the least "modern style." She does not like music according to the latest Willy,[1] but according to her fancy. Her
favorite song is a round in which it is a question of a little
grenadier with scarlet cheeks, who wears his hat over his
ear like an old trooper. . . . This is ineffable and of a not
very aggressive aesthetic.

Debussy's close friends found Lily agreeable company on a
picnic, at the circus or in the Brasserie Pousset. Her lack of musical or other artistic background did not prevent their liking
her; possibly it helped, since there was enough airing of opinions on art subjects whenever several of these cronies got together, without an additional and feminine voice being added to
the disputes. Possibly it was quite enough for Rosalie to be attractive and companionable. As has already been seen, the pretty
picture of Debussy fashioning the character of Mélisande in the
spell of her silent presence, the composer unable to go on with
his work on the opera if she for a moment left his side, is not
to be reconciled with the chronology of events. Nor was Lily's
a personality, if we are to believe some surviving friends who
knew her well, at all mysterious or otherworldly in the Maeter-
linckian manner. She was straightforward, practical, pleasure-
loving, friendly, and affectionate; and there is no testimony to
indicate that she had any such difficulty finding her way about
as to justify any likening of Debussy's discovery of her in Paris
to that of Mélisande by Golaud in the ancient forest of the
Maeterlinck drama.

The apartment to which Debussy and Lily moved, on the
fifth floor of 58 Rue Cardinet, was described by Georgette Le-

---

[1] A reference to the critic, "Willy," otherwise Henri Gauthier-Villars.

blanc as "extremely modest." But for Debussy and his artist friends, it represented a material improvement in the composer's condition as compared to the establishments in the Rue de Londres and Rue Gustave-Doré. René Peter has recalled that it had a balcony and two high windows facing the street. It was furnished in what was then the "modern style" and the composer already was indulging his fondness for oriental paintings and statuettes, as well as for the color green. His chairs and tables had what was described as an "unripe" or "vegetable"-green hue, supplied by a liberal use of paint. The rug in Debussy's study was pale green, the wallpaper another shade of green. Claude even carried, hooked over his arm, a green cane. Peter [2] has told of Debussy's theft of a green necktie which he much admired. Sometime later, when Claude discovered Rosalie wearing it as a hat band, he was struck by it anew, and asked her where she got it, having forgotten not only that he had purloined it, but that he had given it to his wife. There are tales about Debussy which contain more than a hint of kleptomania. But they pertain almost wholly to objects that were green.

If Lily was not Debussy's Mélisande, she may well have been the prototype and the inspiration, such as it was, for a character in a play styled Les F.E.A.[3] which Debussy and René Peter attempted to write together in 1900. The play had been ordered by a Paris theater, and three scenes were on paper before Debussy withdrew from the collaboration, probably because he sensed a risk in appearing before the public in another and untried capacity at the time Pelléas was in preparation. In the play, another of the dramatis personae thus addresses the likeness of Lily:

[2] In recollection of his friend's love of the color, Peter has had his own bookcase, easy chair, and the doors of his bedroom painted green.
[3] Les Frères en Art.

"You don't pretend to be a Muse and to frighten away the sparrows. You don't imitate the women in the frescoes in the way you wear your hair. You are like a peach and you have about you a sweet perfume that doesn't suggest the latest product of Houbigant. You don't go in for dressing up and that gives you so much more time. . . ."

To return to *Pelléas*, the work was put in rehearsal on January 13, 1902. The dress rehearsal, which according to custom was in reality a public performance, was set for April 27 of that year. Therewith came the break with Maeterlinck. There can no longer be reason to doubt that this was the result of Carré's decision to cast Mary Garden as Mélisande, instead of Georgette Leblanc, the celebrated actress and somewhat less celebrated singer, who had then only recently become formally the wife of the Belgian poet. Mme. Leblanc has told how Debussy went to them in the Rue Ranouard in Passy to play the score, late in 1901. Because of the position of the piano, the composer could not see Maeterlinck, who, in an extreme state of boredom as the music progressed, lit his pipe and before the audition was finished was half asleep. There was some talk about the casting and when Maeterlinck urged that his wife should have the distinction of creating his heroine in her new musical dress, Debussy said he would be delighted to have it so. Thereafter were some personal rehearsals at Debussy's abode in the Rue Cardinet. Georgette, deep in the score, took for granted that she would be called upon to undertake the role.

But Albert Carré had his own ideas about casting the opera. Whether Debussy attempted in any way to intercede for Mme. Leblanc has not been disclosed. Presumably, it was not his affair. Why either the poet or the poet's wife should feel that he had "betrayed" them—the word is Georgette's—is by no means clear, save as he may have been hesitant or negligent about breaking the news that he knew would be bad news. Georgette learned of Carré's decision through the newspapers and Maeterlinck was enraged. Brandishing his cane, he jumped through the window of their ground-floor apartment and rushed away with a threat to give Debussy a drubbing. Presently he returned, waving the cane comically, with a story of Debussy's having dropped into a chair at the sight of him and of Lily rushing frantically to her husband with smelling salts; whereupon the irate Maeterlinck departed, because there was nothing else to do.

But Maeterlinck found something else to do with his pen if not with his cane. He attacked the management of the Opéra Comique. In a letter to *Le Figaro*, dated April 14, 1902, he declared this *Pelléas* "a work which is now strange and hostile to me," adding "I can only wish its immediate and emphatic failure." He complained that he had been excluded from his own work, which "from now on, is in the hands of the enemy." His poetic text had been made incomprehensible, he declared, by "arbitrary and absurd cuts," whereas passages which he had desired to suppress had been retained. There was talk of a duel, in which Carré offered to take the place of Debussy, as did Robert de Flers. Nothing came of it and the work went forward in rehearsal.

The cast as announced included Miss Garden as Mélisande; Jean Périer as Pelléas; Jeanne Gerville-Réache, Geneviève; Hector Dufranne, Golaud; Félix Vieulle, Arkel; and one Blondin, Yniold. Messager has left us a description of the first reading of the opera to the artists, who assembled at his house. Debussy played the score and sang all the roles as best he could in a "deep, sepulchral voice" which took the high parts an octave lower. The atmosphere at first was one of mistrust and antagonism, but Debussy's earnestness and expressiveness, together with the strangeness of the drama and the music, were not lost upon the artists. In the end they were in tears and quite carried away. Their eagerness to get to work on the parts was an earnest of victory for Debussy, so far as the singers were concerned. But there was still the orchestra to reckon with. Debussy had entrusted the copying of the parts to an inexperienced friend, with the result that there were many mistakes to irritate and perplex the players. Partial rehearsals were protracted beyond ordinary length and there were some one hundred and twenty ensemble rehearsals in all. As always with a score which divagates from the obvious, this one was termed "unplayable" by some of musicians, in no wise troubled by similar assertions on the part of their predecessors of the days when Beethoven's C Minor Symphony, Schubert's C Major, and Wagner's *Tannhäuser* were new. Among those familiar with the published play, the libretto was described as ridiculous.

All this was abetted by a sarcastic pamphlet, styled "Select Program," which wittily parodied the drama and was sold at the doors of the Opéra Comique at the time of the dress rehearsal, the afternoon of April 27, 1902. Vallas says that "in spite of rumors to that effect, it is impossible to believe that it was inspired by Maeterlinck himself." The rumors persist. Indeed, surviving friends of Debussy will shrug their shoulders and say there is nothing of rumor about it. Had not Maeterlinck expressed himself in the public prints as hoping that the work would fail immediately and emphatically? [4] Offsetting this, Octave Mirbeau did what he could in a newspaper article to present *Pelléas* in a favorable light, in advance of the first performance. With the "Select Program" as an incentive, the dress rehearsal was not permitted to go its way without disturbances that bordered on scandal. The admirable Miss Gar-

---

[4] It is said that the only time the poet heard Debussy's music in the theater was in 1927 when he was present through one act of a performance of *Pelléas et Mélisande* at the Metropolitan Opera House in New York. His interest at that time was in the première at the Metropolitan of Albert Wolf's operatic setting of his *L'Oiseau bleu*.

den's Scotch-American accent evoked laughter, particularly in the phrase "Je ne suis pas heureuse" in the second act. Yniold's repeated "petit père" was an excuse for guffaws in the scene with Golaud. And such was the uproar when Golaud, holding the child up to the tower window, asked whether the suspected lovers were near the bed, that a solicitous officialdom brought about the elision of some fifteen bars of text and score at this point. There already had been some curtailment of the score, as written; including the scene of Yniold with the little sheep. At the first regular performance on the evening of April 30 more laughter and more heated arguments were engendered, with Debussy's friends and certain of the critics, as well as a few of the more open-minded musicians waxing belligerent in his behalf. Thereafter came a rapid calming down and to the surprise of everyone, including Debussy and Carré, the new work took its place as a repertoire opera. If it had failed completely and disappeared from the boards, neither the composer nor the producer would have been surprised, in view of the prevailing attitude of opera patrons and, for that matter, the musical fraternity. Carré saw to it that there was a healthy clacque by filling the stalls and balcony with students and others from the higher levels when the regular occupants departed. It is of record that people were turned away from the seventh performance. *Pelléas* had fourteen representations at the Opéra Comique in May and June of that year and was given ten times in the course of the new season that opened in October, with Henri Büsser as conductor during an absence of Messager.

Meanwhile *Pelléas et Mélisande* was inspiring feuilletons and magazine articles that went beyond the ordinary newspaper reviews in their analysis of the new work.[5] The critiques which followed the dress rehearsal and the first regular performance

[5] For extended quotations from the reviews of *Pelléas*, see Vallas, *Claude Debussy, His Life and Works*.

were about evenly divided between praise and censure. Certainly it is not true that *Pelléas* was condemned or ridiculed indiscriminately in the press, as careless speakers and writers on occasion have asserted. Debussy himself found reason to thank publicly Gaston Carraud of *La Liberté*, Camille de Saint-Croix of *La Petite République*, Gustave Bret of *La Presse*, André Corneau of *Le Matin*, and Henry Bauer of *Le Figaro* for their laudatory and understanding reviews. Ironically, he confesses to having greatly alarmed one of the fraternity (M. d'Harcourt), whom he finds evoking the holy trinity of melody, harmony, and rhythm as "three things which are unknown to M. Debussy," but in a public statement tells him not to be uneasy. He adds that after reading the gentleman's observations three times, he has been unable to fathom their meaning, which no doubt shows that "they are exceedingly profound." In reply to an assertion that the score contains "no trace of melody" he begins by saying that in the first place the statement isn't true. "Besides," he continues, "the feelings of a character cannot continually be expressed in melody" and adds that dramatic melody should be totally different from "melody in general."

Among those hostile to the work were writers who found the music "decadent," "morbid," and "pernicious"; it was declared that nowhere in it could be recognized "a single phrase, a single motive, a single form, a single outline." The score was described as "spineless," "invertebrate," possessed of "a minimum of vitality." The singers were referred to as "unnecessary," since their task was merely to "drone out the words" in "a monotonous, moribund recitative." Here was "a nihilistic art," here also was preciosity of an order that might "distract the ears of the blasé" but could not touch the hearts of those of normal, healthy emotions. One reviewer went so far as to liken this velvety, filmy, evanescent music to the noise of a squeaking door or a piece of furniture being moved. The redoubtable Willy spoke of the harmonic harshness of rasping dissonances; then gallantly took it back, by appending: "I am wrong. I am behaving like those painters who were so accustomed to the most mournful bituminous colors that they revolted against the luminosity of the impressionists." Camille Bellaigue regarded this harmony as treated in a haphazard manner, and described the composer as "qualified to preside over the decomposition" of the musical art.

On the commendatory side Saint-Croix pointed out how the rhythm of the music followed the melopoeia of the language, syllable by syllable; Carraud dwelt upon the beauty of the harmonic concatenations, which, he said, defied analysis; and declared that Debussy took his place—more definitely than Wagner—among the great sensualists of music, "of whom Mozart was the greatest"; Henry Bauer said boldly that, today or tomorrow, Debussy's music must prevail, describing it as youthful, pure, tender; intensely artistic and full of originality. "It grows on you, never seeming monotonous, the inspiration never weakening for an instant," wrote Gustave Bret. Among composers, Paul Dukas and Vincent d'Indy wrote articles of discriminating praise. Though d'Indy was reported to have expressed himself unfavorably toward the work at the dress rehearsal, when he came to put his reactions on paper he remarked on "the sonorous rendering of the text" as "marvelously adapted to the inflections of the language" and observed further that the "many-coloured waves of music" in which the drama had been steeped "enhance its design, reveal hidden meanings, and intensify its expression, while always permitting the words to be discernible through the fluid element of the music."

Debussy felt called upon to explain his purposes in his setting of the text. "I have tried to obey a law of beauty," he said, "which appears to be singularly ignored in dealing with dramatic music. The characters in this drama endeavor to sing like real persons," rather than in the traditional manner of operas constructed on some arbitrary and antiquated pattern. "I do not pretend to have discovered anything in *Pelléas*," he added. "But I have tried to mark out a path which others may follow and make broader with their own discoveries, in such a way, perhaps, as to liberate dramatic music from the heavy yoke it has been wearing for so long."

Of more personal appeal today than his answers to his critics is Debussy's comment on the emotions that came to him when he saw his characters take on life. Writing for *Musica* of January, 1908, six years after the première, he said that the stage realization of a work of art,

> no matter how beautiful, always is at variance with the inner vision. . . . Consider the charming existence in which you and your characters have lived together for so long; when sometimes they seemed about to rise, in tangible form, from your manuscript's silent pages! If you are bewildered when you behold them come to life through intervention of this or that artist, is it any wonder? Something like fear is experienced. They are like phantoms; one scarcely dares to address them. . . . Nothing remains of the old dream. Another's mind is interposed between you and it. . . .

Curiously enough, as performances of *Pelléas* followed one another, some consideration was given to a notion of having the character of Pelléas played by a woman. Debussy seems to have been sympathetic to it, remarking that Pelléas had not the love-making ways of a Hussar. But this seems to have been something more of curiosity than conviction; to construe it as a criticism of M. Périer, who was to create the role for America as well as for France, would be unfair. Next to Messager, Debussy was particularly grateful to Miss Garden, concerning whom he wrote that at rehearsals he almost never had occasion to make any suggestion to her. As, little by little, the character of Mélisande took shape for her, he waited with confidence and interest, mixed with curiosity; until at last, when they had come to the death of Mélisande, he was indescribably amazed. "That was the gentle voice I had been hearing within me, faltering in its tenderness, captivating in the charm for which I had scarcely dared to hope."

Debussy was tendered and accepted a government decoration,[6] his reason for taking it, as he told Louÿs, being that it would make happy his old parents and might please others who were dear to him. But he soon found that his new-won celebrity had its distasteful side. Complaining of being thrust into public life, he left Paris for the summer, to stay with his parents-in-law at Bichain in Burgundy. The craze of Debussyism had begun. At forty Claude Debussy was to take his place beside Richard Strauss as one of the great controversial figures of the music of his day.

[6] Thanks to the interest of Jules Combarieu, the musicographer, then in the Ministry of Education.

CHAPTER XII

NOCTURNES AND BIBELOTS

"The Despair of Critics"—Music for the Piano—A Troublesome
Commission from America—"L'Affaire Ravel"

AWAY from *Pelléas* and the Opéra Comique, other performances
and the publication of some of his works had been accruing to
Debussy. On December 9, 1900, two of the three *Nocturnes*
were played at the Concerts Lamoureux and on October 27 of
the next year the complete triptych was presented under the
same auspices. Though Debussy repeatedly expressed an aversion
to program annotations which had the effect of lessening the
essential mystery of a work, he himself prepared an explanatory
note for the second of these concerts. The title, *Nocturnes*, he
said, was to be interperted in a general, and more particularly,
in a decorative sense, without thought of the musical form which
ordinarily bore the designation. Applicable, instead, were the
various impressions and the special effects of light which the
word suggests. In other quarters, many analogies were to be
drawn between Debussy's *Nocturnes* and those of Whistler.
Though Vallas has found in *Nuages* an instance of unconscious
borrowing, with the opening statement regarded as taken, note
for note, from Moussorgsky's song, *Sunless;* and yet another in
Fêtes, where two "motives"—"in fact," he writes, "the whole
atmosphere"—are "obviously reminiscent" of Charpentier's
Louise,[1] these companion pieces have held their place as the
purest Debussy. Lockspeiser relates how, at a rehearsal in Berlin, one of the orchestral musicians remarked admiringly of
Fêtes that it was "echt französisch." And he might have added,

---

[1] An opera Debussy despised. See page 196.

"echt Debussy."

The *Nocturnes* were a success, in spite of the bewilderment and dismay of some of the academicians. Other of the professorial gentry analyzed the works with highly favorable comment, even imputing to them qualities of form in the classical sense that Debussy had not intended. Though Pierre de Bréville, writing in the *Mercure de France*, spoke of this music as "the despair of critics," in that it "defied analysis," he found it enchanting and lauded Debussy for not demanding of Music *all* that she could give, but, instead, asking from her what she *alone* was capable of suggesting. The reviewers for the *Guide Musical, Ménestrel, Courrier Musical, Revue Hebdomadaire*, and *Monde Artiste* were commendatory. Gaston Carraud acclaimed Debussy in *La Liberté* as "one of the most original artists of the day," one who was "guided by a refined and unerring taste" and one who "seems to have attained to complete lucidity of thought and accuracy of expression." Among composers, Paul Dukas and Alfred Bruneau wrote laudatory articles, Dukas declaring that Debussy must henceforth be regarded as having a place unique and distinctive among the musicians of his time.

In 1900 *La Demoiselle élue*, the Quartet and the *Chansons de Bilitis* were performed with success at the official concerts of that year's Paris Exposition. Debussy's fellow composer and kindred spirit, Alfred Bruneau, wrote of him, in the musical section of a report made to the Minister of Public Instruction, as "the very exceptional, the very peculiar, the very solitary M. Claude Debussy." Among piano compositions which had occupied Debussy in the course of the ten years of *Pelléas* was the suite, *Pour le piano*, begun in 1896 and completed in 1901. The three pieces of the set, *Prélude, Sarabande*, and *Toccata*, were played at the Société Nationale on January 11, 1902, by Ricardo Viñes, who subsequently came to be regarded as an accredited interpreter of Debussy. The *Toccata* was encored and all the indications were that these whimsical, nonchalant compositions had come into the world under favorable circumstances.

In 1903 appeared the group of piano pieces called *Estampes* —*Pagodes, Soirée dans Grenade* and *Jardins sous la pluie*—favorites with a whole generation of keyboard Debussyists. They were published forthwith and won immediate recognition when Viñes played them at the Société Nationale on January 9, 1904. *Jardins sous la pluie* had to be repeated. Inner circles of the art world of Paris had one of their periodical tempests in a teapot shortly thereafter. Resemblances were found between *Soirée dans Grenade* and the *Habanera* of Maurice Ravel. The latter had been brought out in two-piano form, with *Entre Cloches*, its companion piece of the *Sites auriculaires*, at the Société Nationale on March 5, 1898, when Ravel was twenty-three years old. Debussy, it developed, had borrowed the manuscript of the *Habanera* from Ravel and had mislaid it. He was not to put hands upon it again, according to his own testimony, for several years and he had never so much as examined it. And as for the resemblances—including harmonic effects that were novel in that time, a particular treatment of a pedal-note and the voluptuous Habanera rhythm—they were to be found also in an earlier Debussy work (like Ravel's, for two pianos), *Lindaraja*, which Debussy had composed in 1901 but which was not published until 1926. *Lindaraja* had lain forgotten between the pages of one of his other manuscripts. In incorporating the old *Habanera* in his *Rapsodie espagnole* of 1907, Ravel took care to give it the date of 1895, possibly in fear that posterity would suspect him of having borrowed from Debussy!

To 1903 also is credited *D'un cahier d'esquisses*, a still relatively unfamiliar piano work which was not performed until 1910, when Ravel played it at the first concert of the then new Société Musicale Indépendante. The next year brought *Masques* and *L'Ile joyeuse*, the latter inspired by Watteau's painting, *Em-*

barquement pour Cythère.

Four days before Christmas in 1902 Mary Garden sang the soprano part of *La Demoiselle élue* at one of the Colonne concerts. Debussy, never comfortable on the podium, declined to conduct. But, needy as ever, he accepted a post as music critic and a fortnight later (January 12, 1903) his first feiulleton,[2] concerned with d'Indy's opera, *L'Étranger,* appeared in *Gil Blas.* He held this journalistic post for the remainder of the season. As he was later to serve other publications in a similar capacity, his critical writings will be dealt with in another chapter.

In 1903 was celebrated the centenary of the Académie de France in Rome. It was then that Debussy, writing savagely about the festivity, spoke of having narrowly escaped poisoning and rebuked those in charge for not having improved the meals at the Villa Medici. In that year he heard the cantatas composed by the Rome competitors, and expressed himself to Messager as disgusted by the theatrical style of the scores sent in to the Institut. The work of a certain laureate prompted him to remark that the fellow was Leoncavallo's best pupil. "Heavens, what music! It might have been written by a pork-butcher!"

On his mind for nearly eight years was a commission from Mrs. Eliza Hall of Boston for a fantasy for saxophone. Debussy, who confessed to his friends that he was ignorant of the technique of the instrument, procrastinated; though, as he wrote to Messager, he assured his patron that "with the exception of Rameses II," the rhapsody alone occupied his thoughts. It seems that the "saxophone lady," as he styled her, had paid him an unexpected and, under the circumstances, not altogether welcome visit at his Rue Cardinet abode, to inquire about progress. These Americans, he observed to Messager, "are proverbially

---

[2] He had, however, written earlier for the *Revue Blanche* and *Musica.*

THE FIRST PAGE OF THE MANUSCRIPT OF *NUAGES*.
FROM THE ORIGINAL IN THE LIBRARY OF CONGRESS,
WASHINGTON, D. C.

tenacious." So there was nothing to do but renew the search for novel combinations "calculated to show off this aquatic instrument." In another letter, to Louÿs, Debussy wonders "whether the saxophone indulges in romantic tenderness like a clarinet." He described the composition as "ordered, paid for and eaten" more than a year before. A draft for saxophone and piano finally was written out in 1905, when, in a letter to Durand, Debussy reported having received a polite demand for the script. "Her patience deserves reward," he said, in expressing what no doubt was an honest wish that he could satisfy the demand. Six years later, in 1911, he made desultory efforts to orchestrate the work. Apparently abandoning the task in despair, he sent the rough draft, obviously incomplete, to Mrs. Hall. Subsequently orchestrated by Roger-Ducasse, the work was brought to performance at the Société Nationale on May 11, 1919. At first styled *Fantaisie*, it was known as *Rapsodie orientale* and then *Rapsodie Mauresque* before the title finally became simple *Rapsodie*.[3] Debussy's dilatory conduct may have been due partly to the effect upon him of a performance in which Mrs. Hall played the *Choral varié* of Vincent d'Indy, which she had similarly commissioned. For him, the instrument was ungainly and its use by a woman ridiculous.

In the spring of 1904 were composed the *Danse sacrée* and *Danse profane* for chromatic harp and string orchestra. The work was done on order from the firm of Pleyel, which desired the two pieces for use in competitions at the Brussels conservatory, which had inaugurated a class in the chromatic harp. A performance of the dances in November at the Concerts Colonne led to further critical use of the term "impressionism," one writer finding a counterpart for this music in the painting

[3] The saxophone rhapsody is not to be confused, of course, with the clarinet rhapsody of 1910.

of Carrière, where, as he saw it, suffering predominated and subjects were so submerged in misty atmosphere as to be barely visible.

Two sets of songs, a new series of *Fêtes galantes* to texts by Verlaine, and *Trois Chansons de France*, on poems by Charles d'Orléans and Tristan Lhermite,[4] bear date of 1904. Embraced in the former set are *Les Ingénus*, *Le Faune*, and *Colloque sentimental*. The resemblances they bear to the first set of more than a decade earlier have survived the comment evoked by Debussy's supposed change of style; a change whereby a love of persistent patterns asserts itself more predominantly. (Of the first set, *Clair de lune* had been worked over and improved since 1892.) The *Trois Chansons de France*, another supposed marker of the new manner, have a literary significance in that they show Debussy by now more interested in medieval and classical poetry than in the verses of his erstwhile favorite Symbolists. Two rondels, *Le temps a laissié son manteau* and *Pour ce que plaisance est morte*, are settings of lyrics by the fifteenth-century duke who held court at the Château de Blois, whereas *La Grotte* derives from the seventeenth-century conceits of Tristan Lhermite, whose world was that of nymphs and fountains and all the paraphernalia of what was classicism in the well-bodiced and heavily wigged era of the "grand monarque."

With the dedication of both the *Trois Chansons de France* and the new series of *Fêtes galantes* to Mme. S. Bardac, we are brought to a new chapter in the personal story of the man whose heart, as he had said some years before, was still capable of fluttering. On the manuscript of the *Nocturnes* he had written, for the eye of Rosalie Texier Debussy, the following:

This manuscript belongs to my little Lily-Lilo. All rights reserved. It is proof of the deep and passionate joy I have in

---

[4] Also written L'hermite and l'Hermitte.

being her husband, Claude Debussy. At the peep of January, 1901.

On that of the *Fêtes galantes* is to be read:

With thanks, the month of June, 1904. A. l. p. M.
The initials stand for "À la petite Mie," "To my little darling."
The little darling was Emma Bardac.

CHAPTER XIII

A TIME OF TRIAL

Flight from Lily, an Attempted Suicide, Double Divorce, and Marriage to Mme. Bardac—Chou-Chou and The Children's Corner

THE wife of a wealthy banker, Mme. Sigismond Bardac was known socially as a singer, particularly of the songs of Gabriel Fauré.[1] A previous attachment in that quarter was to cause bad blood between Fauré and Debussy. Mme. Bardac was a Jewess whose maiden name was Emma Claude Moyse. The Bardacs had two children, a son and a daughter; the former, Raoul Bardac, achieved a measure of success as an amateur composer, though, after having studied at the Conservatoire, he took up a business career and at this writing is connected with an automobile-manufacturing concern. It was through Raoul's piano lessons, when he was a boy, that Debussy met Mme. Bardac. In one of his needy periods Debussy was the lad's teacher. One day in 1904, having left his book of exercises at his mentor's home, the boy found it necessary to call for them. His mother decided to go with him to the Rue Cardinet address. Raoul found his music where he had left it, on Debussy's piano. Pupil and teacher walked down the steps together, Debussy having put on his hat and picked up his cane, intending to go for a walk. In front of the house introductions were made and Mme. Bardac invited Debussy to drive through the Bois de Boulogne with them in their carriage. Debussy accepted and that was the be-

---

[1] Fauré dedicated his *Bonne Chanson* to her in 1892. She was the first to sing it in public.

ginning of the end for Lily-Lilo. Godet has described the new flame as "an accomplished *femme du monde*, a brilliant conversationalist, an artist who sang exquisitely."

At the time when Rosalie's voice was becoming more and more unpleasant in Debussy's ears—he told Robert Godet that the sound of it froze the blood in his veins—Mme. Bardac was singing his songs at social gatherings, sometimes accompanied by Debussy, to the undisguised irritation and resentment of Fauré. The salons of Paris were, of course, full of such jealousies. This case differed from many or most of the others in that the ill feeling between Debussy and Fauré was manifested openly.

Debussy was on the point of leaving Rosalie a number of times before he made the break in June, 1904, deserting her for flight with Mme. Bardac. Only a month or two before the elopement, Louis Laloy had called to see Debussy, who was not at home.

The door of the apartment was opened for me by a young woman, pale and thin, very timid and evidently anxious for me to go away. When I saw Debussy again, he spoke tenderly of her, complaining only of having no children. I answered: "Don't get discouraged" and could see that aside from the desire for children he was happy . . . within his domain where he was free and master. One could conceive, however, of a happier marriage where all one's thoughts are understood and shared.

Of a visit for luncheon, a few weeks later, Laloy wrote:

I was their only guest and both gaily showed me their faience pieces which they had modeled on their own stone to suit their own artistic tastes. This was Saturday, July 2. Nothing presaged the storm that was to come. Twelve days later, as I afterward learned, on the evening of the 14th, occurred the thunderstroke.

Rosalie tried to commit suicide, shooting herself with a revolver and inflicting a dangerous wound near the heart. She was removed to the Rue Blomet clinic and there Debussy, accompanied by his father, came to see her—the accepted story among his friends being that he came only once, departing when he learned that Lily was going to live. There are several versions of what happened. One, as brought out in Henri Prunières's article, "Autor de Debussy" in the May, 1934, number of the *Revue Musicale*—an article which was largely an attack on the Vallas biography—quotes a remark attributed to Debussy and on which his enemies battened. Lily, recovering from her wound, tried to tell Claude that she could not live without him. "But, after all," he replied, "you are still young and pretty." Prunières endeavors to give the remark a more favorable interpretation than many fellow Parisians had accorded it.

Another story of an even meaner character was widely circulated. As recounted by Prunières, Lily was supposed to have left in the apartment some two hundred francs, which she had put in an envelope addressed to the friend who had lent her this sum. In the confusion following the shooting and the transporting of Lily to the clinic, the envelope with the money disappeared. As Debussy and his father, arriving at the clinic too late to be admitted that day, had gone to the apartment, Lily came to the conclusion that "they had found the money and shared it between them." In a footnote to the article in which the story is recounted, Prunières presents what presumably is another version of the same story. According to this tale, Mary Garden left a one-hundred-franc bill at Lily's bedside in the hospital. This was said to have been taken by a relative of Debussy, under the pretext that the wounded woman did not have long to live and the money would be of no use to her.

However little truth there may have been in these and other stories, which only proof positive would justify the disinterested person in accepting, the sympathy of Debussy's friends was overwhelmingly for the deserted wife. Most of them contributed to a fund for her, when it was learned that she had not sufficient money to pay the hospital bills. The subscription was led by one of Debussy's pupils, Nico Coronio. To give to the fund was, in the eyes of these friends, like saying openly that Debussy was in the wrong; and René Peter, for one, refused to contribute on this ground. Pierre Louÿs, who had been very fond of Lily, participated with the proviso that his name be not disclosed.

If Debussy's close friends felt thus strongly—and some of them were alienated from him for the rest of his life—it is not surprising that enemies and scandalmongers contrived to place him in the light of a cad who had thrown over an adoring helpmate, for the sake of the moneybags of one who could relieve him of his pressing financial worries. Mme. Bardac, it was said, expected to inherit a fortune from a rich uncle named Osiris. As Laloy has related, busybodies, carried away by the agreeable pastime of judging their neighbors, made a sport of pitying the victim and blaming the culprit. People whose past was unknown slurred Debussy unmercifully. Some journalists and actors were compassionate, but so maudlin in their sympathy that to Laloy it seemed a mere show to mark their superiority. After several months there was an exchange of letters between these friends. Under date of April 14, 1905, Debussy wrote to Laloy from his new abode, 10, Avenue Alphaud:

My Dear Friend,
I want to tell you first that you have never ceased being my friend. And your friendship has become even dearer by the simple test—but yet so rare!—that you have just made by writing me with a clairvoyant sympathy. I have seen so many desertions around me! Enough to be forever disgusted by anything that bears the name of man. . . .
I want to tell you what all I've gone through. It's ugly, tragic. I have suffered greatly, morally. Was it because I had

to pay some forgotten debt to life? I don't know, but often I have had to smile, so that people wouldn't suspect that I was on the verge of tears.

I will try to find again the Claude Debussy of old. If he seems a little worse off for worry don't be too angry with him, but think of his friendship for you, which remains unshakable.

In August, Debussy made a brief visit to England, after which he again wrote Laloy.

Dear Friend,

After several days spent in London without much joy, except for the music of the grenadiers who used to pass every morning with their joyful bagpipes and the wild little fifes, playing marches in which the Scotch song seemed to melt into the cakewalk—then two days as a stranger in Paris —here I am, situated for I don't know how long yet. This is a place rendered heavenly by the absence of crowds. There are only a few Americans, heartbroken at not being able to find their customary brand of whiskey, and two or three Russians forgotten by the Japanese. [Presumably a reference to the Russo-Japanese war.]

At an earlier date (September 19, 1904) he wrote of his life being "strange and bizarre," much more so than he could have wished. The particulars, he said, would be rather embarrassing; perhaps he had aimed too high. But "whatever the cause, I have had many a fall." He spoke of mourning the Claude Debussy of the past, "the Claude Debussy who worked so joyously at *Pelléas*," adding that he had never been able to recapture him, "and that is one of my sorrows."

Double divorce proceedings had been instituted and had dragged on for months. On August 2, 1904, Rosalie Texier obtained her decree and, save for some further negotiations over the royalties which Debussy signed over for her support, passed out of his life. There were additional legal complications before

DEBUSSY WITH HIS FIRST WIFE, ROSALIE TEXIER

DEBUSSY WITH THE SECOND MME. DEBUSSY
(EMMA BARDAC)

Mme. Bardac was freed and even then the litigation brought on by the affair was not ended. Debussy was involved in law-suits, of one kind or another, until the end of his days. For eighteen months before Bardac agreed to the divorce, Debussy and Mme. Bardac had been together. The financier, whose interests were elsewhere, his name being coupled at the time with that of a well-known actress, finally agreed to an arrangement whereby he was to settle fifty thousand francs a year on Mme. Bardac. For that time, this was a handsome sum—the equivalent of about ten thousand dollars a year—though no more than would have been regarded as adequate to maintain Mme. Bardac's previous standard of living. That the money soon stopped flowing, with the result that Debussy eventually was compelled to return to all manner of hackwork to piece out a living, was an ironic commentary on the charge that he had married for money.

The daughter born to the Debussys in the autumn of 1905 was named Claude-Emma, but was to be known through her short life chiefly as "Chou-Chou." She early gave musical promise and took piano lessons from a woman teacher. To Chou-Chou, when she was less than four years old, Debussy dedicated *The Children's Corner*; and she was the inspiration, also, of the children's ballet, *La Boîte à joujoux*, composed in 1913 to a scenario by André Hellé. She died in a diphtheria epidemic in 1919, a year after her father, when she was fourteen years old. Louis Laloy has said that the birth of Chou-Chou was the fulfillment of one of Debussy's dearest hopes. In the terrible suffering of his own last years, he at least was spared the knowledge that his only child so soon would follow him to the grave. *The Children's Corner* dedication reads: "To my dearest Chou-Chou, with her father's affectionate apologies for what follows." From 1904 on, dedications to Chou-Chou's mother were to include, besides the *Fêtes galantes* and *Trois Chansons de France*, already referred to, the songs of *La Promenoir des deux amants*, the

Rondes de printemps of the orchestral *Images*, and the three Sonatas of the final years.

Four years after Debussy's marriage with Emma Bardac there was published a play called *La Femme nue*, the work of Henry Bataille, which was widely accepted as a dramatic paraphrase of the Debussy-Lily-Bardac embroglio. In it, a painter, Pierre Bernier, deserts his wife, Loulou, for the luxurious Princesse de Chabran. Various parallels have been drawn from the text, with disillusionment stressed as the inevitable resolution of chords of vanity, snobbery, and greed. Apparently there was no protest of any kind from Debussy or his bride. To have complained of the play might have meant airing in court all the circumstances of the elopement and there was no pressing need for the living composer to regard the make-believe painter as other than a purely fictitious personage of the theater.

CHAPTER XIV

THE CREATION OF *LA MER*

The Hills of Burgundy and the Shore at Eastbourne—*Images* for Piano, *Ibéria*, and the *Ballades* of Villon—*Pelléas* Abroad

"You will remark that the ocean does not exactly bathe the hills of Burgundy," Debussy wrote to André Messager from Bichain, Yonne, on September 12, 1903, in telling of a new work that was occupying him during a holiday at the home of Rosalie Texier's parents. Messager had inquired about a purported quintet. "There is no plan for a quintet in my books," Debussy replied. "I am working on three symphonic sketches entitled: (1) *Mer belle aux îles Sanguinaires*; (2) *Jeux de vagues*;[1] (3) *Le vent fait danser la mer*—under the general title of *La Mer*. You do not know, perhaps, that I was intended for the fine career of a sailor and that only the chances of life led me away from it. Nevertheless, I have still a sincere passion for it." And lest his friend should fancy that this Burgundian sea might resemble a studio landscape, he recalls his "innumerable memories"—"they are worth more, in my opinion, than a reality which in general weighs too heavily on one's thought."

But Debussy was to wrestle with his sea in places other than the Burgundian hills. He worked at it in the chaotic days of his flight with Mme. Bardac. He took it with him to England in the summer of 1905. From Jersey he wrote to the publisher, Jacques Durand, a letter in which he said: "The sea has been very good to me. She has shown me all her moods." The work was finished in Eastbourne, which he described to Laloy as "a little English seaside place, silly as these places sometimes are"—complaining

[1] The only one of the three titles retained in the final score.

in the same breath of "too many draughts and too much music."

October, 1905, brought the birth of Chou-Chou and the first performances of *La Mer*. Debussy, back in Paris under a cloud that separated him from many of his friends, moved with his wife and infant daughter to the house at the end of what is now the Avenue Foch (then Avenue du Bois de Boulogne) which is frequently pointed out to tourists as his home. He was to live there the remaining twelve years of his life; the house was to become Debussy's mansion, his ivory tower against the world, and, in the cruel extremities of his final illness, his hospital and his prison.

To Camille Chevillard, as conductor, fell the distinction of introducing *La Mer* at one of the Concerts Lamoureux on October 15, 1905. His conception of the three imaginative pieces seems to have been a realistic one, with no lack of vigor or of contrast. Whether it accorded with Debussy's desires is not of record. Nor was Debussy's own presentation of *La Mer* at the Concerts Colonne, three years later, productive of agreement as to just how a conductor should go about realizing the composer's intentions. No one could question that Debussy's treatment of his own work was "authoritative," in so far as he had the technique and the command of his ensemble to communicate what he had in mind. But, as he himself was to concede, he had little talent for orchestral leadership. The performance in 1905 found hostile and friendly forces arrayed against each other, both in the public prints and in that private world where Debussy was striving to rehabilitate himself. There was a favorable critique in the *Guide Musical* from the pen of M. D. Calvocoressi, who regarded *La Mer* as marking a new phase in Debussy's evolution. The inspiration, he thought, was "more robust, the colors stronger, the lines more definite." He expressed the view that Debussy, after exploring the realm of sonorities, had "condensed and clarified the sum total of his discoveries" and he found in the work something of the "absolute eurythmic quality that characterizes all masterpieces."

Against this may be set a review by Pierre Lalo, who wrote in *Le Temps*, "I neither hear, nor see, nor feel the sea"; supported in a measure by Gaston Carraud, who declared that the "sketches" were misnamed, in that they neither gave any complete idea of the sea nor expressed its essential characteristics. He found less originality and inventiveness in *La Mer* than in those other Debussy works he had praised. For him the atmosphere was less subtle, the vision less fresh, the scintillations of the score less mysterious. "It almost suggests," he said in a final fling, "the possibility that some day we may have an Americanized Debussy." There was a similar division of opinion when Debussy conducted the work in 1908, with Jean Marnold extolling it in the *Mercure de France* for its "power and charm," its "grandeur and delicacy," its "extraordinary verve and brilliant fantasy"; and Luc Marvy declaring in the *Monde Musical* that the score revealed "a complete, systematic absence of all unity of ideas." [2]

At one of the concerts at which Debussy appeared as conductor of *La Mer*, that of January 19, 1908, hisses and shouts of bravo were mingled in a commotion that lasted for ten minutes at the conclusion of the new work. After Jacques Thibaud, the violinist, had begun to play the Bach *Chaconne*, the disturbance began anew and was so persistent that he was obliged to stop and wait for eventual calm. A few weeks later, on February 1, Debussy was enabled to contrast English politeness with French impetuosity in affairs of art. Conducting *La Mer* in London, he was applauded heartily, if not excitedly; and there were no hisses to upset the decorum of the event.

Between the 1905 and 1908 performances, Debussy is found writing from Puys to Durand [3] as follows:

[2] See Vallas for more detailed reviews.
[3] The letter is dated August 8, 1906.

Here I am again with my old friend, the sea; it is always endless and beautiful. It is really the thing in Nature which restores one best to one's place. But, people do not respect the sea sufficiently. . . . It should not be permitted to bathe in it these bodies deformed by work-a-day life: it is enough to make the fishes weep. In the sea, there should be only Sirens, and how do you suppose those estimable persons would consent to return to waters frequented by rather low company?

And in 1915, three years before his death, to the same friend:

I have slandered the sea, which has been sullen enough in these last days to make one weep! To-day, it is beautiful enough to defy all comparisons. . . . Victor Hugo himself would have exhausted his arsenal of images! . . . The trees are good friends, I tell you. Better than the sea, which is stirred up, wants to dash up across the land, tear out the rocks and has the tantrums of a little girl, singular for a person of her importance. . . .

In 1905 the first of the two series of *Images* for piano appeared, with the second to follow in 1908. The 1905 set contains the first of those "hommages"—*Hommage à Rameau*—which enable the pianist of catholic tastes to make his genuflections international. In 1909 followed *Hommage à Haydn*; and four years later, well down in the second book of *Préludes*, the Dickensian obeisance of *Hommage à S. Pickwick, Esq., P.P.M.P.C.* The Rameau "hommage" and its companion "images," *Reflets dans l'eau* and *Mouvement*, pleased the composer, who expressed in a letter to his publisher his belief that "these three pieces will live," taking their place "either to the left of Schumann . . . or to right of Chopin." The first set was played by Ricardo Viñes at the Société Nationale on March 3, 1906; the second, embracing *Cloches à travers les feuilles, Et la lune descend sur le temple qui fut* and *Poissons d'or*, at the Cercle

Musical on February 21, 1908. The composer is known to have planned a third series which never materialized.

Meanwhile Debussy had begun work on the three orchestral *Images*, of which only *Ibéria* has won a substantial place in the continuing répertoire of symphony orchestras. With the companion *Gigues* and *Rondes de printemps*, this most coloristic of Debussy's orchestral compositions was originally planned for two pianos. He wrote of being in doubt which of three endings he should use. "Shall I toss up between them—or try a fourth?" Six years—1906-11—were required to shape these *Images* to the composer's satisfaction. December 25, 1908, is the date written at the end of the rough draft of *Ibéria*. *Rondes de printemps* was completed in 1909, *Gigues* in 1911. In the course of his labors, Debussy wrote of trying "to achieve something different—an effect of reality" and then expressed himself tartly concerning "what some idiots term impressionism, a word that is altogether misused, particularly by the critics, since they do not hesitate to apply it to Turner, the finest creator of mysterious effects in all the world of art."

The Children's Corner, with the last of its six little pieces taking notice of the fad for the American cakewalk that had interested a group of serious French musicians—in much the same way that American jazz was to interest their successors—was among the products of 1906-08,[4] when Debussy's little daughter was learning to talk and walk. Also of this period were the songs of *Le Promenoir des deux amants* (1904-10), the *Trois Ballades de François Villon* (1910), and the *Trois Chansons de Charles d'Orléans* for unaccompanied chorus. *La plus que lente*, composed for piano and later orchestrated by Debussy, is credited to 1910, as is also the first book of *Préludes*, in which such pieces as *Voiles*, *Des pas sur la neige*, and *Les sons et les parfums tournent dans l'air du soir*, together with the weightier *La Cathé-*

---

[4] *Sérénade à la poupée* was published separately in 1908.

drale engloutie, did as much as any others to affix to his music
the term "impressionism" that he opposed.

Other engagements as conductor of his own works followed
his performances of *La Mer* at the Concerts Colonne. Early in
1908, at the age of forty-six, he again visited London and there
mounted the podium at Queens Hall for the first English performance of *La Mer,* already referred to, given in company with
L'Après-midi d'un faune. A year later in the same surroundings
he conducted the *Nocturnes, Fêtes* being repeated because of a
first reading marred by Debussy's inexperience with the stick.
Though illness caused him to cancel dates in Edinburgh and
Manchester, he was back in London in May, 1909, so as to be
present at rehearsals there for *Pelléas.* Debussy had a personal
success with the English, some of whom were struck by what
they fancied was a strong personal resemblance between Debussy and Rossetti.

On March 25, 1909, clashing demonstrations marred a performance of *L'Après-midi* at the Concerts Sechiari, in Paris,
conducted by the composer. On Good Friday, a fortnight later,
Debussy led his Orléans choruses (two of which were repeated), at the Concerts Colonne. The program also included
La Demoiselle élue. The new and the old works were lumped
together as old-fashioned pre-Raphaelitism by the reviewer for
the *Guide Musical,* who referred to the "Blessed Damozel" as "a
wrinkled, insipid, irritating old maid." Debussy, he said, conducted his music "with a weary arm." In December of this year
the *Chansons de Bilitis* achieved a success perhaps not altogether
to the composer's liking, since the interpretations with which
Lucienne Breval won hearty plaudits at the Châtelet were described as of a passionate, romantic, and rather theatrical order.

Just before his departure for London in February, 1909, Debussy was appointed a member of the supreme council of the
music section of the Paris Conservatoire. Gabriel Fauré is said to

FIRST PAGE OF THE ROUGH DRAFT OF *LA MER* **IN THE LIBRARY OF THE EASTMAN SCHOOL OF MUSIC AT ROCHESTER, N.Y.**

have been largely responsible for the appointment, although, as we have seen, the two composers had not been bosom friends. Interviewed, the new supreme councilor criticized the prevailing methods of teaching harmony and said some sharp things about public competitions and the *Prix de Rome*.

But as a public official he now manifested a measure of personal interest in the Conservatoire. Two years earlier (1907) he had been one of the judges of the wind-instrument tests and his interest in the particular sonorities of the wood winds had led him to compose his *Rapsodie* for clarinet and piano (1909–10) and *Petite pièce* for the same combination, both of which he later orchestrated. The *Rapsodie* was intended as a test piece for the clarinet competitions, of which he was an adjudicator; the *Pièce* was for sight-reading purposes. The *Rapsodie* was played by P. Mimart, to whom it is dedicated, at a concert of the Société Musicale Indépendante on January 16, 1911.

Debussy's new-won eminence plagued him in many ways. Parallels were found in his music not only to Ravel's *Habanera* but to an opera by Debussy's friend, Paul Dukas. *Ariane et Barbe-Bleue*, like *Pelléas*, was a setting of Maeterlinck. In the course of much critical argument over the two works, Debussy was to complain to Durand that Pierre Lalo seemed to regard *Pelléas* as music "for debauchees." So-called Franckists were pitted against so-called Debussyists, the former preferring *Ariane* to *Pelléas* because of its supposed superiority in architectural design. Complaints were aired about the issuance of old compositions under new titles, for which the publishers, not Debussy, would seem to have been to blame. Performance of an orchestral transcription of *Jet d'eau*, a vocal work of 1887, led to criticism and Debussy made clear to Durand his opposition to any such use of old compositions. When the publisher offered Édouard Colonne the march and dance from *L'Enfant prodigue*, Debussy wrote to him that this seemed hardly interesting or worth while.

Paris was impatient for more masterpieces, the more contro-
versial the better. Imitators were everywhere, writing more like
Debussy, it would appear, than he himself could write. In time,
Debussy even was accused of imitating his imitators. When René
Peter told Debussy that the Debussyists were getting on his
nerves, Debussy replied: "They are killing me!"

But he must have found solid satisfaction in the continued success of *Pelléas*, which had begun to make its way abroad. The
music drama achieved something like a triumph when first un-
curtained in Brussels on January 9, 1907, with Mary Garden
once more in the title role. George Ekhoud, reviewing the performance for *L'Eventail*, declared that the play should never be
given without Debussy's music. Debussy was present to assist at
rehearsals and was much disturbed by a bell that rang on C instead of G. Germany also had its first *Pelléas* in 1907, the work
being given at Frankfurt in a translation by Otto Neitzel. The
press was divided, with Hugo Schlemmer declaring in *Signale*
that he had heard nothing but chord successions, consecutive
fifths, and false relations, to which he added stronger words like
"outlandish" and "monstrosities." In 1908 Munich and Berlin
had performances and the *Allgemeine Musik Zeitung* printed
an article by Theodore Tagger in which he borrowed Schumann's famous line about Chopin—"Hats off, gentlemen, a
genius!"

New York heard *Pelléas* before it was taken up in France outside of Paris. On February 19, 1908, Oscar Hammerstein produced his much-bruited novelty at the Manhattan Opera House,
with four of the original Paris cast. Mary Garden was, of course,
the Mélisande. Jean Périer made his American debut as Pelléas.
Hector Dufranne, also appearing in this country for the first
time, was Golaud and Jeanne Gerville-Réache, Geneviève. Vit-
torio Ariminiondi appeared as Arkel, Ludmilla Sigrist as Yniold,
and Armand Crabbé as the doctor. Cleofonte Campanini con-

ducted, as he was to do when London had its first *Pelléas* during the next season. The opera at Lyons was the first in France to follow the lead of Paris. Three performances there (the first on April 1, 1908) found the public apathetic in spite of the fervor of the Belgian conductor, Philippe Flon, who brought to Debussy's music the same consecration of spirit that he had devoted to the first complete French performance of Wagner's *Ring* only four years before.

Under the aegis of Giulio Gatti-Casazza, Arturo Toscanini conducted Italy's first *Pelléas* at La Scala, Milan, in April, 1908. Pasquale Amato sang Golaud in a cast headed by Fiorello Giraud as Pelléas and Cesira Ferrani as Mélisande. There were hostile demonstrations at the dress rehearsal and the audience at the first performance drowned out much of the music. When the work was staged in Rome a year later there was much hissing from the start. Yet reviews were favorable and some at least of the show of hostility was regarded as for an unpopular management, with the new French work used as a pretext.

CHAPTER XV

A COMPOSER-CONDUCTOR

Engagements in Vienna, Budapest, and Turin—Interpretations
via an Interpreter—A "French Festival" and *Le Cas Debussy*

THOUGH the cancer which was to take Debussy's life in 1918 is
believed to have made itself known to him as early as 1909, the
years leading on to the World War were characterized by exceptional physical activity, with more of travel than he had
known since he was household accompanist for Nadejda von
Meck. He had left London, ill, soon after conducting the *Nocturnes* there in 1909, but had returned for *Pelléas* at Covent Garden later in the same year. In 1910 he conducted in Vienna,
taking part also in a concert in Budapest. In 1911 he conducted
in Turin. In 1913 he returned to Russia, which he had last seen
as a member of Mme. von Meck's musical entourage, thirty-odd
years before.

Nor was he as inactive in composition during the prewar years
as is sometimes assumed. For piano he completed the second
book of *Préludes* (1910–13) and the children's ballet, *La Boîte
à joujoux* (1913).[1] To his catalogue of songs he added *Trois
Poèmes de Stéphane Mallarmé* (1913), dedicated to the memory
of the poet, five years dead. Aside from various theater projects
which never reached the stage—among them, *Le Diable dans le
beffroi, La Chute de la maison Usher, Le Roman de Tristan*, and
Khamma—Debussy was occupied with the ballet *Jeux* (1912)
for which the Russian dancer, Vaslav Nijinsky, then at the height
of his career, supplied the scenario and the choreography. To
be credited to this time is another and more momentous theatrical

[1] Orchestrated by André Caplet.

score, *Le Martyre de Saint-Sébastien* (1911), composed as incidental music to the mystery play by Gabriele d'Annunzio, and
by reason of its form still the great question mark among Debussy's major endeavors. Debussy is not ordinarily thought of
as one of those facile and prolific composers who had only to
brood a little over a piano or a desk to bring forth a new opus.
Yet he must be credited with something like sixty songs, more
than eighty piano pieces, including works for two pianos; a
String Quartet, three Sonatas, and several other works which
can conveniently be classed as chamber music, and five completed choral and dramatic works (with two more that other
hands were to finish)—all this aside from *Pelléas et Mélisande*,
L'Après-midi d'un faune, the *Nocturnes*, *La Mer*, *Ibéria*, and its
companion *Images*, *Gigues*, and *Rondes de printemps*. This is
not the record of an idler or a plodder. And as for the period
immediately preceding the war, *Saint-Sébastien* alone might have
seemed a task to spread out over a year or two, whereas Debussy wrote all his music for it within a few weeks.

Before departing for Vienna on the first of his continental
adventures as a composer-conductor, Debussy had declined to
participate in the 1910 "French festival" in Munich, largely because he considered the financial arrangements unsatisfactory.
On arrival in Vienna in December he found the rehearsal time
too short for all the compositions he had intended to conduct
and felt compelled to eliminate *La Mer* and the *Nocturnes*,
while retaining on his program the *Petite Suite*, *L'Après-midi*,
and *Ibéria*. Of these *Ibéria* was new, having had its first performance in Paris under Gabriel Pierné earlier in the same year.
Vienna had heard the *Faun* at least twice before, on one occasion under the baton of Richard Strauss as a companion piece
for his own *Sinfonia domestica*. Rehearsals were held under
difficulties. Debussy had to communicate his wishes through a
Herr-Doktor-Professor-Interpreter or by gesticulating, as he

said, "like a character in an Italian pantomime." In a letter to Durand he told of being recalled at the concert "like a ballet dancer," adding that the only reason the idolizing crowd did not unyoke the horses of his carriage was that this carriage was a taxicab. As many another conductor has done, he took occasion to praise the Austrian orchestra. But he was none too well pleased when, at a banquet in his honor, a well-meaning speaker referred to his great achievement "in having abolished melody"! Debussy added to the confusion by protesting, "But, Monsieur, my music aims at nothing else but melody."

From Vienna Debussy went to Budapest where, before an audience of fifteen hundred, he took part in a miscellaneous concert, the program of which included the Quartet and *The Children's Corner*. From Hungary, with its gypsy musicians in the cafés, he is supposed to have derived the idea for the use of the tympanon as solo instrument in an orchestral version of his waltz, *La plus que lente*.

In Turin the next year Debussy conducted a program of French music, on which he was represented as composer by *Ibéria*, *L'Après-midi*, and Caplet's transcription of *The Children's Corner*. The other items were the Overture to Chabrier's *Gwendoline*, Roger-Ducasse's *Sarabande*, and the prelude to the third act of Dukas's *Ariane et Barbe-Bleue*. A few months later Vincent d'Indy conducted Debussy's *Nuages* and *Fêtes* in the same surroundings.

Debussy's visit to Moscow and St. Petersburg in 1915 was at the behest of Serge Koussevitzky, who engaged him to conduct a concert in each of the capitals, the old and the new. He was warmly received and had high praise for Koussevitzky's orchestra; but he was too late to meet any of the Russian composers in whose work he was chiefly interested, only César Cui remaining of the famous "Cabinet"—Rimsky-Korsakoff having died in

1908; Balakireff in 1910; Borodin and Moussorgsky long before. The young Stravinsky had written *L'Oiseau de feu, Petroushka, Le Rossignol* (as opera) and *Le Sacre du printemps* and Debussy had particularly praised the first of these. In 1913, Debussy was to resume criticism as reviewer for the *Revue S.I.M.*, a post he occupied until the end of the next season. During this time took place the successive first performances of orchestral *Images*, which were disclosed separately and on different dates.

The six years required for the completion of the *Images*, the intervals that elapsed between completion and first performance of one and then another, and the different levels of inspiration to which they attained have denied them any such continuing fellowship as has persisted for at least two of the *Nocturnes*. From the first, *Ibéria* seemed fated to go its way individually, and happily so, considering the inferiority of *Rondes de printemps* and *Gigues*, the orchestration for the last named furnished not by Debussy but by André Caplet. *Ibéria* was the first of the three to have public performance, Gabriel Pierné including it in a program presented at the Châtelet on February 20, 1910. As Pierné was about to comply with an apparent demand for its repetition, a hostile demonstration interfered. The first reviews were not encouraging, the work being described in one critique as just another Spanish rhapsody, "neither better nor worse" than others of the type. On March 2 *Rondes de printemps* had the composer as conductor of its introductory performance at the Concerts Durand. Some of the critical comment was bitterly ironical and the audience reacted with no marked show of enthusiasm. *Gigues* came to completion the next year, so far as Debussy himself was to complete it. First called *Gigues tristes*, and believed to have been inspired by memories of England, the work was published by Durand in the form of a transcription for piano duet by Caplet. In orchestral form it was played at one of the Concerts Colonne on January 27, 1913, and again the next year at the Concerts Monteux. One review spoke of the work as being merely "the small change" of an incomparable talent.

The upshot of the successive first performances of the *Images* was to supply ammunition for those who already were contending that Debussy's powers were waning, though here and there *Ibéria* was declared worthy of its creator. Alfred Bruneau found "these delicate Spanish sketches" truly representative of Debussy's musical personality. He described them as "delightfully poetical," "exquisite" in their coloring, and of a "marvelous artistry." But perhaps the most notable praise this work has received was that bestowed upon it by the Spanish composer, Manuel de Falla, in the course of an article written for the *Chesterian* of London. Though he regarded the work as typically French, in spite of its title and subject matter, he found in it "the intoxicating spell of Andalusian nights," the festive gayety of a people dancing to the joyous strains of guitars and bandurrias.

André Caplet was faithful, if almost alone in his fidelity, to *Gigues*—"Sad gigues, tragic gigues" he called them in an article written some years after Debussy's death. At that time he sought to explain the lack of favor with which the work had been received as due to difficulties of interpretation presented by its ever-changing, merging, and clashing moods. And yet, he contended, *Gigues* revealed under pitiful shudderings and sorry grimaces the true soul of Debussy. Caplet felt for it a special affection and could not regard it as eclipsed by *Ibéria*. *Rondes de printemps* he described as "a youthful, shimmering vision of spring."

Debussy himself described the music of *Rondes de printemps* as "ethereal," and consequently, he told Durand "you cannot handle it as you can a robust symphony which walks on its four feet (sometimes three, but it walks all the same)."

He adds: "I am getting to believe more and more that music in its essence is not a thing that can be poured into a rigorous and traditional mold. It is made of colors and rhythmical beats. All the rest is a fraud, invented by cold-blooded imbeciles riding on the masters' backs."

His own new compositions subject to all manner of disparagement, Debussy found himself warmly applauded for a labor of friendship, when he conducted the orchestral arrangement he had made of Erik Satie's *Gymnopédies*. This was at the Cercle Musical on March 25. Also received with favor was Caplet's transcription of *The Children's Corner*, then given for the first time in France, though New York had heard it previously under the transcriber's baton. In groups of songs, Debussy acted as accompanist for Jean Périer and Maggie Teyte, the latter having succeeded Mary Garden as Mélisande.[2] A few days later, on March 29, Debussy appeared as pianist at the Concerts Durand, playing a group of preludes, *Les sons et les parfums*, *Le vent dans la plaine*, *Des pas sur la neige*, and *Minstrels*. The Villon *Ballades* were sung in the original version, with piano accompaniment, by Paul de Listany on February 5, 1911, and in the orchestral form, by Charles Clarke, with Debussy conducting, just a calendar month later at one of the Concerts Sechiari. Jane Bathori sang the songs of *Promenoir des deux amants* at a Société Nationale concert early in this year (January 14, 1911) and a year later Debussy accompanied Miss Teyte in them, together with the *Fêtes galantes*, at one of the Concerts Durand, when he also played several of the *Préludes*.

With the second book of *Préludes* Debussy was said not to have been altogether satisfied, the assumption being that some had been written just to make up another set of twelve, so as to

[2] The amusing story persists that when Miss Garden's successor was about to be chosen it was thought advisable to have another Mélisande whose accent would be slightly foreign, therefore mysterious.

have twenty-four in all. Three were played by Debussy on April 5, 1913, *La Terrasse des audiences au clair de lune, Les Fées sont d'exquises danseuses,* and *Feux d'artifice.*

On April 2, 1913, Debussy was one of the composer-conductors of the inaugural concert given at the new Théâtre des Champs Élysées,[3] the program designed as a "Festival of French Music." As Gabriel Astruc tells the story: [4]

> . . . the pure voice of Rose Favart sang. . . . Claude Debussy, Paul Dukas, Vincent d'Indy, Gabriel Fauré, each conducted one of his own works. . . . Saint-Saëns likewise. But he almost failed to answer the call. I had telegraphed to him at the Balearic Islands inviting him to take his place at the head of the illustrious cohort. He had answered me: "There must be two concerts. One for me, with *La Lyre* and *La Harpe,* entire, one for all the others." I had retorted: "Impossible," and he: "It will be thus, or nothing." I cabled: "In that case, it will be nothing." Two hours afterwards, the famous maëstro agreed to conduct *Phaéton,* close to the "comrades."
>
> Then, it was *Lucia di Lammermoor* and *Le Barbier* with Barrientos, unknown to Paris, and with Sammarco, Carpi, Vanni Marcoux. Fernand Ochsé had created for Rosina and Lucia, idols revived from the Salle Ventadour, costumes, wigs, accessories, a whole set, which by a sort of magic restored the atmosphere of the former Théâtre Italien and caused to live again the ghost of Patti, the phantom of Masini. During the entr'acte, exclamations, cries of enthusiasm. The emotion scarcely calmed, there appeared the divine *Péri* of Dukas. Next, Loïe Fuller and her children invaded the scene where the *Nuages* rolled. The billows of *La Mer,* which we were to see again twelve years later on the staircase of the Grand-Palais, slowly unfurled and Debussy told Inghelbrecht and me this secret: "This is the first time that I really have heard my music played!"

[3] It was opened, however, on March 30.
[4] *Le pavillon des fantômes,* by Gabriel Astruc.

Also in April, 1913, a concert given in honor of Debussy at the Comédie des Champs-Élysées enlisted as soloists Ricardo Viñes, Ninon Vallin, and Gaston Poulet. Segouret, the actor, read a paper written by Émile Vuillermoz. On October 15 of that year took place the first performance of the *Marche eccossaise*, composed twenty-two years earlier. It was played on a program given at the Nouveaux Concerts des Champs-Élysées. Also presented were *La Demoiselle élue* and *Ibéria*, the latter conducted by Debussy.

Two years earlier, Saint-Saëns had written for the *Courrier Musicale* an article called "L'anarchie musicale" [5] which had been construed as aimed particularly at Debussy. He noted ironically how under the new dispensation everyone was to be free to make his own rules, how there was no such thing as a dissonant chord, or even a common chord, much less a wrong chord; how any combination was legitimate—and this, he exclaimed, "is what they call developing one's sensibility." Throughout these years conservatives found ways to scold or ridicule Debussy and his followers. The latter were dubbed "the Pelléastres" [6] and described as snobs and poseurs, who tried to make a new religion out of Debussy's music. Admirers of Debussy were referred to as victims of a disease called "Debussitis." The composer himself was said to be "possibly the victim of some nervous affliction difficult to classify," this being the conjecture of one who averred that he suffered physically when he heard Debussy's music performed.[7] Sundry such opinions were brought together by two enterprising journalists,[8] to form a symposium which they styled *Le Cas Debussy*. Several times in the course of the thirty published letters of the collection, the charge that De-

[5] January, 1911.
[6] Title of a posthumous novel by Jean Lorrain, published in 1904. It incorporates an article in which he coined the term.
[7] Sar Péladan in *Le Cas Debussy*.
[8] C. Francis Caillard and José de Bérys.

bussy's music was innocent of melody was repeated, also that it was deficient in rhythm. The composer was described as "a deformer of music and impressions." It was predicted by one contributor that in ten years there would be very little mention of *Pelléas*. Camille Bellaigue and Édouard Tremisot dreaded the establishment of a Debussy school, founded, said Tremisot, "on the accumulation of solecisms." Siegfried Wagner, writing from Bayreuth, pleaded total ignorance of the works in question. Josef Joachim confessed that he could not account for the success of *Pelléas*; for him it was disordered, haphazard, like improvisation. Rimsky-Korsakoff was free to say that he had not liked anything in *Pelléas*; the harmonic combinations were incomprehensible, the orchestra lacked body and firmness of texture, the whole was monotonous; and he could see no future for this "curious experiment."

Romain Rolland, answering a question as to whether Debussy was the leader of a school, expressed the opinion that "every great artist has a school and all schools are evil," adding that "it might then be better if there were no great artists." "I don't like your modern French music very much," he said. "But what I can't understand is that, being so poor in artists, you have to quarrel with the greatest one you have."

There were only a few letters on the credit side. Among these that of Ernest Ansermet pointed out that Debussy's contemporaries were making use of his contributions to technique. Repercussions or reflections of Debussy's innovations were to be found, Ansermet said, in nearly every page of Richard Strauss's *Elektra*—which may well have been a matter of as much indifference to Debussy as it probably was to Strauss. But Debussy showed his irritation on more than one occasion over the assertion that his music lacked melody. Rimsky-Korsakoff's inability to grasp the essentials of his harmonic system contrasted with Debussy's own admiration for the Russian's *Antar* symphony and, less certainly, for *Shéhérazade*. The novelist Colette contributed to the program of the 1932 "Debussy festival" a letter, in which she tells of being present with Debussy and others at the first hearing of *Shéhérazade* in Paris. "On returning to the home of Louis de Serres," she said, "Debussy was exultant. He sang scraps of this new music, accompanied himself with a glissando on the piano, imitated the tympani on a pane of glass, the glockenspiel on a crystal vase. He hummed, like a swarm; he laughed with his whole astonishing visage—and we were delighted."

A letter to Raoul Bardac, dated Feb. 25, 1906, would appear to register a change of heart. Debussy wrote of having heard *Shéhérazade* again and remarked that the work didn't improve with age. "It reminds me more of a bazaar than of the Orient," he said.

An article by René Lenormand on the harmony of Debussy, in which he dissected *Pelléas*, drew from the composer a characteristic, ironical reply. Debussy found it "all quite correct" and "mercilessly logical," if "almost savage" in its use of quotations. But think of the indiscriminating, inexpert hands, he warned Lenormand, waiting to make use of his study, "for the sole purpose of annihilating those charming butterflies which are already somewhat crumpled by your analysis." In his own critical writing, Debussy was not given to detailed technical analysis. He preferred to be pictorial, as when he spoke of Bach as a ringmaster putting his "rascally little subjects" through their paces.

CHAPTER XVI

DEBUSSY AS CRITIC

Caustic Views of Contemporaries and a Few Resounding Tributes for Great Ones Past—A Lively Estimate of Strauss

DEBUSSY's critical writing was scattered over fourteen years, 1901–14, though he held a regular post as reviewer in only four seasons. His first work of this kind was for the *Revue Blanche*, which he served from April to December 1, 1901. He took a similar position with *Gil Blas* in 1903, beginning with the issue of January 12 and continuing until June 28. He contributed articles to *Musica*, October, 1902, May, 1903, July, 1906, January, 1908, and March, 1911; to *Mercure de France*, January, 1903; to *Le Figaro*, May 8, 1908 and February 14, 1909; and to *Excelsior*, March 9, 1911. Ten years after he had written his last feuilleton for *Gil Blas* he returned to the fold as a regular reviewer for the *Revue S.I.M.*, being employed by that publication through the seasons of 1912–13, November to May; and 1913–14, November to March. There was also a series of interviews from his pen in *Comœdia;* the issues of November 4, 1909, January 31 and December 17, 1910, January 26 and May 18, 1911, and February 1, 1914.

Only about a year before his death, Debussy prepared for publication in book form a selection of critical articles, some twenty-five in all, variously adapted from his writings of the preceding sixteen years. They were introduced by two essays of a conversational, disputatious character, built about an *alter ego* whose imaginary identity gives to the book its name, *Monsieur Croche, Antidillétante*. Paul Valéry's *Soirées avec M. Teste* had supplied Debussy with the idea. M. Croche says he tries to

forget music because it obscures his perception of what he does
not know or will know only tomorrow. M. Teste remarks that
he hasn't read any books in twenty years and has burned his
papers; the difficult thing is to remember what he will want tomorrow. Though Debussy sent proofs of his articles to G. Jean-
Aubry in 1917, difficulties due to the war held up actual publication until 1921, at which time Debussy had been dead three
years.

Debussy was nearly forty when, in the season of 1901–02, he
took employment as critic for the *Revue Blanche*. Behind him
were *L'Après-midi*, the String Quartet, the *Chansons de Bilitis*,
and other works which at the time were looked upon as revolutionary. *Pelléas* had its première in this season. Debussy was not
an "every-nighter," like so many of the critical fraternity. He
wrote, in fact, only eight articles in as many months for the
Revue Blanche. They were not widely read. In Paris, then as
now, the leading critics were composers. Usually, the more important the publication, the more important the composer chosen
to lend the weight of his name to the paper's musical verdicts.
These celebrities were not expected to write about the eternal
small fry in the concert halls or the routine performances of
opera. Some lesser journalist made the rounds of the daily events.
Just when reviews would appear was—and is—something so uncertain as to defy conjecture. Days, weeks, even a month might
pass before a review dealing with a particular performance
would be found in print. Then there might be no mention as to
when it took place, or where; the artists performing might not
be named; the factual side of journalism, which is so strongly
emphasized in American and English reports of musical doings,
did not greatly burden some of these composer-critics. They
wrote about as they pleased, indulging in rhapsodical flights of
language, if that was their bent; or playing tag with what they
had heard, in bravado displays of highly personal brands of sar-

castic humor. If it is quite generally assumed that criticism, particularly that which involves the fortunes of individual artists,
has no such record of integrity in France and Italy as it has in
America, England, and Central Europe, this can scarcely be
construed to apply to the group of more or less illustrious musicians called on to act as critics because of their eminence as
composers. Often, of course, they had to write about interpreters, as well as about the music interpreted; the ability to compose
did not, of itself, qualify them to pass judgment on a new pianist,
singer or conductor. Every country has produced its freaks of
criticism and France need not be regarded as an exception. Debussy was perhaps as well equipped as most of his confrères for
the varied aspects of critical appraisal. He knew the piano, he
had tried his hand at conducting, he had acted as accompanist
for singers. When he had needed money badly, he had taught
both piano and voice. As a prose writer he had a gift for the
ironical, the paradoxical, the picturesque. His early reviews exemplified all this. Their mocking tone irritated those who hoped
for praise from all quarters, the while it amused the otherwise
small circle of readers who turned to his articles because of
friendship, curiosity, or professional esteem.

Debussy's feuilletons for the daily paper, *Gil Blas*, in the
1902–03 season, were more numerous than those for the *Revue
Blanche* had been, but the total of twenty in six months would
scarcely retain a critical desk for an American, British, or German critic employed by a similar publication. The articles usually
appeared on Mondays. There were four critiques of first performances, beginning with one devoted to the première of
L'Étranger, which Debussy described as "Vincent d'Indy's pure
musical drama." In balancing against its blemishes and excesses
its "many pages of unforgettable beauty," he paid tribute to "the
serene goodness which hovers over this work," referring to it
further as "an admirable lesson for those who pin their faith

DEBUSSY AT THE SEASHORE. THE LITTLE GIRL
IS CHOU-CHOU

to the odious imported fashion for aesthetics, which crushes music between the wheels of realism."

The paper sent Debussy to England and from London he dispatched two articles dealing with the *Ring*. The conductor, Richter, was described as the hero of the performance, while Wagner was satirized. "Richter," Debussy wrote, "looks like a prophet, but when he conducts . . . he is the Almighty." Wagner's music is "worse than an obsession—it is possession. You no longer belong to yourself. You are but a *leit motif* moving in an atmosphere of tetralogy." He ridiculed the "pretense" that certain chords in series were representative of a certain feeling, episode, or character, describing it as "an unexpected game of anthropometry." This was not the first, nor by any means the last, of his critical attacks on Wagner. If it is true that the earlier critical writings have more of impertinence than later ones, the spirit of contradiction remained. As a critic Debussy was not always taken seriously by his readers, who regarded his irony and his paradoxes as something of a game. Nor was he always as conscientious about the work as he might have been; in some instances simply rewriting for *Gil Blas* older criticisms that had appeared in the *Revue Blanche*. He was free to say that he wearied of any work so regular, and the hours devoted to it were a drain upon his vitality.

In promulgating his critical credo, Debussy said that he would endeavor to confine himself to "some impressions actually experienced . . . to discover in works the various impulses that gave them birth, and what they contain of inner life." He insisted on the use of the term "impressions" because it would enable him to shield his emotion from what he described as "parasitic aesthetics." As far as possible, his endeavor was to keep these arbitrary aesthetics out of his criticisms and he aimed to avoid the game which consists in taking impressions to pieces "as though they were watches of curious construction." The beauty of a work of art, he contended, must always remain mysterious. "Let us at all costs preserve this magic peculiar to music, since of all arts it is the most susceptible to magic." Analytical dissection of music, he said, "is practically what Thomas de Quincey, the celebrated opium eater, calls 'murder as a fine art.'" "Children were forbidden to open the insides of dolls" or pull jumping jacks to pieces, such behavior being treason against the mysteries. "They no longer cut open the doll, perhaps, but they take it to pieces . . . and thus kill the mystery in cold blood."

Debussy's return to criticism in the winter of 1912–13 was at the behest of Émile Vuillermoz, editor of the *Revue S.I.M.*, who was by then one of his most fervent disciples. Vincent d'Indy also was a critic for the Vuillermoz review and the opinions of the two composers were sometimes pitted against each other. This resulted in a species of rivalry and of partisanship not altogether conducive to calm deliberation and careful weighing of opinions on the part of the irritable Debussy, whose health was soon to give way before the mysterious and malignant enemy that had been stalking him since his illness in England in 1909. Debussy knew that some of his writing was not up to his former standard; he confessed that certain reviews were mere notes and too hastily written. Along with their haphazard construction and looseness of style, were to be discerned signs of indifference, even of annoyance. To friends he confessed that he was reluctant to hear new music, a sorry state of mind for a reviewer to whom, because of his celebrity, the readers of the Vuillermoz review looked for guidance; or, if not that, for amusement, because of his pungent and often contemptuous expressions of opinion. Often it was only at the eleventh hour that he could goad himself into putting on paper in his small but widely spaced handwriting, always precise and conspicuously regular, the views he was expected to set before his readers. The ten articles published in the *S.I.M.* in the two years immediately preceding the World War doubtless left untouched much of the music that came to his attention and his reviews are scarcely to be taken as the basis for assuming that he knew little of this or that composer. Robert Godet has taken issue, for instance, with the assumption of Vallas that Debussy was virtually ignorant of Schönberg in 1914. In the Prunières-Vallas controversy of 1934, in which liberal use was made of notes communicated to Prunières by Godet, there is reference to a letter written to Godet by Debussy twenty years before, in which the composer expresses the fear that Stravinsky is inclining dangerously toward Schönberg. In conversations with Godet, Debussy showed familiarity with more than one of the quartets, with the *Gurre-Lieder* and—although on this point Godet was less certain —with *Pierrot Lunaire*.[1] One can only wonder whether Debussy had examined the score of the Austrian's early symphonic poem, *Pelléas und Mélisande,* completed in 1903, within a year of the Paris première of Debussy's music-drama.

As has already been mentioned, Debussy was enthusiastic about Stravinsky's *Firebird,* which had its first performance in Paris in 1910, when it was produced by the Diaghileff company. It was after the stir created by *Le Sacre du printemps* (1913) that Debussy wrote to Godet of his fear that the Russian was going the way of Schönberg.

Of other atonalists, the German Paul Hindemith (born 1895) was too young to come within Debussy's survey of the contemporary scene. The Hungarian Bela Bartok, with his compatriot Kodaly, had a favorable word from him, though he considered that the time had not come to pass judgment on their work.

[1] Schönberg's first quartet is credited to 1905, his second to 1907, the *Gurre-Lieder* to 1910–11, *Pierrot Lunaire* to 1912.

Of Richard Strauss, less than two years his junior, but earlier catapulted into world fame,[2] Debussy wrote with insight and apparent relish.

"One of the dominant geniuses of our time" was Debussy's summation of the gifts of the Münchner after hearing a performance of *Tod und Verklärung* in 1912. Not that he gave undiluted praise to this work. He found its oboe cantilena "Italian" in its inflexions. Certain parts of it, he wrote, appeared empty, as if they no longer justified the title. He had scant sympathy for program music of such literal implications. "If people insist on wanting to understand what happens in a symphonic poem," he remarked, "we may as well give up writing them." Yet he found that "transfiguration" did take place in Strauss's music "before our very eyes."

If the Strauss of *Tod und Verklärung* was a genius without reservations for the Debussy of 1912, he was "very nearly a genius" in *Ein Heldenleben* for the Debussy of 1903. He found in this work a "kind of tortured Italianism" and regarded it as a book of pictures "or even a cinematograph." But what impressed him most—and it was here that he put his finger on the real secret of Strauss's success—was the cyclonic energy of this music, its unbounded vitality. In the face of its continuous high pressure, the listener, he said, was no longer master of his emotions.

Till Eulenspiegel, which Debussy heard, with Nikisch conducting, in the same year as *Heldenleben*, drew from him one of his most characteristic and entertaining reviews.

> This piece [he wrote] might almost be called "An hour of music in a lunatic asylum." Clarinets trace addled parabolas; trumpets are stopped up with mutes so that the horns, in anticipation of a sneeze, hurry to utter the customary "God bless you!" A big drum goes boum-boum, as if to call

[2] *Don Juan* (1889) *Tod und Verklären* (1890), *Till Eulenspiegel* (1895), *Don Quixote* (1898), *Heldenleben* (1899) all preceded *Pelléas* and the turn of Debussy's fortunes.

attention to the kicks of clowns. You do not know whether to roar with laughter or groan with pain and you are filled with wonder when you find anything in its customary place. If the double basses were to blow through their noses, if the trombones were to be stroked with imaginary bows, and if M. Nikisch were to be discovered seated in the lap of an attendant, it would not seem at all extraordinary.

But in spite of all this Debussy found genius in the work, commenting on its "amazing orchestral assurance" and "the mad rhythm that sweeps us along from beginning to end and forces us to share in the hero's pranks."

Debussy seems not to have heard any of the Strauss music-dramas in the theater, though *Salome* (1905), *Elektra* (1909), *Rosenkavalier* (1911), and *Ariadne auf Naxos* (1912) all achieved their premières in his middle and later life. He did hear an excerpt from *Feuersnot* and commented on "a veritable orchestral torrent" which he said probably was justified in the drama but which seemed very formidable as the music of a love scene. The beauty of the orchestral coloring of *En rade de Sorrente*, the third part of the *Aus Italien*, appealed strongly to him and he saw in this early work, overlong and overobvious though he considered it, a clear indication of Strauss's future eminence. He summed up Strauss's love of descriptive detail by saying that the German undoubtedly thought in color pictures. Remarking that Strauss must have imbibed his energy from the superman-teachings of Nietzsche, he added: "I say again that it is impossible to withstand his irresistible domination"

Debussy met Strauss and Elgar when he conducted a concert in Turin in 1911. He has left us no comment on the music of Sir Edward, quite possibly because he may never have heard any of it, though this cannot be stated as fact in view of his several visits to England. The only known enthusiasm expressed by Debussy for any English composer was that for Sullivan, whose

Pinafore he had heard in London when he first visited that city as a youth. After he had heard the complete *Ring* at Covent Garden in the course of a much later visit, made in his capacity as critic for *Gil Blas,* he spent an evening at the Empire Music Hall "as a reward for good behavior," the reward taking other forms than the substantialities of things Edwardian and Elgarian. Of some songs by Delius, presented in Paris at the Société Nationale, he wrote that they were "very sweet and innocent songs, music to rock the convalescents of rich neighborhoods." There was always a note hanging over a chord, he said, like a water lily or a little balloon—something for those who think of Delius as strongly influenced by Debussy, to ponder at their leisure. In a later review Debussy used almost these identical words to describe a song by Grieg.

Another of Grieg's compositions was described as resembling "a pink bonbon filled with snow." When Grieg appeared as soloist at the Concerts Colonne, Debussy wrote that apart from being a gifted interpreter of the folk music of his country, he was only a clever musician "more concerned with effects than with genuine art." The offended Grieg wrote a protest to M. D. Calvocoressi in which he observed that "a genuine artist . . . ought to respect the point of view of other artists." But Debussy, the critic, was longer on wit than respect, as when he wrote that "from the front he [Grieg] looks like a genial photographer; from behind [because of his way of wearing his hair] . . . like the plants called sunflowers." . . . Of the concerto, played on this occasion by Pugno, he wrote that it had little individuality, beginning with Schumann and ending with "an apotheosis worthy of 'Excelsior.' " On another occasion he declared the end of the concerto to be reminiscent of Leoncavallo and, in saying that the performer, Mme. Carreño, was talented, could not resist appending, "much more so than Grieg, who rather takes advantage of the circumstance that he is Norwegian." Still, he praised the *Peer Gynt* suite: "The ideas are charming and the rhythms ingenious."

Among composers of an older time who were not to be escaped in the concert halls, Chopin was dear to Debussy; Liszt, he both scolded and admired. Debussy found "Chopin's charming soul, rather than that of Liszt," reflected in *Tristan und Isolde,* "directing its passion." In the preface for the edition of Chopin's work which he undertook in 1915 he described Chopin's music as properly taking its place with "the most beautiful ever written." In Liszt's work also he found "undeniable beauty," along with vulgarity. Fire and abandon tended to compensate for Liszt's faults. Debussy wrote that he preferred these qualities to "white-gloved perfection," even though Liszt, in his adoration of the muse, "sometimes addresses her with unseemly familiarity and unceremoniously takes her on his knees."

Schumann, though he does not come through unscathed, fared rather better in Debussy's critical writings than either Schubert or Mendelssohn. The last named he termed a "facile and elegant notary." Some songs by Schubert were described as inoffensive and likened to dried flowers, with the effect repeated through endless verses. He jibed at the B Minor Symphony as not being able to make up its mind to remain unfinished. Of the Germanic masters of the Lied, all were regarded by Debussy as having failed to understand the poetry they set to music; Schumann particularly in the *Dictherliebe.* Both Mendelssohn and Schumann, he admits, were influences in the shaping of Gounod.

Of the great German symphonists he writes not only as Debussy, with his personal theories and convictions, but as the "musicien français." Of Brahms he seems to have had little to say, other than to describe the violin concerto as a bore; apparently he shared the typical French musician's indifference or antipathy of the time; an attitude that led Émile Vuillermoz to protest and plead eloquently in an article designed to pry open the

eyes of his countrymen to the melodic beauty and the emotional
warmth of the music they persisted in regarding as drab and
cerebral.

Though he rebelled against the lengths to which Beethoven
went in his development sections and otherwise found reason to
regard the Bonn giant's music as anything but a model for
twentieth-century artists, Debussy paid the mighty Ludwig
some resounding tributes. The Ninth Symphony, which he favored above the others, he described as "the most triumphant
example of the molding of an idea to the preconceived form."
This music, he said, "sprang from a soul drunk with liberty."
He pitted Beethoven against Wagner, thus: "The stern and
loyal mastery of our great Beethoven easily triumphed over this
vague and high-flown charlatanism." But he did not relish the
Pastoral Symphony, the popularity of which, he wrote, "is due
to the widespread misunderstanding that exists between man
and Nature." He considers the Nature suggestions of the symphony unnecessarily imitative and the interpretation purely arbitrary. He instances the scene at the brook—"a stream to which
it appears the oxen come to drink, so at least the bassoons would
have us suppose; to say nothing of the wooden nightingale and
the Swiss cuckoo clock." . . . In this symphony, as he views it,
Beethoven inaugurates an epoch in which Nature is to be seen
"only through the pages of books." Elsewhere, however, he
writes: "The true lesson taught by Beethoven was not the pre-
serving of the ancient forms . . . rather, he would invite us to
gaze through open windows to the clear sky." Like Wagner,
Beethoven became for him something of an incubus. French
composers were out of their element, he believed, in trying to fill
with their "short and breathless inspiration" the vast mold of a
Beethoven sonata. Anyway, in Debussy's opinion, the Beethoven
sonatas are badly written for the piano; the last ones he regarded as orchestral transcriptions for which a third hand is

needed. The most caustic of his references to Beethoven has to do with the song *Adelaide:* "I think the old master must have forgotten to burn this melody, and the greed of his heirs is probably to blame for its mistaken exhumation."

Mozart he placed with Leonardo da Vinci—"these are great artists," he said, in the course of what was in reality a defense of Massenet, though he did not always extol his compatriot. "Music," he wrote, "must humbly seek to please . . . extreme complication is contrary to art. Beauty must appeal to the senses . . . must insinuate itself into us without effort on our part." Such, for him, was the beauty of the music of Mozart. Of one of the piano concertos, he wrote that it was impossible to play badly, because it was so well written for the instrument; and he found a luminous lightness, which he likened to children laughing in the sunshine, in one of the symphonies. In citing Beethoven as an instance of genius being able to dispense with taste, he wrote that Mozart, "his equal in genius, has, in addition, the most delicate taste."

Bach he described as "that benevolent god, to whom musicians should offer a prayer before starting to work, so that they may be saved from mediocrity." But he refused stubbornly to accept everything written by Bach, Mozart, Beethoven, or anyone else as possessing the quality of genius. In a letter to Durand [3] he remarked that "when the old Saxon Cantor runs short of ideas he makes a start with anything at all and he is really merciless. In truth, he is bearable only when he is altogether admirable. . . . If some friend or publisher had advised him tactfully to stop writing, say, one day a week, we should have been spared hundreds of pages through which we must wander between long rows of dreary bars." . . . Bach's mastery he described as primarily "a gymnastic feat"; often it did not enable him to fill "the awful void" which only increased as the old master insisted

[3] April 15, 1917.

on "turning some insignificant idea to account." Yet he turned to Bach for corroboration of the artist's right to go his own way, saying: "You may be sure that old Bach, in whom is all music, snapped his fingers at harmonic formulas." For him, Bach was master of the "free and adorable arabesque"—the arabesque which, as he lamented, had all but vanished from music. "When Bach went back to the arabesque," said Debussy, "he made it more pliant and more fluid; and in spite of the stern discipline which the great composer imposed on beauty, there was a freshness and freedom in his imaginative development of it which astonishes us today." Debussy referred to the Violin Concerto in G as containing, almost intact, "that musical arabesque, or rather that principle of ornament, which is the basis of all forms of art"—explaining that the word "ornament" as used here had nothing whatever to do with the meaning attached to it by definition makers; but rather to the principle discovered by Palestrina, Vittoria, and di Lasso in the Gregorian chant, and utilized by them in delicate traceries strengthened by sturdy counterpoint.

In Bach's music [he wrote] it is not the character of the melody that stirs us, but rather the tracing of a particular line, often, indeed, of several lines, whose meeting, whether by chance or design, makes the appeal. Through this conception of ornament the music acquires an almost mechanical precision of appeal to which the audience reacts. Let no one think that there is anything unnatural or artificial in this. It is infinitely more "true" than the wretched whimperings and the tentative wailings of lyric drama. Above all, the music keeps its dignity. . . . It is most noticeable that no one whistles Bach. Such lip service has not been denied to Wagner.

Always it is Wagner to whom Debussy returns when there is a point to make for some other! Yet he could not consistently condemn the music which in his youth and young manhood had held him in thrall, much as he resented its domination over French art, and contrary as he found it, both as to means and ends, to the aesthetic he had of a muse that should be "always discreet." "Wagner's art," he wrote, "can never completely die. It will suffer that inevitable decay, the cruel mark of time on all beautiful things; yet noble ruins must remain, in the shadow of which our grandchildren will brood over the past splendor of this man, who, if he had been a little more human, would have been altogether great." He terms Wagner "the master symbolist," but avers that the vision of a fusion of the arts which the symbolist poets in France derived from Wagner had become little more than a formula for the advancement of literature.

In writing about *Parsifal*, Debussy distinguished sharply between the drama and the music. He ridicules the characters, declaring the "old gaol-bird," Klingsor, the only human and the only moral personage of the lot; Parsifal he found insipid; Kundry, "that ancient rose of Hell," a "sentimental doggle-tail"; Amfortas a creature who "whines like a shop girl and whimpers like a baby." But all this, he confessed, has "nothing to do with the musical beauty of the opera, which is supreme. It is incomparable and bewildering, splendid and strong. *Parsifal* is one of the loveliest monuments of sound ever raised to the serene glory of music."

Elsewhere he described Wagner's music as "beautiful, singular, impure, seductive." He explained in detail his opposition to the *leit motif* and the attempt, by means of it, to have the music parallel details of the action. "Either the music gets out of breath in running after a character," he said, "or else the character sits down on a note to allow the music to catch up with him." And when all is said and done, he contended, "the application of the symphonic form to the dramatic action might end by killing dramatic music." He speaks of "the grandiloquent hysteria of the Wagnerian heroes." He declared the manifold repetitions and transformations, by which the musical material of the *Ring* sustained these heroes through four evenings, to be "inadmissible for those who love clarity and conciseness." The inability of the characters to appear without reiteration of their "accursed *leit motif*"—"some of them even sing it!"—suggested to him "a harmless lunatic, who, on presenting his visiting card, would declaim his name in song." . . . He finds Wotan the most stupid as well as the chief of gods. Brünnhilde, being "more or less a sister" to Siegfried, betrays him with "regrettable consequences. . . . Ho-yo-to-ho! Bravo. . . . Ho-yo-to-hei! Serves her right." When a princeling of Bavaria, who played in the orchestra at the Munich festivals, acclaimed Wagner as the greatest of Germanic composers, Debussy fumed. "What about Bach?" he asked. "Was he just a man who had many children? Beethoven? Another nobody who was so bad-tempered that he decided to become deaf so as to be of greater annoyance to his contemporaries in his last quartets? And Mozart? Merely a little libertine who wrote *Don Juan* to aggravate the Germans?"

Wagner, he declared in one of his extreme statements, "was never of service to music"; when Wagner cried out to the Germans in a mad gesture of pride, "and now you have an art!" he might just as well have said, "And now I leave you the void. Find your way out of it as well as you can." Wagner was "a beautiful sunset that was mistaken for a dawn."

As already has been said, much of Debussy's irritation where Wagner was concerned must be attributed to the slavish and inept imitation of the Bayreuth Titan by Frenchmen, little and big. "Nothing ever was more dreary," he said, "than the neo-Wagnerian school in which the French genius has lost its way among the sham Wotans in Hessian boots and the Tristans in velvet jackets." If Weber aspired to be a Wagner, it was fortunate for him, so far as the opinions of Debussy were at stake, that he did not realize his ambition. The French composer retained throughout his life his early admiration for Wagner's precursor. As Debussy described it, "His work had a sort of dreamy melancholy, characteristic of his time," but never marred by "the crude German moonshine in which nearly all his contemporaries were bathed"; and he was "perhaps the first to face the problems of establishing the due relationship of the infinite spirit of Nature to the finite spirit of the individual." If it could be charged against Weber that he had a weakness for ostentation and florid arias, there was an extenuating circumstance, said Debussy—"he married a singer."

Perhaps quite as much as Wagner—and for a similar reason—Gluck drew the fire of Debussy's critical artillery. This may well have been less an instinctive dislike of the basic qualities of Gluck's music and of the preachments of Gluck's operatic "reform" than a protest against Gluck's alien influence on French music. For Debussy, Gluck was essentially Germanic, yet he was traditionally looked upon as one of the pillars of French opera. In his application of the theory that music should be handmaiden of the text, Gluck set French words in what Debussy denounced as a Germanic, not a French way, with heavy word stresses and emphatic accents on syllables instead of in the undulatory, little-accented manner of French prosody; yet his operas became models for the French composers who were to follow him, and particularly for the academicians!

As Lawrence Gilman has pointed out,[4] if Debussy is not always just, justice does not, in fact, seem to have been his aim. He attacked Gluck, as champion for those French composers whom Gluck, he felt, had wrongly overshadowed. "Long live Rameau, down with Gluck!" he made a critical battlecry. Gluck's position in French music had been made possible by

[4] In the preface to the American edition of *Monsieur Croche, Dilettante Hater*.

the intervention of Marie-Antoinette, an Austrian, he wrote: "A curious analogy to the case of Wagner, who owed the production of Tannhäuser in Paris to Mme. de Metternich, also an Austrian."

To what, he asked, does the Gluck tradition owe its survival? "The false and pompous recitative is enough, but there is also his habit of rudely interrupting the action, as, for example, where Orpheus, having lost his Eurydice, sings a song which does not precisely indicate a very mournful state of mind. But because it is Gluck, we bend the knee. Rameau need only have changed his nationality—that was his mistake."

Gluck, he declared, was a court musician, whose music had an almost uniformly pompous bearing, adhering to a grand, ceremonious style. "Common people participated at a distance"; he represented to them "a wall behind which something was happening." His direct influence was to be found in Spontini, Lesueur, Méhul; he stood for "Wagnerian formulas in embryo, which is intolerable." Rameau could have taught him how to treat declamation so as to preserve inflexion instead of interposing accentuation. He was found an evil influence also, because of the theories he brought to his "reform" of the lyric theater. It was due to Gluck, Debussy said, "that the action of the drama now dominates the music. Is that really desirable?" To the shade of Gluck, he said, "I prefer Mozart to you; the splendid fellow entirely ignores you and thinks of nothing but music."

To bring about the domination of drama over music, Gluck decided upon Greek subjects, which, Debussy says, "accounts for the solemn nonsense that is talked about the alleged connection between your music and Greek art. Rameau was infinitely more Greek." . . . Many false interpretations have been given to the word "classic"; but to have "invented a purring accompaniment to drama, sacrificing any attempt at music," does not entitle Gluck to be called a "classic"—"Rameau has more

serious claims to such a title." There is much more about the
Greeks. The sympathetic but not altogether convinced reader
may feel that what Debussy has at heart is the French. Gluck,
like Wagner, was for him the hereditary enemy of French art;
through Gluck and what he imposed on the French taste, the
beautiful traditions of French music became warped, the French
desire for clarity was stifled, and via Meyerbeer, the French "arrived quite logically at Richard Wagner."

No Frenchman was ever so berated by Debussy, though Saint-
Saëns was the object of recurrent and often stinging satire. Couperin and Rameau, from whom Debussy felt that he stemmed,
were exalted; Massenet and Gounod were defended, even though
Debussy's ways of doing this left no doubt of his recognition of
their deficiencies and, more particularly, their sentimentality.
He admits that music "was never for Massenet the cosmic voice
heard by Bach and Beethoven," but rather a delightful avoca-
tion. He points to Massenet's eternal curiosity about the feminine soul and notes that his harmonies are "like enlacing arms,"
his melodies "the necks we kiss." He takes occasion, however, to
reproach Massenet for "his infidelities to Manon," since with
this opera he had discovered "a suitable form for his flirtatious
inclinations." And which, Debussy asks, is it better to please—
the cosmopolitan old ladies of Wagner or some sweet-scented
young things?

Massenet, he said, "seems to have been the victim of the fluttering fans of his fair hearers, who flirted them so long to his
glory. . . . His influence on contemporary music is obvious,
but admitted grudgingly by certain persons who owe much to
him, though they have the hypocrisy and ingratitude to deny it."

Gounod is praised for having "escaped the imperious genius
of Wagner"—in spite of his failings, Debussy says, he "is necessary"—he "makes room for Bizet, which is well. Unfortunately,
Bizet died too soon; and although he left one masterpiece, the

future of French music remained in doubt." . . .[5] If Gounod made a travesty of the character of Faust, as Germanophiles had charged, that was forgivable, since Goethe was German and Gounod French; but if Wagner distorted the legendary Tannhäuser, that was inexcusable, since both the character and the composer were German.

The literary, otherwise programmatic, leanings of Berlioz, whom he pictured as fastening a romantic curl to old wigs, incurred Debussy's censure. The passion of this master's music was likened to leaves that had dried between the pages of a book. "His genius found bitter pleasure in airing its longings in an artificial flower shop." However, Debussy disliked the dramatic music of Berlioz more than he did the symphonic. The *Fantastique* he described as "that feverish masterpiece of romantic ardor which leaves one amazed that the music can interpret such extravagant situations without losing its breath." Though he found real beauty in *Les Troyens*, it lacked originality and had, for Debussy, the great misfortune of suggesting Gluck.

Debussy seldom disguised his scorn for the Italian opera composers of his day whose careers were to some degree parallel to those of Gounod, Bizet, and Massenet. Mascagni, Leoncavallo, and Puccini, deriving from the Verdi of *Traviata*—an opera wherein the listener, he said, travels "from ballad to ballad"— lacked Verdi's gift of "giving the lie to life in heroic fashion." It was not to be expected that Debussy would have any sympathy for the two Italian settings of Murger's *Vie de Bohème*. In Debussy's view of them, the *verismo* composers made use of "a film formula, whereby the characters fling themselves on one another and tear their melodies from each other's lips."

This may be the place to take note of the striking commentary credited to Puccini at the time of Debussy's death. As printed in

[5] For digests of Debussy's opinions of Franck, d'Indy, Lalo, Dukas, Fauré, and various other French and foreign composers of his time, see Vallas: *The Theories of Claude Debussy*.

translation in the *Musical Times* of London, for July 1, 1918, the Italian composer's "tribute" could only be construed as lending distinguished support to those in France who liked to think of Debussy as in a cul-de-sac of his own contriving. Said Puccini:

> Debussy had the soul of an artist, capable of the rarest and most subtle perceptivities, and to express these he employed a harmonic scheme that at first seemed to reveal new and spacious and prescient ideas for the musical art. When nowadays I hear discussions on Debussyism as a system to follow or not to follow, I feel that I would like to tell young musicians of what I personally know concerning the perplexities that assailed this great artist in his last years. Those harmonic processes which were so dazzling in the moment of their revelation, and which seemed to have in reserve immense and ever-new treasures of beauty, after the first bewitching surprise always surprised less and less, till at last they surprised no more: and not this only, but also to their creator the field appeared closed, and I repeat I know how restlessly he sought and desired a way of exit. As a fervid admirer of Debussy, I anxiously waited to see how he himself would assail Debussyism; and now his death has rendered impossible that we shall ever know what would have been the outcome that indeed might have been precious.

Among the Russians, Debussy gave most attention to Moussorgsky, without apparently mentioning Borodin at all. Debussy proclaimed the *Nursery* song cycle "a masterpiece." "No one," he wrote, "has given utterance to the best within us in tones more gentle or profound. He is unique and will remain so." . . . The art of Moussorgsky was declared "free from arid formulas . . . it is like the art of an inquiring savage discovering music step by step through his emotions." Rimsky-Korsakoff interested him as a technician. The *Antar* symphony he hailed as "a pure masterpiece," in which Rimsky renovated (at the same time that he discarded!) the symphonic form. He defied anyone to remain insensible to the spell of this music, extolling its "charming themes" and its "dazzling orchestral and rhythmic effects." But like most Frenchmen, he seemed to look on Tchaikovsky as representing a compromise with traditional elements that largely nullified his Russian origin. He had sympathy for certain Spanish predecessors of Manuel de Falla (too much his junior to come within his purview as a reviewer and commentator), placing Isaac Albéniz highest in a group that included also Turina, Casas, Del Campo, and Arbós. "There are few works," he said, "to compare with *El Albaicín* in the third book of *Ibéria*." He praises also the *Procesión del Rocio* by Turina and *Á mi Tierra* by Casas.

Reverting to the French scene and to opera, and turning to his private correspondence rather than to his published criticisms, those who relish strong words will find them in a letter to Pierre Louÿs [6] about Charpentier's *Louise*. Debussy speaks of having been "to the show of the Charpentier family. . . . It seems to me that this work had to be. It supplies only too well the need for that cheap and idiotic art that has such an appeal." He particularly resented what Charpentier had done in taking "the cries of Paris, which are so delightfully human and picturesque" and turning them "into sickly cantilenas with harmonies underneath, which, to be polite, we will call parasitic." He declared the Charpentier opera a thousand times more conventional than Meyerbeer's *Huguenots;* and observed that if this was what was to be called "Life," he would prefer to die, then and there. "It is so silly that it is pitiful . . . more silly than harmful." And so, he told Louÿs, he would very much like to have *Pelléas* given in Japan; then the eclectics might approve and he, the composer, could be properly ashamed!

[6] Of date, February 5, 1900.

CHAPTER XVII

OPERAS THAT NEVER WERE WRITTEN

As You Like It and Incidental Music for *Lear*—Poe's *Devil in the Belfry* and *Usher*—A Phantom *Tristan*

SHAKESPEARE and Poe were to alternate in Debussy's plans for a stagework to succeed *Pelléas et Mélisande*, throughout the remainder of his life. But *Pelléas* was to remain his only completed opera. Had Debussy been a rapid worker and a prolix producer of the order of Donizetti or Rossini, the years after *Pelléas* might have seen the first performances of an opera called *Comme il vous plaira* (*As You Like It*), another styled *Le Diable dans le beffroi* (*The Devil in the Belfry*), a third named *La Chute de la maison Usher* (*The Fall of the House of Usher*) and a fourth, *Le Roman de Tristan*, based on Joseph Bédier's *La Légende de Tristan*. Still another opera project, one which resulted in Arthur Honegger's *Amphion*, must be included among the possibilities for such a repertoire; likewise, an *Orphée-roi*, to text by Victor Ségalen, which seems to have interested Debussy primarily as anti-Gluck propaganda. There might also have been yet another *Don Juan*. That all of these were fated to take their place beside the uncompleted *Rodrigue et Chimène* of pre-*Pelléas* years— though no one of the lot progressed so far as that work, and some may never have had a bar of music written for them— indicated more than that Debussy was no Rossini, no Donizetti. His progressive ill health, his indecision, his procrastination may all have amounted to the same thing. There may be good reason to believe, also, that in spite of his bursts of enthusiasm for first one subject and then another, he never felt really assured that any of these subjects represented for him what the Maeterlinck

197

drama of *Pelléas et Mélisande* had represented, a natural and eminently suitable medium for his music, with text calling for just such a tonal envelope as was his to bestow on it.

The unfinished *Rodrigue et Chimène*, as we have seen, occupied him in 1891–92 and was laid aside when he took up *Pelléas*, which claimed his attention through ten years, 1892–1902. It was in 1900, when *Pelléas* was virtually all written, that Paul Valéry—the writer whose *Monsieur Teste* had suggested to Debussy the idea of *Monsieur Croche*—proposed to Debussy that they collaborate on a lyrical drama that would carry on the action by miming, against a background of choral and instrumental music. Debussy apparently was agreeable to the proposal, but did nothing about it. Valéry subsequently took Honegger, thirty years the junior of Debussy, as his collaborator. A little later than the Valéry project appears that of the *Orphée-roi*, about which Ségalen and Debussy consulted over a period of two years. Ségalen, a close friend, apparently was convinced of the sincerity of Debussy's promise of collaboration, since he completed a libretto, published in 1921, three years after Debussy's death. Debussy regarded Gluck's *Orfeo* as dealing primarily with the sentimental aspects of the classic myth and standing in some such relation to it, let us say, as Gounod's *Faust* stood to Goethe's. He conceived Orpheus as being more than a man; he was a symbol—the voice of desire, an expression of power in the world of sound. The music, as planned, apparently was to be largely choral. But no one knows of the existence of any such music. The hint that Debussy thought of writing a *Don Juan* is contained in a letter from Albert Carré to René Peter, in which he expresses the opinion that the bitter memories which Debussy retained of the dress rehearsal of *Pelléas et Mélisande* preyed upon him and weakened his resolution and courage with respect to new works for the theater. In 1912, the French press gave notice to a projected opera to be called *Crimen amoris;* nothing further was heard of it.

Debussy's enthusiasm for Shakespeare dated back at least to his years at the Villa Medici, when he read the plays aloud in company with Paul Vidal and Xavier Leroux, using, of course, a French translation. In the early days of his work on *Pelléas*, Pierre Louÿs had suggested *Hamlet* to him as the subject for a suitable libretto—one "discret, mais énergique"—saying that if they had "the cheek" they would do it together, since, in his opinion, it was just what Debussy would do best. But there is nothing to indicate that Debussy considered the use of this play, already travestied for operatic purposes in the Hamlets of Ambroise Thomas (1868) and Faccio (1865). During the Villa Medici days the poet, Maurice Vauclair, had invited Debussy to collaborate in a version of *As You Like It* and from that time dates an interest in this comedy as a subject for his music, an interest that persisted—though with long intervals when it had no outward manifestation—until Debussy's death. That no such opera was written can be attributed partly to circumstances that took from Debussy the collaboration he was counting upon, at two different periods when he apparently was ready and eager to go to work upon a musical score. The poet, Paul-Jean Toulet, a fanciful and sensitive writer who became addicted to opium, was the man who disappointed Debussy on both occasions. The two artists put their heads together, with *As You Like It* as the reason for their consultations, soon after the production of *Pelléas* in 1902. So far had they progressed by October of that year that they were discussing off-stage choruses and the choice of words, as between the literal and the lyrical. In the quest of originality Debussy proposed comments from the wings, in the form of excited exclamations, during Orlando's wrestling bout. "I would have some of the songs sung by a group of people"—

adding in his incorrigible banter, that "the Duke is rich enough
to have the Chanteurs de Saint-Gervais and their conductor
come to the forest of Arden." But Toulet was soon to depart for
Tongking in Indo-China. "I am frightened," wrote Debussy, "to
have you leave so soon. You have made me impatient to get in
hand the complete scheme of this human little fairy-play."

Some idea of what Debussy had in mind visually for *Comme
il vous plaira* is given by a letter written from Bichain in 1902,
in those weeks after the production of *Pelléas* when he sought
refuge there with the parents of Rosalie Texier. Debussy tells
Toulet that he desires a joyous ending; cheerful, attractive cere-
monies for the betrothal rites; an elaborate scenic treatment with
personages marvelously attired, the whole to be "interspersed
with songs in the antique manner, thus forming part of the action." He was particularly anxious not to repeat *Pelléas et Mélisande*, which, too, had a forest, though of quite another aura
than the forest of Arden. Toulet, who had previously submitted
some sketches to Debussy, wrote out his libretto for *Comme il
vous plaira* while in the French Far-Eastern colony whither he
had gone to visit the Hanoi Exposition. Though he was absent
only about a year, it was not until 1917 that Debussy is again
found discussing the subject with him, this time in connection
with a series of productions given by the actor, Gémier, at the
Odéon. Gémier's staging of *The Merchant of Venice* there
prompted Debussy to take up with him the presentation of *As
You Like It* with music. Toulet told his colleague that he didn't
trust Gémier, who, he thought, would want a severely literal
translation. Debussy hastened to intercede for the actor. Evidently, the musician was more interested than the poet. "I am
too anxious to write the music not to consent to sacrifices," he
wrote to Toulet. A letter of November, 1917, from Debussy to
Durand, indicates that Gémier came to an agreement with Toulet. But if Debussy wrote any music as the result of that agree-

ment no scrap of it has come to light. Within a few months he was dead.

In the small quantity of incidental music composed by Debussy are two souvenirs of still another Shakespearian adventure —a Fanfare and a Berceuse for *King Lear*. These are credited to 1904, and, so far as is known, represent all that Debussy completed in fulfillment of an agreement to supply a score for a production of this drama by the actor Antoine. That worthy was frank to say that he regarded musicians as terrible bores, but if the music didn't take up too much time or distract attention from the play he wouldn't mind having some—certain people might even like it! Debussy, perhaps none too much heartened by the attitude of Antoine, and at that time deep in the meshes of the troubles attendant on his desertion of Lily for Mme. Bardac, procrastinated. In the end the play was given with incidental music by Edmond Missa. Debussy's two fragments,[1] to neither of which can be accorded any importance, were discovered and published in 1926, the Berceuse under the title of *Le Sommeil de Lear*.

La Légende de Tristan was taken up in 1907, apparently seriously, when Gabriel Mourey and Debussy discussed converting Joseph Bédier's poetic text into an opera of a chivalresque character, presumably as different from Wagner's *Tristan und Isolde* as a purely French conception could make it. The title of the work, as reported in the press at the time, was to be *Le Roman de Tristan*. The only trace of any music for this *Tristan* is a musical quotation from a slip of music paper inserted in a letter of 1907, inscribed "For J. Durand from his friend Claude Debussy (one of 363 themes of 'The Romance of Tristan')." The theme is a simple one of twelve measures; and it is assumed that Debussy sent it merely as an ironical allusion to Wagner and

---

[1] Lockspeiser states that there are rough notes in manuscript for six further pieces.

his system of leading motives, which Debussy derided, though he himself used representative themes in the score of *Pelléas et Mélisande*.

Debussy had as a spur to their composition definite assurance of performance for *Le Roman de Tristan* and the two Poe subjects, *Le Diable dans le beffroi* and *La Chute de la maison Usher*. The success achieved by *Pelléas et Mélisande*, when produced at the Manhattan Opera House in New York by Oscar Hammerstein, rival of the Metropolitan, prompted Giulio Gatti-Casazza, the Metropolitan's generalissimo, to seek the rights for any other operas Debussy might write. In May, 1908, (Hammerstein having produced *Pelléas* in February of that year), Gatti-Casazza, then newly engaged as Heinrich Conried's successor in New York, went to Paris.

> One of my first visits [he said in an interview in the New York *Times* [2]] was to Debussy, who received me in the most cordial manner and asked me in much detail about the production of *Pelléas* at La Scala [where Gatti- Casazza had been general manager for ten years before going to the Metropolitan in 1908].
>
> When I asked him to grant me the production rights for the Metropolitan for his three operas, the titles of which had already appeared in the newspapers—i. e., *La Légende de Tristan*, *La Chute de la maison Usher*, and *Le Diable dans le beffroi*, Debussy said: "I must tell you honestly that of the three works, there barely exists the sketch of the librettos; and as to the music, I have written only some vague ideas. How can I honestly sell you such embryonic compositions?"
>
> "Never mind," I answered. "The Metropolitan is happy to obtain the rights for what you can do and I beg you to sign an agreement with me."
>
> It was only through great efforts that I succeeded in ob-

[2] March 15, 1925, six days before the Metropolitan's first production of *Pelléas*.

taining the signature of Debussy and made him accept an advance of money which he himself wanted to be very modest.
I recall that when I was leaving him he said: "Do not forget
that I am a lazy composer and that I sometimes require
weeks to decide upon one harmonious accord in preference
to another. Remember also that you are the one who insisted on making this agreement and that probably you will
not receive anything."

Alas! Poor Debussy was, in this instance, a prophet.

Every year, when I was going to Paris, I would not fail
to pay him a visit, as we had for each other much sympathy
and friendship. And each time he would say to me:

"I am so happy to see you again, the more so because you
do not ask me if I have finished one of my three operas. I
must tell you that what increases in me is not geniality but
uncertainty and laziness."

The last time he saw Debussy, the opera manager said, was at
a performance of the Russian Ballet in Paris. Of that meeting,
Gatti-Casazza related:

"You know," he told me, "the operas that I am to write
for you will be further delayed on account of a new fact."

"But what fact?" I asked.

"I will not write an opera, but a ballet, because, after all,
it is better to have to do with mimes than with singers."

"Well," I said, "let us make an agreement also for a
ballet."

"Oh, no," interrupted Debussy. "Never! I have already
abused enough of your courtesy, faith and patience. No
contract; and when the ballet is finished I shall offer it to
the Metropolitan before any one else."

I recall that after the performance I accompanied Debussy to his house in the Avenue du Bois. He spoke to me
at length about *Le Diable dans le Beffroi* and *La Chute de
la maison Usher*, the libretti of which, as is known, had been
taken from the tales of Edgar Poe.

"But you know," he continued, "Edgar Poe possessed the

most original fantasy among the literature of all lands; he found a note absolutely new and different."

To this I replied: "It is true, and that is the precise reason why such a poet's ideas need to be clothed with the music of a unique composer like yourself, maestro."

"Perhaps, my dear Gatti," he rejoined, "this investiture will never be heard by anyone. I fear as much. I am getting older and more lazy than ever. Good-night and adieu!" . . .

I never saw Claude Debussy again, and, alas! I never saw even a note of the operas of which the Metropolitan had been so proud to procure the rights.

The records of the Metropolitan Opera Company show that on October 15, 1908, the company paid Debussy two thousand francs for an option on performing rights for the two Poe works, but with no mention made of *Le Roman de Tristan*.

The remarkable thing about Debussy's plan of setting *The Devil in the Belfry* was that the devil was to be a whistling, rather than a singing character. Such singing as was contemplated was to be entrusted to the chorus. The devil was to resemble as little as possible the evil spirits of the brimstone variety who paraded their way through the Gounod *Faust*, the Boïto *Mefistofele* and the Berlioz *Damnation of Faust*. He was to be, in fact, not the spirit of evil, but the spirit of contradiction—"perhaps it is he," Debussy said in a letter to Messager, "who inspires those who fail to think the same way as everybody else." Regarding "the red clown" as an illogical tradition, Debussy wanted something much more devilish and cruel—the whole work to be a blending of the real and the fantastic—though he fancied, he said, that "people will think it scandalous of me to have deserted the shade of Mélisande for a cynical, pirouetting devil"—even those same people who went about assuming that he would never be able to escape from *Pelléas*. They were very much mistaken in this assumption, he declared, adding that if such a thing were to happen he would immediately devote himself to growing pineapples. "It is disastrous to repeat oneself."

Debussy was quite as much concerned with his singing crowd as he was with his whistling devil. He had in mind, he told Lalo, something quite different from the large choral ensembles in *Boris Godounoff* and *Meistersinger*. The populace in *Boris*, he said, did not form a real crowd, since first one group sang, then another; or this alternation was replaced by unison. There was no populace in *Meistersinger*, he contended, "but an army, highly organized in the German manner and marching in ranks." What he sought to achieve was a more scattered effect, more divided, more detached, more indefinite—an effect that would appear disorganized, yet would, of course, be regulated—"a real human crowd, each voice independent," but with the voices in reality so united as to produce an impression of movement. In 1903 Debussy reported to his publisher that his scenario was nearly finished and that he had almost decided on the coloring of the music. In 1906 Debussy wrote to tell Durand about finishing *Ibéria* at once and returning to the *Belfry*, "near that devil who ought to end by having a grudge against me." Of his plan for treating the voices, which he said must remain a secret, he wrote: "I am always in fear of finding, some rotten morning, that it is idiotic." In 1911 he was still struggling with musical ideas that seem never to have been put on paper; a letter to Robert Godet shows that he rejoiced because the pressure of work on *Le Martyre de Saint-Sébastien* compelled him to put aside his other labors.

The second Poe subject, *La Chute de la maison Usher*, began to occupy Debussy's thoughts seriously early in 1908, and, perhaps partly as the result of the Metropolitan Opera's promise of production, soon became something of an obsession. In a letter of the early summer of 1908 he wrote that the external world scarcely existed for him, so deeply was he immersed in the fate of the heir of the Usher family; "I am guilty," he said, "of about ten acts of incivility an hour." He tells Durand of working hard; of moments when he so lost the feeling of things around him that if the sister of Roderick Usher had appeared before him in his house he would not have been surprised. A month later, in mid-summer, he wrote of having almost finished "a long monologue of poor Roderick," adding that "it almost makes the stones weep." In confidence he told Durand of a novel effect of scoring he had in mind. What he described as "the mustiness" was to be achieved by contrasting the low notes of the oboe with the harmonics of the violin; Durand was asked not to speak of it to anyone. He confessed he was very much taken with the device; he was striving, he said, to represent a progressive sense of mental anguish and remarked that if he could succeed he would be doing a real service not only for music but for his publisher. "I spend my existence in the House of Usher . . . and leave it with my nerves taut, like the strings of a violin."

There were interruptions as he turned to *Le Martyre de Saint-Sébastien* and the ballet *Jeux*. But in 1912 he wrote of having gone back to his *Maison Usher*, "very tired," yet with the hope of deriving new strength from it. Four years later, he recast the libretto and in 1917 sent it to Durand. The two versions of the text find place in the list of Debussy's unpublished literary works. It is by no means certain that there are no more musical manuscripts or sketches to be disclosed, though Durand, to whom Debussy wrote repeatedly about progress on the Poe operas, has said that he knows of no sketches or fragments of music for these works. Did Debussy destroy a score or parts of a score for *La Chute de la maison Usher*—including that trick of pitting the low notes of the oboe against the harmonics of the violin, which might have rivaled the famous double bass "pinch" of the Strauss *Salome*—as he had threatened to destroy even the revised score of *Pelléas?* He warned Giulio Gatti-Casazza that he was a lazy composer; but his letters to Durand indicate that he was a busy one, deeply absorbed in his subject and—the long monologue of Roderick as a reminder—one who was going ahead definitely with the actual writing of the music in hand.

In 1910, when the Metropolitan Opera Company presented a guest season at the Châtelet in Paris, with Enrico Caruso heading a notable array of singers and Arturo Toscanini dominating the ensemble as conductor, Debussy had opportunity to see what he might expect in the way of production, casting, and orchestral performance for his operas, if completed and given over to the American institution. Gabriel Astruc has told of a meeting between Debussy and Toscanini.[3]

The day of the dress rehearsal of *Aïda* at the Châtelet, Debussy was in a box. During the intermission, I went to seek the author of *Pelléas*, that *Pelléas* of which, a short time before, Toscanini had in a single night read over the score, and directed the first performance—listen well: by heart! replacing, at a moment's notice, the maestro of the Turin opera, confined to his bed. *Propter hoc*, Debussy and Toscanini, without knowing each other, adored each other. I did not forewarn Toscanini, who made a ten-minute retreat to a dressing-room, thinking with his forehead in his hands, and I arrived with Claude. . . . When the door opened and he saw Debussy, Toscanini stood up. The two men looked at each other for a long time, and, speechless with emotion, threw themselves into each other's arms.

Giulio Gatti-Casazza also has left a little story of that time. The Metropolitan's general manager had Debussy as guest in his box at a performance of *Falstaff*, in which Antonio Scotti sang the name part, and over which Toscanini presided with a mastery that exhibited at every bar the genius of the amazing score. "But was Verdi really going on his eightieth year when he wrote music of this kind?" Debussy asked the Italian at his side.

[3] *Le Pavillon des Fantômes.*

"At my affirmative answer," Mr. Gatti related,[4] he exclaimed: 'It is unbelievable! Prodigious! That old man must have made some pact with the devil, like Faust!' "

"But the man for the public," he said to the opera director—one may suspect with a certain concealment of disdain out of respect for the nationality of the person he addressed—"is that amazing Puccini."

"Your genius," Gatti-Casazza replied, "is très aristocratique."

"Très aristocratique?" Debussy echoed—looking at his companion, as Mr. Gatti described it, "oddly." And then, with a shrug and a gesture: "Trop aristocratique!"

[4] Interview in the New York *Times,* March 15, 1925.

CHAPTER XVIII

ADVENTURES IN THE THEATER

Music for d'Annunzio's *Martyrdom of Saint Sebastian—Jeux,* a Tennis Ballet for Nijinsky, and *Khamma* for Maud Allan

IF it was procrastination that deprived Giulio Gatti-Casazza and the Metropolitan Opera House of the promised operatic novelties by Debussy, no such factor entered into the creation of the musical score for Gabriel d'Annunzio's *Le Martyre de Saint-Sébastien.* The composer who had labored for ten years on *Pelléas et Mélisande* lived up to an agreement to provide a specified quantity of instrumental and choral music in a given number of weeks. In accepting the commission at the beginning of 1911, he was bound to deliver the score for performance on May 21 of that year. When he was first approached by d'Annunzio with the scheme for the work, which assumed the form of a mystery play rather than an opera, Debussy confessed that he was plunged into a state of fever, "so happy and proud was I to illustrate in music M. d'Annunzio's work." All other projects were set aside, including *Gigues* and *Le Diable dans le beffroi.* So short the time and so great the need of the music for rehearsal, that the manuscript was turned over page by page, the last touches filled in with pencil. But Debussy did not attempt the orchestration in his haste. Noting down hints and essentials, he left the details of the instrumentation to André Caplet, who had been chosen to conduct. The last bars reached the publisher Durand only shortly before the performance. Debussy wrote that he was not displeased with what he had written, but told his friend, "I'm at the end of my tether." For two months he had lived a hermit's existence in his house, denying himself to callers,

writing and rewriting parts of the music. The tendency among
those who knew something of the nature of the work on which
he was engaged was to regard it either as a piece of hackwork,
of something that would never really materialize, save for a
fragment or two, like the *King Lear* music. To Henry Malherbe,
a journalist who sought him out in his retreat in the Bois de
Boulogne, he complained of being hampered by lack of time,
though he was enthusiastic over the subject as one uniting the
worship of Adonis with that of Christ. It has been said that Debussy was an atheist. In his student days he confessed that he had
not the religious feeling for one of the cantatas undertaken. But
the figure of the Archer of God, the fair "athlete of Christ,"
as bodied forth in d'Annunzio's somewhat unidiomatic French
verse, appealed to the mystic in Debussy and the sensualist as
well. "I have long dreamed of the bleeding youth," d'Annunzio
wrote, "transfigured in the Christian myth, like the beautiful
wounded god mourned by the women of Byblus before the
catafalque of ebony and purple, in the vernal equinox." His mystery play, he explained, was a development of a theme derived
from the writings of Veronica Gambara, a woman poet of the
Renaissance. Taking from these a line, "He that loves me most,
wounds me," he has his saint utter, as he holds fast the laurel in
the hour of his execution by the archers of Emesa:

> I say unto you, I say unto you,
> He that wounds me the more deeply, the more deeply
> loves me.

Writing against time, and in the final weeks with Caplet at his
elbow to carry out his indications for the scoring, Debussy prepared for each act—or "mansion" as d'Annunzio called each of
the several sections—an orchestral prelude or introduction, that
for the final act serving, in fact, as an interlude because of there
being no pause between the fourth and fifth sections. He also

DEBUSSY IN THE DOORWAY OF HIS HOME,
ABOUT 1910

composed choral numbers and passages for solo voices, the martyrs of the first act being contraltos, the celestial beings, whose commentaries are heard thereafter, sopranos. He decided to depend chiefly on the woodwinds for his orchestral texture and to make little use of the strings save as reinforcement or background.

Debussy, who told an interviewer that he sought to write down his musical dreams in a spirit of utter self-detachment and to sing his "interior visions, with the naïve candor of a child," was visibly affected on several occasions by the sound of his own music. Durand has told of an occasion in which the publisher constituted himself the audience, while Debussy played the *Sébastien* score. "When he came to the magnificent passage of the 'Passion,'" Durand says, "Debussy, at the piano, wept, while I in my armchair was likewise moved." Émile Vuillermoz, who assisted in training the chorus for the first performance, reports that at rehearsal Debussy, "who had to a high degree modesty in emotion, could not maintain his habitual attitude of sarcastic good will; ingenuously he wept."

Though, as Vuillermoz reports, there was respect and veneration for Debussy and his music on the part of the artists, they seem never to have been easy or comfortable about what they were undertaking. D'Annunzio's French troubled them. "The mysterious complexity of the score, as it came in, page by page," said Vuillermoz,[1] "filled the performers with a sort of terror." The fragments were so obscure that no one could appreciate their place in the text until the whole was revealed. The choreographer was Fokine. Léon Bakst designed the scenery. With Caplet as conductor, D. E. Ingelbrecht and Vuillermoz were assigned to the work of preparing the chorus. Vuillermoz also was called upon to rehearse the dances of the principal character, impersonated by Ida Rubinstein.

[1] His *Musiques d'Aujourd'hui.*

In some quarters it was declared that d'Annunzio's infatuation for Mlle. Rubinstein was the sole reason for this work being undertaken in a form that subsequently was to defeat it as a stage venture. Debussy was pitied for having been drawn into an experiment that was foredoomed to fail; the more genius he might conjure up for his hastily written music, the greater the loss. The whole project, they said, was merely one for the glorification of the dancer, and, as such, scarcely worthy of a celebrated Italian poet and an equally illustrious French composer. But however much d'Annunzio may have had the sinuosities of Ida Rubinstein in mind, Debussy, it is fair to say, had before him always the symbol that this Saint-Sébastien was for him— something of sensuous grace quite as much as of the pure flame of faith.

But *Le Martyre de Saint-Sébastien* was not to be produced without the motives of the co-authors being attacked in public. For some high dignitaries of the Roman Catholic Church in France, this musico-dramatic saint was something more challenging than a figure in a stained-glass window. The circumstance that the dancer who was to embody Sebastian was a Jewess may have contributed to a feeling that the venture lacked reverence and should be frowned upon by churchmen. Nominally, at least, d'Annunzio was a Catholic. Debussy was not. "I have made mysterious Nature my religion," the composer told Henry Malherbe in explaining that he did not practice any faith in accordance with prescribed ritual.[2] "I do not believe that a man is any nearer God for being clad in priestly garments," he said, "nor that one place in town is better adapted to meditation than another." Expressions like these, or that in which he told of his enthusiasm for d'Annunzio's work as one in which the worship of Adonis was united with that of Christ, were scarcely calculated to reassure the clergy. On May 16, only five days be-

[2] Interview in *Excelsior*, February 11, 1911.

fore the announced "gala performance," the Archbishop of Paris declared the play "offensive to Christian consciences" and warned Catholics to stay away from it.

D'Annunzio and Debussy jointly published an indignant reply in which they said:

> The Archbishop of Paris, in a manner that was ill-advised, has attacked in his recent decree a work, still unknown to him, created by two artists who, in the course of several years of labor, have given at least evidence of their unremitting aspiration toward the severest forms of art. Without failing in the respect which the Archbishop's note itself fails to accord us, we desire to express our regret at the singular treatment which we have not deserved; and we affirm—upon our honor and upon the honor of all those who are acquainted with "The Martyrdom of Saint Sebastian"—that this work, deeply religious, is the lyrical glorification, not only of the admirable athlete of Christ, but of all Christian heroism.

On May 18 Debussy gave an interview to the *Comœdia*, in which he said:

> Do you imagine that my works do not contain what I may call religious precedents? Do you propose to fetter the soul of the artist? Is it not obvious that a man who sees mystery in everything will be inevitably attracted to a religious subject? I do not wish to make a profession of faith. But, even if I am not a practising Catholic nor a believer, it did not cost me much effort to rise to the mystical heights which the poet's drama attains.
>
> Let us be clear about the word *mysticism*. You see that this very day the Archbishop has forbidden the faithful to assist at d'Annunzio's play, although he does not know the work. But let us not dwell on these annoying details. . . . From the artistic point of view such decrees cannot be considered. I assure you that I wrote my music as though I had been asked to do it for a church. The result is decorative

music, if you like, a noble text, interpreted in sounds and rhythms; and in the last act when the saint ascends into Heaven, I believe I have expressed all the feelings aroused in me by the thought of the Ascension. Have I succeeded? That no longer concerns me. We have not the simple faith of other days. Is the faith expressed by my music orthodox or not? I cannot say. It is my faith, my own, singing in all sincerity.

As church papers took up and repeated the charge that there was something inherently sacrilegious about the play, there was talk of excommunication for those who defiantly or carelessly attended, with the result that Astruc, under whose aegis the work was to be given at the Châtelet, had many cancellations, particularly from Catholic families that had taken boxes.

Other factors conspired against the success of the première. The final dress rehearsal, set for Sunday, May 21, was to have been a brilliant affair, with many notables in attendance. But the French Minister of War was killed in an airplane accident that morning, with the result that the official participation customary at such events was forbidden and a last-minute decision was made to exclude everyone but the press. Others attempted to gain entrance and turbulent scenes ensued. The first public performance was that of Monday, May 22, and it went none too well. The stage direction conceived the idea of dispersing the chorus in the wings and various places about the stage. Léon Bakst, in arranging the groupings with a painter's eye to pictorial effect, ignored the musical requirements, with the result that individual sopranos found themselves among basses, tenors among contraltos. Many were panic-stricken over having to sing Debussy's perplexing music without being able to seek support from their neighbors and, in some instances, without being able to see the conductor. No wonder, Vuillermoz remarked, that listeners quite generally failed to comprehend the "mystery." According to one reviewer, the audience "poured out gradually, like water from a broken vase." A liberal measure of blame has been left at the door of Ida Rubinstein. Vallas has described her interpretation of the principal role as "absurdly inadequate." Mme. Rubinstein reappeared as the saint in the revival at the Paris Opéra in June, 1922, and as she controlled the performing rights those Parisians who contended that the interpretation was at fault had little prospect of seeing any other dancer or mime in the part.[3]

Critical verdicts were again divergent, with one writer—Louis Vuillemin, for *Comœdia*—declaring that there had emerged a new and powerful Debussy, a Debussy "resolved no longer to imitate his imitators. Will they forgive him?" But elsewhere, as in *L'Éclair,* the score was declared "not broadly developed nor of any great importance." One writer found in it the charm of the Île de France, applying to it such terms as "solemn and voluptuous, now vibrating to ardent embraces, now appeased by prayer." One viewed it as a practical joke, a *befa;* another as "sacrilegious" and an "offense to Christian feeling." The *Figaro* reviewer found the music intimately identified with the poem. Pierre Lalo noted in the *Temps* that Debussy had given his ideas an increased breadth and expressiveness; that his idiom was more definite, though with less of restraint and subtlety. Debussy's fellow composer, Alfred Bruneau, praised the skill of the vocal ensembles. In other quarters due notice was taken of Debussy's adept use of Gregorian modes, the diversity of his instrumental combinations, the sustained emotional quality of the work. But pervading these reactions was a feeling that the play, as a play, was not a success; that the music labored under severe handicaps, even to make itself heard; and that the lack of some cohesive form, whereby the music might be regarded as an entity rather

[3] A stage representation was given at the Boston Opera House on March 30, 1912, with Theresa Cerutti miming Saint Sebastian.

than a mere complement for the spoken text, tended to deprive the score of a place among Debussy's major compositions. Subsequent experience would appear to have borne this out. In June, 1912, on the 14th and the 17th, D. E. Ingelbrecht presented the orchestral score at the Société Musicale Indépendante and, thereafter, a symphonic suite arranged by André Caplet, with the choruses omitted, achieved scattering performances without establishing the curtailed work in the orchestral repertoire. That the music lost point and poignance in being divorced from the stage action was the opinion of many who admired it most. Jacques Rouché, director of the Opéra, at one time flirted with the idea of converting the "mystery" into an opera and Debussy was enthusiastic, expressing the opinion that d'Annunzio would gladly cooperate, but nothing tangible was done, possibly because the opera manager was reminded of the Catholic attitude; possibly because Ida Rubinstein had her "mystery" and that, after all, was what d'Annunzio had asked Debussy to help create. There are those in Paris who regard *Le Martyre de Saint-Sébastien* as Debussy's French *Parsifal;* but, as one devout admirer of the score described it, a *Parsifal* without a Bayreuth.

Debussy was to deal with dancers other than Ida Rubinstein in the period between 1909 and 1914. Two years before giving up all other work for *Sébastien*, he had embarked on an Italian sketch in one act for the Diaghileff ballet, fashioning his own libretto for music he was never to compose. Of three proposed titles, *Masques et Bergamasques, L'éternelle avenue* and *L'Amour masque*, the first was utilized when the scenario was published. The action had to do with Scaramouche, Barbarina, Arlequin, and others of their ilk, with the scene laid in eighteenth-century Venice. *Fêtes galantes* and *Le Palais de silence* were other ballet projects that did not materialize. For Maud Allan, an Egyptian subject, *Khamma*, was sketched out in 1911 by Debussy, then turned over to Charles Koechlin for instrumentation. Never danced to, though published in 1916 and after Debussy's death performed as concert music, *Khamma* evoked from Debussy the satirical description, "that queer ballet with its trumpet calls," which he said suggested "a riot or an outbreak of fire."

Two years after *Khamma* was laid aside for *Le Martyre de Saint-Sébastien*, Debussy wrote a ballet that was completed by his own hand and duly produced at the Théâtre des Champs-Élysées on May 15, 1913. This was the so-called tennis ballet, *Jeux*, composed for Nijinsky and with choreography by him. It is not recorded that Debussy was a Nijinsky enthusiast. He objected to the dancer's treatment of *L'Après-midi d'un faune*, describing it as "ugly—Dalcrozian in fact." [4] But the Debussy of this time apparently had more of compromise in his nature with respect to qualities of performance than he had where principles of composition were concerned. *Jeux* has to do with a lost tennis ball and the hide-and-seek of a man and two girls who hunt for it in a garden at dusk, with embraces and quarrels ensuing as the pursuit goes on. Debussy rewrote the ending several times, in an attempt to deal neatly with what he described as a rather risqué situation, though, as he wrote Durand, any hint of the improper in a ballet will escape through the toes of the danseuse and end prettily in a pirouette. The dexterity of the score written for *Jeux* was recognized by some of the reviewers, Émile Vuillermoz even likening the course of the music to a series of volleys in a tennis game, with bound and rebound and "a skillful backhand stroke." But the ballet contributed little to the fame of the composer or to the coffers of the theater. When the music was played without the miming at the Concerts Colonne on March 1, 1914, there were hisses as well as cheers. Its harmonic investiture was regarded in some quarters as harsh and disagreeable, but it was by no means without favor in the press,

[4] Letter to Robert Godet.

Gaston Carraud of *La Liberté* going so far as to rank the music far above *La Mer*—possibly because he was one of those who least liked *La Mer*.

Louis Laloy [5] has told of an afternoon in the spring of 1913 when Stravinsky and Debussy met at his house. Igor embraced Claude, who gave Laloy an amused look over the Russian's shoulder. Then they sat down at a piano to play through a four-hand arrangement of *Le Sacre du printemps* which Stravinsky had brought with him, Debussy undertaking the bass. Stravinsky asked for permission to remove his collar and labored much the more of the two over his thorny pages. When they had finished there were no embraces, not even any compliments. Both Debussy and Laloy were dumfounded.

In his autobiography Stravinsky mentions an incident of the kind, but the composition which he says he and Debussy played together was not *Le Sacre du printemps* but *The King of Stars* (*Zvezdoliki*) which he dedicated to Debussy but which, according to the composer, has never been performed, chiefly because of difficulties of intonation that choruses are not prepared to meet. Stravinsky acknowledges with expressions of gratitude what he felt was Debussy's generally sympathetic atitude toward him and his music. As an instance of keen perception, Debussy was one of the few, he says, who had noted the musical importance of the pages which precede the juggling tricks in *Petroushka* immediately before the final dance of the marionettes in the first act. Stravinsky liked *Jeux*, which Debussy had played through for him. But he speaks of having had a distinct feeling that Debussy was disconcerted by the Stravinskyan idiom when they played *Roi des étoiles* on one piano. Though the Russian later dedicated his *Symphonies for Wind Instruments* to Debussy, he was by no means assured that Debussy would have approved of them. "But this supposition, I will even say this certainty, that

[5] In *La Musique Retrouvée*.

my music would have remained foreign to him was far from dis-
couraging me." Incidentally, he recalls the droll advice which
Rimsky-Korsakoff gave him early in his career when he asked
Rimsky about Debussy. It was this: "Better not listen to him;
one runs the risk of getting accustomed to him and one would
end by liking him."

As a rule, Debussy's attitude toward Americans was one more
caustic than friendly. Typical is this reference in a letter to
Durand at a time Henry Russell was negotiating with him for
performance as opera of *L'Enfant prodigue* as well as of *Pelléas:*
"Between us, Mr. Russell and the Boston people seem to have
the air of having found definitely the only true way of performing 'Pelléas.' Aren't the Americans the Marseillaise of the other
side of the ocean? Are they not the inventors of 'bluff,' which
is so near the spirit of the South of France?"

But he considered making a concert tour of America and was
friendly with Arthur Hartmann, the American violinist, with
whom he became acquainted in 1908. Contemplated in the
American tour were joint concerts with the violinist and for the
purposes of their projected appearances Debussy began a violin
Poème, sketches for which are contained in an autograph book
in Hartmann's possession. Hartmann's first meeting with Debussy was the result of some arrangements he had made of several Debussy songs (the first being *Il pleure dans mon cœur*)
after he had learned from the composer, in answer to a letter of
inquiry, that there were no Debussy compositions for violin. He
has told of being shown into a room decorated with Chinese
vases, wood carvings, draperies, and musical instruments. Debussy's manner as he entered appeared to him "hesitating, timor-
ous and almost petulant." He puffed a cigarette violently, his
eyes half closed. Five times Hartmann played a transcription for
Debussy, then received his approval, the conversation running
to detached sentences and monosyllabic comments. Later, when

Hartmann lived in the same square as Debussy, he was a frequent caller. When he came upon Debussy at work he had the feeling that some spirit must be doing it for him, for his desk—a huge long flat table—was always in perfect order and he never saw an ink spot on the blotter. There were never any manuscripts around and none on the piano.[6] On one occasion, when Hartmann found Debussy with Chou-Chou in his garden, a trowel in his hands, the gate bell rang. Debussy seized his friend and dragged him behind a bush. Winking, he whispered, "Monsieur is not at home." Once when he had returned a visit, Debussy expressed a wish for something in Hartmann's abode, making a mystery of what it was until the wish was granted. What he took, to be placed beside his Chinese and Japanese oddities, was something Hartmann had brought back from Norway—a pebble from the strand.

[6] Robert Godet has contradicted the impression that Debussy composed at the piano. Few composers did so little work at the instrument, he says. (*Revue Musicale*, May, 1934.)

CHAPTER XIX

WAR AND THE LAST YEARS

Conducting Engagements in Italy and Holland—The Final
Works and Appearances—Death and Some Monuments

Soon to realize that the hand of death was upon him, and to see
death all about him as the nations of Europe were lashed into the
fratricidal slaughter of the World War, Debussy entered the
year 1914 harried and perplexed by money matters. His marriage to Mme. Bardac had substituted one type of need for another. Alienated as he was from many of his old friends, and
withdrawn as he subsequently became because of the nature of
his illness, Debussy had moved into a different stratum of life.
To live as he was compelled to live, more money was needed
than when he shared his Bohemian quarters with Gaby or Lily.
The reputed personal affluence of Mme. Bardac turned out to
be a myth, funds which she had expected to receive being tied
up in litigation or otherwise chimerical. It is known that in the
last stages of her husband's illness she pawned her jewels to obtain money to pay doctors and defray other medical expenses;
her diamonds she recovered after Debussy's death. Part, at least,
of the royalties on the sale of Debussy's music went, by legal
agreement, to the divorced wife. Lily, it seems, never went back
to her old employment as a dressmaker, but lived on in a shadowy existence that still brought her into occasional contact with
Debussy's older friends.

For the sake of the honorariums involved, even though he described them as "quite inconsiderable," Debussy accepted additional conducting engagements in Rome, The Hague, and Amsterdam. In Rome he revisited the Villa Medici; "but alas," he

wrote of this experience, "I am no longer twenty." Success attended his appearance at the Augusteo, where he conducted *La Mer*, *Rondes de printemps* and *L'Après-midi*, the reception being so enthusiastic that it all but effaced the memory of the hostile demonstrations which had marred the first performance of *Pelléas* in Rome seven years before. At The Hague Debussy conducted the Concertgebouw orchestra in *L'Après-midi*, *Nuages*, and *Fêtes* and the *Marche écossaise*. In addition he appeared as pianist in three of his own works: *Danseuses de Delphes*, *La Fille aux cheveux de lin*, and *Puerto del Vino*. Compositions by Saint-Saëns and Duparc, conducted by Gustave Doret, occupied the first part of the concert. The same program, with the same orchestra, was given the next day in Amsterdam. The official program referred to him as "an authority," not only in France, but in the entire musical world.

Thus recognized abroad, Debussy was no longer a prophet without honor in his own land. When a vacancy was brought about in the Académie des Beaux-Arts as the result of the election of Widor as permanent secretary of the Institut de France, a move was made to put Debussy in the empty chair. Widor favored him, as did several former laureates at the Villa Medici, Marcel Baschet and Gaston Rédon among them. Delay, attributed to the attitude of Saint-Saëns, cheated Debussy of the honor he was then quite willing to accept. He was barely able to send his letter of candidature. Today, we can see that his death cheated the Institut of more kudos than that venerable establishment could have conferred on him.

To take part in a private concert, for which he was to receive a fee such as "Caruso would demand for his accompanist," [1] Debussy went to London for the last time in June, 1914, two months before England's entry into the all-European shambles on the side of France. The fee, insignificant as Debussy declared

[1] Letter to Jacques Durand.

it to be, was for him "a drop of water in the desert of these dreadful summer months." He was never very happy financially in his English, or, for that matter, his other foreign adventures. In 1906 the secretary of the Royal Philharmonic Society offered fifteen pounds to cover his expenses, if he would honor that august body with his presence, after taking care to point out that the Society "is not in the habit of paying a fee" to those composers who did so honor it. The worthy secretary apparently did not know that *Pelléas* was an opera, for it was this work which Debussy was asked to conduct at a Philharmonic concert. The composer's answer pointed out the existence of five acts, lasting two and a half hours; whereupon the secretary invited him to come over, anyway, and conduct some other work. After an interval Debussy, who quite possibly had come to the conclusion that he was not in the habit of performing without fee for the sake of honoring societies, royal or otherwise, sent a final refusal.

Debussy and Hartmann appeared together in the Salle des Agriculteurs, playing several transcriptions by Hartmann of vocal and piano works by Debussy (*Il pleure dans mon cœur* from the *Ariettes oubliées, La Fille aux cheveux de lin,* and *Minstrels*) as well as Grieg's sonata for violin and piano, the last-named in somewhat tardy championship of the composer whom Debussy, as a critic, had ridiculed, and presumably because of the scorn that had been heaped on the Norwegian in the precincts of the Schola Cantorum, for which Debussy had a minimum of love and sympathy. A little later, in mid-April, Debussy was heard as pianist and accompanist in a concert devoted to his compositions, at which some of the *Préludes* figured, along with a sheaf of songs sung by Ninon Vallin, who was also the vocalist at a concert given in the Salle Gaveau (March 21) when the *Trois Poèmes de Stéphane Mallarmé* were sung for the first time. On this occasion Debussy played *The Children's Corner,*

Feuilles mortes, La Cathédrale engloutie, and *La Fille aux cheveux de lin.*

Debussy began in this year the orchestration of *La Boîte à
joujoux,* written out in piano score in 1913. But it was destined
to be completed by Caplet and was not performed until December, 1919. The scenario for this fanciful little ballet was prepared by André Hellé, a painter whose specialty was the illustration of books for children, and was drawn from a story he had
written, of the same title. It was all about a doll and what goes on
in a toy chest when a brave soldier and a wicked polichinelle
fall in love with the same pretty face of wax. The ending is
happy and there are many children. Debussy once spoke of "ex-
tracting confidences" from Chou-Chou's dolls; but, for all his
sympathy with the subject, he had difficulty in translating these
confidences into music. "The soul of a doll," he wrote to Durand, "is more mysterious than even Maeterlinck supposes; it
does not readily put up with the claptrap that so many human
souls tolerate." He favored the use of marionettes for the projected performance, which had to be postponed until after his
death because of the war.[2] Of about this time, but not published
until 1927, was the flute solo known as *Syrinx.* It was intended as
incidental music for Gabriel Mourey's *Psyche.*

With the outbreak of the war in August, 1914, Debussy's first
conviction was that an artist must forego all creative work during such a time of tragedy and sacrifice. He was fifty-two years
old and for a good many years had cultivated his strongly French
outlook, which more than once had led him into expressions of
repugnance for what he regarded as typical manifestations of
German art. He extolled the true French taste and protested
against its being "smothered under the eiderdowns" of an antagonistic alien culture. Without so much as dreaming of the

---

[2] As completed by Caplet, *La Boîte à joujoux* was first performed at the
Théâtre Lyrique du Vaudeville, Paris, on December 10, 1919.

fearful conflict to come, he had called in 1913 for a French "warfare against the Barbarians," saying that they had become more dangerous since they had taken to parting their hair in the middle. Over a long period he had resisted what he had regarded as German tyranny in music, calling on Frenchmen to worship at their own shrines and to shake off domination from across the Rhine. He made special pleadings for the old French clavecinists, because, as he saw them, they were of all French composers the most French.

For weeks after the guns began belching their vomit of death, Debussy would not so much as touch his piano. He regarded composition as impossible and, with France in such travail, was opposed to performances of his works abroad. France, he said, could neither laugh nor weep while so many of her sons were heroically facing death. There came over him, however, a desire to pay tribute to the gallantry of Belgium, ridiculous though it seemed to have to deal with heroism well out of the reach of bullets. Under the pressure of this desire, he composed in November, 1914, a *Berceuse héroïque*, in homage to King Albert of the Belgians and his soldiers, which, though scored for orchestra, has the character of a relatively simple piano piece. Incorporated is the Belgian anthem, *La Brabançonne*. It conveyed more of a sense of nostalgia than heroism when it was performed at the combined Concerts Colonne et Lamoureux within the next year.

Disinclined, otherwise, to undertake creative work, Debussy accepted a proposal made by Durand that he should revise the works of Chopin for a new French edition. The manuscripts from which he worked, some obviously not in Chopin's hand, caused him no end of trouble, as he tried to reconcile the differences discernible in various publications. Alarmed at having to play the role of adjudicator, he was content to write a preface for the work which was merely a tribute to Chopin rather than a comparative study of conflicting details. He also occupied himself with a revision of Johann Sebastian Bach's violin sonatas, undertaken in 1917 because of his financial straits and with unconcealed distaste. A change of heart in 1915 brought Debussy back to composition. Perhaps it was because he came to feel that this was the one real service he could do for his invaded France. Physically, he was not fit for any sort of war service. He had neither inventive nor organizing talent, he was not even competent to do clerical work. He did not look upon anything he might do as indispensable, he wrote Robert Godet, but it would be cowardice for him to join the ranks of the disabled. So, at long last, he had come to the conclusion that he should do the only thing he could do "more or less well." And because he now felt impelled to work, he found reason to regret his "state of latent death." Thus convinced, he told Godet that he had been "writing like a madman, or one who knows he must die the next morning."

Under the stress of his new resolution there emerged his *Épigraphes antiques*, six in number, and the three pieces styled *En blanc et noir*, the former for piano, four hands, the latter for two pianos. León Vallas has shown that the *Épigraphes*, which also exist in an arrangement for piano solo, were derived from sketches for some incidental music composed in 1900 for poems by Pierre Louÿs and styled *Chansons de Bilitis*, like the series of songs so known, but not to be confused with them. The music, scored for two flutes, two harps, and celesta, was intended to be played as an accompaniment for recitation of the verses, and was written out in three small notebooks but never published. For the *Épigraphes*, Debussy adapted, rearranged, improved, and in some instances expanded the original, which was divided into a dozen small pieces of a hasty, improvisatory character. *En blanc et noir*, which apparently can be credited to 1915 as an entirely new undertaking, represented at the outset still another instance of Debussy's readiness to re-use titles already identified with his music. Though he had published two sets of songs called *Fêtes galantes*—the first ascribed to 1892, the second to 1904—and only recently had considered a stagework to be so styled, he planned to give these two-piano pieces the same name, in further obeisance to Verlaine. He changed, however, to *Caprices en blanc et noir*, then simplified the designation by retaining only the four words by which the published caprices are known. They were not without an echo of the war, the second, which Debussy styled *Ballade de Villon contre les ennemis de la France*, having a tiny carillon effect which he referred to as "a pre-Marseillaise." To his publisher he wrote that he considered this permissible in a time when forests and pavements vibrated to the universal song. He called attention to his use of "Luther's choral" and how the hymn "catches it for having strayed into a French caprice"; how, finally, after some troublesome revision of certain bars, he has succeeded in "cleansing the atmosphere" of "the poisonous fumes" spread for a moment by the choral; "or rather by what it represents," since "after all, it is a fine thing." This caprice is dedicated to the fallen lieutenant Jacques Charlot; the others to Koussevitsky and Stravinsky.

Meanwhile, he was at work on the two books of *Études*, six to the book, which were also to be credited to 1915. Though the twenty-four *Préludes* of 1910–13 were left without dedication, Debussy inscribed the *Études* to the memory of Chopin.[3] These studies were conceived either as explorations in sonorities or as likely to propound unaccustomed problems for the fingers. Not one, he observed, with a return of his old irony, was designed for the delight of pianists, but rather to torment them as they deserve. They will frighten the fingers, he remarked with some show of glee; when he, himself, undertook them, he had to catch his breath, he said, "as after climbing a mountain."

In writing of the *Études* to Durand, Debussy said: "You break

[3] At first he considered a joint dedication to Couperin and Chopin.

your left hand in them, in gymnastics almost Swedish. They all conceal a rigorous technique beneath flowers of harmony where flies are not caught with vinegar!" About the one in sixths he observes: "The continual use of sixths reminds me of pretentious young ladies sitting in a drawing room doing slovenly work on tapestry, while they envy the scandalous laughter of the mad ninths!" Of the one in fourths: "You will find something not heard before, although your ears are trained to many 'curiosities.'" Concerning his general purpose in writing them he says: "You will agree with me that there is no need of making technique any sadder than it is, that it may seem more serious; and that a little charm has never spoiled anything. Chopin proved that, and makes this desire of mine very rash, I realize. And I am not dead enough yet not to know the comparisons that my contemporaries, confrères, and others, will not fail to make, to my disadvantage." The *Études* were completed in August, at Pourville, near Dieppe, where Debussy remained for three months, striving to clarify his mind as to what he should do, while seeking opportunity and incentive for actual work. It was at this time that he reached a decision that has been the cause of endless speculation among those who have tried to explain on other grounds than his illness the change that now came over the little music he was still to produce.

The composer who had built his world reputation largely on his independence of all structural as well as harmonic formulas, now became an avowed exponent of pure music and the traditional forms. Of his published compositions only the String Quartet of 1893 could be regarded as in alignment with the six Sonatas for various instruments planned in 1915, only three of which were written. As completed and published, the first is for 'cello and piano; the second for flute, viola (in substitution for the original oboe), and harp; the third for violin and piano. The fourth, as shown by a note on the manuscript of the third, was to have been for oboe, horn, and clavecin. The three completed sonatas are dedicated to his wife, and this was the last time the name of Emma-Claude Debussy was to appear in his published work. The first Sonata, written without apparent struggle in July and August, 1915, was first played by Debussy and Joseph Salmon. The second, begun in September and finished in October, was performed in April of the next year at the Société Musicale Indépendante by Manouvrier, Jarecki, and Jamet. The third gave the composer more trouble, for he was a desperately sick man before he could do more than sketch it out. Writing from Pourville, he had described his Paris study as a "workshop of nothing." But because of a serious turn for the worse in his health, he was compelled to return to the city. Confronted by the staggering news the physicians had for him, he wrote to his friend Hartmann, the violinist, that he was spiritually ready for the violin-piano Sonata for which Hartmann was waiting, but he did not know when he could get his work under way again.

An operation was decided upon in December, 1915. As he prepared for that distressing event, for it was of a character that might have had fatal consequences, the sick man composed *Le Noël des enfants qui n'ont plus de maison*, conceived as a prayer to Le petit Noël (Santa Claus) on the part of children in the war-devastated sections of Belgium and France. The words of the naïve little poem were Debussy's own. Two versions exist, one for solo voice and one for children's two-part chorus.

Debussy described himself to Hartmann as "a walking corpse." Morphine injections annihilated his will. The operation only temporarily checked the development of what by this time was recognized as an incurable disease. It was cancer of the rectum. Evacuations had to be made through the side. Radium treatments and drugs failed to alleviate materially his pain. He was to grow steadily weaker, but had the courage and the stamina to make several further appearances in public in the little time that was left to him. In July of 1916 he wrote to Durand that he had made up his mind to ignore his tyrannical malady and would work in spite of everything; life was endurable only if he composed a great deal, he said in another letter, even though tapping a hollow brain was not a pleasurable occupation. "If I am doomed to vanish soon, I desire at least to have done my duty." He was very ill at Moulleau-Arcachon, where he went in October to escape the nightmare of wartime Paris. At Cap Féret the musical phrase came to him that was to be "the germ idea," as he described it, of the last movement of the delayed violin-piano Sonata. A week later he returned to Paris, there to make slow progress on the Sonata, the first and second movements of which were finished early in 1917; the third still in an unsettled state. He spoke of trying to realize in it the "simple play of a snake that is biting its own tail," that is, to give sound to an idea that returns upon itself. A fair copy was made of this first version of the conclusion, the so-called "Neapolitan Finale." But Debussy discarded it, dissatisfied, only to return to it after he had begun another. In March, 1917, he felt that he was about ready to play the piano part of his Sonata in public, but the last two measures still troubled him; even in *hora mortis*, as Ernst Decsey has observed, his feeling of responsibility would not slacken; the artist within him demanded that he strike out the measures that in some way seemed to upset the equilibrium of the structure.

Drawing heavily on his slender reserve of vitality, Debussy reappeared as pianist on May 5 at the Salle Gaveau to play the Third Sonata with the violinist, Gaston Poulet. What was a first performance for the new work was a farewell to the public of Paris for the composer. In June he was in the audience that heard a French-Italian concert conducted by Bernardino Molinari, in which was included *La Mer*. In September he came out of his self-immurement at Saint-Jean-de-Luz to play again the piano part of the last Sonata in collaboration with Poulet, consenting reluctantly to repeat the Intermezzo in response to particularly hearty and protracted applause. He was in attendance when the pianist Francis Planté played the toccata from the suite *Pour le piano, Reflets dans l'eau,* and *Mouvement* at the Société Charles Bordes a little later. Back in Paris in October he showed Alfred Bruneau a clutter of sketches, then said, "I cannot compose any more."

In the first stages of his physical collapse, he had experienced the death of his mother.[4] To Durand he wrote: "My poor mother died yesterday afternoon at half past one o'clock. Her struggle was long, although it seems she was without suffering. But does one know what happens in such moments?" In the children's Christmas prayer of that year are the words: "Poor mother died, before she saw all this."

It was in this time that Debussy, whom d'Annunzio dubbed "Claude de France," signed himself "Claude Debussy, musicien français." "Let us get back our freedom and our own forms," he abjured his fellow musicians. "Since we ourselves invented most of them, it is only right that we should preserve them. There are none more beautiful." In his own final Sonatas, the old French forms were what he strove to exemplify; his neo-classicism stemmed not from Italian and German models but from the eighteenth-century compositions of his own countrymen. He championed the light touch of the French as against the ponderosity of the Germans. "Let us be on our guard," he wrote, "against those who accuse us of frivolity." This charge, he averred, always had companioned "the mealy massiveness which has ineffectually concealed its desire to stifle us."[5]

With the libretto to *La Chute de la maison Usher* turned over to the publisher in the autumn of 1917, with Rouché again considering *Saint-Sébastien* as an opera, and with *As You Like It* a

[4] March 25, 1915.
[5] Preface to a series of lectures on French music, written in 1916.

subject of three-cornered negotiations between Debussy, Toulet, and Gémier, Debussy still had thought for one more stage subject, an East Indian music drama which d'Annunzio discussed at length with him, but of which Debussy himself left not so much as a phrase of music, so far as has been disclosed. The Italian poet, himself swept into the vortex of Italy's struggle with Austria and her allies, has told of the eagerness with which he looked forward to meeting Claude again as "the highest reward" for years of ceaseless warfare; but Debussy was to die while the fighting was at its most desperate, seven and a half months before the armistice.

A second operation followed the first, and Debussy, confessing a terrible fatigue, could summon little energy or even inclination for work. "There are mornings," he wrote to Durand,[6] "when the effort of dressing seems like one of the twelve labors of Hercules." In another letter he spoke of his "life of waiting—my waiting room existence, I might call it—for I am a traveler, waiting for a train that will never come now." André Suarès has given us an affecting description of the sick man as he saw him at a charity concert in March, 1917—he was emaciated, his face like wax and the color of ashes. The hand that had been "rounded, soft, episcopal" now "dragged down from his shoulder" and his head "pressed on his whole body." Even more was Suarès struck by his absent-minded, weary expression. He looked at the audience, Suarès said, "with dull eyes under flickering lids; like one who seeks to see without being seen." He seemed confused, as if ashamed of his suffering. It was said that he had permitted his malady to develop through trying to conceal it. "The voluptuous often are more anxious than others to hide their bodies, especially if they are blemished." And Debussy, the artist, had the shyness attendant on his voluptuary desire for perfection.

[6] July 22, 1917.

One more effort at composition was made; Claude de France, the "musicien français," sought to leave behind him, when his hour should come, a patriotic work that would be something more than a preachment in behalf of his country's music. With Louis Laloy, his intimate friend and first biographer, editor of the *Mercure musical*, whilom secretary-general of the *Opéra* and more recently music critic of the *Revue des deux mondes*, he embarked upon a choral work of large proportions, dealing with the martyrdom of Joan of Arc, and to be called *Ode à la France*. Debussy left sketches for solo voice, chorus, and orchestra. Ten years after his death, Laloy accepted the collaboration of Marius-François Gaillard in a reconstruction of the work, based on these sketches, but with orchestration entirely Gaillard's own. A public performance on April 2, 1928, at the new Salle Pleyel called forth much criticism as a gratuitous disservice to Debussy's memory, but had the sanction, it appears, of the composer's heirs.

Gabriel Astruc, his neighbor during the war, has told of how the stricken man suffered from cold because of lack of fuel. "I pointed out his plight to the pretty wife of a coal man. She, in exchange for some sacks of coal, asked for 'a little dedication' on a score of *Pelléas*."

The hand which affixed Debussy's signature on March 17, 1918, to his letter of candidature for the vacant chair in the Académie des Beaux-Arts was that of a man about to die. Through all his last days the war raged on, in its most frightful aspects. Air raids were frequent and such was Debussy's condition that he could not even be carried to the comparative safety of a cellar. The German long-range guns found their mark and, to the bewilderment and horror of France and most of the world, began dropping shells into the heart of Paris. On Good Friday one of these screaming missiles of death, fired from a 'Big Bertha' an unbelievable number of miles distant, fell on the church of Saint-Gervais, killing and maiming the men, women, and children who were worshipers there. The chanteurs of Saint-Gervais had meant as much to Debussy, perhaps, as any musical organization in Paris. Their singing of music from the days of the great masters of liturgical polyphony was a refreshment of spirit that he cherished through many years. But he was never to know of what happened at the church of Saint-Gervais. Four days earlier came, for him, the end.

Debussy died at ten o'clock on the night of Monday, March 25, 1918.[7] In the papers of March 26 there was a bare mention of his passing. For war everything was commandeered, including the space of newspapers greatly reduced in size and published under every conceivable difficulty and strain. Conditions precluded any such solemn obsequies as would have been held in normal times, with eulogies and music. Only a score of persons participated in a funeral held during a lull in the almost incessant cannonading. If no such sorry procession as that which had turned back and left poor Mozart to be buried as a pauper in an unidentified grave, that which followed Debussy's body, traversing the entire breadth of a city that seemed to be holding its breath in expectation of another bombardment, bespoke more the love of a few relatives and close friends, among whom were a few officials, than it did the admiration of his country or his fellow musicians for "Claude de France." First interred at Père Lachaise, the body later was transferred to the cemetery at Passy. There, Chou-Chou was to join him a year later and her mother in 1934. On the black marble vault, along with the composer's name is inscribed: "His wife and daughter are with him."

Of the funeral on Thursday, March 28, the day before the slaughter at the Saint Gervais, Louis Laloy has written:

As in a bad dream, I can see the musicians in their soldiers' uniforms and the coffin near the piano . . . there was no

[7] Not March 26, as stated in various lexicons.

room for flowers. The Minister of Education took his place at the head of the procession. Before me, side by side, Camille Chevillard and Gabriel Pierné, conductors of our two great symphonic societies, walked in silence. . . . The sky was overcast. In the distance was a rumbling . . . a storm or an explosion? . . . in the wide avenues only military trucks . . . people on the pavements pressed ahead hurriedly . . . children in the gutter stared at us . . . shopkeepers . . . glanced at the streamers on the wreaths, saying "Il parait c'était un musicien." There was but one oration.

*   *   *

The world needed a little time to realize that Claude Debussy was dead. Then, in article after article, appeared tributes, all over the world. Ten composers contributed to a *Tombeau de Debussy*, in which were included compositions—one each—from Paul Dukas, Albert Roussel, G. Francesco Malipiero, Eugène Goossens, Béla Bartok, Florent Schmitt, Igor Stravinsky, Maurice Ravel, Manuel de Falla, and Erik Satie.

Memorials in stone were to follow. In June, 1932, there was unveiled at the edge of the Bois de Boulogne on the Boulevard Lannes, and not far from Debussy's last abode, an allegorical monument executed by the brothers Martel, of a complexity of detail that has aroused the most divergent comment. It has been lavishly admired and it has been described as a curiosity, even a monstrosity. Given the form of a portico, the center presents a bas-relief, seven meters high, with a "spiritual interpretation" of Debussy's work; at the right or left appears the figure of an attendant muse. Stylized leafwork frames allegorical pictures; at the top, laurel blooms around the body of Saint-Sébastien. A little lower, trees shroud the castle of Mélisande; below, a vine entwines the faun of Mallarmé and the fugitive nymphs of his languorous dream. There are decorative reminders of the sunken cathedral, the pagoda, the goldfish, the toy box, the sea, the sirens, and the clouds. On the other side of this tapestry in stone, faces of noted friends and celebrated confrères of Debussy are discoverable, playing instruments as if in an orchestra of affectionate acclaim. Seen from behind, with the profile turned away but recognizable from the locks of hair, a suggested Debussy runs his fingers over the keyboard of a piano. About him are the phantom features of André Messager, Ernest Chausson, Gabriel Pierné, Paul Dukas, and twenty others—musicians, painters, poets, virtuosi, critics, singing masters, all partipants in some manner in the life story the monument commemorates. A creature assumed to be Nijinsky leaps above these. Feminine faces—some have guessed Mary Garden, some Ninon Vallin, some Lucienne Bréval—personify song. Higher than the dancer, diaphanous figures of Inspiration and Harmony continue the allegory. The titles of Debussy's works from 1880 to 1917 are cut into the stone, as are the names of fifty French cities and eighty in other lands which responded in some manner to an appeal for participation in this glorification of the departed master. Lightly tinted with rose, and, set off with its four pillars and the entablature, the monument is mirrored in a basin at its foot. It stands against a background of trees and turf, gleaming on a spring or summer day with the green that brought a glint of adoration to Debussy's eye. The central inscription is the signature of the last years:

CLAUDE DEBUSSY, MUSICIEN FRANÇAIS

On July 9, 1933, a second monument was unveiled, this time in the verdant park at Saint-Germain-en-Laye. It takes the form of a nude feminine figure, seated, one knee raised, the head bowed as in reverie, and construed as representative of Debussy's youthful inspiration. At the dedication exercises there was music by Debussy and Rameau. Included were the choral rounds to texts by Charles d'Orléans and fanfares from *Le Martyre de*

Saint-Sébastien. A speaker referred to the martyrdom of Claude of France.

*   *   *

Debussy left no estate, except his author's rights and his manuscripts. His widow had a legacy only of his fame. Her own means, much more slender than the world believed, barely sufficed during the sixteen years in which she survived her husband. She died at 24 Rue Vineuse, having long before given up the house in the Avenue du Bois de Boulogne. Lily Debussy preceded her to the grave by a little more than a year. She was not quite sixty, and nearly half of her life had been lived after Debussy had left her for Mme. Bardac. Certain of the composer's old friends, including Léon Vallas, looked upon her as Debussy's Mélisande, though he was deep in his composition of that work before he met her. In the days of his ramblings from café to café, when it was no uncommon thing for Debussy to remain in a restaurant until six or seven in the morning, she shared his noctambulations. Toulet, the poet, would say at the sight of the pair, "Here comes St. Roch and his dog." After the divorce she all but disappeared for a time. In her possession was the painter's palette charged with colors which Debussy had used in his youth, when he had a transient dream of becoming an artist of the brush. In a newspaper article,[8] Léon Vallas has told a pathetic little story that was not included in his biography of Debussy. In 1927 Vallas gave a series of public lectures on Debussy at the Sorbornne, scattered through a period of four months. Among those who attended was Lily. At every meeting he noticed her, seated inconspicuously high up in the amphitheater, listening to a professor talking about her husband, and about compositions that she had seen in the first sketches that came from his pen. After one of the lectures, in which he had touched

[8] New York *Times,* January 8, 1933.

upon her marriage, she ventured to approach him to tell him that what he had said was true. Thereafter, he wrote, she confided "many a touching intimacy—which I shall never reveal."

The picture of Lily, in the last years of her life, endeavoring to learn something about the genius of the man to whom she was married for five years—years of his most confident strength and most fruitful inspiration—is one to linger in the minds of those who turn the pages of Debussy's story. In its lack of momentous incident, it is the story of Brown or Jones, or of whatsoever name should be substituted to represent the everyday man of the streets and dwellings of Paris. But it has the heartbeat of a life lived to its sorrowful full behind the curtains where were born those visions that were so peculiarly Debussy's own, and which, through his genius, became the common property of mankind.

PART III

THE MUSIC

I

DEBUSSY'S MUSICAL PROCESSES

THE key to everything that Debussy accomplished is in his harmony. All begins and ends with the chord. Though he turned with enthusiasm to oriental music for a freshening of the jaded scale systems of the Western world, he was, of all occidental composers, the one who normally should least interest orientals, with their predilection for melodic nuancing and their abhorrence of harmony. The youthful Debussy had chord obsessions which, in manifesting themselves so early, set him apart from his fellows as one possessed with a revolutionary harmonic sense. He was playing all manner of strange successions before he hit upon the whole-tone scale, which, of course, was by no means new in the music of Europe; and his other adventures in scales were developments out of his chordal explorations. No one knows quite what was disclosed to him in his Russian visits. At the Villa Medici in Italy a leaning toward the old church modes was accentuated, though this never became one of the dominant influences in his music. The seven-note scales of Phrygian and Dorian modes found reflection, respectively, in the String Quartet and the *Suite bergamasque*. There is a phrase at the opening of *Hommage à Rameau* in the Hypoeolian. But neither the plainchant nor medieval organum (the latter finding a tangible echo in *La Cathédrale engloutie*) was at the bottom of Debussy's personal musical idiom, nor was the pentatonic scale, which he was to use in *Pagodes, Voiles, Reflets dans l'eau,* and elsewhere, more often for color than for exotic effect.[1] In *Les sons et les*

---

[1] This scale, of course, is not essentially oriental. It is the basis for sundry Western folk songs.

parfums is a passage that could arbitrarily be regarded as based on a twelve-tone scale. That in his scale browsings Debussy should have become particularly identified with the so-called "organ-tuner's scale," consisting of six whole tones, may be significant of his chordal bias, in that there are theorists who contend that the whole-tone scale ought to be regarded not as a scale but as a chord. But as Debussy employed also what is known as the whole-tone chord, it may be the part of wisdom to call the scale a scale and let it go at that. Of various examples that may be cited of Debussy's use of this scale, the most completely satisfying one remains the piano prelude, *Voiles*, because, with the exception of six measures, the entire piece is constructed on a whole-tone basis. Those six measures are pentatonic. There is a popular notion that Debussy used the whole-tone scale much more prodigally than he did. *Voiles* is an exceptional instance. There are various others in which this scale has only an incidental part to play. If he does not happen on the right compositions, a concert patron may hear entire programs of Debussy and not discover the scale at all. Its limitations are such that Debussy would have been the most monotonous of composers if he had gone about restricting his utterance to this six-tone medium. But its employment in works like *L'Après-midi d'un faune* for orchestra and *Soirée dans Grenade* for piano is like a cooling draught, so freshening is the effect on the surrounding measures. Debussy resorted to chromaticism in the melodic line sparingly as compared to Wagner and certain others of the day but some of his most beautiful effects are achieved chromatically.

Debussy's chord successions may be said to be of first importance primarily because they tend to invalidate rather than to confirm tonalities, irrespective of scales, modes, and other fixities of musical procedure. He was not an atonalist in the postwar sense, but he opened the door for those who were to come. The fundamental of his harmonic revolt was a desire to escape from the accepted use of chord combinations within a given key. A composition with a key signature will retain a determinative key center; yet in every measure may be introduced chords that are foreign to the scale of that key, as in *Les sons et les parfums*. Unrelated triads will be found moving in succession in various compositions. They do not destroy the key but they do tend to produce a vagueness of tonality, a sense of wavering between keys, of hesitation as between major and minor, characteristic of Debussyan harmony.

In Debussy's idiom dissonance came to be regarded as an end in itself and not an episode on the road to a consonance. He used dissonant chords freely, with no thought of resolving them according to the older canons of musical theory. He treated chords as independent units which could be arranged in successions contrary to accepted rules and in arriving at concatenations of his own he created what in the end were to be looked upon as Debussy formulas. Consecutive perfect fifths between two parts, long frowned upon, appealed to him from his student days. Nor could he understand the objections of classicists to various other chord successions, fourths, major thirds, seconds, sevenths, ninths. As examples of Debussy's use of consecutive fifths may be cited passages in *Poissons d'or* and the prelude to *La Demoiselle élue;* fourths, *Jardins sous la pluie*, and *La Cathédrale engloutie;* major thirds, *La Danse de Puck*, the String Quartet; seconds, *Et la lune descend;* sevenths, *Sarabande, La Cathédrale engloutie, Soirée dans Grenade;* ninths, *Nuages*. Debussy made liberal use of what have been styled "gliding chords," in which there is an exact repetition of a given chord formation on different fundamental tones, as in certain measures of *Jardins sous la pluie, Minstrels*, and *Reflets dans l'eau*. Also to be encountered frequently are "escaped chords," in which the bass is comparable to the traditional pedal point, except that it is often a chord instead of one or two notes, and the effect is as though the dissonant chord, or group of chords, had escaped from the established harmony or tonality suggested by the sustained chord.[2] Examples may be found in the opening of *La Cathédrale engloutie* and the close of *Reflets dans l'eau*. A device which Debussy used to enhance the richness of chords and which became a recognized Debussyism was the "added second," in reality a grace note or appogiatura, though written as part of the chord. Examples may be found on the last page of *Mouvement*, *Jimbo's Lullaby*, and the *Golliwog's Cakewalk*. *La Cathédrale engloutie*, which opens with "escaped" chords, is of particular interest for other chord formations which, without thirds, give rise to intervals of fourths, fifths, and octaves, resulting in a return to currency of medieval organum. As Debussy opens the door to atonality, he stands momentarily on the threshhold of polytonality in *La Puerto del Vino* and *Brouillards*. *Jeux*, the tennis ballet, goes further, even raising a question as to whether Debussy's contact with Stravinsky (*Jeux* is contemporaneous with *Le Sacre du printemps*) had not led to deliberate experimentation in this direction. Pedal points, in the bass or elsewhere, and pedal chords were used with characteristic effect by Debussy, as in *La Danse de Puck*. It will be recalled that "L'Affaire Ravel"—the tempest in a teapot over resemblances between Debussy's *Soirée dans Grenade* and Ravel's earlier *Habanera*—had to do partly with the use of a corresponding pedal device in both compositions. Debussy also was fond of using a recurring figure with the effect of a pedal, against a succession of changing harmonies. An example of a "decorated" pedal is found in *La Cathédrale engloutie*. In the prelude of *Jeux*, where Debussy gives lightness to harmonic departures that are harsh in Stravinsky's *Sacre*, there is an interesting use of a pedal point in the strings, against which move a succession of

[2] See Marion Bauer's *Twentieth Century Music*.

descending chords composed of all the notes in the whole-tone scale. (It is in his use of superimposed major and minor seconds, thereafter, that Debussy most clearly heralds the dawn of polytonality.) Of all these adventurings, Debussy could say, as he did in a letter to Laloy, that he was only endeavoring "to rid music of the legacy of clumsy, falsely interpreted traditions, under whose weight the art seemed likely to succumb."

Debussy's time signatures bespeak his quest of rhythmic freedom and although his manuscripts present no such barrage of changes as was rained down on the pages of Stravinsky, there are elaborate alternations of bar values (as in *L'Après-midi d'un faune* and the third movement of the String Quartet) and a plenitude of conflicting rhythms. Long-breathed melody and spacious forms were not for Debussy. He sought, instead, evanescent curves and irregular patterns, mixed, in his songs, with a chantlike presentation of the words. Counterpoint for its own sake did not greatly interest him, as was natural in one who thought of music primarily as an expressive or suggestive medium, rather than architectually or in a decorative sense. Yet he loved the arabesque, not as an ornament, but as an integral part of the melodic or chordal line. He detested variations and obvious devices of formal development. To structure he applied the dictum of art concealing art. For him the framework should not be visible. On occasion, as in the String Quartet, he applied the principle of the cyclic form, but he cannot be regarded as an exponent of it. For the most part his compositions are confined in the ambient of a picture. It is the picture that ordains the form. Hence *La Mer*, instead of being a symphony or a symphonic poem, is three symphonic "sketches"; hence the *Images* and the *Estampes*, and the *Nocturnes* that are nearer to Whistler's concept than to Chopin's. Other individual characteristics duly considered, the student of Debussy is brought back to his harmony as the factor having hegemony over all.

The chord and the chord succession are the identification on his musical passport; and particularly those blocklike processions that eventually came to be almost as much of a formula for him as the stuffy traditional old sequences had been for the academicians against whom he was from boyhood in revolt.

II

THE PIANO MUSIC

As a practical musician, Debussy was primarily a pianist. He had no mastery over any other instrument. He was not a singer. He was an indifferent conductor. In composing for the piano, he composed for the one medium of expression that was responsive to his personal touch, the one he could approach in a companionate way and not vicariously through the intervention of others. He added to, and in some details altered in their application, the resources of piano technique, something that can scarcely be said of his relation to the voice, the violin, the 'cello, the various instruments of the orchestra, or, in a collective sense, the orchestra itself. In the music he gave them to perform, all were called upon to share the innovations of his creative art, but only the piano found these of importance to its individual manner of utterance. For this there were two reasons. First, the piano, being an instrument of harmony and of tonal blending rather than one of simple melodic statement, was the natural medium for experimentation in a personal art built upon harmony and tone blending. Second, the piano, in spite of all that had been accomplished for it by several generations of exploiting virtuosi, was still capable of gradations of color and nuances of accentuation that had been ignored—or perhaps more correctly, used only sparingly—by the high-riding masters of its sonorities.

Only with the piano was it possible to realize, unaided, such a shifting of tonalities as to suggest the absence of tonality, since this was something of chord successions. If Debussy had been an organist or a harpist he would scarcely have dealt with chords as he did; if a violinist, he might never have been a composer at all. As a pianist, his blendings had in them little of the symphonic essence of orchestral music, but the compliment paid him —for it can scarcely be regarded as an accusation—when it was said that he was endeavoring to make the piano *not* the piano, was one that had been bestowed similarly upon Chopin and Liszt before him. Today these three may be regarded as among the most idiomatic of all composers who wrote for the instrument, and at least partly because they did not accept the limitations and the essential characteristics of piano playing as they found it. In Debussy's piano music are to be noted all of the harmonic, rhythmic, and melodic devices peculiar to him, touched upon in the more general comments of the preceding section. The essential to note here is that he made them thoroughly pianistic. As a craftsman and innovator the essential Debussy can be studied in his keyboard compositions perhaps better than anywhere else. A little knowledge of his own playing, as passed on by those who heard and saw him at the piano, in public or private, may be of value not only for the light shed on matters of style and interpretation, but for the insight that may be gained into the personality behind, and *in*, the compositions themselves. Debussy, as has been said, was the supreme monarch of the impalpable. At the same time there was in the sensation of his music something essentially tactile. Both considerations lead to thought of piano touch. His was a new sort of touch. Let us recall the statement in which he was likened to the cat which rubs itself against the hand that strokes it, and see Debussy at the piano "caressing his own soul." Only rarely could he have thought of the piano as a percussive instrument; quite as rarely as a medium for organlike accumulations of sonorities. It was not primarily for him the instrument of cantilena that it was for Chopin. Neither could he look on it as the magnified cimbalom of the Liszt rhapsodies. He was closer to Schumann, sharing his affection for extra-musical titles; but Debussy was the more objective, the more painterlike, the more concerned with sights and sounds, the less concentrated on the nature and destiny of man. As the one was representative of nineteenth-century Romanticism at its most typical, the other bespoke those more specialized art objectives which took on their separate colorings, with an increased emphasis on art for art's sake, when the prism of romanticism was split into separate and successive lights.

Debussy, the pianist, appeared in public chiefly in the role of interpreter of his own music, hence as the protagonist of his own harmonic dispensation. He also played Chopin, whom he regarded as a kindred spirit. For the sake of the fee he could even bring himself to play Wagner—excerpts from the *Ring* as illustrations for lectures. But he avoided the piano music of the German masters, Beethoven particularly, Brahms totally. His studies with Mme. Mauté de Fleurville, a pupil of Chopin, had given him what he felt was a special insight into the piano idiom of that master. When he took up the chore of editing Chopin's works for a new French edition, he recalled what she had said of Chopin's advice to his pupils about the pedal. They should practice without it and not hold it down except in very rare cases. But Debussy's own music played with an absolute minimum of pedal would be unthinkable. At the Conservatoire Debussy fared best in his examinations when he depended upon Chopin; worst when he undertook Beethoven. The tree grew as the twig was only too willing to be bent. The boy, it appears, had a particularly agile left hand but he did not acquire for it or its partner any such perfection of technique as was acquired by some of his fellow students. The truth, as was evident to his teachers, was that he did not relish this particular kind of hard work. His heart was elsewhere. As was said at the time, he was more interested in music than in the piano.

Later, in the time when he occasionally appeared at the concerts of the Société Nationale (where on February 1, 1896, he took part in the first performance of Lekeu's *Quatuor inachevé*), he was frank to say to Chausson that he played with his "usual contempt for principles." Meanwhile he was formulating principles of his own. To quote Vallas, he was "an original virtuoso, remarkable for the delicacy and mellowness of his touch. He made one forget that the piano has hammers—an effect which he used to request his interpreters to aim at—and he achieved particularly characteristic effects of timbres by the combined use of both pedals."

Though Debussy in his youth was described as having strong hands, and although he referred to his *L'Île joyeuse* as embracing every possible manner of treating the piano, "combining strength and grace," his own playing ran to grace much more than it did to strength. After one of his appearances late in his career a reviewer said that he had maintained an almost continuous pianissimo. His tone was described as "dim" and "veiled" and "at times almost inaudible." Throughout, the coloring was subdued, and if the program was not without interest neither was it lacking in monotony. This was the perhaps extreme view of a writer who, in apparent relish, went on to say that an elegant audience enjoyed its nap and woke up to applaud.

At about the same time another reviewer, while confessing that there was something monotonous as well as fluid and insinuating in Debussy's playing—monotonous particularly as to tone—was free to state that he preferred Debussy's playing to that of any other. All questions of technical dexterity were forgotten, he said. Such was the performer's "restraint and discretion," that the "naked soul" of the music was placed before the audience and the interpreter was lost sight of; the work seemed to make its effect direct, not through the interpretation of an intermediary. Like Vallas, Louis Laloy has written of tones that seemed to be produced without the impact of hammers; there appeared to be no vibration of strings. He described the delicate sonorities invoked by Debussy as rising up "into a transparent atmosphere, where they unite without merging and dissolve in iridescent mists."

Elsewhere, Laloy has made known some of Debussy's own injunctions for the performance of his music. The player should avoid all romantic affectation. There should be no effort to particularize or emphasize the melody. Such slight prominence as it should have is provided for it in the music as written and should be left to take care of itself. Likewise there should be no stressing of the chords which form the harmonic framework of the thematic substance. Instead, the player should aim at a blending of patterns so as to produce "a sonorous halo." Where notes are surmounted by a small stroke, these are not to be detached, since what the composer desires is a transparent tone, achievable through a bold but not harsh attack, followed by a release of the keys and a prolongation of the sound by means of the pedal. Anything that disturbs the tonal unity of a work not only is useless but may be fatal to the Debussy style; hence the peril of romanticizing and of particularizing technical details. Yet it must be remembered that Debussy's music does not "develop" in the traditional sense. Each melodic fragment, each chord, has its own expressiveness in the unified succession of sonorities. There is little of building from measure to measure.

A Debussy specialist among pianists of the day, Maurice Dumesnil, quotes the following as one of Debussy's chief instructions: [1] "Play with more sensitiveness in the fingertips. Play chords as if the keys were being attracted to your fingertips and rose to your hand as to a magnet."

Comments Dumesnil: "The little cushions at the fingertips should be extremely sensitive and through their 'feel' you should

[1] In *How to Play and Teach Debussy*, 1932; published with the endorsement of the composer's widow.

almost be able to foretell the quality of tone which is going to come out." Elsewhere it has been said that the fingertips should yield a sensation as if playing through a veil. There should be no percussiveness in the attack and no "edges" of tone in characteristic pieces. For particular pianissimo effects, Dumesnil illustrates what he styles the "indirect attack," a slanting, oblique, caressing attack, with the finger stretched out so as to come *progressively* in contact with the key, the impact being that of the elastic little cushion of flesh which is under the fingertip, whereas in the direct attack the tone is produced by the extreme tip of the finger. This indirect attack softens the tone. Another pianist uses the words "touching off" to describe the desired effect, achieved by a caressing approach that, instead of seeming to strike downward, converts the key into an imaginary springboard. In this way are produced "floating" or bell-like effects of a kind repeatedly demanded by Debussy.

The terms "half-pedal" and "overlapping pedal" are frequently used for the sort of tone modeling that is characteristic of good Debussy playing. The former is a matter of using the damper pedal as a tone modifier by means of which much of the tone is sustained without excess of dissonance. After a chord has been struck with the damper pedal on, it is modified by lifting the foot only a fraction of an inch and immediately depressing the pedal again. The contact of the dampers with the strings is not sufficient to cut off the vibration completely. The device is one for the achievement of the sort of delicate coloring in which Debussy's piano music abounds. In chord successions the player often must slide the hand from chord to chord and "woo" the tone, so to speak; a thickly padded "sinking through" of the weight of the hand.

Ably abetted by other factors, the harmony is the greatest single factor in the achievement of Debussy's new musical concept. The chord, not running counterpoint, is Debussy's reliance in the development of his harmonic individuality. In his quest of new sonorities he gives the greatest possible measure of extension to his chords, often repeating notes of the chord several times at the distance of the octave, often arpeggiating them. The Debussy arpeggio is distinctive, in that it is essentially light and luminous, with an aerial suggestion, far removed from the ponderous, massive, regimented arpeggios of much German music or the brilliantly aggressive and rather noisy ones of Liszt. Finesse invariably takes precedence over muscularity. There is little or nothing that is genuinely heroic in Debussy's piano music; even in the *Berceuse héroïque*, composed in honor of King Albert of the Belgians during the war, he shows his great dread of overemphasis, or, as he described it in this instance, of "blatancy." For Debussy the piano is a confidant, not a herald. It insinuates much; it never proclaims. There are times when it characterizes, even caricatures. But it does not dramatize, in the Lisztian sense. Perhaps *La Cathédrale engloutie* is closest to drama. But it is the drama of a painting like von Böcklin's *Isle of the Dead*, not a drama of events like *Mazeppa*, or a drama of the spirit like the B Minor Sonata.

As the French, particularly, have regarded it, the technique which Debussy developed heightened the sensuous pleasure to be derived from piano playing and restored to it a lyrical quality that was being sacrificed to the austerities of the school of César Franck—austerities that a later age may not be inclined to regard as quite so austere. With Debussy, small details of rhythm and accent render picturesque and evocative the curl of phrase. Fluidity of line and transparency of background are achieved with a new refinement of utterance. Often the effect is of harmonies that dissolve in the moment of their emergence. Tone blends that are like the combinations of chamber music, but which remain essentially pianistic, are achieved in place of carefully articulated counterpoint or the enunciation of an accompanied melody. Everything partakes of the fantasia, even in the short, undeveloped forms which are most common with Debussy. The piano is like an artist's palette, but employed for sketches and not completed landscapes. Debussy's piano lyricism has the momentary lilt of a line quoted from Baudelaire or Verlaine, but rarely that of sustained song. At its most tangible, this art is often most fugitive. As the symbolist poets can be regarded as nearest kin of Debussy, the composer of songs, so the impressionist painters are the blood relatives of the Debussy of the piano *Images* and twenty-four *Préludes*. A little earlier in time, the symbolists most strongly influenced Debussy in his first period—the period in which he composed most of the vocal music. Relatively secondary was the piano music of this first period—extending from about 1880 to 1902. It is small in quantity and rather indeterminate in quality. Not until he was forty was Debussy to become an important composer of music for the piano. To his second period—1902 to about 1910—belong his really memorable works for the instrument.

Much, of course, of what was most characteristic of his piano writing at its peak had previously been worked out and applied in the accompaniments of his songs. His new concepts of sonority, his skillful adjustments of dynamics, his subtle employment of the pedal, his ambiguous treatment of tonalities, his blocklike chord formulas, his quest of unobtrusive dissonance, including the use of the faintly clashing overtones of the lower register, all had figured characteristically in the songs, making of them, in many instances, as interesting examples of the piano idiom of Debussy as are the piano works themselves.

THE PUBLISHED WORKS FOR PIANO

Danse bohémienne. Attributed to 1880, when Debussy was eighteen.
This is the earliest published work for piano from his pen. Tchaikovsky, to whom it was submitted by Mme. von Meck, found

it bungled in form and lacking in unity. As the effort of a youth and an amateur its interest is primarily biographical.

Deux arabesques. Among the earliest works for the piano, dated 1888. This is still music of student character, concise, clear, neatly written, if of no striking quality aside from the impression it yields of an intuitive style. The second of the two is the more straightforward and completely traditional, suggesting the Schumann of the lighter moods in the earlier Fantasy pieces. The first slightly adumbrates the effects eventually developed in a more atmospheric style.

Rêverie. Sold by Debussy in 1890, and ordinarily credited to that year, this work may be older. Its publication after a delay of fifteen years led to a protest from the composer, who described it as written in a great hurry and not only unimportant but bad. Save for a few unusual harmonies, it is placidly orthodox.

Ballade. (Also known as *Ballade slave*.) One of several early compositions on which Debussy realized a little money in 1890 and which seem to point back to his visits to Russia with Mme. von Meck. The thematic material has a Slavic implication and the treatment vaguely suggests Borodin. Certain arpeggio figures recur in the later toccata of the *Pour le piano* suite.

Danse. (Originally called *Tarantelle styrienne*.) Another of the early pieces sold in 1890. The influence is Russian and the feeling tentatively orchestral. The modulations are somewhat daring for their time, the rhythms were unusual in French music, chords of the seventh and ninth are utilized. Ravel orchestrated it.

Valse romantique. Also sold in 1890. An early work of a drawing-room character, with a touch of strangeness in the harmony, due to seventh and ninth chords.

Nocturne. (Also styled *Interlude*.) Debussy received one hundred francs for the manuscript in 1892. In material and style it is a composite work suggesting various French and Russian composers.

SUITE BERGAMASQUE. 1890-1905, consisting of *Prélude, Menuet, Clair de lune, Passepied*. Originally the suite was to have been otherwise constituted, with *Prélude* followed by *Menuet*, *Promenade sentimentale*, and *Pavane*, and at one time it was announced to include *Masque* and *L'île joyeuse*, published separately in 1904. The suite is Debussy's earliest effort to recapture the delicacy and elegance of music of the days of the clavecin. The use of seconds and of unexpected key juxtapositions contributes to a sense of harmonic freshness. This is plainly the music of a stylist, if one as yet unable to free himself of the melodic ideas of others. *Menuet* has a distinctive coloring, as has *Passepied*.

Clair de lune (not to be confused with the song of that title in *Fêtes galantes*) is more than beautifully pellucid writing; it has an emotional feeling as Debussyesque as its title. It is very essential that it be played with a luscious tone and that the tone be kept floating, so to speak, with the overlapping or legato pedal. Of *Clair de lune* Guido Gatti has written: "What an airy flowering of arpeggios ascends the keyboard, to leap up again like a fountain jet which scatters its water on the air, then relapses into calm again in solid tonic and dominant undulations, on which the theme spreads out, ample, sonorous, expressive."

Mazurka. Though ascribed to 1891, this composition has earmarks of Debussy's Conservatoire days and of his Russian sojourns. In the harmonic writing is a feeling of modal uncertainty, suggesting the innovator to come, though Chopin and Borodin were at the young composer's elbow.

POUR LE PIANO. 1896–1901. The suite includes *Prélude, Sarabande, Toccata,* titles that have nothing to convey; although when *Sarabande* originally appeared in somewhat different form in a magazine (*Grand Journal de Lundi*) there was a reference to the movement as being one of "slow serious elegance, rather like an old picture, or a memory of the Louvre," printed as an indication of expression.

Prélude has a rapid martellato theme, encircled by reiterated figures or reinforced by brilliant, overlaid chords. To be noted are successions of augmented triads and an appearance of the whole-tone scale. At the close is a harplike cadenza, light, aerial, unexpected.

Sarabande uses sevenths and ninths in what was a daring succession for the time, though the effect for modern ears is both grave and slightly archaic. The melody is one of Debussy's most serene. Because of the effect produced by its reproduction of a chord on different degrees of the scale it is one of the works that have come to be styled "impressionistic." Analogies have been found to Satie's once much-discussed *Sarabande*.

Toccata is a highly colored work, with decorative arpeggios and an adventurous exploration of sonorities. The persistence of rhythms and the return of the same patterns, but with altered harmonies, gives to these pieces a distinctive personality, while seeming to stem from Bach, Scarlatti, and the French clavecinists.

ESTAMPES. 1903. The component compositions are *Pagodes, Soirée dans Grenade, Jardins sous la pluie*. Among the most diversely colored of Debussy's piano works, and, in a sense, among the most descriptive, they also are among the most highly organized.

Pagodes employs systematically the five-note scale assumed to have been brought to Debussy's attention by Javanese and Cambodian musicians at the Paris exposition in 1889. Amid bell-like effects, the principal theme is reiterated with an oriental sense of fixity but in different octaves and in altered rhythms. The ending is strikingly dissonant. The slender basic design is decorated with successions of fourths and of seconds above held notes in a syncopated accompaniment, trancelike in effect. In the music of its time, here was a new type of exoticism.

Soirée dans Grenade has been described by Spain's foremost living composer, Manuel de Falla, as "characteristically Spanish in every detail." The tempest in a teapot over its resemblances to Ravel's *Habanera* is referred to elsewhere in the text of this volume. There is something kaleidoscopic in its patterns and fragmentary use of themes. In spirit it is the soul of nonchalance, with its sinuous Habanera rhythm and

the curiously drooping effect of chords which turn lan-
guidly about a persistent pedal point on C sharp. There are
momentary effects near the close as of strumming on a mandolin, while the rhythm of the habanera faintly persists; a
whispering as of a summer wind and a final magical glint of
night and stars. This was the first of Debussy's Spanish essays, re-distillations of the spirit and atmosphere of a country he knew only in fantasy. Said Falla: "This music . . .
conjures up the effect of images mirrored by moonlight
upon the limpid waters of the large albercas adjoining the
Alhambra."

Jardins sous la pluie. Two French songs, the ronde, *Nous n'irions
plus au bois* and the lullaby, *Do do, l'enfant do*, are adroitly
utilized by Debussy in this popular work. They are heard
through the splash of arpeggio figures, as the rain patters
down in semiquavers. Modulations change momentarily the
look of the sky. The lawn is drenched, the wind rises, the
sun comes through the mist, away goes the cloud, the grass
seems jewelled in the sunlight. It is for the listener, of
course, to say whether this is what the music conveys to him,
and whether through it all runs a hint of regret for vanished
happiness, as expressed in the plaintive character of the children's songs; or whether here is only a lively exercise for the
fingers, fashioned in what by this time had become definitely
a Debussy style. In performance this work requires a kind of
liquid crispness of touch and in the main part less of the impressionistic "half-pedaling" than *Soirée dans Grenade*.

D'un Cahier d'esquisses. 1903. A lesser work, of facile character but
not often played; taken from one of the notebooks filled with
sketches. It was published in Belgium but had appeared earlier in
an album brought out by the *Paris Illustré*. Ravel played it in a
Paris concert in 1910.

Masques. 1904. One of the longer of Debussy's separate piano pieces,
it was intended originally for the *Suite bergamasque*. There
are passages that recall *Danse* of 1890, and others that have
parallels in the accompaniments of the early Verlaine settings.
The atmosphere of Italian comedy, wherein are encountered
Scaramouche and his companions, is conveyed with a success

that caused a Paris reviewer to write that he was attracted to this music as to "some forbidden pleasure, some vicious habit." He added that he was afraid of growing to like it!

L'île joyeuse. 1904. Also originally announced for the *Suite bergamasque*, this is one of the more carefree and most sensual of Debussy's compositions, as well as one of the more ambitious. A musical representation of Watteau's *Embarquement pour Cythère*, it contrives not only to be suggestive of its subject but to serve the virtuoso purposes which Debussy the pianist sometimes urged upon Debussy the composer. There is a suggestion of orchestral timbres, the play of rhythm is fascinating, and in its gayety and animation the music has a distinctly Debussyan sheen. "Heavens, how difficult to play!" Debussy wrote to the publisher. An orchestral transcription was made in 1917, by Molinari.

IMAGES, first series. 1905. Embracing *Reflets dans l'eau*, *Hommage à Rameau* and *Mouvement (moto perpetuo)*. To the publisher, Debussy wrote: "I think I may say without undue pride, that I believe these three pieces will live and will take their places in piano literature . . . either to the left of Schumann . . . or the right of Chopin. . . ."

> *Reflets dans l'eau.* If there is impressionism in music—and why should so serviceable a term be rejected?—this is one of the most perfect examples of it. The first floating chords establish a mood that is highly suggestive, if something less than directly pictorial. Luminous chords and skimming arpeggios are used in successions that yield a drowsy, flickering effect, as of inverted images in a pool. The basic theme is a slow, trailing one, mirrored, in the course of its transformation, in what may be described as harmonic reflections. Debussy referred to this music as embodying "the newest discoveries in harmonic chemistry." Included are the whole-tone scale and bits of the pentatonic.

> *Hommage à Rameau,* written while Debussy was revising the score of *Fêtes de Polymnie* (and incidentally holding Rameau up as a model of all that Gluck was not), can be construed as a tribute not only to Rameau but to the French genius. Perhaps only the French can see and feel this music as Debussy did. It is one of the graver and stiffer of Debussy's

piano works. Though it may, as has been said of it, "spring from the depths of the soul of the race," it has not Debussy's customary fluidity of utterance. Neither is there much to suggest (whether or not this was intended) the musical personality of Rameau. In effect the work has suggestions of organ music unusual for the composer. As the extreme of French opinion, André Suarès has said that "with the *Sunken Cathedral*, *Hommage à Rameau* is the most beautiful piece for the piano . . . since the last three sonatas of Beethoven." Instead of stiffness, he sees "grandeur and purity of architecture," "gentle majesty of proportions," "simplicity of effect," and "extreme refinement."

Mouvement, "a moto perpetuo," the motion being represented by a succession of triplets which proceed without interruption, except for a place in the middle of the composition, where a slower theme is introduced. The feeling is that of gayety and exhilaration, but with something of humor, even of irony, in the tossing of a motive in octaves and fifths from one hand to another. Near the close, there is a whole-tone staircase upward to the end of the keyboard.

IMAGES, second series. 1907. Embracing *Cloches à travers les feuilles, Et la lune descend sur le temple qui fut*, and *Poissons d'or*. Written on three staves, these compositions can be described as variations of a very free order and they illustrate the continual quest of Debussy for subtle harmonic blendings. A greater condensation of substance and an increased simplicity are to be found in the second series of *Images*, as compared to the first.

Cloches à travers les feuilles has a faint and magical vibration, sustained by the pedals, as of distant chimes resonating through the boughs of slumbrous trees. The impression is that of a silence scarcely broken by the harmonics that penetrate the murmurous rustle of the leaves.

Et la lune descend sur le temple qui fut. The title was conceived by Louis Laloy after the music was composed. Its archaic, perhaps Chinese suggestion, abides in the music to which it was affixed. Rather rigidly moving blocks of hollow-sounding chords—a formula developed by Debussy to suggest the mystery of things ancient and immobile, as in a world that has been drugged and left behind—give it a strange and disquieting character. The effect depends largely on the use of the pedals. The melody is a simple one, clothed in combinations of seconds and fifths, which seem more a part of it than an accompaniment.

Poissons d'or. According to Vallas, this work was inspired by contemplation of a piece of oriental lacquer (Lockspeiser suggests embroidery) in Debussy's possession. Thus viewed, the music is less a description of actual goldfish swimming in a pool than it is a reflection of Debussy's love of Japanese *objets d'art.* But it has the flash of sunlight on water and the gleam of moving fins, rather than any suggestion of static contemplation of line and color. At the outset is a sound as of ripples. Sevenths and ninths, later seconds varied by thirds, with falling arpeggios leading to an upward rush of scales, then plunging downward again, are interlaced in a rich fantasy that races to a calm and restful conclusion. The popularity of this *Image* may be attributed to its vivacity and partly to its pictorial or literary appeal; but partly also to its enticements for the fingers. It requires a touch of the most intimate order.

CHILDREN'S CORNER. 1906–1908. The included titles: *Doctor Gradus ad Parnassum, Jimbo's Lullaby, Serenade for the Doll, Snow Is Dancing, The Little Shepherd, Golliwog's Cakewalk.* It is not reported that Chou-Chou, as Debussy called his little daughter, had more than ordinary talent for music. She took piano lessons at the age of nine from a woman teacher; earlier she had learned the rudiments of music from her father. When Debussy dedicated this suite to her, she was five years old. "To my dear little Chou-Chou," the inscription reads, "with her father's apologies for what is to follow." Chou-Chou, whose name was Claude-Emma Debussy (her mother's, Emma-Claude) died in 1919, when she was fourteen, during an epidemic of diphtheria, only a year after her father's death. The English titles have been explained as suggesting the games played by a little French girl with an English governess. The suite was orchestrated by André Caplet.

Doctor Gradus ad Parnassum. With the first bars is envisioned a child struggling at the piano with the torments devised by the tyrannical Clementi; there are abrupt halts as distractions intervene and there are suggestions of sulks; then liberty to romp, Clementi out of sight, out of mind. Debussy described this piece to the publisher as "a kind of progressive, hygienic, gymnastic exercise, to be played every morning, fasting; beginning moderato and working up gradually to an animato." It presents a delightful parody of academic solemnities.

Jimbo's Lullaby. Jimbo [2] was a toy elephant, made of felt and properly stuffed; as such, one of the infant Chou-Chou's cherished companions. But Jimbo must sleep, and to get him to do that, he must be crooned to and told stories. Debussy left the words to the imagination of Chou-Chou, Jimbo and those who listen.

Serenade for the Doll. The title is so listed in the index at the beginning of the series, but the heading of the piece itself is *Serenade of the Doll,* when it should read, *Serenade to the Doll,* or perhaps *The Doll's Serenade.* The French translation, as Alfred Cortot has pointed out, gives the exact sense; it is *Sérénade à la poupée* and not *de la poupée.* The doll is the one serenaded, not the serenader; the serenade is a child's caprice, not a toy caricature. With the French title, the piece was published separately in 1906, the year of its composition. Lingering in its melodic curve is something of the older Debussy; the Debussy who could not escape a kinship to Lalo, Gounod, and Massenet. It is to be noted that Debussy directed that the soft pedal be kept down throughout the entire serenade.

Snow Is Dancing. The delicate tracery of this work, interpreted as a picture of a child watching the falling snowflakes and waiting for a return of her playfellow, the shining Sun, is typical of Debussy as an exquisite craftsman and a stylist— if slender of substance, otherwise. The piece is perhaps the most difficult of the set to play, demanding, as it does, the lightest, most feathery touch and very sparing use of the pedal.

The Little Shepherd. A toy vignette, with a touch of the sylvan to companion the Noah's Ark figures—shepherd and sheep.

[2] It is thought Debussy really meant Jumbo.

Golliwog's Cakewalk. Gabriel Astruc has told of the enthusiasm which many of Debussy's circle had for the American cakewalk. In visits to America Astruc had studied the strutting phenomenon in its native habitat and he had shared his increased erudition with his confrères. This was some years before *The Children's Corner* was written. Debussy looked backward when he concerned his muse with the lurching Golliwog. Here is rhythm on a rampage. The tune, itself, is one Debussy is said to have heard played by the Grenadier Guards in London, but doubtless made more brusque and jaunty by his droll, even gawkish treatment of it. There is a sardonic fling at Wagner in an interruptive passage, smacking of the *Tristan* prelude and marked to be played "with great emotion."

Hommage à Haydn. (Or, *sur le nom d'Haydn.*) 1909. This was one of six little pieces contributed to the *Revue S.I.M.* by as many composers, the others being Dukas, Reynaldo Hahn, d'Indy, Ravel, and Widor. Each piece was formed by use of notes taken as the equivalent of the letters of Haydn's name, in the fashion of the Germans, who built all manner of musical structures on B-A-C-H.

La plus que lente. 1910. One of the least consequential of Debussy's piano compositions, possibly intended for the projected but soon abandoned third series of *Images*. The spirit is that of half-parody, half-earnestness.

DOUZE PRÉLUDES. First book, 1910. The titles appear at the end of each of the twelve, or in the index, rather than at the beginning of each *Prélude*. The compositions are given a somewhat improvisatory form and can be regarded as summing up the technical and harmonic devices which Debussy had been developing since the *Danse bohémienne* of 1880. Characteristic of Debussy's middle period, these pieces project the results of much experimentation in the subtleties of pianoforte resonance. In the view of Ernest Newman they are in some ways Debussy's most original work and may well prove to be of the utmost seminal force for the future of music. He finds them singularly devoid of humanism, in spite of the programmatic character of their suffixed designations. Theirs is a new sort of realism, in which there is a certain clairaudient as well as clairvoyant seizure of the most delicate sensations in Nature; but a realism directed inward, instead of outward, illustrative by suggestion rather than frank description, and devoid of palpable imitation or intent of reproduction. It is quite possible, he suggests, that in at least some instances a given prelude was written first and the title devised afterward. Certainly, there is little to link these atmospheric compositions to the fiery, concentrated expressions of emotion, the melancholia, and the personal revelation of the *Préludes* of Chopin. In this instance Debussy's is a much more objective art, with very little of the feverish quality that pervades the music of the romantic, consumptive Pole. These *Préludes* are more like sketches than paintings; occasionally they yield the impression of a praxis in which a formula preëmpts the musical thought.

Danseuses de Delphes. The top of a pillar found in the Louvre, on which are sculptured three bacchantes, is the accredited source of inspiration for the first prelude of Book 1. The music is tranquilly slow of rhythm and pace; in its harmonic appeal is something of mystery and akin to incense. Nadia Boulanger has pointed out that its simple three-part keyscheme, (1) tonic key with inflection at the end toward the dominant, (2) dominant, with allusions to related keys, and (3) tonic, is that of many of the Bach preludes.

Voiles. Debussy is here *un visuel*, as elsewhere he is *un auditif*. In writing of marked economy, with the entire composition built upon the whole-tone scale, save for six measures in the pentatonic, and with runs in slow successions ending in a final aerial staccato, is captured the sensation (not the image) of sailboats at anchor in a sunlit port. There is a fluttering as of sails, the air is mellow with the splendor of a sun about to set. Something tactile characterizes this music; the listener seems to touch rather than see the scene. The harmony is peculiarly evocative, due to the persistent and remarkable use of the whole-tone scale, of which *Voiles* is probably the most striking single illustration. Major thirds play their part in producing a floating effect, as of sailing boats anchored to a fixed pedal point.[3]

[3] Voiles can be translated "veils" as well as "sails." Though the music would suit either title, French authorities seem to be agreed that it is "sails" in this case.

Le Vent dans la plaine. The languor of the preceding *Préludes* gives way to the racing lilt of lively breeze, with here and there a momentary gust of biting wind. But this is no tempest. It ends in thin air, wisplike, on a note marked "laissez vibrer," instead of gravitating to an expected cadence.

Les sons et les parfums tournent dans l'air du soir. Baudelaire's voluptuous epigraph is converted into melancholy, languorous music, sensuous in every detail, if not strictly the poet's "vertiginous waltz." The air is heavy with perfumes and vibrant with sounds that seem to swoon in the dying day. All the senses, with those of touch and smell added to those of sight and hearing, seem to enter into the caress and the gentle intoxication of this fantasy. (Nadia Boulanger finds in it "a bit of Chabrier vulgar lyricism.")

Les Collines d'Anacapri. A snatch of folksong and a hint of cowbells, a carefree popular refrain, with its frank tune passed from bass to treble; a songlike middle section with diatonic harmonies leading on to a badinage of tunes and bells, fragmentarily recalled; then a close marked "lumineux," as if there were blazing sunlight in a tonic chord with added sixth—there is no escaping the impressionism of this *Prélude.* The rhythm of the tarantelle contrasts with that of straightforward Neapolitan melody, but not so heartily as to give a really robust meaning to Debussy's words "avec la liberté d'une chanson populaire."

Des Pas sur la neige. According to Debussy's directions, the rhythm represented by a simple appoggiatura "should have the sonorous value of a melancholy ice-bound landscape." If the tonal picture is one of gray melancholy, it is neither bleak nor desolate; to find human sorrow in it may be to convert the thought of steps or footprints into something more subjective than the music implies. Yet, comments Suarès, "this stumbling rhythm, persistent, like a false step on a treacherous surface, the step of a foot which slips and catches itself, evokes marvelously the gray horizon over a pale expanse of ice. But how much more the crushing silence of space where the heart can be heard beating and almost stops, sick with unhappiness, haunted by melancholy, palpitating with doubts and with regrets. The little breath of wind which holds the snowflake every now and then in its falling, only to toss it aside; the long, interminable road; the nostalgia for the light which is not there and for the warm caress: this solitude, infinite, in a word, the solitude of our soul, wandering along absorbed in itself, a solitude which all the deserts and all of the winters of earth never approach."

Ce qu'a vu le vent de l'Ouest. The vision of a hurricane and of a sea lashed to a fury, but retaining the sensation of a nightmare rather than of terror actually experienced.

La Fille aux cheveux de lin. In his youth Debussy wrote an unpublished song of the same title, inscribing it to Mme. Vasnier, but the piano prelude is assumed to be a remote paraphrase of a *Chanson écossaise* of Leconte de Lisle which bears this title. The idiom is one of simple lyricism and recalls that of the earlier period of the *Clair de lune* of the *Suite bergamasque.* Nadia Boulanger again scents the malign influence of Chabrier, "apparent in the melodic turn of theme and the frequent use of cadential formula."

La Sérénade interrompue. Thrumming guitar effects identify the Spanish scene of this nocturnal fantasy, the rhythm and the color of which inevitably suggest *Ibéria.* Was it, in some degree, a preparatory sketch? A note of mockery prevails, the while the diffident serenader is confronted by the sounds of roystering in competitive claim upon the pleasures of the night. "A master work," says Falla, noting its rhythmic suggestion, its guitar characteristics, and its "quite Andalusian grace" in its use of *copla* ornaments.

La Cathédrale engloutie. The most mystic of the *Préludes,* this favorite work makes audible and all but visual the essence of the old Brêton legend that Lalo adapted and expanded for operatic purposes in his *Le Roi d'Ys.* On occasion, so the tale runs, when the sea is transparent in the clear light of morning, out of the waves rises the cathedral of Ys, its bells tolling, its priests intoning; slowly to return again to the depths where is resumed its enchanted sleep. The melodic content is Gregorian; the harmony recollective of the medieval organum. The effect is orchestral and inevitably transcriptions were undertaken, the first by Henri Büsser with Debussy's

consent. There are three principal musical ideas, one suggestive of plain chant and the organ, as if played by phantom
fingers; another representative of the quiet sea; the third like
the slow swelling of the waves. A bell-like figure and a ponderous pedal point are heard at the climax. As the cathedral
recedes beneath rocking waves there is an echo of the plain
chant and the conclusion is like the opening, but with seconds added to the harmonies. The moving blocks of hollow
chords that Debussy employed to express somber mystery
are utilized to suggest the sunken bells. In its chord successions, the composition represents what was then a new concept of dissonance, a conception in which dissonance was
to be regarded as an end in itself and not a mere episode on
the road to a redemptive consonance.

La Danse de Puck. Debussy realizes here, momentarily (as also
in the two fragments of incidental music for *King Lear*), his
deep-seated desire, otherwise thwarted, to make musical the
delights of Shakespeare. The mocking, mercurial meddler of
A Midsummr Night's Dream flits his scherzando way over
the keyboard, in a way to tempt the orchestral transcriber.[4]
For all its quicksilver lightness, the composition is far removed from the Mendelssohn scherzo. Arpeggiated chords
of the major ninth spice the harmony, and rhythmic dis-
placements add piquance to thematic snatches that are discarded successively until the principal melody is reached.
There is a concluding puff. Puck is gone.

Minstrels. These are not troubadours, serenading under castle
windows. The atmosphere is that of a music hall. American
commentators have assumed that Debussy had in mind a
black-faced pair. There are other assumptions that Debussy,
the circus lover, made minstrels of tumblers, gagsters, and
clowns. Black or pasty white, they are no jauntier than
Debussy's rhythms, as he converts them into oddities for
the fingers. A suggestion of an old-time Broadway song, as
well as a certain shuffling effect, are pointed to as corroboratory of the notion that these droll fellows are of American
antecedents.

[4] Grovlez incorporated the *Danse de Puck* in his *Antre des gnomes,* produced
in 1920.

DOUZE PRÉLUDES. Second Book, 1910–13. The second set, delayed in publication longer than was expected, has been regarded, quite generally, as more uneven in quality than the first group. Some few may have been included primarily to round out the dozen, as would seem to be corroborated by Debussy's reluctance to have the complete series played as a whole. "They are not all good," he confessed. Most foreign critics have agreed with Ernest Newman in according a higher estimate to the first book. Still, as Newman has said of the *Préludes*, in describing them as largely attempts to record infinitely delicate auditory and visual sensations in terms of music, "even their failures are interesting, while their successes are marvellous." Guido Gatti has argued that although the first book is superior as to content, the second represents an advance in perfection of means.

Brouillards. A Whistlerian sketch, with moments of luminosity in a fog of tonalities, with the minor second playing its typically Debussyan part. This is one of the compositions pointed to as foreshadowing the polytonality to come.

Feuilles mortes. Dead leaves flutter to the ground by means of the chord formulas that for Debussy represent over and over again the sense of melancholy in Nature. The key signature indicates C sharp minor. But the opening chords are ninths with no apparent connection with the key.

La Puerta del Vino. The townscape here is said to be that of a picture postcard which Debussy received from Manuel de Falla in Spain, showing the famous gate of the Alhambra which bears the name given to the *Prélude*. Certainly there is dancing; Cortot hears mule drivers beating their palms. In what may be considered a prelibation of the polytonalists of postwar modernity, two opposing keys are kept clashing with one another, with no attempt to merge or reconcile their parallel statements. The *Prélude* differs in melodic design from *Soirée dans Grenade*, Falla points out. In *Soirée* the melody is what might be called syllabic; in *Puerta* it frequently appears embellished by the ornaments known to Spaniards as "cante jondo" and which are characteristic of Andalusian "coplas."

Les Fées sont d'exquises danseuses. A work of gossamer lightness and of a darting sort of virtuosity.

Bruyères. A woodland idyl, less evocative than some of its companions in similar vein, but with the now familiar devices to suggest shade and the glint of sunlight through leaves.

General Lavine—eccentric.[5] The general was made of wood and did duty as a vaudevillian at the Folies Bergère. Even for a puppet he was absurdly stiff and ungainly, with a skip in his walk. After meeting various mishaps he concluded his "act" with a surprising pirouette. Debussy indicated the mechanical rigidity required in characterizing his "eccentric" by means of the keyboard. The "General" is not humanized; his is a puppet grimace and a puppet limp, but something of the ironical attends his gait. Again, there is a suggestion of the American cakewalk.

La Terrasse des audiences au clair de lune. Exemplifying a type of Debussyan harmony in which there is a faint suggestion of a dual tonality, this is one of the more sensuous and scented of the *Préludes*, with something also of the ceremonious in its charm. It breathes a faint hint of the old melody of *Au clair de lune*, evanescently floated in sevenths. The sensibility of Debussy is essentially amorous, and in the moon-drenched scene is more of caress than of painting. A phrase from a letter written by René Puaux which appeared in *Le Temps* supplied the title.

Ondine.[6] Murmurous and reticent, the music has the watery suggestion often found in compositions by Debussy in which there is no such obvious reason for water to be present. In her blurred and shadowy way the nymph of the title is elegant, and graceful, with something of mother-of-pearl about her, but no such iridescent creature as the *Ondine* of the later composition by Ravel.

Hommage à S. Pickwick, Esq., P.P.M.P.C. The portrait has amused French admirers of Dickens more generally, it is fair to say, than it has English and American. Ernest Newman has described it as "laboriously humorous," whereas Alfred Cortot has written that "it is impossible to conceive of a wittier musical expression than this." Whether the use of

[5] Another of the Debussy *Préludes* orchestrated by Groulez for *L'Antre des gnomes.*

[6] Also transcribed for orchestra by Grovlez.

God Save the King is, or is not, convincingly comic, may remain a question of national outlook. So, also, the question as to whether there is blood in the veins of this Pickwick or whether he is "the caricature of a cartoon and the cartoon of a caricature," as was once written of him. Arresting is the bit of a whistle he seems to sound before withdrawing.

Canope. Its funereal lyricism has a slumbrous character and its melancholy is that of an impersonal sort of reverie, as of contemplation of antique cinerary urns, together with an abiding tenderness for what is too long gone to pierce the heart.

Les Tierces alternées. Debussy here shows something of his affinity with the old clavecinists whom he was to espouse in his literary work. The interest is purely technical.

Feux d'artifice. Impressionism (for surely here is more that is in alignment with the impressionist painters than with the literary symbolists) goes hand in hand with virtuosity in this, the most superficially brilliant of the *Préludes.* The fireworks of this glittering showpiece are not to be mistaken for any other sort of festivity. There is a fleeting reference to the *Marseillaise* to suggest a Bastille Day celebration. Those who so desire can construe many of the pyrotechnical effects literally, with red fire, pinwheels, rockets, roman candles, and multicolored lights to enliven their interpretation of the scene. The music does not materially suffer thereby. In all that pertains to pianistic display, Debussy is nearer to Liszt in *Feux d'artifice* than in any other composition.

Berceuse héroïque pour rendre hommage à S.M. le Roi Albert 1er de Belgique et à ses soldats. 1914. In its piano form the *Berceuse* was written for King Albert's book in November, 1914, and a month later scored for orchestra. In a letter written in October of that year, Debussy spoke of a desire to compose a *Marche héroïque* but dreaded the blatancy inevitable in that type of composition. The Belgian National Anthem, the *Brabançonne,* supplies the heroic or patriotic content of the work (in the orchestral version, first given out by bassoons, horn, and clarinets, then by viola and 'cellos) which, intentionally or otherwise, is less conspicuous than its sense of war weariness and nostalgia.

DOUZE ÉTUDES. 1915.

BOOK I	BOOK II
Pour les cinq doigts	*Pour les degrés chromatiques*
Pour les tierces	*Pour les agréments*
Pour les quartes	*Pour les notes répétées*
Pour les sixtes	*Pour les sonorités opposées*
Pour les octaves	*Pour les arpèges*
Pour les huit doigts	*Pour les accords*

These two books, of six studies each, are dedicated to Chopin, though Debussy at first intended that the inscription should also include Couperin. The composer described them to Caplet as containing "a thousand ways of treating pianists according to their deserts." These are exercises in technique, each *Étude* dealing with some particular difficulty, the first book beginning with a five-finger exercise, followed by exercises in thirds, fourths, sixths, and octaves and ending with an eight-finger exercise. In the second book are exercises dealing with chromatic intervals, grace notes, reiterated notes, contrasted sonorities, arpeggios and chords. Technical difficulties beset the player on every page. Debussy, with the knowledge that he had altered piano style, and that his compositions called up special problems of touch and fingering, fully expected these studies to occupy a special position, observing meanwhile that "a touch of charm has never spoiled anything—Chopin proved that." To this he added, with characteristic irony, "I am not sufficiently dead to be safe from comparisons." Fingering was omitted, it being Debussy's conviction that the same fingering could not suit differently shaped hands. As music, the studies assemble under one cover all Debussy's characteristic processes, harmonic, rhythmic, pianistic. Clearly, he chooses artifices peculiar to his own manner of expression. There are passages of formalistic obstinacy, when the effect is more rigid than fluid; but the studies are imaginative, not merely mechanical. They have their smiles, as in the opening of the five-finger study, marked "d'après Monsieur Czerny"; and their mead of lyricism, as witness the lilt of the "agréments," a barcarolle mirroring a balmy, meridional sea.

The so-called Czerny study has been described as pitting Debussy against the famous pedagogue in "a personal affair." *Pours les tierces alternées* is not composed of thirds only. These in most cases are preceded by sixths and fourths. The fourth of the set is recollective of Chopin. The fifth, developed in the movement of a valse caprice, has a graceful bell design. The final *Étude* of the first book, that for eight fingers, excludes the thumb as in Bach's time. In the second book Guido Gatti spies nymphs and fauns dancing the measures of No. 8, that for grace notes. And in No. 10, *Pour les sonorités opposées*, he finds presented "in alternatives of light and shade the contrast between lofty, irradiant peaks and deep, shadowed abysses, opposites of sonority heard in the most profound silence. And only the chime of a bell in the distance brings an echo of human life into the solitary mountain regions."

PIANO DUETS

Symphonie en si (one movement). 1880. An arrangement by the young Debussy of what was planned as an orchestral work. Of interest only as a biographical document. Dedicated to Mme. von Meck and discovered in Russia, where it was published in 1933.

Triomphe de Bacchus. Attributed to the early eighteen eighties. An interlude, intended for orchestra. Clearly a work of Debussy's student days.

Petite Suite. 1889. Embracing *En Bateau, Cortège, Menuet,* and *Ballet.* The most popular of Debussy's early compositions, chiefly in the orchestral transcription by Büsser. With its facile and melodious barcarolle, its brilliant march and its pervasive prettiness, it might have been written by any one of a number of French composers of the heyday of Massenet.

Marche écossaise sur un thème populaire. 1891. This is the so-called Earl of Ross March which Debussy subsequently orchestrated and declared good fun when he heard it performed in 1913. Written on commission for General Meredith Read, a descendant of the Earls of Ross and dedicated to him, it makes use of a primitive march tune which the lairds of old had played for the whetting of their fighting appetites in the days when a bagpipe was as much a war weapon as a dirk. The general supplied the tune as well as the honorarium.

SIX ÉPIGRAPHES ANTIQUES. 1914.
   Pour invoquer Pan, dieu du vent d'été.
   Pour un tombeau sans nom.
   Pour que la nuit soit propice.
   Pour la danseuse aux crotales.
   Pour l'égyptienne.
   Pour remercier la pluie au matin.

These pieces, which Guido Gatti has described as six bas-reliefs, grew out of the improvised *Chansons de Bilitis,* hastily written by Debussy in 1899 as accompaniment for recitations of poems by Pierre Louÿs in a Paris newspaper office. The composer also considered converting the series into an orchestral suite. As they stand, the piano writing often implies orchestral coloring, with a tinkling of bells and the timbres of such instruments as the flute and the harp. A detail is a repetition by which the first of the series supplies the conclusion for the last. In the second Debussy set for himself a problem of lending accents as varied as possible to a fundamental elaboration through three entire pages on the whole-tone scale. In the sixth, in an endeavor not to repeat the rain suggestions of *Jardins sous la pluie* of a decade earlier, he contrives a somewhat more positive onomatopoeia. In their four-hand medium, others of the series present momentary parallels with certain of the *Préludes.* But they have rarely had similar recognition as among the most significant of Debussy's compositions. In the view of Edward Burlingame Hill they approach the stylistic perfection of the *Chansons de Bilitis* but are full of clichés, a term also applied to them by Guido Gatti, who notes that they have moments of fleeting beauty but savor of artifice.

The more interesting, therefore, the opinion of André Suarès that they are among Debussy's greatest works. With the late sonatas they make confessions, he has said, which are as harrowing as art ever has wrung from the heart of an artist; "here, the sigh, the strangled cry, the abandonment of the tortured body, the anguish of illness are music. . . . It is suffering which speaks . . . physical suffering, the incurable point which works its way into the course of ideas and comes to interrupt them . . . the mind has not ceased to be master; it only gasps for breath . . . this music lacerates the imagination in all that it tells us of the musician and in what it leaves to be guessed . . . the short breath, the melody interrupted by spasms, broken by

severe shocks, by contractions and tremblings, not a line which
does not reveal the man put to the question on the bed of tor-
ture." And yet among pianists of past and present there has
been found in these *Épigraphes* calm or gayety, if perhaps
something less than the genius acclaimed by Suarès. Ernest
Newman, who discerns nothing of emotion in Debussy's later
works, but notes in them a low physical vitality—"we seem to
be watching some heavy sleeper struggling to burst the thick
veil of dreams that holds him half-paralyzed"—has put the question: "What had his heart been doing all these years?" [7]

FOR TWO PIANOS

Lindaraja. 1901. Discovered years after it was written and not published until 1926, this is the all-but-forgotten work which figured in the controversy over certain resemblances between Debussy's *Soirée dans Grenade* and Ravel's early *Habanera*. Its
importance in "l'Affaire Ravel" was due to the testimony it
gave of Debussy having used the disputed devices several years
before he wrote *Soirée dans Grenade*. Otherwise, this is one
of his most commonplace works and it is not surprising that
he had forgotten it when it turned up between the pages of
another manuscript.

En blanc et noir. 1915. Originally styled *Caprices en blanc et noir*
and at one time thought of by Debussy as a further set of
Fêtes galantes. The three pieces are of differing styles and musically have little or no relation to one another, save in what
might be called their etched quality and the idea they convey,
not of a color palette but of chiaroscuro. There are separate
dedications, the first to Koussevitzky, the second to Lieutenant
Jacques Charlot, the third to Stravinsky. The collective title,
at curious variance with the one-time contemplated obeisance
to Verlaine, is said to have been derived from the grays of
Velasquez.

The first of the three pieces illustrates four lines from *Romeo and Juliet*, not Shakespeare's, but Gounod's:

[7] Article in the London *Musical Times*, August 1, 1918.

Qui reste à sa place
Et ne danse pas
De quelque disgrâce
Fait l'aveu tout bas.

This has been construed as a bitterly ironical commentary on those who, perhaps because of some physical defect like Debussy's, stood aside while the war raged. It takes the form of an elegant valse caprice, rhythmically vivacious and fluid.

The second of the series is of more symphonic character and much more obviously music of the war. The lieutenant to whom it is dedicated fell in battle on March 3, 1915. The piece begins with a signal alarm on a double pedal, the upper note like the faraway beat of a drum. Homesickness and a touch of the liturgical, suggesting funeral rites, have been found in the succeeding measures. At the beginning is the *envoi* from Villon's *Ballade contre les ennemis de la France*. In the music these enemies are characterized by Luther's choral; toward the end is a carillon-like use of what Debussy described as "a pre-Marseillaise."

If the third of the set has a war background, this has not been discerned. It takes as its subject, otherwise unexplained, a line from a poem by the fifteenth-century Charles d'Orléans, "Yver, vous n'estes qu'un vilain." Debussy had already set these words in his choral devoirs to the Duke. Guido Gatti hears in the piano piece the wind whistling as in *Le Vent dans la plaine* and rain beating against the windowpane, as an old castellan relates a terrifying legend. The storm passes and the moon comes out to illume the white and silent landscape.

III

THE SONGS

IF Debussy had been almost exclusively a composer of songs, like Hugo Wolf—if there had been no *Pelléas et Mélisande*, no *L'Après-midi d'un faune*, no *Le Martyre de Saint-Sébastien*, no *Nocturnes*, no *La Mer*, no *Ibéria*, no string quartet, no piano compositions—he still would have been one of the most distinctive and individual figures in music. The essence of Debussy's musical personality is in the songs and they exhibit virtually every facet of his art. There is nothing else like them in song literature. Here and there, of course, a contemporary or a successor has written a song that would pass as Debussy's, but although he was much imitated—and eventually was charged even with imitating his imitators, an absurd accusation—he so far transcended all others in the application of his methods that, whereas the Debussy songs are widely celebrated and often sung, those of other composers who adopted his methods have had little currency. Debussy, to be sure, was not free of influences, echoes, reminiscences, or, it may be, borrowings. Wagner, Borodin, Moussorgsky, Gounod, Massenet, Fauré, Chabrier, even Godard are encountered in his pages. But the reminders and resemblances are fewer than they are (as between one composer and another) in the line of masters of the German Lied. Among song composers of all lands, Debussy was one of the most personal. He achieved a new style in the setting of poetry and poetic prose. In it was a new sensitivity to fantasy and the shadow moods. As with his piano compositions, he demanded and gradually brought about an altered technique of performance. Vocalists had to become Debussy interpreters in a special sense, just as pianists

276

did. And there was required also a special order of accompaniment, involving the same essential piano technique as the piano
solos. Much that is most characteristic of Debussy's writing for
the piano is as readily discoverable in the songs. His harmonic
devices are to be studied there as conveniently as in any of his
purely instrumental compositions. Nowhere is his melodic personality more fully disclosed. And only in *Pelléas* is he equally
the master of the setting of words (with all due respect to his
choral writing and the solo parts of the cantatas). Poetically,
the Debussy songs are an unrivaled exposition of the French
genius both in quantity and quality, though it need not be contended that they impoverish a limited number of other notable
examples of this genius, variously signed with the names of
Franck, Duparc, Fauré, and Ravel.

Debussy's individuality as a song writer begins with his choice
of poets. More than half of his settings—numbering between fifty
and sixty in all—are of works by great poets. For the others he
chose verses by respectable if not internationally celebrated
bards. With a very few exceptions, all were his contemporaries.
He did not set the effusions of friends. His songs are remarkably free of those concessions to association and comradeship
that frequently clutter the output of a composer. There is little
or no casual use of equally casual verses. If in his earlier songs
the choice of subjects is not always of the most literary select-
ness, this was because of adolescent enthusiasms that subsequently were outgrown. Sixteen of the published songs are settings of Verlaine; five of Baudelaire; four of Mallarmé. There
are three which go for their material to François Villon, three to
Tristan L'hermite, and two to Charles d'Orléans, also drawn
upon for the words of three unaccompanied choruses. Victor
Hugo and Alfred de Musset figure once, each, in the catalogue
of lyrics utilized. Théodore de Banville, Vincent Hypsa, Paul
Bourget, and André Girod were early sources of lyrical in-

spiration. Pierre Louÿs was drawn upon when Debussy was ripe
for the *Chansons de Bilitis*. G. le Roy and Paul Gravelot wrote
one poem, each, that found its way into this anthology. Debussy
himself wrote the texts for the four songs of the *Proses lyriques*.
The words for his last song, the wartime *Noël des enfants qui
n'ont plus de maisons*, also were his. There are some mediocre
poems in the lot. But the level is high. Debussy set no poems by
other than Frenchmen and none in any language but French.

Of necessity, the Debussy song will have a clearer definition
of line than the most nebulous of his piano pieces. The words require this; the separate and unblendable vocal part enforces it.
But so important are the accompaniments in the establishment
of the mood and atmosphere of the Debussy songs that it is quite
as possible to talk of "impressionism" in the vocal music as in
the piano music. Debussy, indeed, seems to have settled into his
harmonic stride sooner in the songs than in the keyboard compositions; for one thing, he wrote many more songs than piano
works in the first period of his career and was perhaps more confident of his medium. Fully twenty-five of his published songs
—and possibly about five more of which the dates are not certain
—were composed before 1890. Only seven or eight of the piano
pieces came from the same period and among them is nothing to
compare in importance with the *Cinq Poèmes de Baudelaire* or
the *Ariettes oubliées*—contemporaneous were the *Deux Arabesques*.

If the first songs suggest Massenet or Borodin and the *Cinq
Poèmes de Baudelaire* yield echoes of Wagner, the *Ariettes
oubliées* are indisputably Debussyan. The two series of *Fêtes
galantes*, the *Chansons de Bilitis*, and the *Proses lyriques* possess
an individuality to set them apart in song literature. There are
several appreciable changes of style between the Baudelaire songs
of 1887–89 and the *Trois Poèmes de Stéphane Mallarmé* of 1913,
but they are all different facets of the same distinctive musical

personality, impossible to confuse with any other. With a few exceptions—and those rather dubious ones—these are all songs of fantasy. Theirs is an unreal world, not a mere garnishment of reality; a world that is moonstruck and peopled with lunambulists; a world more often melancholy than happy, though frequently animated; a world that loves shadows and the dusk and shuns the noonday sun. An exquisite tenderness pervades it, companioned by irony and a recurring sense of futility and desolation. There is humor, occasionally hearty as in *Chevaux de bois* —"popular humor à la flamande"—or humor full of the tragic mockery of life, as in *Ingénus*. "Sometimes," says Thérese Lavauden,[1] "the humor traverses the lyrical tissue like a comet, gone in a flash. A brief allusion, an apt word passed in a low voice to the audience, a wink, which, when it has won the desired connivance, ceases to be, having in derision drawn attention to a portrait or a landscape." The epigrammatic quality of the poem and the musical commentary are closely interwoven in such songs as *Colloque sentimental*, *Le Faune*, and *Fantoches* wherein Debussy contrives to overlay sentimentality with a patina of worldy skepticism. There is a twanging irony in the song, *Mandoline*, as there is in the somewhat parallel piano piece, *Serenade interrompue*. Humor is latent, elsewhere, in many unsuspected passages. But there is no unbuttoned laughter.

As Edwin Evans [2] has warned Debussy singers, these songs are not dramatic declarations. They do not purport to tell a story in music or to illustrate an episode. They are not in motion, like a drama. For the brief period of their duration, they are static. As Debussy put no song in his one music-drama,[3] he put no music-drama in his fifty-odd songs. Instead of action there is shining fantasy—and impeccable taste. Debussy's fantasy

---

[1] Article in the *Chesterian*, April–May, 1928.
[2] Article in *The Sackbut*, November, 1921.
[3] An exception must be made, of course, for Mélisande's tower song.

may have failed him at times, but not his taste. The form, the manner, the feeling are right, even if the content is of only secondary inspiration. In no other medium is Debussy more scrupulous, more fastidious, more exacting than in his songs. The singer must have something of Debussy's fastidiousness, literary as well as musical. He or she must share Verlaine's hatred of rhetorical effect and sham eloquence—as Debussy shared it—if the sixteen Verlaine settings are to be given their true effect. Any attempt to dramatize them is wrong. All extremes, all attitudinizing, all pumped-up emotions are destructive of illusion. With songs like *Colloque sentimental* the best effect is to be had by not seeking effect. The poet and the musician have conspired to create their own contrasts. The texts must be scrupulously enunciated and with their allied notes as scrupulously inflected. The minutest nuancing is demanded, but no conspicuous underlining of words or phrases. The effect must be one of simplicity of utterance, a simplicity that bespeaks breeding and intelligence. It is the listener's privilege, if he is so minded, to find this or that Debussy song over-precious. But he also will find it patrician.

Of such songs of intricate imagery as the *Trois Poèmes de Mallarmé* it has been said with wisdom that as much depends on the listener as on the performer. No music could make these poems clear to those not already familiar with their content. For those who know and love the texts, Debussy's music may heighten the pleasure. The interpreter can only assume such familiarity and employ his musicianship and such subtleties of voice as he may command for the purpose of establishing the basic mood. Any conscious effort to "put the points across" is necessarily fatal. If the songs are unintelligible to an audience, the interpreter cannot hope to bridge the gap. In less degree, this is true also of the less involved *Fêtes galantes* of Verlaine, for which simplicity of style is a prerequisite. Without a knowledge of their associations, something, perhaps much, of their charm must evaporate. The interpreter cannot communicate associations. As Edwin Evans has said, it is the listener who needs to know Watteau, Lancret, and the *Comédie italienne*, if he is to revel in the fantasy of these poems in song. The most gifted interpreter cannot supply the deficiency.

Much might be said of the felicities of Debussy's word setting, with here and there a reservation for those instances in which rhythmic considerations or the insistence of a mood have been given preference over the usual naturalness of Debussy's melodic speech. True to his concept of the French language, Debussy avoids heavy stresses and courts an undulous syllabication. The accompaniments are exceptionally varied and illustrate about everything in Debussy's armory of effects, from the whole-tone scale to pedal points festooned with unorthodox chords. One consideration is to be remembered. Debussy sometimes thinks of the song accompaniments in terms other than the piano. There are flute passages and harp figures as in the *Chansons de Bilitis;* and there is a lute or mandolin quality as in *Fantoches*— not without difficulties for the accompanist.

THE PUBLISHED SONGS

Nuit d'étoiles. Circa 1876. Poem by Théodore de Banville. If, as believed, this song was composed by a youth of fourteen, it must be regarded as an exceptional one. That it suggests Massenet more than it prefigures the later Debussy is not surprising, though a fortuitous resemblance to a theme of Mélisande has been discovered in an accompaniment figure. The song is one of broad curves and symmetry, the key E flat major. The poet sees his beloved mirrored in the starry night:

> Nuit d'étoiles, sous tes voiles
> Sous ta brise et tes parfums,
> Triste lyre, Qui soupire
> Je rêve aux amours défunts. . . .

Debussy, at fourteen, was rather young to be dreaming of dead loves. He had not yet made his first proposal to Sonia von Meck. But the sad lyre, the breezes and the perfumes, the secrets of the star-studded vault overhead found ready response in his adolescent sensibility.

Beau soir. Circa 1878. Poem by Paul Bourget. If the date is accepted, this is the product of the fancy and the musicianship of a richly gifted lad of sixteen. Debussy did not publish the song until 1891, a year before *Pelléas*. The young composer shares, musically, in the poet's desire to be happy on this beautiful evening, when the rivers are rose-tinted with the setting sun—

Lorsque au soleil couchant les rivières sont roses,

but he feels a premonition of death. We, too, are but travelers—

Car nous nous en allons
Comme s'en va cette onde
Elle à la mer,—nous au tombeau.

Again the feeling is of Massenet, but the song has warmth and its fair measure of charm.

Fleur des blés. Circa 1878. Poem by André Girod. The youthful Debussy of the Conservatoire, much more Achille than Claude, strives with a decent measure of success to give musical appeal to Girod's *Flower of Wheat*, in which the lover compares his beloved to a bouquet. Where the breeze has stirred the curling grain in waves he has found his flowers and his simile:

Le long des blés que la brise
Fait onduler puis défrise
En un désordre coquet,
J'ai trouvé de bonne prise
De t'y cueillir un bouquet.

The setting is conventional, but fluent and not without its touch of elegance.

Mandoline. 1880–83. Poem by Paul Verlaine. Dedicated to Mme. Vasnier. The most popular of Debussy's early songs, this one bespeaks the progress he made at the Conservatoire in the years immediately preceding his winning of the *Prix de Rome*

(1884), in spite of his antagonistic attitude toward his instruction. The text is from Verlaine's *Fêtes galantes*, but Debussy apparently did not consider the song worthy of place in either of the sets of songs given the Verlaine title and it was published separately. The musical setting is one of engaging spontaneity and it deftly establishes the mood of the text. Serenaders and their ladies dally, amorously exchanging vows, under the singing branches—

> Les donneurs de sérénades
> Et les belles écouteuses
> Échangent des propos fades
> Sous les ramures chanteuses . . .

The serenade is one Gallic in spirit and inflection, this time further from the contemporary influences of Gounod and Massenet than from the Berlioz of the earlier *Damnation de Faust* and the Ravel of the much later *Heure espagnole*. Light-footed in pace and even a little acrid in harmony, *Mandoline* is the earliest example of the twanging irony that was to be found in various later compositions, particularly the *Sérénade interrompue* for piano. It would be too much to say that this song is really typical of Debussy. Nor is it difficult to agree with Evan Evans when he contends that *Mandoline* has been too prominent on singers' programs, considering how little known are many that are of more musical significance. But it is not to be forgotten that the Debussy of *Mandoline* was barely twenty-one. The song attests a distinctive and personal gift for mood evocation.

La Belle au bois dormant. 1880–83. Poem by Vincent Hypsa. This is a French re-telling, in ballad form, of the long-cherished story of the sleeping beauty. The poet of the Chat Noir sends to awaken her a knightly lover whose hair is full of sunlight under a helm the color of the moon—

> Des trous à son pourpoint vermeil,
> Un chevalier va par le brune,
> Les cheveaux tout pleines de soleil
> Sous un casque couleur de lune. . . .

Was Debussy, as has been suggested, haunted by a memory of Borodin's *Sleeping Princess?* But nothing of Borodin, one may be sure, enters into Debussy's use of the popular French round, *Nous n'irons plus au bois*, for which he had so persistent a liking that he employed it twice later, in his *Jardins sous la pluie* for piano (1903) and his *Rondes des printemps* for orchestra (1909). The round is the basis of the entire ballad and serves as its conclusion.

Voici que le printemps. 1880–93. Poem by Paul Bourget. Like *La Belle au bois dormant* and *Paysage sentimental*, not published until 1903. This is one of the early songs in which Russian influences have been sought and, in the view of some commentators, found. Vallas takes note of "festoons of major thirds" "in the Borodin manner" and refers to the theme as possibly of Russian origin. A characteristic detail is found in series of common chords linked in arpeggios, as later in *Chevaux de bois*. In Bourget's poem Spring returns like a banished prince, on his left shoulder a nightingale that sings for lovers, on his right a blackbird to mock at those not loved:

> Voici que le printemps, ce fils léger d'Avril,
> Beau page en pourpoint vert brodé de roses blanches
> Parfait leste, fringant et les poings sur les hanches. . . .

Paysage sentimental. 1880–83. Poem by Paul Bourget. Like a mysterious forest pool, the poet's happiness sleeps in his lonely spirit. The young Debussy is already a landscape artist, but one concerned with the sentimental or emotional promptings of the scene rather than with the scene itself. From the inert winter sky, where the sun wanders among white vapors, is conjured forth the thought of a sad happiness—

> Le ciel d'hiver, si doux, si triste, si dormant,—
> Ou le soleil errait parmi des vapeurs blanches,
> Était pareil au doux, au profond sentiment
> Qui nous rendait heureux mélancoliquement. . . .

Even more than its companions of the group of songs credited to 1880–83, *Paysage sentimental* has been assumed to be reflective of Borodin, though just what music by this Russian composer Debussy really knew at this time has not been made clear. The refrain has been pointed to as a vague prefigurement of the air of Lia in *L'Enfant prodigue*. Some unusual chords forecast the harmonic innovations of the piano works of the next decade. Fault has been found with details of the textual accentuation, a rarity in the criticism of Debussy's songs.

Zéphyr. 1881. Poem by Théodore de Banville. The poet muses wistfully on the intimacies permitted the winged breeze—

> Si j'étais le Zéphyr ailé
> J'irais mourir sur votre bouche. . . .

The song presents a prelude and an epilogue and moves airily over a rather conventional accompaniment.

Rondeau. 1882. Poem by Alfred de Musset. The dedication reads: "Pour mon ami Alexandre de Meck. Souvenir bien affectueux." Alexandre was a son of Debussy's Russian patroness and a brother of the girl to whom he proposed marriage at about the time this song was composed. There is a little prelude and a brief epilogue, not unlike the beginnings and endings of some of the Hugo Wolf songs. The accompaniment, while fluid and mobile, has rather more of a dramatic character than was common with Debussy.

> Fut-il jamais douceur de coeur pareille
> À voir Manon, dans mes dras, sommeiller. . . .

But the happiness of having Manon thus ensconced is not without its wistfulness, since there is not merely the present to consider—

> Hélas, l'amour sans lendemain ni veille
> Fut-il jamais?

Pantomime. 1882–84. Poem by Paul Verlaine. The original version is included in the so-called Vasnier series, embracing also the first of the two songs styled *Clair de lune*, along with *Pierrot* and *Apparition*. All are dedicated to Mme. Vasnier. The manuscript book containing these songs and several others is in a private collection. *Pantomime* was published posthumously, with its companions of the four named above, in the *Revue Musicale* of May, 1926. Pierrot, Cassandra, Harlequin, and Columbine cross the pages of the three tableaux of this miniature spectacle. Columbine has been abducted by Harlequin and obviously likes it. Cassandra is worried over her errant nephew. But Pierrot is hungry, so at the very outset

Pierrot, qui n'a rien d'un Clitandre,
Vide un flacon sans plus attendre,
Et, pratique, entame un pâté. . . .

Debussy was to deal more successfully with the characters of Italian comedy in later works. The interest in *Pantomime* is about that of the vast majority of posthumous publications.

Clair de lune. 1882–84. Poem by Paul Verlaine. Dedicated to Mme. Vasnier. This is not the *Clair de lune* of 1892, and resembles it very little, aside from the circumstance that the text is identical. The later *Clair de lune* was published as one of the songs of the first series of *Fêtes galantes.* The early setting appeared posthumously in the *Revue Musicale* of May, 1926, along with the other three of the Vasnier series. It might have been a by-product of several other French composers, Massenet not excepted.

Pierrot. 1882–84. Poem by Théodore de Banville. Another of the Vasnier songs, published posthumously.

Apparition. 1882–84. Poem by Stéphane Mallarmé. Of the posthumous Vasnier set.
The poet, on the day of his mistress's first kiss, was dreaming sadly. But in the evening she appeared like the fairy that had brightened his childhood dreams.

CINQ POÈMES DE BAUDELAIRE. 1887–89. Dedicated to Etienne Dupin. Poems from Charles Baudelaire's *Fleurs du mal.*

Le Balcon. 1888. One of the most Wagnerian of songs Debussy wrote while under the spell of Wagner. (The time of the *Cinq Poèmes* corresponds roughly with that of Debussy's pilgrimages to Bayreuth.) Debussy uses the same melodic phrase as a refrain each time a line of the text recurs, but varies the accompaniment. Some commentators have even styled this refrain a *leit motif*, but it is scarcely that. Like others of the group, *Le Balcon* is weightier and more declamatory than the typical Debussy song, and with a somewhat longer line. There are reminders of the string quartet in its chromaticism, and the accompaniment suggests the orchestra.

Mère des souvenirs, maîtresse des maîtresses . . .

The song is the impassioned and mystical appeal of a lover to
his mistress, to whom he ardently expresses his hope that
their happiness will rise again like the setting suns they saw
from a balcony on summer evenings.

> Que le soleils sont beaux par les chaudes soirées!
> Que l'espace est profond! que le coeur est puissant!

Harmonie du soir. 1889. As in *Le Balcon,* lines are used as refrains
and the chromaticism suggests a Wagnerian influence. In an
evening reverie a lover turns to thoughts of the loved one
to escape the chill of nothingness and the vague sadness of
Nature—

> Un coeur tendre qui hait le néant vaste et noir . . .

The poem is one of sumptuous imagery—

> Voici venir les temps où vibrant sur sa tige
> Chaque fleur s'évapore ainsi qu'un encensoir. . . .

Debussy was to learn, as other composers have learned, that
the setting of such lines entails a double imagery, verbal and
musical, and propounds problems difficult to solve.

Le Jet d'eau. 1889. Debussy orchestrated the piano part in 1907
and Caplet revised the instrumentation after Debussy's death.
In the sparkling play of a fountain a lover sees mirrored the
fierce intensity and the subtle melancholy of his passion.

> La gerbe d'eau qui berce ses mille fleurs
> Que la lune traverse de ses pâleurs. . . .

Less of Wagner, more of Borodin, is to be found in the setting of this erotic lyric, with its dissonances, its seconds, its
transparent flow.

Recueillement. Circa 1888. One of the most positive of Wagnerian echoes in Debussy's music is found at the opening of
this song, where the effect is reminiscent of the horns of
Tristan und Isolde. At the same time the introduction prefigures the beginning of the last movement of the string

quartet. In meditation the poet regards the coming of the shrouded night and sees struggle and passion fade slowly into darkness of oblivion.

> Sois sage, ô ma Douleur, et tiens-toi plus tranquille. . . .

The poet takes Sorrow by the hand and leads her away from the multitude of mortals who, driven by the whip of Pleasure, gather only flowers of remorse.

La Mort des amants. 1887. The earliest of the Baudelaire songs, it is one of the least Wagnerian. This *Death of the Lovers* is an apotheosis of passion, in which two souls burn out like twin torches in the flame of their final hours together—

> Usant à l'envi leurs chaleurs dernières,
> Nos deux coeurs seront deux vastes flambeaux,
> Qui réfléchiront leurs doubles lumières
> Dans nos deux esprits, ces miroirs jumeaux.

Thus mirrored in their supreme unity, they are awakened by an angel. The same phrase in the accompaniment begins and ends a song rich in texture and intense in feeling.

ARIETTES OUBLIÉES. 1888. Poems by Paul Verlaine. Three are from *Romances sans paroles*, two from *Aquarelles* and one from *Paysages belges*. The set is dedicated to Mary Garden. Originally simply *Ariettes*, the title was changed to *Ariettes oubliées* when the songs were republished fifteen years after their first appearance.

C'est l'extase langoureuse. The poet of this communion with Nature sees the image of his emotions in forest murmurs and shadows, all pervaded by an amorous lassitude.

> Cette ame qui se lamente
> En cette plainte dormante
> C'est la nôtre, n'est-ce pas?

The voice part has an ecstatic quality, as the song moves forward in chromatic successions. The accompaniment is more concise and in a sense more formal than that of the Baudelaire songs.

Il pleure dans mon coeur. The song is prefaced by a line from a poem by Rimbaud. "Il pleut doucement sur la ville." As it rains over the city, there is rain also in the heart of the symbolist; there is an all-pervading sadness—

> Pour un coeur qui s'ennuie
> Ô le bruit de la pluie! . . .

which Debussy has heightened in his setting. "Water pieces," dear to the generality of French artists of the time, found in Debussy a particularly sensitive and adroit exponent, because of a style peculiarly fluid. Rain and fountains were as much his concern as the sea.

L'Ombre des arbres. In this instance the prefatory quotation is from Rostand's *Cyrano de Bergerac.* It concerns the nightingale afraid of drowning because of spying its reflection in the river. Verlaine's imagery pictures a lonely traveler whose sadness is similarly reflected and whose drowned hopes whisper around him.

> L'ombre des arbres dans la rivière embrumée
> Meurt comme de la fumée
> Tandis qu'en l'air, parmi les ramures réelles
> Se plaignent les touterelles. . . .

The music goes through daring modulations that testify to the new independence of the man but recently done with the academicians of the Conservatoire and the Villa Medici. If, as has been contended, the song actually was composed at an earlier period, it must be regarded as surprisingly different from others of its time, since it is altogether Debussyan in harmony and feeling.

Chevaux de bois. Composed about 1885, when the composer was twenty-three or twenty-four years old, this hearty and humorous song was admired by Debussy's associates at the Villa Medici. It was one of the original *Ariettes,* published separately in 1885, and republished under the collective title of *Ariettes oubliées* in 1903. The poem is from Verlaine's *Paysages belges* and the Belgian landscape in this case is that of a merry-go-round. The chevaux de bois are the wooden horses—

> Tournez, tournez, bons chevaux de bois,
> Tournez cent tours, tournez mille tours,
> Tournez souvent et tournez toujours. . . .

The red-faced child and the white mother, the boy in black and the girl in red, slinking sneak thief in the gay crowds, the rush to supper and the descent of the peace of evening succeed one another in the myriad images of the merry-go-round and the fair, hilarity yielding finally to tranquillity—

> Le ciel en velours
> D'astres en or se vêt lentement. . . .

The musical close is a subtle one, after a galloping melody that has undergone striking harmonic transitions. There is a lumbering preamble in uneven time, with the theme strident or raucous as the roundabout gets under way. Whirling arpeggios and series of parallel common chords contribute effects that must have been novel, indeed, for Debussy's fellow laureates in Rome. All manner of literal interpretations have been given details of the music—the cry of a servant girl, the shout of a soldier, coarse hiccoughs from the piston—all swept into a vortex of sounds representative of the intoxication of high spirits. The basic melodic design of the rondo-like song remains unchanged as the merry-go-round slackens and goes to sleep; then, at the close, to quote one French commentator, we see the first star and scent the fragrance of the night.

Green. Verlaine's *Aquarelles* are designed to give the feeling of water colors in verse. Debussy's setting of *Green* transfers this feeling to music. Though there is subtlety as well as warmth in its lyric flow, the song is more straightforward and, in a sense, more conventional than many of its companions, which may explain why it was one of the first Debussy songs to become widely known. *Green* is a love song, not a nature picture—the love song of a symbolist whose ardor has the freshness of the color green, and who seeks its coolness in the arms of his beloved.

> Voici des fruits des fleurs des feuilles et des branches
> Et puis voici mon coeur qui ne bat que pour vous. . . .

The English title is Verlaine's. Debussy knew little English.

Spleen. It is melancholy with which we have to deal in this instance, not "spleen" as the word is understood in English, though the mood is tinctured with a sort of fanciful disgust— disgust for the too beautiful scenes of Nature, disgust for almost everything except the loved one, of whose constancy the poet is none too sure.

> Je crains toujours, ce qu'est d'attendre!
> Quelque fuite atroce de vous. . . .

In the third bar of Debussy's music is an ingenious foreboding of this fear, which takes the form of a sudden sforzando.

DEUX ROMANCES. 1891. Poems by Paul Bourget. Originally given to the publisher without separate titles.

Romance. The Massenet-like character of the music indicates the song is older than the date attached to it.

> L'âme evaporée et souffrante. . . .

Like the odor of lilies blown away by the wind, hope, faith, and love are gone. (An earlier song also called *Romance*, has remained unpublished.)

Les Cloches. Also believed to be of an older period than that in which it was published. Spring and the sound of bells bring memories of past happiness—

> Les feuilles s'ouvraient sur le bord des branches délicatement.
> Les cloches tintaient, légères et franches, dans le ciel clément.

Les Angélus. 1891. Poem by G. le Roy. A simple and not very characteristic song. Christian bells sound for matins, but the poet has abolished all matins in the pain of his heart—there he finds only shadows and night and death.

> Cloches chrétiennes pour les matines . . .
> Aujourd'hui souveraine est ma peine,
> Et toutes matines abolies. . . .

Dans le jardin. 1891. Poem by Paul Gravelot. A graceful and atmospheric song if not of the first order. While taking note of beauty on the other side of a wall, the poet pricks a finger—and enjoys it.

> Je regardais dans le jardin
> Furtif au travers de la haie
> Je t'ai vue, enfant! et soudain
> Mon coeur tressaillit: je t'aimais!

The song yields a hint or two of *Pelléas et Mélisande*, not yet begun at the time *Dans le jardin* was composed.

TROIS MÉLODIES. 1891. Poems by Paul Verlaine.

La Mer est plus belle. Dedicated to Ernest Chausson. The sea, sings the poet, is more beautiful than cathedrals; and so, prayer and reverence for the Virgin are more beautiful on the sea than in churches. Where the breeze sings—

> Vous sans espérance, mourez sans souffrance!

The accompaniment presents another of the instances in which common chords in changing tonalities are a Debussy signature.

Le son du cor s'afflige. Dedicated to Robert Godet. The sound of the horn complains in the woods. In the evening snow is falling, a wolf howls mournfully; the countryside seems to fall into drowsy slumber. Again the use of common chords—a descending series of six at "la neige tombe à longs traits de charpie"—makes clear the harmonic authorship.

L'échelonnement des haies. Dedicated to Robert Godet. The poem may be assumed to have been inspired by hedgerows of the English countryside, familiar to Verlaine in the time when he was a teacher in the South of England. The succession of hedges rolls on the horizon, a clear sea in a clear mist—"mer claire dans le brouillard clair"—an image of rural peace to which Debussy brought music of like clarity and luminosity.

FÊTES GALANTES. First series, 1892. Poems by Paul Verlaine. An earlier version of *Fêtes galantes* dates back to Debussy's days at the Vasniers in the early eighteen-eighties, when he set *Pantomime, En Sourdine, Mandoline, Clair de lune* (the early version), and *Fantoches*. Of these *En Sourdine* and *Fantoches* were retained, the latter little altered, and a new setting made of *Claire de lune*. The others were published separately. These songs have been singled out as the earliest in which Debussy applied the principles of the impressionistic method to vocal music, though this is debatable. The accompaniment is often reduced to a minimum of suggestion; the voice part has sometimes more the character of a rhythmic chanting than of tangible melody. In each poem there is preoccupation, however, with a well-chiseled melodic curve at the close, so as to leave a final sense of satisfaction and elegance.

> *En Sourdine.* The original version, among the so-called Vasnier songs, is credited to 1882–83. The landscape, the feeling, alike are "muted."
>
>> Calmes dans le demi-jour
>> Que les branches hautes font,
>> Pénétrons bien notre amour
>> De ce silence profond. . . .

A dreamlike love song, in orthodox Lied form, with a little motto theme running through it. The song of the nightingale, evoked at the end of the poem, opens and closes the musical setting.

>> Ferme tes yeux à demi
>> Croise tes bras sur ton sein
>> Et de ton coeur endormi
>> Chasse à jamais tout dessein. . . .

The music, too, breathes the peace of the forest where the lovers wait for the despairing lay of the nightingale. The song is one of the most delicate sensibility. But it stands as an example of Debussy's occasional neglect of details of prosody for the sake of rhythmic flow.

> *Clair de lune.* To be distinguished from both the early *Clair de lune* of the Vasnier set and the piano piece of the *Suite berga-*

masque. This mature song has been described as epitomizing the true Debussy, free of the influence against which he struggled throughout the first half of his career. Perhaps the text conveys an ironical twinge that is not to be found in the music. But the latter communicates with affecting subtlety the melancholy that abides under the gayety of a Watteau landscape where half-tragic figures seem to be singing of a fictitious happiness.

> Votre âme est un paysage choisi
> Que vont charmant masques et bergamasques
> Jouant du luth et dansant et quasi
> Tristes sous leurs déguisements fantasques.

A sustained melody moves in an atmosphere of moonlight to an ending of haunting loveliness. The accompaniment is of modal coloring, with unexpected transitions and the type of harmonic blending that was to distinguish Debussy's compositions, from *L'Après-midi* onward.

Fantoches. The original version of the Vasnier set was incorporated, little changed, in the publication of ten years later. The music transcribes in tone the essence of Verlaine's verse. The accompaniment has almost a lute or mandolin quality; there is a characteristic use of thirds. In sheer fantasy, Scaramouche and Pulcinella, having got together with some evil intent, are making black patterns in the moonlight. The reiterated "la-la" gives to the picture its touch of irony.

PROSES LYRIQUES. 1892–93. Texts by Claude Debussy. As the general title indicates, these texts are in prose, but lyrical prose. They have evoked the most conflicting opinions as to their quality and their suitability for song. Criticism of Debussy's settings has included descriptive references of so opposite a nature as "more spacious character—clear lyricism" on the one hand and "new school of musical stippling—universal amorphism" on the other. The literary basis is a variety of symbolism, bordering on allegory, that has been described in one quarter as far-fetched and full of studied abstruseness; in another as somewhat juvenile, but essentially delicate in its imagery.

De Rêve. Echoes of the horns of *Tristan* have been found in this song, as in *Recueillement*. These, with the motif-like recurrence of three themes, have caused the song to be looked upon as older than the date given it (1892). Debussy's dream of the past suggests a confusion of periods. The knights for whom the trees weep their golden leaves in the moonlight have died in the quest of the Grail. The women whose grief the trees have thus taken unto themselves—the "Frêles and Folles" of the text—wear the outward aspects of the eighteenth-century types of Watteau. Delicate arpeggios produce the atmosphere of the dream.

> La nuit a des douceurs de femme,
> Et les vieux arbres, sous la lune d'or
> Songent à celle qui vient de passer. . . .

If the song is a relatively early one, was it to Borodin that the composer turned for the touch of Slavic color at the words "Ils n'ont pas?"

De Grève. Perhaps only a Frenchman of Debussy's time can properly orient himself to this song, which Léon Vallas considers one of Debussy's most perfect. As its title, *Of the Strand*, indicates, it is a sea piece, in the course of which the waves are likened to frightened little girls rushing out of school. The whitecaps are compared to their skirts, blown up by the wind. There are three verses, differently treated, the piano playing a more than ordinarily assertive part. There are somber moments, as at the outset, contrasted with passages in which the voice part is of a fleeting, pattering character, while the accompaniment splashes with a suggestion of the sea. The close, in which one note is repeated against changing harmonies in sixths, brings a hint of the sunken cathedral of the piano prelude—

> Les cloches attardées!
> Des flottantes églises!
> Soie blanche apaisée!

For an alien the imagery of white silk, even in a meditation that has its admixture of humor, leaves something less than completeness of illusion as the distant bells echo through the twilight and the song comes to its end in Debussyan quietude. The music of *De Grève* clearly transcends the text. Vocally, it is more than ordinarily grateful.

De Fleurs. A lover, longing for the return of his loved one, sees in the glaring colors and deadly green of a conservatory the image of his own distress.

Dans l'ennui si desolément vert de la serre de douleur
Les fleurs enlacent mon coeur de leurs tiges méchantes. . . .

The song has something of the dead heat of a greenhouse. Musically, it tends to the dramatic. A chromatic melody is introduced at the outset by common chords that upset any sense of tonality.

De Soir. Another song that possibly only the Parisian can feel as Debussy felt it, though its beautiful close, with a picture of swallows against an evening sky, is of immediate appeal. The song is about "Sunday in the cities, Sunday in the hearts." There are excursion trains, tunnels, signals. In the blue of dreams, thoughts are like defective fireworks. But at length, after all the commotion, comes evening with its solemn stillness. Then the heart is filled with compassion.

> Prenez pitié des villes, prenez pitié des coeurs,
> Vous, la Vierge, or sur argent!

A popular song, *Tour prend garde*, is drawn on for the basic melodic substance. The end is like a brief nocturne, with a suggestion of faint chimes in the evening air. Again, in the variety of the setting, Debussy's music transcends the quality of the text. One can only assume that the humor of the latter asserts itself more convincingly for those whose Sundays are mirrored in the words.

CHANSONS DE BILITIS. 1897. Prose poems by Pierre Louÿs. The three songs of this group, *La flûte de Pan*, *Le chevelure* and *Le tombeau des naïades*, are among those in which the music seems to melt into the text. They place Debussy beside Wolf and Moussorgsky as a supreme master of word setting. Elsewhere he occasionally sacrifices word values for the sake of a continuing mood or for rhythmic flow in the music. The

Chansons de Bilitis must be regarded as among the ripest fruits of an art at once sensitive and voluptuous, reticent and sybaritic.

La Flûte de Pan. Debussy is here the gentle hedonist, as was the imaginary Bilitis before him.

> Pour le jour des Hyacinthes, il m'a donné une syrinx
> faite de roseaux bien taillés. . . .

By modal harmonies, Debussy invokes, as Edward Burlingame Hill has said, "not the atmosphere of the church, but the pagan spirit of Greece." Impalpable but definite, the song contains the essence of Debussy's poetic insight. At the outset is a charming example of the whole-tone scale. Sustained by a mobile accompaniment of alternating common chords, a syrinx-like melody ensues. This leads into a rhythmically more complex section, where the text refers to the chant of the green frogs. A declamatory passage in which the accompaniment employs a succession of fifths brings back, for the conclusion, the flute refrain of the opening. The last phrase of the voice part, "presque sans voix," vanishes, as one commentor has remarked, "in an almost imperceptible vibration."

La Chevelure. The most passionate and the most human in its appeal of the Bilitis set. In a warm flood of sensuous charm, Pan tells Bilitis of his dream and of their ecstatic fusion of body and soul.

> Il m'a dit: "Cette nuit j'ai rêvé,"
> J'avais ta chevelure autour de mon cou. . . .

There is no escaping a thought of *Pelléas*, which Debussy had nearly completed at the time these songs were written—of Mélisande and her gleaming tresses in the tower scene. "I had your tresses and they were mine," said Pan. "I had your locks, like a black necklace, around my neck and over my breast. I caressed them and they were mine and we were tied forever thus. . . ." In recitative that has a touch of the archaic, in harmony that is clear sounding in spite of thick clusters of notes, in subtle rhythms and colors that give to the whole a decorative effect, the song proceeds to a simple, eloquent close, in which is mirrored the tenderness of Pan's utterance and the trembling of Bilitis of the lowered eyes.

Le Tombeau des Naïades. The chantlike voice part moves forward, as across a fresco or a frieze, with the accompaniment conspiring to give it the solemnity of a slow march. The chords which cluster about it give it a harmonic feeling that was unknown in song before Debussy appeared. There are some tingling dissonances. Yet the effect is simple, direct, with something of the archaic and a touch of mystery.

> Le long du bois couvert de givre je marchais; mes cheveux devant ma bouche se fleurissaient de petits glaçons. . . .

The march tells of the slow tramping of Bilitis to the tomb of the naiads. The trail she has been following is that of a goat, Pan tells her. It is a frightful winter; the Satyrs and the nymphs are dead.

FÊTES GALANTES. Second series, 1904. Poems by Paul Verlaine.

Les Ingénus. They are youthful lovers, full of mischief and gay rapture, though their first confidence is a solemn affair.

> Les hauts talons luttaient avec les longues jupes
> En sorte que, selon le terrain et le vent
> Parfois luisaient des bas de jambes, trop souvent
> Interceptés, et nous aimions ce jeu de dupes. . . .

An inexorable succession of sixteenth notes illustrates the fondness of Debussy at this time for persistent patterns in which the rhythmic basis never changes. The accents of the vocal declamation at times are at variance with the accompaniment, which yields the feeling of an old dance transformed for the more sophisticated purposes of a later day. Thérèse Lavauden [4] cites this song as an example of Debussy's humor. After a beginning that apparently holds out the promise of a mood of harmless melancholy, she observes, the notes of a parody are suddenly heard at the phrase "Et nous aimons ce jeu," whose design, "with its appogiaturas of

---

[4] Article in the *Chesterian*, April–May, 1928.

obsequious foolishness, immediately lays bare these hearts benumbed by a thousand arrows."

Le Faune. Flute and tambourine seem to be participants in this ensemble of voice and piano. A flutelike prelude and postlude give the song its savor. There is a drumlike rhythm, but the faun is of plaster, watching over the enchanted wood where two lovers meet, and there is no dancing save in the imagination.

> Un vieux faune de terre cuite
> Rit au centre des boulingrins. . . .

The style is more precise and the harmony less vague than in most Debussy songs of his middle period. The rhythmic bass is an ostinato against which are traced the patterns of the imagined flute.

Colloque sentimental. Edwin Evans has said of this song that in its way it furnishes a Latin contrast for Schubert's *Doppelgänger*. But there is no such drama in the Debussy Lied as there is in Schubert's. In its place is a minute nuancing of feeling within a mood of disillusionment, as two ghostly figures recall their dead love, in a lonely park.

> Dans le vieux parc solitaire et glacé
> Deux formes ont tout à l'heure passé. . . .

A long pedal point sustains the dialogue, which is more declamatory than melodic, but in an episodic, reticent manner, yielding more than a suggestion of a sigh. The words have the naturalness of speech. The song is close to *Pelléas*.

TROIS CHANSONS DE FRANCE. 1904. Dedicated to Mme. Bardac. After the second series of *Fêtes galantes*, Debussy turned for his song texts from the Symbolists of his own day to French poets of older time. The medieval had taken hold of him and he was attracted to Charles d'Orléans and François Villon. That the seventeenth-century Tristan Lhermite also attracted him is readily explainable on the basis of the musicality of his verse. In this set are two settings of poems by the Duke of Orleans, both rondels, and one by Tristan. The last of these he transferred bodily to a subsequent series of songs, *Le Promenoir des deux amants,* made up entirely of settings of poems by Lhermite.

Le Temps a laissié son manteau. Rondel, with text by Charles d'Orléans. Debussy had to deal here with verse of a certain rigidity of form, the refrain of the first verse being repeated three times. In consequence there is a more obvious symmetry of the musical line than is to be noted in the songs of the so-called impressionistic character. The weather, sings the poet, has cast off its mantle of wind, cold, and rain and has clothed itself with shining sunlight. The setting has felicities suggestive of the calls of birds and the fresh colors of spring. The harmonies are bright, the rhythms lively. But in the modal feeling is something of another time.

La Grotte. (See *Auprès de cette grotte sombre,* of *Le Promenoir des deux amants,* below. The same song finds place in both groups.)

Pour ce que plaisance est morte. Poem by Charles d'Orléans. This second rondel from the fifteenth-century court where ruled the rhyming seigneur of the Château de Blois, sees Nature in a joyless mood. Now that Pleasure is dead, the May is clad in black. The setting abounds in harmonic and rhythmic contrasts. The feeling is archaic, though the coloring was "very modern" in 1904.

LE PROMENOIR DES DEUX AMANTS. 1904–10. Poems by Tristan Lhermite.[5] Dedicated to Emma-Claude Debussy. The preciosities of the era of Louis XIV summoned from Debussy equivalent niceties of expression. Grottoes, fountains, zephyrs were quite in his line, even though, as one critic said of these songs, such subjects and methods were productive of "everything except song for the singer with a voice."

Auprès de cette grotte sombre. The same song as *La Grotte* of the *Trois Chansons de France.* The poet sees his dreams in the reflections of the water.

[5] Also written L'hermite and l'Hermitte.

> Auprès de cette grotte sombre
> Où l'on respire un air si doux
> L'onde lutte avec les cailloux
> Et la lumière avec l'ombre. . . .

Clusters of notes in sudden rhythmic impulses play a coloristic part in the accompaniment, which is of rare perfection. But the song is not one of Debussy's most evocative.

Crois mon conseil. Over the poet and Climène, as they linger in the dusk, breathes the fragrant zephyr.

> Crois mon conseil, chère Climène;
> Pour laisser arriver le soir
> Je te prie, allons nous asseoir
> Sur le bord de cette fontaine. . . .

In the accompaniment are harplike figures. The vocal line is firmly etched.

Je tremble en voyant ton visage. Trembling at the sight of his lady's face, the lover of this labored poem fears to entrust his hopes and happiness to a barque which might be shipwrecked. He asks, instead, to be transported to Elysian fields. The setting is sympathetic—more so, perhaps, than it is successful in vitalizing its indifferent subject.

TROIS BALLADES DE VILLON. 1910. Settings, of course, of ballads by François Villon. Of these *Ballades* André Suarès has written that "he who understands this music in its plenitude; he who feels it with the spirit of love in which it was conceived, will understand Debussy at last; and he will know not only the charm, but the veiled power and quiet majesty of his genius." One would choose different words, perhaps, in saluting the genius of the immortal who provided the texts. There is more fire in a line of Villon than an entire Rondel by the Duke of Orleans, or a lifetime of verses by Tristan Lhermite. Debussy's halo formula of earlier years will not do for poems of such thrust and bite. These songs are in what may be regarded his last manner and they are among the most successful creations of a period of increased directness and hardness of line.

Ballade de Villon à s'amye. The friend is of the glamorous sex and there is no lack of manly bitterness in the poet's denunciation of her.

> Faulse beauté, qui tant me couste cher;
> Rude en effet, hypocrite douceur. . . .

In the shadow of age and death, everything has withered for the poet until only a desire for release is left. Debussy's broad melodic phrases mingle anguish with regret, the feeling of the song being established adroitly in the first measures of the piano part. The vocal line has more of declamation than melody and conveys with a considerable measure of intensity the emotion of the poem. To be noted in this song is one of the relatively few passages in his vocal music that Debussy marked *forte*.

Ballade que feit Villon à requeste de sa mère pour prier Nostre-Dame. Debussy has managed to suggest the churchlike character of the ballad without resort to obvious means. The simple faith of the poet's old mother is affectingly phrased in the song, with its hesitant, almost stammering refrain, "In this faith I wish to live and die."

> Dame du ciel, regente terrienne,
> Emperière des infernaulx palux
> Recevez-moy, vostre humble chrestienne. . . .

The music achieves a medieval atmosphere. The style is contrapuntal and the melodic content discreetly modal. The workmanship is exquisite, the text flawlessly set.

Ballade des femmes de Paris. All women of antiquity and of Europe pale before the women of Paris when it comes to chatter, laughs Villon—

> Quoy qu'on tient belles langagières
> Florentines, Veniciennes,
> Assez pour estre messaigières
> Et mesmement les anciennes. . . .

This is one of the raciest of the Debussy songs, with a bounding, propulsive motion and an infectious simulation of chatter in both the voice part and the accompaniment. Debussy has given the right "lift" to Villon's repeated phrase, "Il n'est bon bec que de Paris," emphasizing that the Parisian women carry off all honors. The glissando at the end is more than a charming touch. It is like a final flamboyant gesture on the part of the poet as he takes his leave.

TROIS BALLADES DE MALLARMÉ. 1913. Dedicated to Dr. Bonniot and to the memory of Stéphane Mallarmé. But once before, in *Apparition*, a song of his Conservatoire days, had Debussy set a text by Mallarmé. As this was Debussy's last set of songs, there lingers a thought that he regarded the task he set for himself as one he owed to the author of *L'Après-midi d'un faune*. That he postponed so long the labor of love— or duty, as the case may have been—would seem to indicate that he realized fully the danger courted by any musician who sought to add new sounds to this artist's "tortuous lyre," whose "hermetically sealed poems," so complete in themselves and of such perfection of form, seemed to discourage musical intrusion, save in the independent manner of the *L'Après-midi* prelude.

Soupir. This imagistic and highly involved verse begins:

> Mon âme vers ton front où rêve, ô calme soeur
> Un automne jonché de taches de rousseur. . . .

The cool majesty of Autumn is depicted in a personification, if the personification of a dream. It is an autumn "freckled with russet spots," an autumn of almost untranslatable metaphors, like that of "the tawny agony of leaves" that wander on the dead water where the wind plows a cold furrow. For this allegory Debussy has a thin, furrowlike line of melodic speech, bordering on recitative, skillfully supported by an accompaniment of a melancholy bareness and discursiveness.

Placet futile. This "futile petition" to a lady whose eyes are closed whenever she turns her lover's way partakes of the character of a slow minuet, with even more of the feeling of a sarabande. It is slender and spare, as if the composer sought to give the right of way to the poet's imagery, concerning himself chiefly with an accurate realization of the text and avoiding unnecessary musical competition. In its extreme of fantasy the text is both capricious and baffling, with a type of ironic humor so intellectual and literary as to raise at once a question as to what part music can play in the communication of it.

> Princesse! à jalouser le destin d'une Hébé
> Qui poind sur cette tasse au baiser de vos lèvres
> J'use mes feux, mais n'ai rang discret que d'abbé. . . .

Edwin Evans has recommended the following for the consideration of those who think they must sing Debussy's songs in translation:

> Since I may not be your furry-bearded lapdog,
> Nor lozenge, nor stick of rouge, nor yet the arch-
> forfeit of your games—appoint me shepherd of your
> smiles.

Thérèse Lavauden finds in Debussy's setting a salient example of his musical humor. She points particularly to the phrase "nommez-moi," dropped and taken up again in "the highly bantering tone of pomp married to affectation, while in the background a mocking onlooker stifles the laughter which the 'mauvaudage' arouses."

Eventail. It is the fan that speaks. An authority on Mallarmé, Roger Fry, points out that the real meaning of this poem is to be found in its revelation of a lack of meaning. The fan opens horizons and it closes them. There are red lips but no one to kiss them. Motion and incident make up a pattern and in the fan is symbolized futility.

> O rêveuse pour que je plonge
> Au pur délice sans chemin
> Sache, par un subtil mensonge
> Garder mon aile dans ta main. . . .

In his scherzando setting the composer has been faithful to the task he set for himself. Such complexity as the song possesses is that inherent in the text. For those to whom the poem itself has an appeal he has found a musical parallel that may be said to have enhanced its essential quality. But the test of interest remains an addiction to Mallarmé.

Noël des enfants qui n'ont plus de maisons.[6] 1915. The text is Debussy's own. Words and music were written on the eve of Debussy's first operation, in December of the second year of the World War. The song takes the form of a short prayer addressed by the children of the devastated zone to Le petit Noël, the French Santa Claus.

> Nous n'avons plus de maisons!
> Les ennemis ont tout pris,
> Tout pris, tout pris,
> Jusqu'à notre petit lit!

After a further recounting of the horrors of the war—the school and the teacher burned—the song closes with a prayer for victory. It is not a charitable song, much less one written on the principle of "Love thine enemy." In the naïvete of their supplication the children pray that there be no Christmas for the Germans and that they never see Christ. It is a prayer full of the suffering of the French, whose enemies have taken all, even the little beds. A pathetic melody, simple and direct, is supported by an accompaniment that has a breathless, almost gasping character. Harmonically, the song has touches to recall the era of *Pelléas*.

UNPUBLISHED SONGS

Caprice. 1880.
Chanson espagnole. (For two voices.)
Rondel chinois.
Romance. Poem by Paul Bourget.
Aimons-nous. Poem by Théodore de Banville.   } 1880–84.
La Fille aux cheveux de lin. Poem by Leconte de Lisle.
Eclogue. (For soprano and tenor.) Poem by Leconte de Lisle.

Berceuse. 1908. Poem by René Peter. (For the play, *La Tragedie de la mort.*)
Other songs have disappeared or perhaps were rewritten under different titles. A song called *Les Roses* figured in the Vasnier-Thieberg-Debussy concert of May 12, 1882. One called *Madrid, Princesse des Espagnes* is known to have been composed while Debussy was a student at the Conservatoire. Another song of this

---

[6] Also written for children's chorus.

early period was called *Ballade à la lune* and was a setting of a poem by Alfred de Musset. Originally intended for the second series of *Fêtes galantes* was a setting of *Crepuscule du soir*.

ERRONEOUSLY ATTRIBUTED

Chanson d'un fou. Composed by Émile Pessard to text by Alphonse Daudet; published as by Debussy.

Ici-bas. Composed by Paul and Lucien Hillemacher to text by Sully Prudhomme; published as by Debussy.

IV

THE ORCHESTRAL WORKS

IT was not known that Debussy ever had considered writing a symphony until, more than a decade after his death, there was found in Russia the manuscript of a movement from the youthful work dedicated to Mme. von Meck and headed *Symphonie en si mineur*. As it exists only as a piano duet, it affords no clue as to whether the Debussy of 1880, eighteen years old and for seven years a student at the Conservatoire, could have scored an orchestral work successfully. The cantatas and the *Fantaisie* for piano and orchestra, products of the middle and later part of the same decade, show him able to write clearly and idiomatically in his application of what he had been taught of instrumentation. The individuality of Debussy's scoring, as time progressed, was closely allied with his harmony, a further corroboration that with Debussy the secret of musical personality was to be found in his ear for unorthodox combinations, successions, and concatenations, as witnessed by his fellow students and his instructors very early in his Conservatoire years. But Debussy's orchestra was not a blended orchestra in the sense that his harmony was a blend. He loved pure color and to a degree to ally him with composers of pre-Beethoven times. In this, his scoring was strikingly different from his German contemporaries and represented very different orchestral conceptions than those of Wagner, Brahms, and Strauss.

It has been said of Debussy that he gave back its original quality to each instrument, freeing it from the enormous servitude into which Wagner had forced them all in limning the scenes and portraits of his music-dramas. Wagner's tone colors, to quote André Suarès, are like Kundry on her knees, pleading: "Dienen, dienen!" With Debussy, the families of instruments are emancipated; there is for him no such regimentation as generalissimo Richard Strauss brings about in the battle of "Heldenleben" and elsewhere. Harmonically, Debussy favored the block-like chords that eventually took on the aspect of formulas. His orchestral works share with the others the liberal employment of such devices. But the scoring aims at a transparency or a vaporosity in which basic timbres do not lose their individuality by virtue of group or mass timbre. There is never the thick impasto of the post-Wagnerians. In contrasting Beethoven's orchestra with Wagner's, Debussy referred to Beethoven's as "a formula in black and white, resulting in the whole exquisite gamut of grays," whereas Wagner was declared to rely on "a species of polychromatic putty, spread almost uniformly." With Wagner, said Debussy—speaking in words of *Monsieur Croche* —it was no longer possible to distinguish the sound of the violin from that of the trombone.

Debussy thought of different parts of the compass of a given instrument as if these parts were different instruments. Frenchman that he was, he was particularly drawn to the woodwinds and wrote for them with the acme of taste and sensibility. What Wagner was to the brasses, Debussy was to the woodwind group, which he favored with many of the most exquisite curves of his orchestral melody. The harp, too, has much to thank him for; he rescued it from its latter-day employment as merely a contributor to sonorous climaxes and gave it back a role of its own to play. In all of its aspects Debussy's scoring is essentially French and when utilized as the means of setting off a characteristic harmonic passage it is so distinctive as to settle the identity of the composer then and there. Composers so different as Puccini, Stravinsky, and Strauss—masters all of an individual idiom —have their patches of scoring that to any ordinarily experienced listener prompt at once the mental observation, "Debussy."

In a sense, Debussy created his orchestral forms, a different form for each work, but all are kin. *L'Après-midi d'un faune* is described as a Prélude; *Nuages, Fêtes,* and *Sirènes* are "Nocturnes"; *Gigues, Ibéria,* and *Rondes de printemps* are "Images." But Prélude and Nocturne have had quite different meanings for other composers, Chopin particularly. If there is any such musical form as "image," it would be difficult to define. Orchestrally, Debussy was no miniaturist, but neither did he attempt to fill canvases of heroic proportions. There was nothing of the panorama in his painting. He seized upon some aspect of the sea, the sky, the season, the dream; and this he converted to a state of feeling communicable in music. Much else might have been in view besides that particular aspect, but he was concerned with what he felt and this was what he gave out. In a sense it is music of a detail, but not music of details. There is a limitation of the scene, but little or no delineation of its particularized parts. Debussy's orchestra is never imitative. There is an inescapable consonance between timbre and subject, which, with Debussy, was fundamentally something of taste. If he could never have surrendered to the banal realism of the Straussian sheep-bleating in *Don Quixote,* neither could he have abjured the flute for the drowsy reverie of his faun. If *Ibéria,* as Manuel de Falla said of it, has the intoxication of Andalusian nights, this is because Debussy could summon color glints to match his rhythms, because his was a technique of instrumentation that was equal to his imaginative concepts. Imagination pervades the scoring of all of Debussy's major works for orchestra. *Nuages* and *La Mer* are almost parallels in the suggestive quality of their orchestral sound; the procession midway in *Fêtes,* though easily degraded to a mere "effect" in the reading of a conductoral showman, is one of the most magical moments ever contrived by a master of the orchestra.

Much has been said of Debussy as one who drew veils between the listener and his music. Sometimes he does. But quite as often he withdraws a veil not of his making, and in the felicities of his orchestra are crystallized and made irradiate the nameless sensations that linger on the borders of consciousness behind men's eyes.

ORCHESTRAL WORKS

Printemps. 1887. A symphonic suite for orchestra and chorus. Dedicated to the memory of August Durand. Second of the *Envois de Rome*, the last one really composed at the Villa Medici. It was inspired by Botticelli's painting, *Primavera*, and has nothing to do with the two choruses of the same name written at the Conservatoire. In its modal suggestion and its ambiguity of tonality it foreshadows later works. The humming chorus is a prefiguration of *Sirènes* of the *Nocturnes*. It was the cause of the abandonment of Debussy's concert of *envois* soon after he returned to Paris, as he failed to obtain approval for its inclusion in the program with *La Demoiselle élue*.

PRELUDE A L'APRÈS-MIDI D'UN FAUNE

Composed during the years 1892–94, and dedicated to Raymond Bonheur. The relation of Debussy's music to Mallarmé's poem, *L'Après-midi d'un faune*, is clarified when it is understood that the poet conceived his verse as a monologue to be recited by an actor, thus giving it a stage character. When first announced for a Brussels concert of March 1, 1894, Debussy's composition was listed as *Prélude, Interlude et Paraphrase Finale pour l'Après-midi d'un faune*. This would seem to infer further unfoldments of the text, possibly in connection with its declamation by a speaker in accordance with Mallarmé's intent.

No one has been able to supply an inkling as to what else Debussy had in mind, or whether in abandoning the other sections he may have incorporated in the Prélude certain musical ideas that otherwise would have been encountered in the Interlude or the Finale. So perfect in its unity and manner of progress is the Prélude, and so exclusively elaborated from its own basic themes, that any splicing or telescoping seems most unlikely. But the circumstance that Debussy did plan additional music and had not originally contemplated a Prélude that would stand alone may be a warning against any construction of the Prélude that would make of it a parallel for the complete poem, or in any sense a synopsis of such incident as the poem can be said to possess. Possibly it was because he became convinced that the Prélude did say all there was for him to say in a musical transvaluation of the poem that he discarded the other sections, regarding them as repetitious and superfluous.

Mallarmé's poem was written in 1876 for Coquelin aîné, and when published in the same year was illustrated by Manet. Much has been said of its lack of lucidity, among other descriptions being that which dubs it a "famous miracle of unintelligibility." Mallarmé sought to refresh the languid current of French literary style by the use of odd, exotic, and archaic words, meanwhile rejecting terms that were worn with use and lacking in luster. As Edmund Gosse has summarized it, Mallarmé aimed "to use words in such harmonious combinations as will suggest to the reader a mood or condition which is not mentioned in the text, but is nevertheless paramount in the poet's mind at the moment of composition." Mallarmé wrote to Gosse, saying: "I make music and do not call by this name that which is drawn from the euphonic putting together of words—this first requirement is taken for granted; but that which is beyond, on the other side, and produced magically by certain dispositions of speech and language, is then only a means of communication with the reader, as are the keys of the pianoforte to a hearer."

The English scholar, confessing that for him to say that he understood the poem bit by bit and phrase by phrase would be excessive, even though he cherished it and had read it many times, prepared a précis that has been widely quoted in program annotations on both sides of the Atlantic. Lawrence Gilman has suggested that if Debussy had been an Englishman he might have been tempted to set music to this "inimitable paraphrase." But paraphrase it is, leaving to the reader of the original French or the translations of Alexander Cohen and A. I. Ellis the reward of such discoveries as the faun's imagined seizure of the Naiads who have troubled his memory, of the struggle and escape of one and the vanishment of his illusion, of the pursuit of a vision of Venus herself on the summit of Mount Etna, and of the Nemesis that so impious a desire must bring upon him. All this and more in the transitions of the daydream conjured forth by a febrile imagination, ere the faun returns to his slumber in the noontide haze of a drowsing countryside, must be ascertained apart from Gosse's transcript. Familiarity with the original makes it less difficult to understand why, after the second performance of the Prélude in Paris—seventeen years before the commotion aroused by Nijinsky's choreographic interpretation of the work—there was printed in the *Annales du Théâtre* the note: "Written after a poem by Stéphane Mallarmé so sadistic that M. Colonne did not dare to print the text; young girls attend his concerts." That was 1895, and in Paris. Debussy, in describing his Prélude as a very free illustration of Mallarmé's poem, said merely that his music sought to evoke "the successive scenes in which the longings and the desires of the faun pass in the heat of the afternoon."

But is the poem so miraculously unintelligible, after all? The many thousands of American and English concert patrons who have thought of it almost solely in the words of the Gosse paraphrase may obtain at least an approximation of the original in an admirable translation by Alex. Cohen which has the virtue—or will it be found a fault?—of being entirely understandable. By permission, Mr. Cohen's English version is reprinted here from *Musical Opinion* for September, 1935.

From *Musical Opinion* for September, 1935.

L'APRES-MIDI D'UN FAUNE

Stéphane Mallarmé

Eclogue

I would perpetuate those nymphs.
                Their rosy
Bloom's so light, it floats upon air drowsy
With heavy sleep.
           Was it a dream?
                  The mound
Of my old dark uncertainty was crowned
By subtle boughs and leaves which, still remaining
Woods, alas, persuade me that the feigning
Roses shaped my fleeting dream for me.
Reflect......
           Are then those nymphs that came to thee
Desires that from thy fabled senses rise?
Illusion wells forth from the chaste blue eyes
Of the first, cold as weeping springs: and she,
The second, made of sighs, O can she be
The sultry breeze that stirs thy fleece at noon?
Ah no! Athwart the still and weary swoon
That stifles the freshness of the struggling breeze,
No water murmurs, save what dews the trees
In sound poured from my flute. Amid the hush
The only puff of wind to stir's the gush
That from my twin pipes blows an arid rain
Of music, save that where upon the plain
The skyline circles tranquilly there floats
The breath that artifice transmutes to notes,
Seeking at length the home it left on high
When inspiration called it from the sky.

Calm mere, whose shores are pillaged by my pride
That with Sicilian suns has more than vied,
But now is mute 'neath flowering sparks, tell how
"I here cut reeds that I did then endow
With genius; how, upon the distant wold

That wreathes its limpid springs with green and gold,
A wave of white flesh resting idly stirred:
How, when the first slow notes I piped were heard,
The swans, no! naiads, flew off helter-skelter,
Or swiftly dived" ......
      Around this woodland shelter
The tawny hour is burning fiercely, so
That all things lie inert, and none doth know
How that great rout of hymen fled from me,
Whose all consuming quest is for the SHE.
Let me then wake old ardours and, upright
And lone, lilies, flooded neath ancient light,
Let me be one of you for artlessness!

In no wise like the lips' lightsome caress
—The kiss with which false love calms doubt and fear—
My breast attests a mystic imprint here,
Although no mark of queenly teeth it bears.
—Enough! such secrets must be told in airs
Played by the confidant who sings my fires,
Twin-reed that, fluting of languor and desires,
Dreams, in an arabesque, we were amusing
The beauty hereabout by falsely confusing
Its charm with the illusion art creates:
Scaling the heights to which love modulates,
My music veils those forms, naked and white
—Through closed eyes I pursue the flock in flight—
Blurring the starkness of the tedious line.

Essay then, instrument of flight—malign
Syrinx—to bloom again beside our lake!
I'll paint adorëd goddesses and make
The girdle fall from many a shadowy shape:
Proud of my fame, their forms I shall undrape.
Thus, when the grape's radiance I drain,
To quench regret I fill the globes again,
Laughingly puffing the empty grape-skins tight
And gazing through the glowing spheres till night
Athirst for drunkenness and ecstasy.

O, nymphs, let's plump the grapes of MEMORY!
"Piercing the reeds, mine eye speared each immortal

Bosom that slakes a rage unknown to mortal
Within that lake, and cries from wood to sky;
In a sun-shot flash of shuddering jewelry
The glitter of their tresses sinks from view!
I run: when, at my feet outstretched, lo two
Maidens with languor laden I see sleeping,
Wounded with love, each in the other's keeping,
Their arms twined in a casual fond embrace.
I pick them up, not seeking to unlace
The pair, and bear them to this rosebush where
Sweet sun-drained perfume fills the ambient air
And where our play and sun-drunk pleasure may
Be rose-flecked like the heavens of burnt-out day."
I love thee, virginal fury, shrinking rapture
Of sacred naked burdens that I capture
Fleeing my fiery lips that drink like quivering
Lightning the secret terror of the shivering
Flesh. From the elder's feet my kisses dart
Their fire to the younger's timid heart,
And both together with their kindling sense,
Forsaken are by erstwhile innocence,
Wild tears, or some less piteous dew, in eyes
From which the old ingenuousness dies.

"But herein lay my trespass and my guilt;
Quelling their traitor fears I did exult,
And the tangled tuft of kisses I unwound
That gods about the guileless pair had bound.
By her hand I held the younger of the twain
So that her sister's quickened sense might stain
Her dove's unblushing whiteness: straight thereafter,
Seeking to suppress my burning laughter
In the happy bosom of the elder one,
I felt as though some vague death had undone
The prison of my drunken arms. My prey,
Ingrate, deaf to my sobbing, slipped away."

No matter! Others will drag me to caresses,
Binding my horns with bonds of amorous tresses.
Desire, thou knowest, that to quench the thirst
Of murmuring bees, the pomegranates will burst
Their ripe and purple fruit; and that our blood,

In love with all that seeks it, is in flood
For all the everlasting swarms of passion.
At evening, when this wood grows gold and ashen,
The dying foliage blazes festively.
Etna! 'tis then that Venus visits thee,
Withdrawn as is her wont from her retreat,
To tread thy lava with her artless feet
When thy flames die in slumbrous thunder, spent.
I hold the goddess!

      O sure chastisement!......

Quelled at length by conquering silent noon,
My speechless soul and heavy body swoon.
On thirsty sand be now my sin in sleep's
Oblivion stilled. I'd drain with parted lips
Dream's starry wine. Farewell! I go to see
O Nymphs, the shades that ye already be.

Revised translation by ALEX. COHEN

The background thus considered and in some degree assimilated for association's sake, Debussy's music is to be listened to primarily as music and certainly with no effort to relate any particular passage to a corresponding idea in the poem. *The Afternoon of a Faun* is scored for three flutes, two oboes, English horn, two clarinets, two bassoons, four horns, two harps, small antique cymbals, strings. The antique cymbals, tiny plates of definite pitch, are the only departures from the usual ensemble. Two themes supply the basic substance of the work. The flute enunciates the first in its softest and most dulcet accents at the beginning. It is a subject compounded of scale-wise passages, chromaticized within a narrow gamut of three whole tones. With oboes, clarinets, and horn responding and the harp adding a glissando, the theme passes through mutations of color, the while a slumbrous haze is created by muted strings and horns, mindful of the summer day. Debussy's love of the arabesque is not to be denied as this first section of the work expands in the shimmer and iridescence of Debussy's harmonic coloration. The music grows more sensuous, more desirous, as flute yields to clarinet and clarinet to oboe; and the second subject, much the more positive of the two, is chanted among the woodwinds. The new theme is brought to a climax, with the harp and woodwinds accompanying the strings, and, as its passion subsides, a solo violin leads beautifully on to a passage suggestive of a fleeting vision of the nymphs. The first theme returns, more languorous even than before, as fresh chords take possession and the vision seems to pass. A solo 'cello that attaches itself to the flute, two stopped horns that take up in thirds the pattern of the opening and trancelike harmonies of violins and clarinets are woven into an enchanted close, with repeated phrases for harps against full soft chords and the tiny, bell-like tone of the antique cymbals glinting through the fading dream. Of *The Afternoon of a Faun* can be said without hesitation what has been said of the *Lohengrin* Prelude: that at the time it was written nothing like it existed in music.

NOCTURNES. 1893–99. (1) *Nuages.* (2) *Fêtes.* (3) *Sirènes.* Dedicated to Georges Hartmann. The original manuscript of the sketches, in the form of a condensed score, is now in the Library of Congress in Washington, D.C. It contains a notation to the effect that the composer finished them on December 15, 1899, at three o'clock in the morning. But he was later to make many changes in the scoring. In Debussy's own explanation of his purposes, "the title *Nocturnes* is intended to have a more general, and above all, a more decorative meaning" than that ordinarily accorded it in its use for musical purposes. "We, then, are not concerned with the form of the Nocturne, but with everything that this word includes in the way of diversified impression and special lights.

Intended originallÿ as a triptych for solo violin and orchestra and with the thought of Ysaÿe as their interpreter, the *Nocturnes* are so notably an example of precisely the right treatment that one can only wonder today how Debussy could have thought of them otherwise and particularly as music for a solo instrument. Nowhere else in his orchestral music has he been more essentially the painter, more characteristically the impressionist. That a kinship should be found to the *Nocturnes* of Whistler was inevitable, particularly in the gray tones of *Nuages*. Debussy wrote of them, at the time the *Nocturnes* were being formulated for the violin, as "a study in gray painting." But Renoir and Claude Monet likewise have been drawn into discussions of this music as something singularly close to the parallel art; though the pictures presented are not the literal ones that musical realists would have essayed. They are evocations rather than descriptions, reflections rather than specific images; but it is not to be denied that both *Clouds* and *Festivals* have a scenic quality. In them Debussy again demonstrates his ability to achieve much with little; there is an economy of resource, together with logic and coherence of form, all without a superfluous bar or gratuitous note. Only *Sirènes* departs from the customary scoring in its use of wordless women's voices. The resources utilized in the three nocturnes are as follows:

Nuages: Two flutes, two oboes, English horn, two clarinets, three bassoons, four horns, kettledrums, harp, and strings.

Fêtes: Three flutes, two oboes, English horn, two clarinets three bassoons, four horns, three trumpets, three trombones, bass tuba, two harps, a set of three kettledrums, cymbals, snare drum (in the distance), and strings.

Sirènes: Three flutes, oboe, English horn, two clarinets, three bassoons, four horns, three trumpets, two harps, eight soprano voices, eight mezzo-soprano voices, and strings.

NUAGES

Debussy's thought, as he explained it, was of "the unchanging aspect of the sky, with the slow and melancholy passage of the clouds dissolving in a gray vagueness [1] tinged with white." Two clarinets and two bassoons move across the orchestral canvas at the opening. Vallas and some others have found an unconscious souvenir of Moussorsgky in this opening, regarding the theme as a note-for-note borrowing from the song, *Sunless*. The feeling of the phrase, as enunciated by Debussy, is so very different that the likeness is more convincing on paper than it is when the phrase is made audible in the orchestra. Stravinsky also is credited with having employed the same notation for a theme in his *Rossignol*. (Ernest Newman once traced a given figuration back through virtually every important composer of several centuries to the very beginnings of art music, then followed it forward again along a different course.) The circumstance remains that *Nuages* is one of the most personal, the most individual, the most original, the most Debussyan of the masterpieces on which his reputation rests. Again, it is the harmony that creates the mood; harmony that employs discords in a manner to suggest the vibrations of light sought through conflict of color in the works of the impressionist painters. The orchestral sonorities remain peculiarly lucent, whatever the minute clashes of harmonic blending.

Unforgettable is the moment of song when the English horn, languorous but forthright, fashions a delicious fragment of melody against an undulous background in which the strings have returned to the design of the original theme. If, as has been said, this passage for the *cor anglais* was suggested by the tooting whistles of the little Seine steamers, Debussy's imagination carried him a long way from the original. The music is inescapably cloudlike, as one vista melts into another. The tone fades imperceptibly and there is silence where but a moment before was the faint glow of horns and a final soft pizzicato against an almost inaudible drum roll. One commentator thinks of Baudelaire's prose poem, *The Stranger*, and of the Enigmatical Man's reply, when asked what it was he really loved in this world, since he had neither father, mother, sister, brother, friends, or country. "I love the clouds, the clouds that pass yonder,

[1] Philip Hale, who remarked upon the difficulty of finding an English equivalent for some of Debussy's expressions, translated this as "a gray agony tinted with white."

the marvellous clouds." Debussy also loved the leafy arbor and the
sea. He returned several times to these, but *Nuages* was his one
avowed adventure in the drifting mansions of the sky.

FÊTES

The second of the *Nocturnes* is as brilliant and animated as the
first is dream-bound and reticent. If *Nuages* is something of merging grays, suffused with delicate hints of warmer colors, *Fêtes*
is iridescent and vibrant with ever-changing lights that quiver
in their momentary intensity. Debussy's imagination dwelt upon
"the restless dancing rhythms of the atmosphere, interspersed with
abrupt scintillations." Midway is an incidental procession, which he
described as "a wholly visionary pageant—passing through and
blended with the revelry; but the background of the uninterrupted
festival persists; luminous dust participating in the universal
rhythm." Finely powdered sonorities, produced by an instrumentation in which there is much subdivision, produce a glitter that
was new in a world heavy with the Germanic type of rich and
massive scoring. In *Fêtes* is a luminosity of vibration that even with
Debussy was to stand alone. Muted brass assumed a new importance
in scoring. The harp became something aerial and atmospheric
rather than an accompaniment or a decoration. The play of rhythm
is no less dazzling than that of instrumental color. Wisps of melody
jostle one another in a tonal *Mardi Gras*. The spirit is that of high
revelry until there comes upon the auditory carnival a miracle as
from another sphere, the visionary procession which the composer
likened to "luminous dust." There is a sudden hush in the gay swirl
of the celebrants; from the harps, drums and pizzicato basses comes
a marchlike accompaniment above which are sounded faint fanfares, approaching nearer and mounting to a scintillant but still dis-
embodied climax, a phantom *divertissement* in a world of pure
fantasy. Muted trumpets and cymbals tingle in the air. As the vision
passes, echoing from afar, the dancelike swirl of the opening is resumed, there is an amorous interlacing of woodwinds in the sultry
evening air and the music dies away, leaving, like *Pelléas et Melis-
ande*, the afterglow of "a dream within a dream."

SIRÈNES

The last to be decked out and formally introduced, *Sirènes* has
remained the Cinderella of the sister *Nocturnes*. Its infrequent

performance has separated it from *Nuages* and *Fêtes* and this, no doubt, has influenced many to believe that it is a work of inferior quality, else why so seldom performed? Its employment of a women's chorus is at once its distinctive element and its handicap. Symphonic institutions are loath to undertake works which require them to augment their forces with a vocal ensemble; choral groups either do not possess the symphonic resources for performance of music of this type or they turn by preference to compositions of contrapuntal or chordal upbuildings in which the feeling is essentially vocal and primarily choral. The voices of Debussy's sirens are wordless. They are used instrumentally, perhaps with more of the intent of the originally projected violin than seems conceivable to anyone who knows this *Nocturne* in its final form. Debussy had a similar choral idea for his *Printemps* of the middle 'eighties.

The intonation of *Sirènes* always has troubled singers. Of the first performance in Paris Louis Laloy wrote that the enchantresses, confused by the chromatic inflections, sang augmented and diminished semitones that were not unpleasing; they caused him to think "of the flat diatonic and the sesquilateral chromatic so dear to the contemporaries of Pericles."

Debussy's summation of *Sirènes* reads like the program for a tone poem: "The sea and its unnumerable rhythm; then amid the billows silvered by the moon the mysterious song of the sirens is heard; it laughs and passes." The voices do much of the silvering. About their melodic line the orchestra billows and casts up arabesques of spray. All is undulant, spacious, airy. The tonal structure is built largely of two notes which rise or fall a tone, with something of the fixity and monotony of waves, but with harmonies as changing as the incessantly moving sea. Rhythmically altered, the motive of rising and falling moves against backgrounds of varying lights and shadows. About it all is a deceptive simplicity. The singers find that they are not merely so many violins, violas, and 'cellos; they also are momentarily clarinets or horns.

Ordinarily regarded as one of the least successful of Debussy's larger works, *Sirènes* yet has evoked rhapsodical praise, as in this comment by André Suarès. "Never before," he says in his recent study of Debussy's music, "never before so much genius; never with a taste which penetrates so deeply into the soul and is so unusual. When one has just heard *Sirènes*, one is tempted to sigh: 'Music before Debussy and music after Debussy.' Of course, nothing which has been a masterpiece in previous centuries ceases to be one; but this one palpitates and breathes in us. It opens the doors, so hard to discover, of our own emotion; they are no longer obscure or distant. Debussy is on the threshold which invites us to enchantment; we are there with him; he is with us. . . . Never has a choir of women had more of languid beauty or been more adroitly given over to the delicious pleasure of song. . . . Happy or disillusioned, wild with desire or weeping, the sirens are ever calling, ever calling . . . they disappear little by little in the distance, but they carry away with them their precious torment . . . the harmony accompanies them and follows them . . . one no longer knows if they are two different things. . . . One sees the shimmer in these instrumental pearls . . . an infinite melancholy, an eternal ardor which covers itself with ashes in order to last longer; so much ravishing tenderness in which the most sensual caress seems to be only the shadow of the intoxication of the soul. . . ." All leading to the crowning of Achille-Claude Debussy as the King of Sirens!

LA MER

Trois Esquisses symphoniques. Composed 1903–1905. (1) *De l'aube à midi sur la mer* (*From Dawn till Noon on the Ocean*), (2) *Jeux de vagues* (*Play of the Waves*), (3) *Dialogue du vent et de la mer* (*Dialogue of the Wind and Sea*). The dedication is to Jacques Durand. This is Debussy's most extended separate orchestral work. It is also the one nearest the symphony, by reason of the relation of its complementary movements, no one of which, however, can be regarded as in symphonic form except as the term may be loosely applied to the generality of large-scale orchestral music. Though any one of the three sketches could be played alone, and there would be both musical coherence and imaginative communication in such a performance, the tie between the three is so close, and the manner in which they complete one another so satisfying in all that pertains to unity and fitness, that to separate them seems as dubious a procedure as to separate movements of symphonies. This is not true of the *Nocturnes* or the *Images*. In the one instance *Nuages* and *Fêtes* go their way unabashedly without *Sirènes*. In the other *Ibéria* seems to have parted company permanently with *Gigues* and *Rondes de printemps*, so far as public performance is concerned. Doubtless there is a somewhat different principle involved. *Nocturnes* and *Images* are collective titles for compositions dealing with different subjects, one from another. There is only one sea; the three movements present three different aspects of the same subject.

In the scoring the composer has treated the movements somewhat differently, but that, of course, has been true of the movements of many symphonies.

From Dawn till Noon on the Ocean is scored for piccolo, two flutes, two oboes, English horn, two clarinets, three bassoons, four horns, three trumpets, three trombones, bass tuba, a set of three kettledrums, cymbals, tam-tam, two harps, and strings.

Play of the Waves is scored for piccolo, two flutes, two oboes, English horn, two clarinets, three bassoons, four horns, three trumpets, cymbals, triangle, a Glockenspiel (or celesta), two harps, and strings.

Dialogue of Wind and Sea is scored for piccolo, two flutes, two oboes, English horn, two clarinets, three bassoons, double-bassoon, four horns, three trumpets, two cornets-à-pistons, three trombones, bass tuba, a set of three kettledrums, bass drum, cymbals, tam-tam, Glockenspiel, two harps, and strings.

According to the notation on a rough draft of the orchestral score in the library at the Eastman School of Music in Rochester, N.Y., Debussy finished *La Mer* on Sunday, March 5, 1905, at six o'clock in the evening. Another date is scratched out.

Perhaps no other work from his pen has so completely baffled those musical analysts whose burden it has been to put into words something comprehensible about his musical processes. Program annotators, almost to a man, have foregone all but a literary and interpretative description of the sketches, on the basis that anything that might be written about the thematic and structural aspects of the work would probably remain unintelligible. Yet it has been said of *La Mer*, both in commendation and in regret over an apparent change of style, that it is more robust, more definite as to line and color, more complex of texture, more dense, and more polyphonic than his earlier orchestral compositions.

The difficulty seems to be that in going its own way, instead of following the traditional procedure of the symphony or the tone poem, it lacks those fixed points which can be recognized in the description of a symphony and to which can be related details of departure from, as well as conformity with, the familiar patterns. It is not feasible to refer to tonalities, since there is a kind of incessant modulation. To attempt to particularize thematic material is also futile, because of equally incessant transformation. Yet *La Mer* is anything but amorphous; there is a tighter holding of the reins of form—Debussy's kind of form—than in the earlier works. As a detail, there is a partial community of theme. Indeed, some of the disappointment the work produced among confirmed Debussyists in

France was due to what they regarded as its increased tangibility. For them the true Debussy must remain nebulous.

In some quarters, *La Mer* has been regarded as the beginning of a return to classical form, of a kind, as represented much more fully by Debussy's final Sonatas. It has been looked upon as the first fruit of a new style in which the composer sought to shake off the purposely indefinite dreaminess of such works as *L'Après-midi* and *Nuages*. Others have viewed it as a direct outgrowth of *Sirènes*. Ironically enough, Debussy was criticized for not varying his style and then for varying it. With Wagner, the circumstance that each of his great music-dramas (regarding the *Ring* as one work) brought some great departure has been regarded as vastly significant of his genius; with Brahms, the essential oneness of goal and procedure in his symphonies, varied as they are in spiritual aspiration and musical content, has been a similar monument to his character as a composer.

The three movements of *La Mer* are technical achievements not elsewhere surpassed by Debussy. If they are still in some sense a battleground—perhaps more so in France than in America—this is chiefly because of disagreement over their expressiveness, both as music *per se* and as a species of tone painting illustrative of their literary or scenic subject; a disagreement in which questions of realism, symbolism, impressionism enter in, as well as quite other questions that hark back to a more orthodox sort of thematic creation. The finesse, the dexterity, the surety, and the unity of the work, and of each of the component movements, are beyond dispute.

De l'aube à midi sur la mer was preceded as title for the first movement by *Mer belle aux îes Sanguinaires*, though Debussy, as has been pointed out, had never been to Corsica. It was said that he liked the discarded designation because of the contrast between "belle" and "sanguinaires." The rising-falling figure of *Sirènes* is expanded into the wavelike suggestion which pervades this and the subsequent movements. There is a mysterious, eerie quality in the undulations with which this sketch begins. In the music are at once an incantation and an awakening. The chief subject—for subject of course it has—is declaimed by muted trumpet and English horn. Thereafter, as the light seems to grow clearer and Nature more boisterous, the waves of this chimerical sea ride higher, throwing their spume into the sunshine, with all manner of glint and refraction, exultant, tumultuous, but not menacing or cruel. Toward the end, wind instruments intone a solemn and noble theme that has been described as "the chorale of the depths." Above it continues the pitching of the waves; there comes a momentary lull, then a last shake of the mane of these horses of the sea.

Jeux de vagues is the one original title retained. Here Debussy limns his now thoroughly awakened sea at play. There are waves of every color and mood in a capricious sport of wind and spray. In a contrastive sense this is the scherzo of Debussy's heretical symphony. The elements dance, they romp and race through immemorial games the secrets of which never will be known to man. The waves become coryphées or they gambol like dolphins. About all is an aura of the remote and the unreal. This is a world of sheer fantasy, of strange visions and eerie voices, a mirage of sight and equally a mirage of sound. On the sea's vast stage is presented a trancelike phantasmagoria so evanescent and fugitive that it leaves behind only the vagueness of a dream.

Dialogue du vent et de la mer, originally *Le vent fait danser la mer*, presents a gustier and a wilder sea, with a stronger dramatic emphasis and something more closely akin to human quality in the impersonation, however incorporeal it may be, of wind and ocean. The use of the whole-tone scale is more conspicuous in this movement than elsewhere in *La Mer*. There are two clear recollections of the first movement, the first subject being whisked back in one of countless necromantic transformations of fragments of song, and the chorale returning again for a climax of glowing sonorities. This climax has few parallels in Debussy's usually reticent scoring. The brass peals forth in shining splendor. At the close is again the undulation of harmonies suggestive of the sea that rolls and will not cease to roll, whatever the puny destinies of man. The dialogue of wind and wave is of cosmic things, of which Debussy's arabesques are cabalistic symbols. The music only hints at the immensities it does not attempt to describe. "Yet beneath these elusive and mysterious overtones," writes Lawrence Gilman, "the reality of the living sea persists: the immemorial fascination lures and enthralls and terrifies; so that we are almost tempted to fancy that the two are, after all, identical—the ocean that seems an actuality of wet winds and tossing spray and inexorable depths and reaches, and that uncharted and haunted and incredible sea which opens before the magic casements of the dreaming mind."

KING LEAR. Incidental music. 1904. (1) *Fanfare.* (2) *Sommeil de Lear.* The only fragments remaining of the music Debussy undertook for a stage revival of Shakespeare's play.

IMAGES. For orchestra. 1906–12. The musical relationship between the three orchestral works of this group, *Ibéria*, completed 1908, *Rondes de printemps*, 1909, and *Gigues*, 1911 (with orchestration in 1912 by André Caplet) is no more apparent than that existing between the pieces of the first set of piano *Images* (1905) or the second set (1907). Save in Debussy's own grouping of them under a common title, they have had a minimum of association together, anywhere, *Ibéria* having gone its separate way as the only one widely performed. With *Rondes de printemps*, *Ibéria* was originally planned and announced as for two pianos, but like the *Nocturnes* (intended for violin solo and orchestra) it never saw the light of public performance in its first form. Debussy was a long time finishing these scores, which were to have been ready in 1906, a year after the completion of *La Mer*. They are a product of the same time as the *Images* for the piano and there are similarities, both as to ends and means. One of the links between the three parts of the triptych, if it can, indeed, be so regarded, is the use of music of a folk order in each of the works, though that of *Ibéria* is so completely a re-distillation as to be something of feeling rather than quotable phrases. As *Ibéria* is basically and atmospherically Spanish, *Rondes de printemps* is French and *Gigues* is English.

Debussy's own attitude toward these works is reflected in a statement contained in a communication of March, 1908, to the effect that he has been "trying to achieve something different," with that something different described as "an effect of reality." This effect of reality, he added, was "what some imbeciles call 'impressionism,' a term that is utterly misapplied, especially by the critics; for they do not hesitate to apply it to Turner, the finest creator of mysterious effects in the whole world of art."

IBÉRIA

Ibéria is scored for piccolo, three flutes (one interchangeable with a second piccolo), two oboes, English horn, three clarinets, three bassoons, double bassoon, four horns, three trumpets, three trombones, bass tuba, kettledrums, side drum, tambourine, castanets, xylophone, celesta, cymbals, three bells (F, G, A), two harps and the usual strings. There are three sections of contrasting mood, each with its literary designation, but connected by the repetition of thematic material and played without a break. (1) *Par les rues et par les chemins (In the Streets and By-Ways)*, (2) *Les Parfums de la nuit (The Fragrance of the Night)*, (3) *Le Matin d'un jour de fête (The Morning of the Festival Day)*.

Manuel de Falla has commented on Debussy's unusual thematic processes in *Ibéria*, the initial subject of the first section giving rise to all manner of subtle transformations. This generic theme is a kind of Sevilliana which, to Falla, "seems to float in a clear atmosphere of scintillating light." Castanets and tambourine play a recognizable part in immediate identification of the locale; the former being heard at the outset, when the first of the three evocations begins with a burst of brilliant color. A swaggering little melody for two clarinets, accompanied by oboes and bassoons, with the tambourine marking the rhythm in a persistent triplet rhythm, rises out of the once-forbidden consecutive fifths, played pizzicato by the strings. Various instruments—clarinet and bassoon, violins, 'cellos, and English horn, sing successively and alternately, with the piccolo adding its shrill voice in a fortissimo repetition of the main theme. The piccolo then doubles harmonics of the violin in a faintly dissonant melody (G flat over a seventh chord in A). This leads on to a melody sung by viola and oboe that will be heard again in the succeeding movement. Four unison horns proclaim a marchlike theme which yields to a return of the first subject, now sung by oboes, and the music evaporates in the clear air.

The second section or movement invokes (in Falla's phrase) "the intoxicating spell of Andalusian nights." Dreamlike is the opening, with the oboe murmuring against muted strings and flute, sustaining an ethereal G. Out of chromatic runs and glissandi rises the oboe's song, a melody that was foreshadowed in the first movement, but now of penetrating sweetness. Muted and divided strings prepare the way for the melancholy song of a solo horn, presently followed by a recollection of the chief theme of the first movement in which muted trumpets sound in three-part harmony. After a climax of full orchestra and a new melody played by horns and violins and a return of material already heard, there is a sound of bells, and without pause the music passes into the third movement.

The morning of the festival day, thus ushered in with the chiming of brazen voices, takes on a marchlike rhythm, with the tambourines marking the pace for the other instruments. These enter gradually but eagerly and joyously. The romance and the tenderness of what has gone before are recalled in fragments from the first two movements, now given a jovial and even ironic turn, the woodwind repetition of the night song being a frank parody. The end is jubilant, turbulent, festive. Again to quote Falla, "the gayety of a people dancing to the joyous strains of a banda of guitars and bandurras . . . whirls in the air."

Falla is authority for the statement that Debussy's one visit to Spain was to San Sebastián, near the frontier, where he spent a few hours, primarily to see a bull fight. There seems to be no other record of Debussy's having ever so much as set foot on the Iberian peninsula. Falla has written of the lasting impression made on Debussy by the peculiar light of the Plaza de Toros; the striking contrast between the part flooded by sunlight and that covered by shadow. The third movement in particular, he observes, might be accepted as an evocation of that afternoon spent on the threshold of Spain. But Debussy's fancy carried him further, into the heart of Andalusia, with which he was acquainted only through books, pictures, songs, dances, and the tales told by friends. Without knowing Spain, he has written better and truer Spanish music, Falla is so generous as to say, than Spanish composers who have known their native land only too well.

Falla has this to add of certain harmonic phenomena which the French master made his own: "The Andalusians obtain these sounds from their guitars; needless to say, in a rudimentary form and quite unconsciously; and curiously enough, Spanish composers have neglected and even despised these effects, which they looked upon as something barbaric, or they might have at most sought to reduce them to old musical forms, until the day on which Claude Debussy showed them how they could be used."

Bolder of line, and more positively polyphonic in various details than Debussy's earlier orchestral writing, *Ibéria*, none the less, has been declared as representing the peak of Debussy's impressionistic practice. Particularly has this thought been applied to his harmonic and orchestral coloring. As one Paris reviewer described it, "he puts his timbres side by side, adopting a process like that of the *Tachistes* or the stipplers." Elsewhere it is noted that "his coloring is now that of the pointillistes," who painted with a multitude of fine points rather than with free brush strokes. Debussy the harmonist was never to escape these analogies to painting and its practices.

GIGUES

Though the last to be completed and performed, *Gigues* is listed as No. 1 of the *Images*. The rough draft is dated January 4,

1909; the orchestration, done by Caplet in conformity with Debussy's indications, was finished in 1912. The work was first performed, with Caplet conducting, at the Concerts Colonne, on January 26, 1913. The title was originally *Gigues tristes*, implying a contrast, even a contradiction of terms, since the gigue—or jig—is traditionally a merry dance. The orchestra includes an oboe d'amour and the scoring has, as a detail, the grouping of the woodwinds in four. Before the publication of the orchestral score, the work appeared in the form of a transcription for piano duet.

There is no very tangible basis, aside from the individual's reaction to the "feeling" of the composition, for the assumption that *Gigues* may represent some memory of England. It is built upon a plaintive melody that presumably could have been derived from English folk song. Wayward in mood, it breathes both nostalgia and a kind of forced humor, with a few rather violent outbursts to vary the prevailing sense of melancholy. The jerky rhythm of the dance persists, but there are counter-rhythms as well as a lively interplay of sonorities, mostly of a subdued coloring.

"Sad Gigues—tragic Gigues," wrote Caplet, describing the music as "a portrait of a soul in pain . . . a wounded soul, so reticent that it dreads and shuns all lyrical effusions and quickly hides its sob behind the mask and the angular gestures of a grotesque marionette." The ever-changing moods, varying from torment to phlegmatic indifference, together with the rapidity with which they merge, clash, and unite again, make the interpretation, Caplet pointed out, very difficult. But he finds here the soul of Debussy.

RONDES DE PRINTEMPS

Published as No. 3 of the *Images*. The score bears as an inscription a quotation from *La Maggiolata*: "Vive la mai! Biennvenu le mai avec son gonfalon sauvage!"

When first played at the Concerts Durand, on March 2, 1910, with the composer conducting, program notes by Charles Malherbe supplied what may have been the composer's own view of this work. Malherbe wrote that these "are real pictures" in which the composer endeavors to convey impressions received by the eye. He likened the melody to the multiplicity of lines in a drawing, the orchestra to a huge palette wherein each instrument supplies its own color. The musician, he says, asks his listeners to visualize what the music gives forth in sound; the pen in his hand becomes a brush and he takes pleasure in the shock of unexpected dissonances and the fusion of unusual timbres, just as a painter delights in contrasts of color and the play of light and shade.

With this, Debussy's music is brought squarely back to the moot issue of "impressionism"—that same impressionism that he repudiated in words, if not in music, when he told of his purposes in connection with the orchestral *Images*. For the third time, Debussy makes use of the old French lay, *Nous n'iron plus au bois;* if less obviously than in his song, *La Belle au bois dormant,* of the early eighties; or in the piano piece, *Les Jardins sous la pluie.* In the words of Laloy, this is "the single idea which now glides, now runs through light fronds of melody, till it joins in a breathless dance, whirls wildly for a moment, then grows calm and vanishes in clear air." Structurally, the work has been criticized as labored and self-conscious. Like *Gigues,* its performances have been relatively few.

FOR SOLO PIANO AND ORCHESTRA

Fantaisie. 1889. Dedicated to René Chansarel. Published posthumously and first performed in 1919, after Debussy's death. This is the work which Debussy removed from the stands when Vincent d'Indy had placed it in rehearsal in 1890; his reasons were never made public, although he wrote a letter to d'Indy at the time. It was written after his return to Paris from Villa Medici but never sent in to the Institut. In character it is the nearest to a concerto of any work composed by Debussy. In size and weight it is his most ambitious composition for the keyboard. Thematic material which in itself has the character of the scholastic sonata, is submitted to cyclical treatment with variations that make use of devices known to have been unpalatable to the Debussy of a later time. That Debussy never again composed piano music of similar weight of structure and such visible framework is perhaps the best clew to his reasons for keeping it from the public, though there are those, particularly in France, who find in it a delightful freshness of approach and many evidences of personality.

FOR SAXOPHONE AND ORCHESTRA

Rapsodie. 1903–05. Debussy's score is for saxophone and piano; the orchestration is by Roger-Ducasse. The dedication is to "Mme.

Elise Hall, President of the Orchestral Club of Boston." The organization was more properly the Orchestral Society and was founded in 1899. Georges Longy was conductor. The "Femme-saxophone" as Debussy described her in a letter to his publisher, Jacques Durand, was Mrs. Richard J. Hall and it was to her support that the society was chiefly indebted for being. Special arrangements of music of various types were made for her and she commissioned other French musicians of note besides Debussy to contribute original compositions to the repertoire of the concerts which she sponsored or supported. There were also compositions for groups of instruments, including saxophone, in the performance of which Mrs. Hall participated. Debussy's *Rapsodie*, which at one stage was to bear the title of *Rapsodie orientale*, at another, *Rapsodie mauresque*, is a melodious work of definite lines and Moorish or Spanish rhythmic suggestion. Its history, as retold on another page of this book, has called more attention to the work because of Debussy's amusing outlook on the task he had undertaken than the none too distinguished character of the music otherwise would justify. In 1932 the *Rapsodie* was performed at concerts by the Boston Symphony Orchestra with the saxophone part entrusted to English horn.

FOR HARP AND STRINGS

Danse sacrée and *Danse profane*. 1904. Written for chromatic harp at the instance of the house of Pleyel. De Falla finds a Spanish element in this music, with a suggestion of the ornaments of Andalusian *coplas*. Admirably written for the instrument, these dances are among the works which illustrate the more facile but commonplace aspects of Debussy's art.

V

THE CHAMBER MUSIC

In the accepted sense of the term, but four of Debussy's compositions qualify as chamber music: the String Quartet of 1893 and the three Sonatas of the six he planned "pour divers instruments," composed in the last years of his life. Had he lived to complete the Sonata set and possibly to compose also the second Quartet which he mentioned in a letter to Chausson soon after the completion of the first, this meager list of chamber compositions would have been converted into a fairly extensive one, though it is scarcely to be lamented that he was unable to undertake more than he did, in view of the state of his health when he finally returned to chamber music after a lapse of twenty-two years. The early Quartet was to remain his supreme achievement in this field; the only one of his chamber works to retain a place of eminence in the year-to-year repertoire of those who must play for the public and not for specialists.

Also grouped with the Quartet and the Sonatas in some listings of Debussy's works—chiefly because they do not come readily within any other classification—are the two clarinet pieces written for examination and study purposes when Debussy resumed his ties with the Conservatoire: *Rapsodie* for clarinet and piano and *Petite Suite* for the same combination. Mrs. Hall's made-to-order *Rapsodie* was intended for saxophone and orchestra, in which form it exists by virtue of the instrumental dress given it by Roger-Ducasse. The clarinet *Rapsodie* was orchestrated by Debussy. Both may be given place, therefore, among the little group of works for solo instrument and orchestra. The solo for unaccompanied flute, *Syrinx,* composed

332

in 1912 as incidental music for a play, is not chamber music, as the designation ordinarily is understood.

That Debussy should have written so little music to qualify in this rubric is significant; so is the further circumstance that he turned to the one field he had most neglected when, in the eyes of the world, he seemed "written out." Chamber music, more than any other, has preserved the classic forms. Chamber music, to a greater extent than any other, has retained in its form the traditional schemata of "development." And chamber music, more consistently than any other form of instrumental music, has relied upon counterpoint in its construction. Debussy was an individualist in all that pertained to form; he evinced an aversion for the development section, as symphonists and sonata writers had established it in the standardized sonata form; he was no contrapuntist, as contrapuntists went, and expressed his musical personality by chord formulas rather than by dexterity and variety in the employment of parallel voices. Moreover, his utterances were seldom of the long-breathed order. The fleeting impression, the miniature, the vignette, the mosaic were his particular province. For reasons of timbre and color, he turned to the orchestra when he had ideas to fill a larger canvas. The fantasia was freer there. Chamber music made him more conscious of what through most of his career he regarded as a rule of thumb.

The degree of his success in the four works he contributed to the repertoire of chamber combinations is disputed, with reservations even in the case of the quartet. Where the individual listener or commentator will align himself may depend on the degree to which he is ready to concede that Debussy accomplished something else, and that with distinction, in place of the particular things wherein it is contended that his chamber music is deficient. If the development is not of the most masterly order, must there be development? If the form still lacks the long line,

must there be length of line? If the counterpoint is spare and unorthodox, is there not another form of harmonic interest more
important than this counterpart in effecting the purposes of the
composer? The issue may be one of whether Debussy accomplished precisely what he sought to accomplish, not what he
would have needed to accomplish if he had been seeking something else; and whether, having accomplished the end intended,
the results are of such musical quality as to constitute a con-
tribution of value to the world's store of beautiful or significant
music. The success of the Quartet with players and the public
seems to have settled the point, so far as it is concerned. The
Sonatas have not grown materially in world estimation, though
plentifully debated, and in the case of that for violin and piano,
not infrequently played. It seems fair to assume that if they had
come from the pen of a lesser composer their distinction of
workmanship, particularly in the second and third sonatas, would
have called attention to them at once. The disappointment they
engendered was in direct relation to the eminence of the composer; Debussy was expected to write only masterpieces. For
an unknown composer to achieve such finesse and clarity, such
a poised, balanced, and idiomatic play of instruments would
have been something noteworthy. It was expected of Debussy.
With him other considerations outweighed those of taste and
skill, to a degree that might not have been true had the composer been any other than Debussy.

Granting all this, there remains the equally pertinent consideration that a greater effort undoubtedly has been made to keep
this music alive, because of its having emanated from Debussy,
than otherwise would have been the case. Every year brings
forth promising work by men who have not acquired world
reputations. It is played, praised, and thereafter ignored. The
number of sonatas produced over a period of a decade would be
appalling to anyone who stopped to ponder the figure. That

all are hopeless in point of craftsmanship is beyond belief. Yet how many, even including those of Debussy's contemporaries who were by no means unknown, have fared as well as the Debussy violin-piano Sonata? Would it have fared so well if it had been the product of Dukas, Roussel, Chausson, d'Indy even, or the ill-starred Lekeu? There is this difference between the sonatas and the quartet: the early work for string foursome would have made a reputation for any composer, however he spelled his name. Without denying the violin-piano Sonata and that for flute, viola, and harp their measure of exceptionally fine writing, it may be doubted that any continuing place of importance would have been accorded their composer on the strength of these works alone.

THE STRING QUARTET

Prèmier quatuor. 1893. Though Debussy wrote no other of its kind, the work has retained its original listing as his "First Quartet." It is enumerated as Opus 10 and as in G Minor. It is dedicated to the members of the Ysaÿe quartet, which first performed it. Of all Debussy's compositions, it most nearly corresponds to classic form, in the internationally accepted sense, since the form of the sonatas has a more particularized relation to that of the old French school which Debussy so ardently espoused. The Quartet is not free of influences, Franck and Borodin among them, but its determinative qualities are purely Debussyan. An individual application of the principle of community of theme, as then much publicized in connection with the cyclic form of Franck and his disciples, is one of the salient features of the structure. To fill out the form in the required dimensions, Debussy undertakes a kind of development not characteristic of his methods. Without foregoing admiration for the beauty of the writing, or one whit of the pleasure to be derived from an expert performance, it is possible to agree with Ernest Newman that the form, small as it is, taxes Debussy's capacity. The impression left is that, as a form, it is too big for him; but by substitution of jeweled detail not inherent in the form he accomplishes his ends, to the delight of the fastidious. Debussy seems to have recognized as much in his letter to Chausson; when he wrote his Second Quartet, he said, he would try to bring to it more of dignity of form. Though couched in language apparently designed to placate or flatter his friend, who had "grieved" the composer by what he had said about the First Quartet, Debussy's statement may be taken as an indication that he was not altogether satisfied with the results, particularly since he was not to return to music of a similar order until more than two decades had elapsed.

First movement. "Animé et très decidé." In the first bar is stated a germinal theme which is to figure in three of the four movements, or, if a more liberal attitude is taken toward metamorphosis of theme, in all four. The flattened second degree of the minor scale imparts to it the flavor of the Phrygian mode. For Debussy it is a theme of vigorous character. The harmony is quickly modernized and after some interesting chord successions in bridge passages, the first theme gives way to a tranquil second subject, with solo parts for violin and viola that move frequently in ninths and octaves. When the development is reached there is an arresting restatement of the principal themes with double-stopping for all four instruments. The second subject is omitted in a curtailed recapitulation, but there is reference to it in the coda, followed by a stormy passage in octaves, based on the first three notes of the first subject.

Second movement. "Assez vif et bien rhythmé." This is a scherzo in ternary form. The generating or motto theme of the first movement, changed from four-four to six-eight time, supplies the material. First entrusted to the viola against a pizzicato of the other instruments, in a section of great rhythmic vivacity, it becomes a solo in long notes for the violin, after which it is freely transformed, with "shakes" figuring in the accompaniment. Subsidiaries are given little prominence. An elfin energy, recalling what Franck once said of Debussy's music, that it was music "on needle points," characterizes the movement.

Third movement. "Andantino doucement expressif." There are three sections, of which the middle one is the most extended. Thematically, the movement has the least in common with its companion movements, the generating theme being ignored, unless a triplet figuration in the second section is to be construed as a transformation. At the beginning all of the instruments are muted and, after a brief introduction, give out a lusciously harmonized melody, with the inner voices frequently moving in sixths. The middle part begins like a two-part invention, but subsequently changes to accompanied melody taken by violin, later the 'cello, no longer muted. This is built into a climax that is the high point of the entire work. The harmonization of the modal material with which this section begins makes striking use of fifths; there is another of Debussy's personal signatures in the employment of consecutive major thirds as accompaniment for the characteristic passage leading up to the climax of the movement, where the theme is entrusted to the violin. At the close, the first subject returns with richer scoring.

Fourth movement. "Très modéré." The generating theme can be traced forward through the introduction to a fugato built from the 'cello upward. There are clear references to the scherzo. The first three notes of the motto appear in inversion in the viola part, presently in syncopation in long notes, then in the accompaniment. At the climax of the movement the motto is given to the violin, against conflicting rhythms and a tremolando for the viola. As heard in the scherzo, the motto then supplies the basic substance of the conclusion, topped off with a precipitous scale passage for the first violin. The movement is the most conventional in feeling of the four. One suspects that Debussy made concessions to contrapuntal traditions he could not wholeheartedly embrace. With the development section of the first movement, which is largely a mosaic of minute variations on the second subject, this finale bespeaks achievement in spite of, and not because of, the medium chosen to express the composer's ideas.

In their essence, these ideas are altogether charming. Their harmonic investiture is uncommonly personal and distinctive. There are felicities in the use of the instruments that retain a surprising freshness. In its sheen, the scoring is Debussyan all through; the texture a delight. Emotionally, the work makes no pretense to profundity. But its finesse is such as to place it among the smoothest and most aristocratic creations of its time. With the later Ravel quartet and perhaps the Fauré quartet on which the ink had scarcely dried when its composer was whisked away, the Debussy quartet represents the most notable manifestation of latter-day French genius in its particular genre, the more notable because of its difference in feeling and manner from the favorite D Major Quartet of César Franck.

Première rapsodie. For clarinet and piano. 1909–10. Orchestrated by Debussy. This work was intended as a test piece for students participating in the wind-instrument competitions of the Paris Conservatoire. The clarinet is treated with sympathy and insight.

Petite pièce. For clarinet and piano. 1910. Orchestrated by Debussy. Intended as a sight-reading test, and like the clarinet *Rapsodie* it is less noteworthy for its musical substance than for its good writing for the instrument.

Syrinx. For unaccompanied flute. 1912. Dedicated to Louis Fleury, the flautist who gave it a first performance on December 1, 1913. *Syrinx* was composed for Gabriel Mourey's play *Psyche*, for which Debussy planned other incidental music that apparently never was written. The original title was *Flûte de Pan.* This was discarded because of duplication with the title of the first song of *Chansons de Bilitis.*

THE THREE SONATAS

The First Sonata. For 'cello and piano. 1915. Debussy is said to have sought in this work to evoke the character of old Italian comedy, as he did in some of the piano pieces. He liked its proportions and its form, conceived in the spirit of French composers of the clavecin period, particularly Leclair and Couperin. There are three movements: Prologue, Serenade, and Finale, the last two being linked. As in the Quartet, there is an obeisance to the principle of the cyclic form but less of what is recognizably sonata-like in the treatment of the material. The theme of the Prologue, the effect of which is largely declamatory, recurs in the two subsequent movements. The instrumental writing is often widely spaced, with employment of extreme registers, and the general effect is modal and slightly medieval. In spirit the work is sarcastic at times to the point of facetiousness. There are parallel chords illustrative of what by this time was formulistic with Debussy. The Serenade has a bantering air, with the 'cello providing harlequinesque effects against an almost continuous pizzicato. The Finale leaves a fragmentary impression on those who look for the usual degree of organization in such movements. It is said to find its inspiration in old French song and there is some suggestion of *Fantoches*, wherein the kinship, of course, is not to Leclair or Couperin, nor yet the Comédie Italienne, but to Verlaine. This Sonata is ordinarily regarded as the least effective of the three. Ernest Newman has described it as "consisting mostly of a fog opening now and then and giving us a momentary glimpse of ravishingly beautiful country." Perhaps the most striking detail is to be found in a passage of twelve bars in the Finale marked "con morbidezza."

The Second Sonata. For flute, viola,[1] and harp. 1915. The three parts are Pastorale, Interlude and Finale. Of these, the first gives its color to the entire work and succeeds in conveying an eighteenth-century (or, as Edwin Evans has described it, a "Trianon") suggestion. *Interlude* is of the character of a minuet. The themes of the three movements are closely related and the ending of the last movement recalls the first. In the opening measures, Debussy uses a device which also figures in the ballet *Jeux* (composed two years earlier), whereby he produces a double series of changing intervals of the second in parallel lines. In this and other details, the writing is polytonal. There are suggestions of Gregorian chant, and French commentators have found in the melodic substance a heritage from the trouvères and troubadours. The work exemplifies Debussy's love of the arabesque and is rhythmically one of his most complex compositions. The mood is one of gentle melancholy, evoking from the composer the comment that he hardly knew whether to laugh or cry, "perhaps both." Again, the texture is of exceptional refinement—a texture which Ernest Newman describes as possessing "the combined delicacy and strength of refined porcelain." Whether the basic ideas have a strength at all commensurate with their delicacy has remained a moot point, not only for this but for its companion Sonatas.

The Third Sonata. For violin and piano. 1917. The most viable of the three and the one written for the most frequently utilized combination of instruments, is also the one which most nearly

[1] The viola part was originally conceived for oboe.

approaches orthodox sonata form. The three movements are marked "Allegro vivo," "Intermède" (fantasque é leger) and "Finale." Stravinsky now appears among the influences, along with recollections of *Ibéria* and *La Flûte de Pan*. Widely divergent views have been held of this work. Perhaps it is significant that in many instances its staunchest defenders are those who have played it repeatedly, though knowing from experience that it will evoke only the politer sort of applause. It is animated, melodious, vehement. Like its fellows, it has the asset of the most meticulous taste and the most refined workmanship. The issue as to its degree of inspiration is by no means a closed one, even though various commentators, Frenchmen among them, attribute to it a laborious quality, an artificial straining after originality, that they do not find in the trio Sonata. As has been well said by Vallas, the three sonatas constitute Debussy's last will and testament.

UNPUBLISHED CHAMBER WORKS

Trio in G. For piano, violin, and 'cello. About 1880. The youth dedicated it to his harmony teacher at the Conservatoire, Émile Durand. It has remained unpublished. Presumably this is the trio mentioned by Mme. von Meck in a letter to Tchaikovsky.

Chansons de Bilitis. 1900. Incidental music hastily sketched for use with recitations of the poems by Pierre Louÿs, and not to be confused with the songs of 1897. The material afterward was utilized in *Épigraphes*.

WORKS FOR THE THEATER

DEBUSSY composed the music of four works for the theater which achieved stage performances: the music-drama, *Pelléas et Mélisande*, the mystery play *Le Martyre de Saint-Sébastien*, the ballet *Jeux*, and the children's ballet *La Boîte à joujoux*. Of these, the second and fourth were orchestrated in large part by another, André Caplet, and the last of the series was not publicly performed until after Debussy's death. A fifth stagework, the ballet Khamma, was completed with orchestration by Charles Koechlin, but performed only in concert form. Though *L'Enfant prodigue* has been presented as opera it was not intended as a stagework. Other plans for operas and ballets have been discussed in the biographical section of this book. Only *Rodrigue et Chimène*, on which Debussy was at work at the time he took up *Pelléas*, progressed far enough to represent in any sense an uncompleted score. Two acts of this work were written out. There are two versions of a libretto for *La Chute de la maison Usher*, but like its companion Poe subject, *Le Diable dans le beffroi*, all that is known of any music is derived from Debussy's letters or conversations. There is one purported sketch for the proposed *Roman de Tristan*, described by Debussy as one of the 363 motives for that work—an obvious jibe at Wagner. No scrap of music has been uncovered for *Cendrelune*, which Debussy projected to a libretto by Pierre Louÿs. Nothing came of the proposed *La Saulaire*, *Crimen Amoris*, and *Daphnis et Chloe*. If Debussy wrote any music for *As You Like It*, it is not known. Two fragments, *Fanfare* and *Sommeil de Lear*, with a few rough notes in manuscript for six further pieces, survive of the incidental music undertaken for a production of *King Lear*. Among Debussy's literary works is the manuscript of three scenes of a play, *F.E.A.* (*Frères en art*), written with René Peter, but abandoned at the time Debussy was finishing the orchestration of *Pelléas*, then nearing production at the Opéra Comique.[1]

[1] See under these titles in the biographical text.

PELLÉAS ET MÉLISANDE. 1892–1902

Lyrical drama in five acts and twelve tableaux. The text is substantially that of the play of the same name by Maurice Maeterlinck. Debussy's score is dedicated to the memory of Georges Hartmann, the publisher who befriended him in his early years as a composer, and to André Messager, who prepared and conducted the première. This took place at the Opéra Comique, Paris, on April 30, 1902. The original cast was as follows: Pelléas, Jean Périer; Mélisande, Mary Garden; Arkel, M. Vieulle; Golaud, Hector Dufranne; Geneviève, Jeanne Gerville-Réache; Le Petit Yniold, M. Blondin; Un Médicin, M. Viguié. The history of the work has been related in the biographical section of this volume.

The action of the play, as adapted by Debussy, may be briefly outlined. The composer omitted certain portions of the original, including the scenes at the beginning of Act I and Act V, in which the serving women of the castle appear; the fourth scene of Act II, in which Pelléas is persuaded by Arkel to postpone his journey to the bedside of his dying friend Marcellus; and the opening scene of Act III, between Pelléas, Mélisande, and Yniold. There are other condensations and elisions, all relatively small and unimportant, including some that were made in the course of rehearsals for the première. The customary elimination in performance of one entire scene for which Debussy wrote music, that of Yniold and the little sheep (the third scene of the fourth act of the play), has remained a question of dubious theatrical wisdom and musical rectitude, though apparently made originally with Debussy's acquiescence.

The characters are these:

ARKEL, King of Allemonde
PELLÉAS⎱ half-brothers, grandsons of Arkel
GOLAUD ⎰
MÉLISANDE, an unknown princess who becomes the bride of Golaud
LITTLE YNIOLD, son of Golaud by a former marriage
GENEVIÈVE, mother of Pelléas and Golaud
A PHYSICIAN
Servants, Beggars, etc.

Act I. Scene I. An autumnal forest in an unknown land. The stern, gray-bearded, iron-bodied Golaud has lost his way while hunting wild boar. In the depths of the forest he comes upon a young girl weeping by a spring. She is frightened and tries to flee. Golaud reassures her. Though torn as by briars, her raiment is that of a princess. Her golden crown has fallen into the spring, but although she weeps for it, she would rather die than have Golaud get it for her. Golaud learns her name, Mélisande, but little else when he questions her. She was born far away, she is a fugitive, lost in the woods. He persuades her to accompany him. "Where are you going?" she asks. There is something portentous and fatalistic in his answer, as they leave together. He tells her he does not know. "I, too, am lost."

Scene II. A hall in a castle near the sea, half a year later. Geneviève, the mother of the half-brothers, Pelléas and Golaud, reads to the ancient Arkel a letter Golaud has written to Pelléas, in which he tells of his impending return with his bride, Mélisande. Although six months have passed since he married her, he says that he knows as little about her past as on the day he met her.

Scene III. Gardens near the sea. Mélisande and Geneviève, walking together, are joined by Pelléas. Their talk has an undercurrent of foreboding as they watch the departure of the ship that brought Golaud and Mélisande, and Pelléas foresees a storm. Pelléas takes Mélisande's arm as they enter the castle, her hands being full of flowers. "Oh! Why do you go away?" she asks, when he tells her of his intention to go to the bedside of his friend.

Act II. Scene IV. An old fountain among the great trees of the park, called "The Fountain of the Blind." "One can hear the water sleep," says Pelléas as he and Mélisande bend over it. Mélisande plays with her wedding ring, tossing it into the air and catching it. Finally it falls into the deep water of the fountain. She asks Pelléas what she is to say to her husband. The truth, he responds. "La vérité, la vérité."

Scene V. An apartment in the castle. Mélisande bends over Golaud, who is in bed as the result of a hunting accident. He discovers that she is not wearing the ring and asks her harshly where it is. Frightened, she dissembles, saying she must have lost it while with little Yniold at a grotto on the seashore. Golaud commands her to search for it at once and, since she is fearful of going alone, to take Pelléas with her.

SCENE VI. The interior of the grotto. Mélisande and Pelléas, well knowing the ring is not there, take note of the place, so that they can describe it to Golaud. When a moonbeam eerily reveals three old beggars sleeping on a ledge, Pelléas silently leads the uneasy Mélisande away.

ACT III. SCENE VII. The exterior of one of the towers of the castle. A winding staircase passes beneath a window, where, combing her unusually long tresses, Mélisande is singing as Pelléas enters. As she leans toward him from the window, her hair streams down upon his head. Enraptured, he seizes it and kisses it. "Do you hear my kisses?" he asks. "They mount along your hair." Frightened doves fly about them. "They will be lost in the dark," says Mélisande, whose utterances seem always to hint of some tragedy to come. Mélisande finds that her hair has been caught in the branches of a tree, just as Golaud descends the winding staircase and comes upon the pair. He tells Mélisande not to lean so far out of the window and not to play in the darkness. "Quels enfants!" he remarks with a nervous laugh. "Quels enfants!"

SCENE VIII. The vaults in the depths under the castle. Golaud, carrying a lantern, leads Pelléas to a place where they look down on stagnant water. "Do you smell the death odor?" Golaud asks, urging Pelléas to lean far over. Both are agitated as they leave the noisome place in silence.

SCENE IX. The terrace at the entrance to the vaults. When they have emerged into the sunlight, Golaud warns Pelléas that Mélisande is perhaps with child. What he overheard and saw the night before was only play but must not be repeated. He tells Pelléas to avoid Mélisande as much as possible, but not too pointedly.

SCENE X. Under one of the towers of the castle at dusk. Golaud questions little Yniold about Mélisande and Pelléas. The child's answers quicken his jealousy at the same time that they leave him baffled and uncertain. "They always weep in the dark," the boy says. In trying to show how they had kissed once when it rained, the boy pricks his face on his father's beard. "Why, your beard— your hair—are all gray, all gray," he exclaims to the exasperated Golaud. A light appears in Mélisande's room above them. Golaud lifts the boy to the window and asks him what he sees. He says Pelléas is there with Mélisande, looking at the light. In unexplained terror, the boy asks to be let down as Golaud, baffled and excited, vainly enjoins him to "Look! Look!"

Act IV. Scene XI. An apartment in the castle. Pelléas tells Mélisande that he is leaving and must speak to her alone that night. She
agrees to meet him at the fountain. As Pelléas goes out, Arkel enters. The old man tells Mélisande he has pitied her and kisses her.
"The old need sometimes to touch with their lips a woman's forehead or the cheek of a child, that they may still keep faith in the freshness of life and avert for a moment the menaces of death." Golaud
comes suddenly upon them. There is blood on his forehead. It is
nothing, he says; he has passed through a thicket of thorns. But he
is nervous and violently repulses Mélisande when she seeks to wipe
his brow. He demands his sword, which she brings to him from the
prie-dieu. "Why do you tremble so?" he asks. "I am not going to
kill you." Turning to Arkel he asks him what he sees in Mélisande's
eyes. Arkel answers: "I see a great innocence." "A great innocence!"
echoes Golaud in a frenzy. As Mélisande shrinks from him, he seizes
her by the hair and throws her from side to side. "Absalom! Absalom!" he cries. "Already I laugh like an imbecile." The helpless old
Arkel is appalled. "Golaud!" he cries. Regaining his composure,
Golaud releases Mélisande, utters a cryptic warning, and leaves.
"What ails him—is he drunk?" asks Arkel. "No, no," cries Mélisande,
weeping. "He hates me. I am wretched." "If I were God," muses
the compassionate Arkel, "how I would pity the hearts of men."

Scene XII. The fountain in the park. Night is coming on. The
scene in which Yniold sees the sheep, customarily omitted, though
included in Debussy's score, precedes the final fateful meeting of
Pelléas and Mélisande. "Where are they going to sleep tonight?"
cries the child when the shepherd calls out that it is no longer the
road to the fold. The boy departs, exclaiming that he must find
someone to talk to. Pelléas arrives before Mélisande. He must look
well at her, he muses. It is for the last time. And he must tell her
all that he has never told her. Mélisande joins him. Golaud is sleeping, she says. It is late and within an hour the castle gates will be
closed. Pelléas tries to tell her why he must go away, and so tells
her that he loves her. "I love you too," she says quietly. Interrupting the explanations that follow is the harsh sound of the closing
of the gates. The lovers realize that they cannot return. "So much
the better," cries Mélisande, as they embrace. She senses that there
is someone in the shadows and whispers to Pelléas that Golaud is
behind a tree—and with drawn sword. Pelléas has no weapon. They
kiss desperately as Golaud comes up behind them. "The stars are
falling," cries Pelléas. "Upon me also!" she cries back. Golaud

strikes Pelléas down with his sword and pursues Mélisande as she tries to escape.

Act V. An apartment in the castle, which is to be the death chamber of Mélisande. Only slightly wounded by Golaud, she has been prematurely delivered of a puny child, and lies unconscious on a bed, with the baby in a basket beside her. Golaud, who had been found with his sword in his side after an effort to kill himself, is present, broken, remorseful, self-tortured. Arkel attends, as does a physician. When Mélisande regains consciousness Golaud staggers to her bed, begging the others to leave him alone with her. He entreats her to answer truthfully his questions. Did she love Pelléas? Yes, she answers, where is he? Was it a guilty love? No, not guilty. Why should he ask her that? "I shall never know," groans Golaud as Arkel and the physician return. The child is shown to her. Mélisande cannot lift her arms to hold her. Women servants enter the room. Why have they come? asks the distracted Golaud. Arkel interposes when he seeks to return to Mélisande. "Trouble her not . . . we must speak in low tones now . . . the human soul is very silent. The human soul likes to depart alone. It suffers so timidly. But, oh, the sadness, Golaud . . . the sadness of all we see."

At the faint sound of a distant bell, the servants drop to their knees. Mélisande is dead. Arkel tells Golaud that he must not remain. "Now she needs silence. . . . It was a poor little being, mysterious, like everyone." He takes up the child. "It is the turn of the poor little one."

THE MUSIC OF PELLÉAS

In detail, the music of Pelléas et Mélisande is preeminently and characteristically Debussyan, possessing many points of contact, harmonically and otherwise, with the songs, the piano pieces, and the orchestral compositions. But the place of Pelléas in the upper brackets of the lyric drama depends on qualities which are peculiar to it, and which are momentous in their relation to the operatic form, even more than on the individuality of the musical idiom. The work holds its unique position in the theater because of (1) the word setting, which enables the sung text to move with almost the naturalness of speech; (2) the suggestive background of the orchestra, which supplies for the drama what may be termed a tonal envelope, without constituting itself either an accompaniment for the singers or a series of symphonic expansions in competition with them; (3) the mood expressiveness of the score, which in its reticence and lack of emotional stress takes on the mystery of the otherworldly, and ends in being profoundly human in its sympathy and its pathos.

Pelléas et Mélisande is an opera of *leit motifs,* curiously at variance though this may seem with Debussy's frequently expressed opposition to the Wagnerian system. His characters do not sing their motives—one of the irritations of which he complained in writing about the *Ring*—and the representative themes are so imbedded in the orchestral fabric that an ordinarily perceptive listener might hear a dozen performances and never know that they exist. Indeed, reviewers and commentators have been known to state in so many words that *Pelléas* has no leading motives; twenty-three years after the Paris première, M. D. Calvocoressi felt called upon to devote an article to the subject,[2] because of the persistence of the erroneous notion. Yet when Lawrence Gilman wrote his illuminating little book on *Pelléas* in advance of the first American performances in the season of 1907–08 he was able to cite more than a score of representative themes and to label them, "The Forest," "Fate," "Mélisande," "Mélisande's Naïveté," "Golaud," "Golaud's Love," "Pelléas," "The Fountain," "Awakening Desire," etc., after the manner of thematic designation customary for *Tristan und Isolde* or *Meistersinger.* He took pains to point out that these themes are often so indeterminate, so shadowy and elusive, as to rebuke the analyst who would disengage them and expose them in accordance with the ruthless methods applied to Wagner or Strauss. He styled them "soundwraiths"; misty and evanescent rather than clearly articulated; harmonic half-lights and melodic shreds more suggestive and evocative than descriptive or definitive. But they are there. They are recurrent, essential strands in the fabric of the score. And they are used for a purpose, or a variety of purposes, musical, structural, coloristic, atmospheric and, beyond all doubt, for character and mood suggestion. The music of *Pelléas* is like a halo for each of its personages; each moves in an aura that serves as a new kind of characterization in music. This is also a scenic aura; and, call it symbolism or impressionism, the music contrives to establish, partly by means of its almost unrecognized leading motives, an intimacy of feeling for the stage characters and places rare indeed in opera since Mozart and Rossini.

The representative themes or motives of *Pelléas* often are given out by the orchestra just as the characters appear, or just before.

[2] Article in the *Musical Times,* London, August 1, 1925.

Perhaps the one most readily identified is that which attends *Pelléas* throughout the opera. Three flutes and a clarinet announce it, over a viola accompaniment, at the time of his first entrance. A variant of it closes the scene and it is utilized many times thereafter, rather prominently in the first measures of the brief introduction to the second act, when it is sung by two flutes and repeated, interwoven with harp arpeggios. Of various recurrences, that which marks the entrance of Pelléas in the scene that leads to his death by the fountain takes on an impassioned character (woodwind, horn, and strings) and as the tragedy impends, with the lovers rapturously seizing upon the brief moment left to them before Golaud shall strike, it is sounded by the 'cellos, as Mélisande's theme is by the violins. There is a like return many times of the Mélisande theme; first sung "doux et expressif" by the oboe over tremolos in divided strings in the first prelude, before the curtains open on the forest scene. As Calvocoressi has pointed out, these motives are not organized wholes, but brief units or cells which go to make up the musical tissue. They are not building blocks in the sense of the chief themes of symphonies and they are not expanded symphonically as are some of the Wagner motives, either singly or in combination. Dramatically, they may be taken as standing not for the characters as individuals but for what the characters stand for in the play. Nor can they be looked upon as associated entirely with a single character. That of Pelléas, for instance, is used for purposes of illusion when he is not on the stage and when others hold discourse, though the thought is of him. A motive which Calvocoressi calls "Wisdom" is closely associated with Arkel, but could scarcely be regarded as his personal theme. The fragment which Gilman names "Mélisande's Naïveté" is a derivative, based on the Mélisande theme which immediately precedes it. Closest to the Wagnerian *motifs* in feeling and use is the "Threat motive," as Calvocoressi terms it. After a first appearance in the interlude between the first and second scenes, it plays an important part in the scene between Golaud and Yniold and is heard when Golaud is about to mistreat Mélisande. The names given these themes, of course, are arbitrary and the same motive will be found differently designated in the comments of different authors. The importance of the motives to the listener must not be exaggerated; recognition of their individual contours and glints is by no means necessary to enjoyment of the opera as opera or the music as music. The fact is that the motives are so fragmentary, so fugitive, and so unobtrusive as almost to defy identification except in company with the printed page, even for specialists. They are part and parcel of the score, like any chord formation or succession; that noted, it is just as well that they be left to work their spell upon the ear indirectly, in the relative obscurity the composer contrived for them.

Harmonically, the composer's processes in *Pelléas* represent the full fruition of ideas to which he had clung in spite of the rebuffs of the *Envois de Rome*, and which he had seen justified in *L'Après-midi d'un faune* and the *Nocturnes*. The feeling of tonality is largely negatived by the shifting character of his chord successions. Rhythmically, there are minute changes of accent and, in the avoidance of heavy stresses, a fluidity of movement quite different from the successive patterns of past operatic writing. Melodically, *Pelléas* takes on the superficial aspects of chant, but so undulous is the line that the description scarcely applies. Certainly nothing could be further from the truth than to say that *Pelléas* lacks melody. What it lacks, and by clear intention, is sustained song, whether vocal or instrumental. There are no rounded-out vocal forms, if an exception be made for the unclassifiable lay, with its archaic, runic suggestion as of some distant time, which Mélisande sings from her tower window while combing her unbound hair. A little later in this scene, Pelléas in his ardor over the tresses he carries to his lips is close to the recognizable sort of set air, and he approaches this again in the second fountain scene. In both instances Debussy halted when another step would have carried him over into the domain of Massenet. His own explanation of his melodic purposes has been cited elsewhere in this book. Would *Pelléas*, indeed, have been less *Pelléas* if he had gone that additional step? The Debussyist who is more than content with the score as it stands will shrug his shoulders, knowing that others will disagree with him, as some will continue to disagree with the confirmed lover of Verdi's *Falstaff* who has no regrets to waste on the set airs the composer might have written but willfully would not. *Pelléas* is marvelously of one piece. It can be analyzed as being compounded of several styles, so far as its antecedents are concerned, but it has so blended the lyrical and the dramatic, so interwoven the melodic and the orchestral with the principle of recitative, that it yields an effect of continuity and of freedom from formulistic constraint such as can be attributed to only a handful of operas, at the most. That any melodic exfoliation which went beyond those mentioned would have impaired this continuity and freedom seems self-evident, and no one can say whether something really compensatory in the way of musical beauty would have been added if Debussy had made any further concession to the insatiable appetites of opera-lovers for more or less glorified tune. His songs indicate that in *Pelléas* he wrote the one way in which he really was happy when dealing with the voice.

The care with which the text is made musical, not only in the treatment of words and syllables so as to give to their utterance the simple directness of speech, but in the handling of the orchestra, which is never permitted to obscure the vocal declamation, unimpeachably merits the world admiration it continues to receive. Flyspeck faults can be found in details of accentuation; perhaps no two experts would agree on some of the nice points of prosody that could be (and have been) raised. But, to mention only a detail, the score is remarkable in its avoidance of those long notes for words or syllables that in Wagner and, yes, Moussorgsky, distort the verbal flow and prove that, after all, the musical pattern was given first consideration by these accredited champions of the word. Of the many dramatic felicities of the score, that in which the avowal of love at the fountain is made with the orchestra silent, could have sprung only from Debussy. Wagner and probably any other composer of opera who can be named would have built some sort of vocal or orchestral climax on Pelléas's "je t'aime" and Mélisande's "je t'aime, aussi." If Debussy's effect is no less climactic, it is infinitely more convincing.

On occasion the orchestra has revelations to make that must be relished for their own sake, and for the sake of the harmonic beauty entrusted to the delicately utilized instrumental sonorities. There is the famous passage for the strings alone, when Mélisande's unloosed hair streams down on Pelléas. Built on the whole-tone scale, this passage is a descending flight of seventh-chords, precipitous and shining like the gold of the tresses thus symbolized. Debussy's orchestra for *Pelléas* is the usual one, but with the brass very much subdued, with little doubling in the woodwinds, with the strings divided into eight, ten, twelve parts, and with the timpani enlisted almost exclusively for soft, rolled effects. The bassoons are given an expressive role of their own and the scoring exemplifies Debussy's desire to retain the individual timbres of the instruments rather than density or weight. Transparency is essential if the song-speech is to have the subtlety and clarity he sought for it, and which it notably achieves. Largely by means of the orchestra, Debussy heightens the sense of mystery and foreboding in Maeterlinck's play. He creates a background of Nature which is none the less valid for being Nature in a dream. The suggestion of the sea, as Pelléas and Mélisande discuss the departure of the ship in which she came to the castle as Golaud's bride, is one of Debussy's most necromantic touches. It is more than a literal sea or yet a sea of fantasy. It is a sea of some shrouded, unguessed destiny. The murmuring of the "Fountain of the Blind," the flight of the doves about Mélisande's tower, are felicities that remain suggestive rather than descriptive. The music evokes the shadows when Pelléas and Mélisande meet for the last time; and it bathes in a faint luminosity the entire scene of Mélisande's death. It is full of the compassion of Arkel and it contrives, more than the drama, to build sympathy for every being who comes upon the stage. Curiously unreal and remote as the play is, the effect is that of a greater naturalness and a closer personal identification with the subject than is true of operas that strive for the most frank and immediate realism. As lyric drama, Debussy's *Pelléas et Mélisande* unquestionably achieves in enhanced fullness and poignance what Maeterlinck's symbolic dialogue could only partly achieve as a spoken play.

LE MARTYRE DE SAINT-SÉBASTIEN. 1911

Incidental music to the mystery play of this title by Gabriele d'Annunzio. For solo voices, chorus, and orchestra. The instrumentation was completed by André Caplet, and it was first performed in Paris, May 22, 1911. The music consists of a prelude for each of the five acts, that to the fifth serving as a bridge or interlude, and other orchestral passages, choruses, and incidental soli. Each act is treated separately, with little attempt to carry musical ideas over from one act to another. A theme expressive of the divine summoning of Sébastien to his high mission recurs frequently throughout the course of the play.

Each prelude is intended to evoke the necessary atmosphere for the ensuing tableau. The work has the characteristics of Debussy's last period, when the melodic line was more positive, the structure more polyphonic, the orchestral color higher and more concentrated than was characteristic of compositions of the middle period. Though there is here no tangible imitation of ancient forms, the music makes frequent use of Gregorian modes. In the tierlike dispositions of the choral voices it conveys the suggestion of medieval or Renaissance frescoes. In feeling it is both solemn and voluptuous, "now vibrating to ardent embraces, now appeased by prayer." It has more of poignance than of religiosity, but is pervaded by a sort of adoration to be expected of one who loves Nature as well as mystery. Whatever his modifications of style, Debussy never escaped his background of sensuousness and fantasy. Musically, *The Martyrdom of Saint Sebastian* is well named a "mystery." But the play, with the chief character mimed by a dancer, failed from the first to exert an appeal to lend glamour to that appellation.

Act I. *La Cour des lys.* The five acts are given the medieval designation of "mansions," each played in a different locality. The first is the Court of Lilies, a sumptuous court in a Roman palace, through the seven arcades of which are to be seen sheaves of growing lilies. True to its purpose, the prelude surrounds this opening with an atmosphere as of Christian purity and exaltation. This purpose has been further literalized to represent the vision of the Good Shepherd appearing to Sebastian. Debussy has altered the usual equilibrium of his orchestra, allotting the most important parts to the woodwinds and giving prominence to the harp. At the outset an archaic theme in diatonic progressions is given out by the woodwinds, a theme that in its rectangular outlines has been likened to the first crude efforts of early Christian art. Mysterious tones rise from the orchestra in a succession of ascending intervals. It is this theme which recurs as a summons to Sebastian to fulfill his divine mission. The oboe and English horn sound thus early the note of suffering and martyrdom, but the prelude has been well described as possessing "the cool, even-toned sonorities of an organ." With the parting of the curtains, the twin brothers, Marcus and Marcellus, are seen bound to two columns, "like caryatids in some ancient temple." Before a marble altar consecrated to the pagan gods slaves rake the embers of a fire for Christian sacrifices. The song of the twins, "Frère, que serait-il le monde," is charged with physical suffering and weariness. Sebastian stands with his archers as in a trance. He shoots an arrow into the sky. When it does not return the mixed crowd of Romans and Orientals accepts this as a proof of his sanctity. As evening falls Sebastian advances toward the flaming coals. In the fragrance of the lilies and the glow of the embers he dances, his feet moving in ecstatic rhythm over the carpet of fire. This is the *Danse extatique.* In the songs of the twins, in the chorus, and in the orchestra sorrow is transformed into joy. A seraphic chorus rises above the earthly choir; a vision of realms celestial brings with it the halleluias of angels. The music is built up through a gradual crescendo until it reaches climactic sonorities without parallel in Debussy's work.

Salut! O lumière,
Lumière du monde,
Croix large et profonde,
Signe de victoire,
Et Palme de gloire,
Et Arbre de vie.
Voici les sept témoins de Dieu,
Les chefs de la milice ardente.
Tout le ciel chante!

Act II. *La Chambre magique.* A glittering brilliance irradiates the beginning of the second act where is shown a magic chamber in which necromancers and astrologers seek to decipher the future, hidden behind a mystic door. A young woman whom Sebastian has converted is tortured to her death. In her extremity she sings a prayer which, on the authority of André Caplet, is an Italian song of the Middle Ages.

Je fauchais l'Epi de froment, oublieuse de l'asphodèle;
Mon âme, sous le ciel clément, était la sœur de l'hirondelle;
Mon ombre m'était presqu'une aile, que je traînais dans la moisson,
Et j'étais la vièrge fidèle à mon ombre et à ma chanson.

Sebastian enters and batters down the mystic door. A new force, Christianity, rises behind it. Here there is no word spoken; to Debussy's music is left the battle of Christ's teachings against the pagan spirit. It is dramatic music; as dramatic, in the usual sense of the term, as Debussy wrote at any time in his career. Celestial voices supply the choral element of this act.

Act III. *Le Concile des faux dieux.* The prelude of the third act is preparatory for a scene of splendor, picturing the court of Caesar Augustus. The choral passages take on something of the movement and character of opera. Caesar offers honors to Sebastian, who refuses them. A hymn to Apollo is sung and then Sebastian portrays the march of Christ to Calvary. In the music is described the varying emotions of the saint, the tyrant and the throng. Stirred by the saint, the crowd takes up the plaint of suffering and pity. There is a strange chorus—

Il es mort, le bel Adonis.
Pleurez, pleurez.
Il se meurt, le bel Adonis!
Pleurez, pleurez.

Il descend vers les noires Portes,
Tout ce qui est beau l'Hades morne l'emporte.
Renversez les torches.
Eros! Pleurez.

One remembers here the words of a French critic who described
Le Martyre de Saint-Sébastien as "the work of a pagan musician
who sees God in all things."

ACT IV. *Le Laurier blessé.* The actual martyrdom is depicted in
the fourth act. There is an ecstatic quality in the music, both in
the prelude and the laments of the chorus, the latter repeating the
"Eros! Pleurez" from the third act. The orchestra describes the
affecting meeting of Sebastian and an old priest just before the death
of the saint, who is bound to a cross and made the living target of
archers who shoot straight at their marks.

ACT V. *Le Paradis.* The orchestral prelude serves as a bridge or
interlude, there being no pause between the fourth and fifth acts.
The scene is in Paradise and the music carries the entire burden.
Chorus follows chorus, without a word being spoken.

The final chorus, "Louez le seigneur," closing with a repeated
"Alleluia" has no parallel elsewhere in Debussy's music. The composer found it necessary to alter his orchestral texture and to build
vocal sonorities of a kind only hinted at in the early cantatas and
the *Trois Chansons de Charles d'Orléans.* So interwoven is this
music with the progress and meaning of the play that it has always
seemed episodic and disconnected when presented separately. Yet, as
one commentator [3] has said:

"Whoever attempts to stage the 'Martyrdom of Saint Sebastian'
does it a great wrong. The wonderful scenes, the magnificent tableaux which enchant the reader's visual imagination become under
the borders the merest tinsel; the sapphire dome is a blue back-cloth;
the whirling signs of the zodiac, discs of wood; the dance of the
Saint in imitation of the Passion a grotesque and blasphemous mum-
mery. Those who praise the play confine themselves to its literary
qualities; those who find fault with it are mainly discussing its
dramatic aspects."

This French *Parsifal*, waiting, as has been said of it, for its Bayreuth,
waits also for some decision on the part of conductors and public
as to what is the most satisfactory manner of producing it. It is in-

---

[3] Lander MacClintock in *Contemporary Drama of Italy.*

conceivable that the music should go unheard merely because the world is not clamorous for revivals of d'Annunzio's play.

JEUX. 1912.

Ballet, with scenario and choreography by Nijinsky. Written for the Russian Ballet, it was first performed in Paris on May 15, 1913. In some details Debussy followed the advice of Diaghileff, rewriting the ending and revising the score almost up to the hour of the première. It was this ending which he described as difficult, since the music had to convey a rather risqué situation. The inconsequential story of the ballet enabled Debussy to employ an extreme lightness of touch as well as to make use of characteristic harmonic devices to suggest the gathering dusk.

The scene is a garden at evening. A tennis ball has been lost and a young man and two girls pretend to be searching for it. But they are more interested in one another and there is an amorous game of hide and seek. They sulk, they quarrel, they embrace, the while large electric lights shed fantastic rays upon the scene. Ironically, someone in the shadows throws out another ball and the three, conscious of being spied on, vanish into the dark of the garden. Delicate as is Debussy's scoring, he has written harmonies that were regarded as stringent, even disturbingly harsh, when the work was first heard. The question has been raised as to whether he was not conscious of effects in Stravinsky's *Sacre du printemps*, which, although not brought out at the Théâtre des Champs-Elysées until May 29, two weeks after the *Jeux* première, is said to have been familiar to Debussy in score. (See page 218.) Presumably, however, it was Debussy who influenced Stravinsky and not the other way round, and it is easier to find traces of Debussy in Stravinsky's *Pagan Night* than the reverse in Debussy's light-footed tennis score.

Jeux can be regarded as a direct forerunner of the polytonal scores of the postwar period. Major and minor seconds are superimposed; there is a double scale passage in which the parallel lines are a semitone apart; there is an instance in which a melody is doubled so as to achieve a similar effect, its changing elevations retaining in their relation, the one part to the other, the interval of a second. At the outset, in the prelude, is introduced a succession of chords composed of all the notes of the whole-tone scale, against a pedal point in the strings. The harshness of this harmony led one reviewer to remark that the listener felt as if he had penetrated into a thorny bush, hoping to discover some rare flower and had come away with bleeding hands, exasperated and disheartened. The delicacy and grace of the writing proved in curious contrast with this feeling of harmonic acerbity. Though the music has been performed separately, the shelving of the ballet for which it was designed has meant also the desuetude of the score.

KHAMMA. 1912.

"Egyptian" Ballet, commissioned by Maud Allan. Scenario by W. L. Courtney and Miss Allan. Orchestrated by Charles Koechlin. The dancer desired the work for London and Debussy agreed to compose the music for it. This was before he took up *Le Martyre de Saint-Sébastien*. When Miss Allan returned from South Africa in 1912 the score was not ready and Debussy called in Charles Koechlin to help him finish it, Koechlin doing most of the orchestration under Debussy's supervision. In a letter to his publisher, Durand, Debussy asked for haste in the engraving of the plates, "for a woman who fearlessly makes such perilous voyages ought not to know obstacles to her will." Though completed in 1913, *Khamma* still awaits a dance performance. As an orchestral work, it was played in Paris in 1924, six years after Debussy's death. The composer wrote disparagingly of it as "that queer ballet, with its trumpet calls, which suggest a riot or an outbreak of fire, and give one the shivers."

LA BOÎTE À JOUJOUX. 1913.

Children's Ballet, with scenario by André Hellé. Orchestrated by André Caplet. First performed at the Théâtre Lyrique du Vaudeville, Paris, on December 10, 1919, after Debussy's death. Debussy completed the piano part in October, 1913, and sketched the orchestration in the spring of 1914. Though sometimes listed among the piano compositions and, of course, playable from Debussy's own piano score, the work was intended for the stage and in orchestral form.

The action takes place in a toy box. A soldier falls in love with one of the dolls he sees dancing. But the fair one has bestowed her affections rather prematurely on a quarrelsome polichinelle. There is a mobilization of forces and a battle is fought between soldiers and the followers of polichinelle. The particular soldier who loves the particular doll is wounded. She nurses him and comes to love him, having meanwhile been deserted by the shiftless polichinelle.

There is a happy ending, with the soldier marrying the doll and the polichinelle becoming a garde-champêtre. The happy married couple have many children and life goes on in the toy box as before. And toy boxes, we have it on the authority of Hellé, a painter whose specialty was children, both with the brush and the pen, "are really towns in which the toys live like real people."

Debussy sought in his music to achieve, first of all, an affect of naturalness and simplicity. The cardboard characters, he told an interviewer, must retain the air of burlesque or the play becomes meaningless. He conceived the work, he said, in a characteristically French spirit, aiming to be clear and even amusing, without indulging in acrobatic feats. He referred to pantomimes of a kind he had written at Christmas or New Year's for children's albums as his models. This was to be just "a little work to amuse the children, nothing more."

He was, of course, understating his case. After his death, when the work was finally performed, it was even described by one of the reviewers as "a masterpiece of French music." The score employs *leit motifs*, these being of the most obvious character and used to identify each of the characters. There are music-box effects, bugle calls, parodies of familiar tunes. Rhythmically, the music is lively and varied; melodically it is naïve and occasionally a little bizarre. The harmony, however, is Debussyan in a discreetly advanced manner, its subtlety masking what in a bolder work might have been regarded as daring. In spite of the praise with which it was first received, the work has taken its place among those examples of Debussy's decline, wherein the artistry of the workmanship is seen to be more noteworthy than the substance.

UNFINISHED OPERA

Rodrigue et Chimène. Text by Catulle Mendès.

VII

CANTATAS AND CHORAL WORKS

Printemps. 1882. Text by Comte de Ségur. A chorus for female voices, written by Debussy at the Conservatoire for the *Prix de Rome* contests.

Invocation. 1883. Text by Lamartine. Chorus for male voices. One of the student works for the *Prix de Rome* contests at the Conservatoire.

L'ENFANT PRODIGUE. 1884.

Cantata for soprano, tenor, and baritone. Text by Édouard Guinand. The work with which Debussy won the *Prix de Rome.* Dedicated to Ernest Guiraud. The first performance was at the Paris Conservatoire on June 27, 1884, with a second on the following day at the Institut. The singers were Mme. Caron (Lia), Van Dyck (Azaël), and Taskin (Simeon). There are just these three characters in the cantata, the mother, the prodigal son and the father. The narrative is of the simplest. The mother laments the loss of her son. The son returns exhausted and falls unconscious outside the paternal door. Presently he is recognized by the mother and forgiven by the father. There are rejoicings in which all three partake. The scenes of the cantata are thus arranged: recitative and aria of Lia, the mother, *L'année en vain;* recitative of Simeon, the father, *Eh bien! encore des pleurs;* procession and dance; recitative and air of Azaël, the returning prodigal, *Ces airs joyeux;* recitative of Lia, *Je m'enfuis;* duet, Lia and Azaël, *Rouvre les yeux à la lumière;* recitative and air of Simeon, *mon fils est revenu;* final trio, *Mon coeur renait.*

The introduction is short and compact. In the first bars is a prefiguration of the curious chords, seemingly colorless, that Debussy was to employ as late as 1911 in *Le Martyre de Saint-Sébastien.* There are faint indications of the mature Debussy's vagueness of tonality, as well as transient use of the whole-tone scale. The melodies are recollective of Massenet and the vocal writing has fewer of the hallmarks of the true Debussy than some of the early songs. In the scoring is to be encountered frequent division of the strings.

Twenty-five years later Debussy reorchestrated the score and laughed at thirds and fifths in the original English-horn part. The *Cortège* and *Airs de danse* were completely rewritten as was the Air of Azaël, with its recitative. Though the later Debussy referred to his score as "theatrical, amateurish, and boring," it has remained a tribute to his early powers. The Air of Lia, the popularity of which he particularly protested, might have been written by Massenet or Lalo; if so written, neither would have had cause to be ashamed. A student work, *L'Enfant prodigue* had dignity as well as a high degree of artistry for a composer of twenty-two years. Debussy happily escaped the pitfalls of a subject and text that were a continual invitation to the sentimental. He had not yet matured sufficiently as a composer, however, to escape a mixture of styles. The bulk of the cantata is in the current French idiom of the day, hence the satisfaction of the judges, who gave it twenty-two of a possible twenty-eight votes. In the prelude are suggestions of orientalism that may represent half-assimilated ideas brought back from Russia. And in harmonic details, such as successions of sevenths and effects of fourths and fifths attenuated by sixths, as well as in the hazy coloring of the scoring, there are prelibations of the future brew. *L'Enfant prodigue* is not a masterpiece. But, viewed as a youthful effort, it probably justified the judges in regarding it as the most promising trial composition submitted in the *Prix de Rome* contests in a good many years.

LA DEMOISELLE ÉLUE. 1887–88.

Cantata for solo voices, chorus, and orchestra. French text by G. Sarrazin, a translation of *The Blessed Damozel* by Dante Gabriel Rossetti. The work is dedicated to Paul Dukas. Debussy scored the cantata for three flutes, two oboes, English horn, two clarinets, bass clarinet, three bassoons, four horns, three trumpets, three trombones, two harps, and strings. The narrative portions of the poem are divided between the chorus of women's voices and the solo voice of a contralto Narrator ("Une récitante"). The Blessed Damozel is a soprano.

The third of Debussy's *Envois de Rome*, the cantata was written entirely after Debussy's return to Paris in 1887. It was published in 1893, in a limited edition, with a cover designed by Maurice Denys and was performed for the first time that year under the auspices of the Société National. As Debussy's music is a setting of Sarrazin's French text, performances in English require either the editing of Debussy or of Rossetti—the latter being the customary course—in order to obtain the requisite mating of words and notes. To illustrate the variation between the French verses and the original, the first two stanzas of each will suffice:

The blessed damozel leaned out
  From the gold bar of Heaven;
Her eyes were deeper than the
  depth
Of waters stilled at even;
She had three lilies in her hand,
  And the stars in her hair were
    seven.
	La damoiselle élue s'appuyait
	  Sur la barrière d'or du Ciel;
	Ses yeux étaient plus profonds
	  Que l'abîme des eaux calmes
	    au soir.
	Elle avait trois lys à la main
	  Et sept étoiles dans les che-
	    veux.

Her robe, ungirt from clasp to
  hem,
  No wrought flowers did
  adorn,
But a white rose of Mary's gift,
  For service meetly worn;
Her hair that lay along her back
  Was yellow like ripe corn.
	Sa robe flottante n'était point
	  Ornée de fleurs brodées,
	Mais d'une rose blanche, présent
	  de Marie
	  Pour le divin service justement
	  portée;
	Ses cheveux, qui tombaient le
	  long des ses épaules,
	Étaient jaunes comme le blé mûr.

Sarrazin shortened the poem and Debussy made some further elisions of his own.

When *La Demoiselle élue* was written, Pre-Raphaelitism was already going out of fashion. Lily-bearing ladies were even less the mode by the time the work was first performed. The poem was more than forty years old when Debussy first turned to the translation for the subject of his final *envoi*. Whether the music has aged similarly is a matter of by no means unified critical opinion. In 1909 a Parisian reviewer spoke of the once-beautiful maiden having become "a wrinkled, insipid old maid." Viewed, however, in the light of its time, the score is not only an exquisite one—"too exquisite," was the verdict of Alfred Bruneau—but a daring one. A succession of fifths in the opening bars is evidence of the younger composer's eagerness to be done with academic rules. His restless modulations indicate similarly his desire to escape the fixity of tonalities. Fluctuations of rhythm prefigure the later Debussy as does the sensuous feeling of the work, which some critics at once pronounced decadent, effeminate, corrupt. The melodies languish, as do Rossetti's words. "A symphonic stained-glass window" perhaps, but one delicately and sensitively wrought. In the prelude are outlined three themes that are developed harmonically as the music progresses with at least a nod of acquiescence to formalistic procedure. The solos are graceful, the choral writing somewhat orchestral in the nicety of certain coloristic effects. The young composer is said to have completed the score in haste but the musical syllabication is expert and all is orderly and in faultless taste. *La Demoiselle élue* is not, of course, a score in which to look for signs of the hot blood of youth, much less the convictions of a mature artist. But it deserves high place among the *Envois de Rome* and it is full of harmonic prophecies that no subsequent generation can fail to recognize.

UNACCOMPANIED CHORUSES

TROIS CHANSONS DE CHARLES D'ORLÉANS. 1908.

> *Dieu! qu'il fait bon regarder!*
> *Quand j'ai ouy le tabouren.*
> *Yver, vous n'estes qu'un villain.*

Written for sopranos, tenors, contraltos, and basses in a contrapuntal style, but modern in the harmonic effect. First performed in Paris on April 9, 1909.

Ode à la France. 1916–17. Text by Louis Laloy. Cantata for solo, chorus, and orchestra. After Debussy's death, completed from sketches by Marius-François Gaillard.

UNPUBLISHED CHORAL WORKS

Daniel. 1880–84. Cantata to words by Émile Cécile. A student work.
Le Gladiateur. 1883. Student cantata to words by Émile Moreau.
Printemps. 1884. Student chorus to text by Jules Barbier.

ARRANGEMENTS

Debussy made the following arrangements for piano solo:
  Gluck. Caprice on airs from the ballet of *Alceste.*
  Raff. *Humoresque en form de valse.*
  Tchaikovsky. Three dances from *The Swan Lake.*

For two pianos:
  Saint-Saëns. Extracts from the opera, *Etienne Marcel, Introduction et rondo capriccioso,* and Second Symphony.
  Schumann. *Am Springbrunnen:* Six Studies in canon form.
  Wagner. Overture to *Der Fliegende Holländer.*

For orchestra:
  Satie. *Deux Gymnopédies.*

BIBLIOGRAPHY

BIOGRAPHICAL

Boucher, M., 'Debussy.' (Paris, 1930.)

Chennevière, D., 'Claude Debussy et son oeuvre.' (Paris, 1913.)

Daly, W. H., see section "Other Books About Debussy and His Works."

Decsey, Ernst, 'Debussy.' (Vienna, 1933.)

Fábián, L., 'Claude Debussy und sein Werk.' (Munich, 1923.)

Gianturco, E., 'Claude Debussy.' (Naples, 1923.)

Koechlin, C., 'Debussy.' (Paris, 1927.)

Laloy, L., 'Debussy.' (Paris, 1909.)

Lépine, J., 'La Vie de Debussy.' (Paris, 1930.)

Liebich, L. S., 'Claude A. Debussy.' (London, 1908.)

Lockspeiser, E., 'Debussy.' (London, 1936.)

Peter, R., 'Claude Debussy.' (Paris, 1931.)

Suarès, A., 'Debussy.' (Paris, 1922.)

Vallas, L., 'Debussy.' (Paris, 1926.)

——, 'Claude Debussy et son temps.' (Paris, 1932.)

——, 'Claude Debussy: his Life and Works.' English translation by Maire and Grace O'Brien. (London, 1933.)

Vuillermoz, E., 'Claude Debussy.' (Paris, 1920.)

OTHER BOOKS ABOUT DEBUSSY AND HIS WORKS

Arconada, M., 'En torno a Debussy.' (Madrid, 1926.)

Bérys, J. de. See under Caillard, C. F.

Caillard, C. F. and Bérys, J. de, 'Le Cas Debussy.' (Paris, 1910.)

Cortot, A., 'The Piano Music of Debussy.' English translation by Violet Edgell. (London, 1922.)

Daly, W. H., 'Debussy: a Study in Modern Music.' (Edinburgh, 1908.)

Dumesnil, M., 'How to Play and Teach Debussy.' (New York, 1932.)

Emmanuel, M., 'Pelléas et Mélisande.' (Paris, 1926.)

Gilman, L., 'Debussy's Pelléas et Mélisande. A Guide to the Opera.' (New York, 1907.)

Jardillier, R., 'Pelléas.' (Paris, 1927.)

Liess, Andreas, 'Claude Debussy. Das Werk im Zeitbild.' 2 vols. (Strasburg, 1936.)

Perracchio, L., 'L'Opera pianistica di Claude Debussy.' (Milan, 1924.)

Santoliquido, F., 'Il dopo-Wagner: Claude Debussy e Richard Strauss.' (Rome, 1909.)

Setaccioli, G., 'Debussy è un innovatore?' (Rome, 1910.)

——, 'Debussy. Eine kritische-ästhetische Studie.' Translated from the Italian by F. Spiro. (Leipzig, 1911.)

Shera, F. H., 'Debussy and Ravel.' (London, 1925.)

Suarès, A., 'Debussy' (The Music). (Paris, 1937.)

Therval, P., 'Pelléas e Mélisande. Guida per gli spettatori.' (Rome, 1909.)

Vallas, L., 'Les Idées de Claude Debussy, musicien français.' (Paris, 1927.)

——, 'The Theories of Claude Debussy, musicien français.' English translation by Maire O'Brien. (London, 1929.)

OTHER BOOKS DEALING PARTLY WITH DEBUSSY

Antoine, A., 'Mes souvenirs sur le Théâtre Antoine et sur l'Odéon.' (Paris, 1928.)

Astruc, G., 'Le Pavillon des Fantômes.' (Paris, 1937.)

Aubry, G. Jean-, 'La musique et les nations.' (Paris and London, 1922.)

——, 'La musique française d'aujourd'hui.' (Paris, 1916.)

Barre, A., 'Le Symbolisme.' (Paris, 1911.)

Bernard, R., 'Les tendances de la musique française moderne.' (Paris, 1930.)

Boschot, A., 'Le mystère musical.' (Paris, 1929.)

Boulanger, N., 'Lectures on Modern Music.' (*Rice Institute Pamphlet*, Houston, 1926.)

Bowen, C. D., see Meck, B. von.

Bruneau, A., 'La musique française.' (Paris, 1901.)

——, 'Musique de Russie et musiciens de France.' (Paris, 1903.)

Calvocoressi, M. D., 'Musicians' Gallery.' (London, 1933.)

Chantavoine, J., 'De Couperin à Debussy.' (Paris, 1921.)

Cœuroy, A., 'Appels d'Orphée.' (Paris, 1928.)

Cortot, A., 'La musique française de piano.' (Paris, 1930.)

——, 'French Piano Music.' Translated by H. Andrews. (London, 1932.)

Dubray, J. P., see Vuillermoz, E.

Durand, J., 'Quelques souvenirs d'un éditeur de musique.' (Paris, 1924.)

Ellis, A. I., 'Stéphane Mallarmé in English Verse.' (London, 1927.)

Gatti, G. M., 'Musicisti moderni d'Italia e di fuori.' (Bologna, 1925.)

Godet, R., 'En marge de Boris Godounov.' Vol. II. (Paris and London, 1926.)

Gosse, Sir E. W., 'French Profiles.' (London, 1905.)

Gray, Cecil, 'A Survey of Contemporary Music.' (London, 1924.)

Heyman, K. R. W., 'The Relation of Ultra-Modern to Archaic Music.' (Boston, 1921.)

Indy, V. d', 'Richard Wagner et son influence sur l'art musical français.' (Paris, 1930.)

Kurt, E., 'Romantische Harmonik und ihre Krise in Wagners Tristan.' (Berne and Leipzig, 1920.)

Laloy, L., 'La Musique retrouvée.' (Paris, 1928.)

Leblanc, G., 'Souvenirs.' (Paris, 1931.)

——, 'Maeterlinck and I.' English translation by Janet Flanner. (London, 1932.)

Leoni, Sergio, 'L'arte pianistica in Martucci, Brahms, Grieg, Novak, Debussy.' (Padua, 1915.)

Mason, D. G., 'Contemporary Composers.' (New York, 1918.)

Mauclair, C., 'Histoire de la musique européenne.' (Paris, 1914.)

Meck, B. von and Bowen, C. D., 'Beloved Friend.' (New York, 1937.)

Meck, N. F. von, see under Tchaikovsky.

Niemann, W., 'Die Musik seit Richard Wagner.' (Berlin and Leipzig, 1913.)

Norton, Mrs. C. M. and others, 'Modern Drama and Opera.' (Boston, 1911.)

Paglia, C., 'Strauss, Debussy e compagnia bella.' (Bologna, 1913.)

Pizzetti, I., 'Musicisti Contemporanei.' (Milan, 1914.)

Poueigh, J., 'Musiciens français d'aujourd'hui.' (Pseudonym, Octave Séré.) (Paris, 1921.)

'Pour la Musique française. Douze causeries, avec une préface de Claude Debussy.' (Paris, 1917.)

Rebois, H., 'Les Grands Prix de Rome de musique.' (Paris, 1932.)

Rolland, R., 'Musiciens d'aujourd'hui.' (Paris, 1908.)

——, 'Musicians of To-day.' Translation by M. Blaicklock. (London, 1915.)

Salazar, A., 'Musica y músicos de hoy; ensayos sobre la musica actual.' (Madrid, 1928?)

Séré, O. See: Poueigh, Jean.

Symons, A., 'The Symbolist Movement in Literature.' (London, 1908.)

Tchaikovsky, P. I., 'Peripiska s N. F. von Meck.' Vol II. (1879–81; Moscow, 1935.)

Templier, P. D., 'Erik Satie.' (Paris, 1932.)

Tiersot, J., 'Un Demi-siècle de musique française.' Entre les deux guerres.' (Paris, 1918.)

Verlaine, M., 'Mémoires de ma vie.' (Paris, 1935.)

Vermeulen, M., 'De twee muzieken.' (Leiden, 1918.)

Vuillermoz, E., 'Musique d'aujourd'hui.' (Paris, 1923.)

Vuillermoz, E. and Dubray, J. P., 'Seize figures de la musique.' (Paris, 1919.)

Walch, G., 'Anthologie des poètes français contemporains.' Vol. II. (Paris, 1927.)

Waterhouse, F. A., 'Random Studies in the Romantic Chaos.' (New York, 1923.)

Woolley, G., 'Wagner et le symbolisme français.' (Paris, 1934.)

MAGAZINE ARTICLES ABOUT DEBUSSY

Ambrière, F., 'La Vie romaine de Claude Debussy.' (*La Revue musicale,* Paris, January, 1934.)

Aubry, G. Jean-, 'Claude Debussy et la musique française moderne en Angleterre.' (*La Revue S. I. M.*, Paris, March, 1909.)

——, 'Some Recollections of Debussy.' (*The Musical Times*, London, May, 1918.)

——, 'Claude Debussy.' (*Musical Quarterly*, New York, 1918.)

——, 'Claude Debussy.' (*Forum*, Stockholm, 1919.)

——, 'L'Oeuvre critique de Debussy.' (*La Revue musicale*, Paris, December, 1920.)

——, 'Claude Debussy.' (*Revue des idées*, Paris, February 15, 1910.)

Barbey, V., 'Projet de mise en scène pour Pelléas.' (*La Revue Musicale*, Paris, 1927.)

Barini, G., 'Claude Debussy.' (*Nuova Antalogia*, Rome, 1918.)

Behrend, W., 'Claude Debussy.' (*Tilskveren*, Copenhagen, 1918.)

Bellaigue, C., 'Pelléas et Mélisande.' (*Revue des Deux Mondes*, Paris, May 15, 1902.)

Bonheur, R., 'Souvenirs et impressions d'un compagnon de jeunesse.' (*La Revue musicale*, Paris, May, 1926; special number entitled 'La Jeunesse de Debussy.')

Brian, H., 'The Theories of Claude Debussy.' (*Musical Opinion*, London, 1929.)

Brussel, R., 'Claude Debussy livre aux bêtes.' (*Revue d'art dramatique*, May, 1902.)

——, 'Claude Debussy et Paul Dukas.' (*La Revue musicale*, Paris, May, 1926.)

Burk, J. N., 'Estimating Debussy.' (*New Music Review*, New York, 1919.)

Calvocoressi, M. D., 'Claude Debussy.' (*The Musical Times*, London, 1908.)

——, 'Debussy and the leit motiv.' (*The Musical Times*, London, 1925.)

——, 'The Tragedy of Claude Debussy.' (*Nineteenth Century*, London, 1933.)

Cardinne-Petit, L., 'En écoutant Pierre Louÿs.' (*Les Nouvelles litteraires*, Paris, December 22, 1934.)

Casella, A., 'Claude Debussy.' (*Monthly Musical Record*, London, January, 1933.)

Casella, A., 'Claude Debussy.' (*Ars nova,* Rome, April, 1918.)

Coeuroy, A., 'Debussy et l'harmonie romantique d'après un livre recent.' (*La Revue Musicale,* Paris, 1921.)

Cortot, A., 'La musique pour piano de Claude Debussy.' (*La Revue musicale,* Paris, 1920.)

'Debussy en Belgique, Claude Debussy et l'Espagne, La musique de Debussy et les Anglais, Debussy et la jeune ecole italienne, Debussy à Petrograd.' (*La Revue musicale,* Paris, 1920.)

'Claude Debussy et la pensée contemporaine.' (*Grand Revue,* July 25, 1913.)

'Debussy as Musical Critic' (extracts from his criticisms). (*The Musical Times,* London, 1918.)

'Debussy as Critic.' Translated by Mrs. F. S. Liebich. (*The Musical Times,* London, 1919.)

'Debussy's Pelléas et Mélisande—A Masterwork in Music.' (*Musical Courier,* New York, 1908.)

Destranges, E., 'Pelléas et Mélisande.' (*Revue musicale de Lyon,* Lyon, 1910.)

Dukas, P., 'Les Nocturnes.' (*Revue hebdomadaie,* February 9, 1901.)

Durey, L., 'The Songs of Claude Debussy.' (*Arts,* New York, 1931.)

Eaglefield-Hull, A. See Hull, A. Eaglefield-.

Emmanuel, M., 'Les Ambitions de Claude-Achille.' (*La Revue musicale,* Paris, May, 1926.)

Evans, E., 'Debussy for Singers.' (*The Sackbut,* London, 1921.)

——, 'Debussy's Pelléas et Mélisande.' (*Musical Standard,* London, 1909.)

Falla, M. de, 'Claude Debussy and Spain.' (*Chesterian,* London, 1920–21.)

Farwell, A., 'The Debussy of Saint Sebastian.' (*Musical America,* New York, February, 1912.)

Garnier, G. L., 'Correspondence de Claude Debussy et P.-J. Toulet.' (*Le Menestrel,* Paris, 1929.)

Gatti, G. M., 'The Piano Works of Claude Debussy.' (*Musical Quarterly,* New York, 1921.)

——, 'L'Opera pianistica di Claude Debussy.' (*Revista Musicale Italiana,* Milan, 1920.)

Gatti-Cassazza, G., 'Debussy.' (*New York Times*, March 15, 1925. Interview.)

——, 'Apropos Claude Debussy's Musical Setting of Maurice Maeterlinck's Pelléas et Mélisande.' (*New York Times*, March 15, 1925. Interview.)

Gilman, L., 'The Music of Claude Debussy.' (*Musician*, Boston, 1907.)

——, 'Wagner and Debussy.' (*Musical Standard*, London, 1908.)

Godet, R. (see also under Prunières, H.), 'Claude Debussy.' (*La Semaine littéraire de Genève*, April 13, 20 and 27, 1918.)

——, 'Le Lyrisme intime de Debussy.' (*La Revue musicale*, Paris, December, 1920 and January, 1921.)

——, 'En marge de la marge.' (*La Revue musicale*, Paris, May, 1926.)

——, 'Weber and Debussy.' (*Chesterian*, London, June, 1926.)

Gui, V., 'Debussy in Italia.' (*Musica d'oggi*, Milan, December, 1932.)

Gysi, F., 'Claude Debussy.' (*Neujahrsblatt*, Allgemeine Musikgesellschaft, Zurich, 1926.)

Hale, P., 'Prelude to The Afternoon of a Faun.' (Boston Symphony Orchestra Program, 1909.)

——, 'Prodigal Son in Music.' (Boston Symphony Orchestra Program, 1909/10.)

Hartmann, A., 'Claude Debussy as I Knew Him.' (*Musical Courier*, New York, 1918.)

——, 'Claude Debussy as I Knew Him.' (*Canadian Journal of Music*, Toronto, 1919.)

Hill, D. B., 'Debussy's Pelléas et Mélisande, an Inquiry.' (*Musical Standard*, London, 1908.)

Hol, J. C., 'Kamermuziek van Claude Debussy.' (*De Gids*, Amsterdam, 1918.)

Hull, A. Eaglefield-, 'Debussy and Musorgsky.' (*Monthly Musical Record*, London, 1918.)

——, 'Debussy's Forerunner.' (*Monthly Musical Record*, London, 1918.)

Indy, V. d', 'A propos de Pelléas et Mélisande.' (*L'Occident*, Paris, June, 1902.)

Indy, V. d', 'A propos de Pelléas et Mélisande.' (*Revue musicale de Lyon*, Lyon, 1908.)

Inghelbrecht, D. E., 'Souvenirs.' (*La Revue musicale*, December, 1920.)

Italian Appreciation of Debussy; by Tucagliati, Puccini, Mancinelli, Vessella, etc. (*Musical Times*, London, 1918.)

Jardillier, R., 'La vérité de Pelléas.' (*Revue Musicale*, Paris, 1927.)

'La Jeunesse de Claude Debussy.' Articles by Raymond Bonheur, M. Vasnier and others. (*La Revue musicale*, Paris, 1926.)

Klingsor, T., 'Les Musiciens et les poètes contemporains.' (*Mercure de France*, Paris, November, 1900.)

Knosp, G., 'Claude Debussy.' (*Neue Zeitschrift fur Musik*, Leipzig, 1905.)

Koechlin, C., 'Quelques anciennes mélodies inédites de Claude Debussy.' (*La Revue musicale*, Paris, May, 1926.)

——, 'La Leçon de Claude Debussy.' (*La Revue musicale*, Paris, January, 1934.)

——, 'Souvenirs sur Debussy, la Schola et la S. I. M.' (*La Revue musicale*, Paris, November, 1934.)

——, 'Sur l'évolution de la musique française avant et après Debussy.' (*La Revue musicale*, Paris, April, 1935.)

Krummeich, P., 'Claude Achille Debussy. A Study in Experience and Reflection.' (*General Magazine and Historical Chronicle*, Camden, N.J., 1930.)

Ladmirault, P., 'Pelléas et Mélisande.' (*L'Ouest-Artiste*, May, 1902.)

Laloy, L., 'Claude Debussy.' (*La Revue musicale*, Paris, 1904.)

——, 'Claude Debussy und der Debussysmus.' (Der Merker, Vienna, 1911.)

——, 'Le Théâtre de Claude Debussy. (*La Revue musicale*, Paris, December, 1920.)

——, 'La Dernière oeuvre de Claude Debussy: *L'Ode à la France*.' (*Musique*, Paris, 1928.)

——, 'Debussy.' (*La Revue des deux mondes*, Paris, July 15, 1932.)

Landormy, P., 'Is Debussy an Impressionist?' (*Musical Opinion*, London, 1927.)

Lavauden, Thérèse, 'Humor in the Work of Debussy.' (*Chesterian*, London, 1928.)

——, 'L'humour dans l'oeuvre de Debussy.' (*La Revue musicale*, Paris, 1930.)

Liebich, L. S., 'An Englishwoman's Memories of Debussy.' (*The Musical Times*, London, June, 1918.)

Liess, Andreas, 'Claude Debussy und Seine Zeit.' (*Anbruch*, Berlin, 1930.)

——, 'L'harmonie dans les oeuvres de Claude Debussy.' (*La Revue musicale*, Paris, 1931.)

Lilley, G., 'Debussy's Pelléas et Mélisande.' (*Contemporary Review*, London, January, 1911.)

Lockspeiser, E., 'Debussy and Shakespeare.' (*Musical Times*, London, March, 1936.)

——, 'Debussy, Tchaikovsky et Mme. von Meck.' (*La Revue musicale*, Paris, November, 1935.)

——, 'Some Projects of Debussy.' (*Chesterian*, London, September–October, 1935.)

——, 'Debussy, Tchaikovsky and Mme. von Meck.' (*Musical Quarterly*, New York, January, 1936.)

——, 'Claude Debussy in the Correspondence of Tchaikovsky and Mme. von Meck.' (*Musical Opinion*, London, May, 1937.)

——, 'Moussorgsky and Debussy.' (*Musical Quarterly*, New York, October, 1937.)

Lualdi, A., 'Claudio Debussy la sua arte de e la sua parabola.' (*Rivista Musicale Italiana*, Turin, 1918.)

Marnold, J., 'Les Nocturnes.' (*Courrier musical*, Paris, November 1 and 15, March 1, December 15, 1902; January 15 and February 15, 1903.)

Mason, D. G., 'Great Modern Composers. No. 14. Debussy.' (*New Music Review*, New York, 1915.)

Maus, O., 'Pelléas et Mélisande.' (*L'Art moderne*, May 20, 1902.)

Messager, A., 'Les Premières Représentations de Pelléas.' (*La Revue musicale*, Paris, May, 1926.)

Newman, E., 'The Development of Debussy.' (*The Musical Times*, London, May and August, 1918.)

Neisser, A., 'Claude Debussy.' (With a catalogue of his works.) (*Neue Musik-Zeitung*, Stuttgart, 1907.)

Niemann, W., 'Der französische Impressionismus; Debussy's malerische Stimmungsmusik; seine Jünger und Zeitgenossen.' (*Musik*, Berlin, 1913.)

Obit. (*Musical Courier*, New York, 1918.)

Obit. (*Musical America*, New York, March 30, 1918.)

Oulmont, C., 'Deux Amis. Claude Debussy et Ernest Chausson. Documents inédits.' (*Mercure de France*, Paris, December 1, 1934.)

'Pelléas et Mélisande.' (*Chronique des arts*, May 10, 1902.)

'Pelléas et Mélisande at the Manhattan.' (*Musical America*, New York, February 29, 1908.)

Perrachio, L., 'Debussy Claudio Achille.' (*Boll*, Bibiliografico Musicale, Milan, 1927.)

Peter, R., 'Claude Debussy; vues prises de son intimité.' (*Oeuvres libres*, Paris, 1931.)

Peyser, H. F., 'First Hearing for Debussy Sebastian.' (*Musical America*, New York, February 24, 1912.)

Phillips, C. H., 'The Symbolists and Debussy.' (*Humberside*, Hull, 1930.)

Pierné, G., 'Souvenirs d'Achille Debussy.' (*La Revue musicale*, Paris, May, 1926.)

Prod'homme, J. G., 'Claude-Achille Debussy.' (*The Musical Quarterly*, New York, October, 1918.)

Prunières, H., 'À la Villa Médicis.' (*La Revue musicale*, Paris, May, 1926.)

——, 'The Youth of Debussy.' (*The Sackbut*, London, October, 1926.)

——, 'Autour de Debussy.' (*La Revue musicale*, Paris, May, June and September, 1934.) A detailed criticism of Léon Vallas's 'Claude Debussy et son temps,' incorporating notes by Robert Godet. The June and September numbers contain a rejoinder from Léon Vallas.

Régnier, H. de, 'Souvenirs sur Debussy.' (*La Revue musicale*, Paris, May, 1926.)

Revue de Paris, 'Debussy's Pelléas and Mélisande.' Translated article. (*Musical World*, Boston, 1903.)

La Revue musicale. Special number entitled 'Wagner et la France.' (October, 1923.) Other numbers listed under names of contributors.

——, Special issue, December, 1920.

La Revue Wagnérienne. (Paris, 1885–88.)

Ryelandt, J., 'Pelléas et Mélisande.' (*Durendal,* February, 1907.)

Sabaneev, L., 'Claude Debussy.' (*Music and Letters,* London, 1929.) Translated by S. W. Pring.

Salvador, M., 'La Demoiselle Élue de Debussy.' (*Revista Musical de Mexico,* Mexico, 1919.)

Saunders, W., 'Debussy and Shakespeare.' (*Musical Times,* London, 1930.)

Stanley, M., 'Debussy, the Man, as Maggie Teyte Knew Him.' (*Musical America,* New York, April 13, 1918.)

Suarès, A., 'Debussy.' (*La Revue musicale,* Paris, 1920.)

Talamón, G. O., 'Claudio Debussy y el impresionismo musical.' (*Nosotros,* Buenos Aires, 1918.)

'Les Tendances de la musique française contemporaine.' (*Apollon,* Petrograd, February, 1911.)

Ternant, A. de, 'Debussy and Brahms.' (*The Musical Times,* London, July, 1924.)

——, 'Debussy and Some Italian Musicians.' (*The Musical Times,* London, September, 1924.)

——, 'Debussy and Some Others on Sullivan.' (*The Musical Times,* London, December, 1924.)

Thomas, L., 'M. Claude Debussy.' (*Revue musicale de Lyon,* Lyon, 1910.)

Tiersot, J., 'Promenades à l'exposition universelle.' (*Le Ménestrel,* Paris, May 26, June 30, July 14, 1889.)

Une opinion anglaise sur 'Pelléas et Mélisande.' (*Revue musicale de Lyon,* Lyon, 1910.)

Vallas, L. (see also under Prunières, H.)

——, 'Autour de Debussy.' (*Musique,* Paris, 1928.)

——, 'En feuilletant les partitions manuscrites de Debussy.' (*Musique,* Paris, 1927.)

Vasnier, M., 'Debussy à dix-huit ans.' (*La Revue musicale,* Paris, May, 1926.)

Vidal, P., 'Souvenirs d'Achille Debussy.' (*La Revue musicale*, Paris, May, 1926.)

Vuillermoz, E., 'Debussy et les debussystes.' (*Nouvelle presse*, Paris, February 26, 1907.)

——, 'Claude Debussy. Conférence prononcée le 15 avril 1920 aux Concerts historiques Pasdeloup. (1).' (*Le Ménestrel*, Paris, 1920.)

——, 'Autour du Martyre de saint Sébastién.' (*La Revue musicale*, Paris, December, 1920.)

Watelin, L., 'La genès d'un monument; le monument à Claude Debussy.' (*Art et les artistes*, Paris, 1924.)

Literary and Critical Works of Debussy

1901   *La Revue blanche*, April 1 to December 1.
1902   *Musica*, October.
1903   *Gil Blas*, January 12 to June 28.
       Mercure de France, January.
       Musica, May.
1904   *La Revue bleue*, March and April.
1906   *Musica*, July.
1908   *Musica*, January.
       Le Figaro, May 8.
1909   *Le Figaro*, February 14.
       Comoedia, November 4.
1910   *Comoedia*, January 31, December 17.
1911   *Comoedia*, January 26, May 18.
       Excelsior, March 9.
       Musica, March.
1912–13   *La Revue S. I. M.*, November to May.
1913–14   *La Revue S. I. M.*, November to March.
1914   *Comoedia*, February 1 (interviews).

Monsieur Croche antidilettante—a selection of Debussy's articles made by him in 1917, published posthumously. (Paris, 1921.)

——, 'Monsieur Croche the Dilettante-hater.' English translation (anonymous). (London, 1927.)

Masques et Bergamasques—Ballet scenario, written 1910.

The Published Correspondence of Claude Debussy

LETTERS PUBLISHED IN BOOKS

To	*Published in*
Antoine, A.	'Mes souvenirs sur le Théâtre Antoine et sur l'Odéon,' by A. Antoine. (Paris, 1928.)
Aubry, G. Jean-	'La Musique et les nations,' by G. Jean-Aubry. (Paris and London, 1922.)
	'Debussy,' by M. Boucher. (Paris, 1930.) (Facsimile.)
Bardac, R.	'Debussy,' by E. Lockspeiser. (London and New York, 1936.)
Calvocoressi, M. D.,	'Les Idées de Claude Debussy, musicien français,' by Léon Vallas. (Paris, 1927.) (Facsimile.)
Debussy, C. E. (Chouchou)	'Terres latines.' (Brussels, March, 1936.)
Durand, J.	'Lettres de Claude Debussy à son éditeur.' (Paris, 1927.)
Godet, R.	'Dissonances.' (Geneva, December, 1923.)
Hartmann, A.	'Claude Debussy et son temps,' by Léon Vallas. (Paris, 1932.)
Huvelin, P.	'Pour la musique française,' edited by Paul Huvelin. (Paris, 1927.)
Laloy, L.	'La Musique retrouvée,' by Louis Laloy. (Paris, 1928.)
Lenormand, R.	'Claude Debussy et son temps,' by Léon Vallas. (Paris, 1932.)
Louÿs, P.	'Catalogue d'autographes.' Simon Kra, publisher. (Paris, December 13, 1928.)
Messager, A.	'Pelléas et Mélisande,' by Maurice Emmanuel. (Paris, Mellottée.)
	'Claude Debussy et son temps,' by Léon Vallas. (Paris, 1932.)

To	*Published in*
Peter, R.	'Claude Debussy,' by René Peter. (Paris, 1931.)
Royal Philharmonic Society, London	'Debussy,' by E. Lockspeiser. (New York and London, 1936.)
Toulet, P.-J.	'Correspondence de Claude Debussy et Paul-Jean Toulet.' (Paris, 1929.)

LETTERS PUBLISHED IN MAGAZINES

Aubry, G. Jean- 'Some Recollections of Debussy.' (*The Musical Times*, London, May, 1918.)

Baron, E. 'La Vie romaine de Claude Debussy,' by F. Ambrière. (*La Revue musicale*, Paris, January, 1934.)

Chausson, E. 'Correspondance inédite de Claude Debussy et Ernest Chausson.' (*La Revue musicale*, Paris, December, 1925.)

'Deux lettres de Debussy à Ernest Chausson.' (*La Revue musicale*, Paris, May, 1926.)

'Deux amis. Claude Debussy et Ernest Chausson. Documents inédits.' (*Mercure de France*, Paris, December 1, 1934.)

Godet, R. 'Claude Debussy,' by Robert Godet. (*La Semaine littéraire de Genève*, April 20 and 27, 1918.) (Excerpts.)

'Le Lyrisme intime de Debussy,' by Robert Godet. (*La Revue musicale*, Paris, December, 1920, and January, 1921.) (Excerpts.)

'En marge de la marge,' by Robert Godet. (*La Revue musicale*, Paris, May, 1926.)

'Autour de Debussy,' by Henry Prunières. (*La Revue musicale*, Paris, May, 1934.)

To	*Published in*
Guéritte, T. J.	'Some Recollections of Debussy.' (*The Musical Times*, London, May, 1918.)
Gui, V.	'Debussy in Italia,' by Vittorio Gui. (*Musica d'oggi*, Milan, December, 1932.)
Lockspeiser, E.	See section, "Magazine Articles."
Louÿs, P.	'Correspondance de Claude Debussy et Pierre Louÿs.' (*L'Esprit français*, Paris, July to December, 1931.)
Malherbe, C.	*La Revue S. I. M.* (Paris, February, 1910.)
Toulet, P.-J.	'Correspondance de Claude Debussy et P.-J. Toulet,' by G.-L. Garnier. (*Le Ménestrel*, Paris, 1929.)
Vasnier, M.	'A la Villa Medicis,' by Henry Prunières. (*La Revue musicale*, May, 1926.)
Ysaÿe, E.	'Lettres inédites de Claude Debussy à Eugene Ysaÿe.' (*Les Annales politiques et littéraires*, Paris, August 25, 1933.)

INDEX

INDEX